AF695195

OECD Labour Force Statistics

2016

BETTER POLICIES FOR BETTER LIVES

This work is published on the responsibility of the Secretary-General of the OECD. The opinions expressed and arguments employed herein do not necessarily reflect the official views of the Organisation or of the governments of its member countries.

This document and any map included herein are without prejudice to the status of or sovereignty over any territory, to the delimitation of international frontiers and boundaries and to the name of any territory, city or area.

Please cite this publication as:
OECD (2017), *OECD Labour Force Statistics 2016*, OECD Publishing.
http://dx.doi.org/10.1787/oecd_lfs-2016-en

ISBN 978-92-64-27116-6 (print)
ISBN 978-92-64-25243-1 (PDF)

The statistical data for Israel are supplied by and under the responsibility of the relevant Israeli authorities. The use of such data by the OECD is without prejudice to the status of the Golan Heights, East Jerusalem and Israeli settlements in the West Bank under the terms of international law.

Corrigenda to OECD publications may be found on line at: *www.oecd.org/publishing/corrigenda*.

© OECD 2017

You can copy, download or print OECD content for your own use, and you can include excerpts from OECD publications, databases and multimedia products in your own documents, presentations, blogs, websites and teaching materials, provided that suitable acknowledgment of OECD as source and copyright owner is given. All requests for public or commercial use and translation rights should be submitted to *rights@oecd.org*. Requests for permission to photocopy portions of this material for public or commercial use shall be addressed directly to the Copyright Clearance Center (CCC) at *info@copyright.com* or the Centre français d'exploitation du droit de copie (CFC) at *contact@cfcopies.com*.

Table of contents

Conventional signs and abbreviations 6

International comparisons 7

1. Civilian labour force, thousands 8
2. Civilian labour force, index 9
3. Female civilian labour force, thousands 10
4. Male civilian labour force, thousands 11
5. Civilian employment, thousands 12
6. Civilian employment, index 13
7. Female civilian employment, thousands 14
8. Female civilian employment as a percentage of civilian employment 15
9. Male civilian employment, thousands 16
10. Male civilian employment as a percentage of civilian employment 17
11. Civilian employment in agriculture, thousands 18
12. Civilian employment in agriculture, index 19
13. Civilian employment in industry, thousands 20
14. Civilian employment in industry, index 21
15. Civilian employment in services, thousands 22
16. Civilian employment in services, index 23
17. Civilian employment by sector: agriculture as a percentage of civilian employment 24
18. Civilian employment by sector: industry as a percentage of civilian employment 25
19. Civilian employment by sector: services as a percentage of civilian employment 26
20. Self-employment, thousands 27
21. Self-employment as a percentage of civilian employment 28
22. Female self-employment as a percentage of female civilian employment 29
23. Male self-employment as a percentage of male civilian employment 30
24. Part-time employment as a percentage of employment 31
25. Female share of part-time employment 32
26. Female part-time employment as a percentage of female employment 33
27. Male part-time employment as a percentage of male employment 34
28. Unemployment, thousands 35
29. Unemployment as a percentage of civilian labour force 36
30. Duration of unemployment: less than one month 37
31. Duration of unemployment: more than 1 month and less than 3 months 38
32. Duration of unemployment: more than 3 months and less than 6 months 39
33. Duration of unemployment: more than 6 months and less than 1 year 40
34. Duration of unemployment: 1 year and over 41

Country tables 43

Australia 44
Austria 47

Belgium 50
Canada 53
Chile 56
Czech Republic 59
Denmark 62
Estonia 65
Finland 68
France 71
Germany 74
Greece 77
Hungary 80
Iceland 83
Ireland 86
Israel 89
Italy 92
Japan 95
Korea 98
Latvia 101
Luxembourg 104
Mexico 107
Netherlands 110
New Zealand 113
Norway 116
Poland 119
Portugal 122
Slovak Republic 125
Slovenia 128
Spain 131
Sweden 134
Switzerland 137
Turkey 140
United Kingdom 143
United States 146
Brazil 149
Colombia 152
Russian Federation 155

Follow OECD Publications on:

http://twitter.com/OECD_Pubs

http://www.facebook.com/OECDPublications

http://www.linkedin.com/groups/OECD-Publications-4645871

http://www.youtube.com/oecdilibrary

http://www.oecd.org/oecddirect/

Conventional signs and abbreviations

Signs and abbreviations

Totals may not add up due to rounding.

..	Not available or not relevant
0	Nil or negligible.
.	Decimal point
e	Estimated value
|	Break in series

Main country groupings

G7	Canada, France, Germany, Italy, Japan, United Kingdom, United States.
Euro area (19 countries)	The 19 countries of the euro area.
European Union (28 countries)	The European Union of 28 countries.
OECD-Total	The 35 OECD countries.

Classification

The International Standard Industrial Classification (ISIC) Rev. 3 classification is available on line: *http://unstats.un.org/unsd/cr/registry/regcst.asp?Cl=2.*

The International Standard Industrial Classification (ISIC) Rev. 4 classification is available on line: *http://unstats.un.org/unsd/cr/registry/regcst.asp?Cl=27.*

Note

Data on population are no longer updated by OECD, but are available from the United Nations database (*https://esa.un.org/unpd/wpp/Download/Standard/Population/*).

OECD Labour Force Statistics 2016
© OECD 2017

International comparisons

Table 1. Civilian labour force, thousands

	2006	2007	2008	2009	2010	2011	2012	2013	2014	2015
Australia	10 633	10 912	11 206	11 442	11 628	11 815	11 973	12 137	12 278	12 510
Austria	4 028	4 113	4 154	4 192	4 209	4 237	4 284	4 326	4 347	4 390
Belgium	4 647	4 733	4 780	4 800	4 895	4 856	4 893	4 947	4 967	4 974
Canada	17 502	17 847	18 122	18 250	18 451	18 620	18 810	19 038	19 125	19 278
Chile	6 671	6 944	7 203	7 299	7 763	8 061	8 150	8 277	8 443	8 560
Czech Republic	5 183	5 184	5 216	5 272	5 254	5 242	5 239	5 289	5 280	5 296
Denmark	2 919	2 915	2 954	2 948	2 924	2 924	2 907	2 890	2 906	2 933
Estonia	688	686	691	684	679	686	681	678	672	680
Finland	2 638	2 666	2 694	2 670	2 662	2 673	2 681	2 668	2 671	2 680
France	28 079	28 242	28 220	28 421	28 509	28 702	28 978	29 177	29 297	..
Germany	41 206	41 364	41 481	41 507	41 495	40 997	41 153	41 522	41 779	41 971
Greece	4 972	4 981	5 004	5 040	5 041	4 940	4 893	4 863	4 819	4 806
Hungary	4 203	4 177	4 139	4 137	4 175	4 206	4 282	4 315	4 425	4 502
Iceland	175	181	184	181	181	180	180	185	187	191
Ireland	2 128	2 237	2 271	2 243	2 191	2 171	2 152	2 164	2 150	2 165
Israel[1]	2 817	2 904	2 964	3 073	3 147	3 204 |	3 606	3 678	3 778	3 846
Italy	24 164	24 126	24 512	24 357	24 325	24 420	24 991	25 017	25 278	25 249
Japan	66 640	66 840	66 740	66 500 |	66 320	65 910	65 550	65 770	65 870	65 980
Korea	23 978	24 216	24 347	24 394	24 748	25 099	25 501	25 873	26 536	26 913
Latvia	1 109	1 126	1 143	1 101	1 057	1 028	1 031	1 014	992	994
Luxembourg	329	343	360	367	375	385	394	404	414	424
Mexico	43 234	44 063	45 121	45 416 |	49 133	49 482	51 477	51 896	51 837	52 624
Netherlands	8 597	8 741	8 836	8 900	8 760	8 726	8 861	8 932	8 896	8 933
New Zealand	2 217	2 251	2 271	2 287	2 308	2 340	2 346	2 375	2 446	2 501
Norway	2 429	2 491	2 574	2 573	2 588	2 617	2 668	2 692	2 717	2 756
Poland	16 938	16 859	17 011	17 279	17 123	17 221	17 340	17 361	17 428	17 388
Portugal	5 471	5 499	5 505	5 458	5 465 |	5 397	5 352	5 259	5 201	5 167
Slovak Republic	2 655	2 649	2 691	2 690	2 707	2 680	2 707	2 715	2 722	2 738
Slovenia	1 022	1 035	1 042	1 042	1 041	1 019	1 013	1 008	1 015	1 008
Spain	21 692	22 336	22 966	23 150	23 258	23 331	23 345	23 102	22 858	22 831
Sweden	4 671	4 838	4 898	4 907	4 948	5 016	5 060	5 116	5 183	5 223
Switzerland	4 469	4 567	4 666	4 733	4 758	4 845	4 925	5 004	5 103	5 182
Turkey	22 751	23 114	23 805	24 748	25 641	26 725	27 339	28 271 |	28 786	29 678
United Kingdom	30 540	30 729	31 116	31 268	31 394	31 728	31 981	32 210	32 513	32 630
United States	151 428	153 124	154 287	154 142	153 889	153 617	154 975	155 389	155 922	157 130
OECD-Total	**572 821**	**579 033**	**585 174**	**587 470 |**	**593 040 |**	**595 101 |**	**601 717**	**605 562 |**	**608 840**	..
G7	359 559	362 273	364 478	364 446 |	364 382	363 993	366 437	368 123	369 783	..
Euro area	155 363	156 927	158 548	158 889	158 103	158 312	159 472	159 718	160 719	161 009
European Union[2]	235 335	237 249	239 536	240 255	238 860	239 176	240 906	241 531	243 149	243 729
Brazil	95 643	96 829	98 824	100 551	..	100 219	101 184	102 170	105 537	..
Colombia	19 206	19 258	19 655	20 935	21 777	22 446	23 091	23 292	23 654	24 173
Russian Federation	74 419	75 289	75 700	75 694	75 478	75 779	75 676	75 529	75 428	76 588

Disclaimer: http://oe.cd/disclaimer

1. Information on data for Israel: http://oe.cd/israel-disclaimer.
2. European Union refer to European Union with 28 countries.

Table 2. Civilian labour force, index

2010=100

	2006	2007	2008	2009	2010	2011	2012	2013	2014	2015
Australia	91.4	93.8	96.4	98.4	100.0	101.6	103.0	104.4	105.6	107.6
Austria	95.7	97.7	98.7	99.6	100.0	100.7	101.8	102.8	103.3	104.3
Belgium	94.9	96.7	97.6	98.1	100.0	99.2	100.0	101.1	101.5	101.6
Canada	94.9	96.7	98.2	98.9	100.0	100.9	101.9	103.2	103.7	104.5
Chile	85.9	89.5	92.8	94.0	100.0	103.8	105.0	106.6	108.8	110.3
Czech Republic	98.6	98.7	99.3	100.3	100.0	99.8	99.7	100.7	100.5	100.8
Denmark	99.8	99.7	101.0	100.8	100.0	100.0	99.4	98.8	99.4	100.3
Estonia	101.4	101.0	101.8	100.8	100.0	101.1	100.4	99.9	99.0	100.2
Finland	99.1	100.2	101.2	100.3	100.0	100.4	100.7	100.2	100.3	100.7
France	98.5	99.1	99.0	99.7	100.0	100.7	101.6	102.3	102.8	..
Germany	99.3	99.7	100.0	100.0	100.0	98.8	99.2	100.1	100.7	101.1
Greece	98.6	98.8	99.3	100.0	100.0	98.0	97.1	96.5	95.6	95.3
Hungary	100.7	100.0	99.1	99.1	100.0	100.7	102.6	103.3	106.0	107.8
Iceland	96.5	100.3	101.8	100.0	100.0	99.6	99.6	102.2	103.4	105.8
Ireland	97.1	102.1	103.7	102.4	100.0	99.1	98.2	98.8	98.1	98.8
Israel[1]	89.5	92.3	94.2	97.6	100.0	101.8 |	114.6	116.9	120.1	122.2
Italy	99.3	99.2	100.8	100.1	100.0	100.4	102.7	102.8	103.9	103.8
Japan	100.5	100.8	100.6	100.3 |	100.0	99.4	98.8	99.2	99.3	99.5
Korea	96.9	97.8	98.4	98.6	100.0	101.4	103.0	104.5	107.2	108.7
Latvia	105.0	106.5	108.2	104.2	100.0	97.3	97.6	96.0	93.9	94.1
Luxembourg	87.9	91.6	96.1	97.9	100.0	102.7	105.2	107.8	110.5	113.1
Mexico	88.0	89.7	91.8	92.4 |	100.0	100.7	104.8	105.6	105.5	107.1
Netherlands	98.1	99.8	100.9	101.6	100.0	99.6	101.2	102.0	101.6	102.0
New Zealand	96.1	97.5	98.4	99.1	100.0	101.4	101.6	102.9	106.0	108.4
Norway	93.9	96.3	99.5	99.4	100.0	101.1	103.1	104.0	105.0	106.5
Poland	98.9	98.5	99.3	100.9	100.0	100.6	101.3	101.4	101.8	101.5
Portugal	100.1	100.6	100.7	99.9	100.0 |	98.8	97.9	96.2	95.2	94.6
Slovak Republic	98.1	97.9	99.4	99.4	100.0	99.0	100.0	100.3	100.6	101.2
Slovenia	98.1	99.4	100.0	100.0	100.0	97.9	97.3	96.8	97.5	96.8
Spain	93.3	96.0	98.7	99.5	100.0	100.3	100.4	99.3	98.3	98.2
Sweden	94.4	97.8	99.0	99.2	100.0	101.4	102.3	103.4	104.8	105.6
Switzerland	93.9	96.0	98.1	99.5	100.0	101.8	103.5	105.2	107.2	108.9
Turkey	88.7	90.1	92.8	96.5	100.0	104.2	106.6	110.3 |	112.3	115.7
United Kingdom	97.3	97.9	99.1	99.6	100.0	101.1	101.9	102.6	103.6	103.9
United States	98.4	99.5	100.3	100.2	100.0	99.8	100.7	101.0	101.3	102.1
OECD-Total	**96.6**	**97.6**	**98.7**	**99.1 |**	**100.0 |**	**100.3 |**	**101.5**	**102.1 |**	**102.7**	..
G7	98.7	99.4	100.0	100.0 |	100.0	99.9	100.6	101.0	101.5	..
Euro area	98.3	99.3	100.3	100.5	100.0	100.1	100.9	101.0	101.7	101.8
European Union[2]	98.5	99.3	100.3	100.6	100.0	100.1	100.9	101.1	101.8	102.0
Brazil	..	..	..	..	..	..	..	..	..	..
Colombia	88.2	88.4	90.3	96.1	100.0	103.1	106.0	107.0	108.6	111.0
Russian Federation	98.6	99.7	100.3	100.3	100.0	100.4	100.3	100.1	99.9	101.5

Disclaimer: http://oe.cd/disclaimer

1. Information on data for Israel: http://oe.cd/israel-disclaimer.
2. European Union refer to European Union with 28 countries.

Table 3. Female civilian labour force, thousands

	2006	2007	2008	2009	2010	2011	2012	2013	2014	2015
Australia	4 801	4 938	5 083	5 208	5 285	5 392	5 475	5 560	5 645	5 773
Austria	1 844	1 885	1 914	1 947	1 959	1 981	2 009	2 032	2 048	2 064
Belgium	2 065	2 115	2 148	2 167	2 220	2 206	2 223	2 265	2 290	2 297
Canada	8 209	8 405	8 527	8 629	8 746	8 817	8 924	9 041	9 053	9 096
Chile	2 384	2 518	2 675	2 747	3 064	3 249	3 315	3 374	3 476	3 517
Czech Republic	2 287	2 267	2 266	2 287	2 279	2 289	2 298	2 335	2 328	2 346
Denmark	1 372	1 369	1 387	1 390	1 381	1 385	1 380	1 378	1 375	1 380
Estonia	341	335	339	337	338	340	336	334	327	333
Finland	1 281	1 295	1 303	1 300	1 286	1 287	1 297	1 292	1 296	1 303
France	13 331	13 454	13 541	13 703	13 785	13 877	13 961	14 056	14 120	..
Germany	18 735	18 893	18 947	19 037	19 083	19 034	19 073	19 316	19 448	19 557
Greece	2 044	2 058	2 062	2 113	2 144	2 113	2 125	2 119	2 122	2 144
Hungary	1 935	1 916	1 902	1 903	1 941	1 949	1 986	1 988	2 039	2 070
Iceland	80	83	84	84	86	86	86	88	89	91
Ireland	901	960	983	983	975	971	965	975	963	973
Israel[1]	1 313	1 355	1 382	1 448	1 483	1 505 |	1 688	1 722	1 781	1 813
Italy	9 864	9 850	10 124	10 082	10 117	10 230	10 623	10 663	10 822	10 740
Japan	27 610	27 680	27 710	27 820 |	27 830	27 680	27 660	28 040	28 240	28 420
Korea	10 001	10 092	10 139	10 076	10 256	10 416	10 609	10 802	11 149	11 370
Latvia	542	548	564	552	535	517	520	510	495	495
Luxembourg	144 e	153 e	156 e	158 e	163 e	168 e	..	..	..	..
Mexico	16 069	16 594	17 031	16 978 |	18 485	18 543	19 735	19 957	19 660	19 940
Netherlands	3 878	3 977	4 038	4 089	4 026	4 034	4 100	4 128	4 094	4 137
New Zealand	1 029	1 049	1 065	1 078	1 088	1 107	1 117	1 133	1 166	1 188
Norway	1 149	1 182	1 221	1 223	1 222	1 241	1 258	1 272	1 284	1 299
Poland	7 655	7 626	7 694	7 824	7 677	7 717	7 789	7 793	7 835	7 820
Portugal	2 582	2 610	2 618	2 618	2 639 |	2 588	2 588	2 558	2 542	2 535
Slovak Republic	1 184	1 184	1 203	1 193	1 209	1 184	1 199	1 210	1 212	1 234
Slovenia	472	473	476	478	476	468	468	462	467	463
Spain	9 161	9 523	9 932	10 217	10 394	10 563	10 694	10 662	10 582	10 592
Sweden	2 227	2 299	2 324	2 326	2 328	2 371	2 400	2 428	2 459	2 487
Switzerland	2 008	2 051	2 113	2 155	2 151	2 181	2 219	2 271	2 327	2 373
Turkey	5 916	6 016	6 330	6 850	7 383	7 859	8 192	8 674 |	8 729	9 225
United Kingdom	14 104	14 130	14 334	14 457	14 587	14 717	14 841	15 009	15 205	15 293
United States	70 173	70 988	71 767	72 019	71 904	71 642	72 648	72 722	73 040	73 509
OECD-Total	**248 689 e**	**251 871 e**	**255 382 e**	**257 475 e**	**260 525 e**	**261 706 e**	..	..	..	..
G7	162 025	163 399	164 951	165 747 |	166 052	165 997	167 730	168 848	169 926	..
Euro area	68 912	69 912	70 974	71 622	71 677	72 125	72 958	73 356	74 023	74 220
European Union[2]	105 480	106 552	107 868	108 786	108 443	109 032	110 162	110 774	111 756	112 054
Brazil	42 033	42 459	43 294	44 385	..	43 597	44 041	44 630	46 670	..
Colombia	7 795	7 788	7 985	8 699	9 197	9 513	9 907	10 009	10 173	10 452
Russian Federation	36 825	37 170	37 106	37 193	36 877	37 063	36 956	36 809	36 700	37 155

Disclaimer: http://oe.cd/disclaimer

1. Information on data for Israel: http://oe.cd/israel-disclaimer.
2. European Union refer to European Union with 28 countries.

Table 4. Male civilian labour force, thousands

	2006	2007	2008	2009	2010	2011	2012	2013	2014	2015
Australia	5 832	5 974	6 123	6 234	6 343	6 424	6 498	6 577	6 633	6 737
Austria	2 184	2 228	2 239	2 244	2 250	2 256	2 275	2 294	2 299	2 326
Belgium	2 583	2 618	2 631	2 633	2 675	2 650	2 670	2 682	2 677	2 677
Canada	9 293	9 442	9 596	9 621	9 705	9 803	9 886	9 997	10 072	10 182
Chile	4 286	4 426	4 528	4 553	4 698	4 812	4 835	4 903	4 967	5 042
Czech Republic	2 896	2 917	2 951	2 985	2 975	2 953	2 940	2 954	2 952	2 949
Denmark	1 548	1 545	1 567	1 557	1 544	1 539	1 527	1 512	1 530	1 553
Estonia	348	351	352	347	341	347	345	344	345	347
Finland	1 357	1 371	1 391	1 369	1 375	1 385	1 383	1 375	1 375	1 377
France	14 748	14 788	14 679	14 718	14 724	14 825	15 017	15 121	15 177	..
Germany	22 471	22 472	22 535	22 472	22 412	21 963	22 081	22 206	22 331	22 414
Greece	2 928	2 923	2 942	2 927	2 898	2 827	2 768	2 744	2 697	2 661
Hungary	2 267	2 261	2 238	2 234	2 234	2 257	2 296	2 327	2 386	2 432
Iceland	95	99	100	97	95	94	94	97	98	100
Ireland	1 226	1 277	1 289	1 260	1 216	1 200	1 187	1 189	1 186	1 192
Israel[1]	1 504	1 549	1 582	1 625	1 664	1 699 |	1 918	1 956	1 998	2 032
Italy	14 300	14 277	14 388	14 275	14 208	14 190	14 368	14 355	14 456	14 509
Japan	39 030	39 170	39 040	38 690 |	38 500	38 220	37 890	37 730	37 630	37 560
Korea	13 978	14 124	14 208	14 318	14 492	14 683	14 891	15 071	15 387	15 543
Latvia	567	578	580	550	521	512	511	504	497	499
Luxembourg	186 e	191 e	204 e	209 e	213 e	219 e	..	..	..	..
Mexico	27 165	27 469	28 091	28 438 |	30 648	30 939	31 742	31 939	32 177	32 684
Netherlands	4 719	4 765	4 798	4 810	4 734	4 691	4 761	4 804	4 802	4 795
New Zealand	1 188	1 202	1 205	1 209	1 220	1 233	1 229	1 242	1 280	1 313
Norway	1 280	1 309	1 354	1 351	1 366	1 376	1 410	1 420	1 432	1 458
Poland	9 283	9 234	9 317	9 455	9 446	9 504	9 551	9 568	9 593	9 569
Portugal	2 890	2 889	2 887	2 839	2 825 |	2 810	2 764	2 701	2 659	2 632
Slovak Republic	1 471	1 465	1 488	1 497	1 497	1 496	1 507	1 506	1 510	1 505
Slovenia	551	562	566	564	565	551	546	546	548	545
Spain	12 530	12 813	13 035	12 933	12 863	12 768	12 651	12 440	12 276	12 239
Sweden	2 444	2 540	2 574	2 581	2 621	2 645	2 660	2 688	2 725	2 736
Switzerland	2 461	2 516	2 553	2 578	2 608	2 665	2 706	2 733	2 775	2 808
Turkey	16 836	17 098	17 475	17 897	18 257	18 867	19 147	19 597 |	20 057	20 453
United Kingdom	16 437	16 600	16 781	16 811	16 808	17 011	17 140	17 200	17 309	17 336
United States	81 255	82 136	82 519	82 123	81 985	81 975	82 327	82 667	82 882	83 620
OECD-Total	**324 133 e**	**327 177 e**	**329 803 e**	**330 008 e**	**332 525 e**	**333 386 e**	..	..	..	..
G7	197 534	198 885	199 539	198 711 |	198 341	197 986	198 708	199 276	199 857	..
Euro area	86 450	87 015	87 574	87 267	86 426	86 187	86 514	86 363	86 696	86 789
European Union[2]	129 855	130 698	131 667	131 469	130 418	130 144	130 744	130 758	131 393	131 676
Brazil	53 610	54 370	55 530	56 166	..	56 622	57 143	57 540	58 867	..
Colombia	11 411	11 470	11 670	12 236	12 580	12 933	13 183	13 283	13 481	13 722
Russian Federation	37 594	38 119	38 594	38 501	38 601	38 717	38 720	38 720	38 729	39 433

Disclaimer: http://oe.cd/disclaimer

1. Information on data for Israel: http://oe.cd/israel-disclaimer.
2. European Union refer to European Union with 28 countries.

Table 5. Civilian employment, thousands

	2006	2007	2008	2009	2010	2011	2012	2013	2014	2015
Australia	10 124	10 434	10 731	10 806	11 022	11 215	11 347	11 451	11 532	11 752
Austria	3 816	3 912	3 982	3 969	4 006	4 043	4 075	4 094	4 102	4 138
Belgium	4 264	4 380	4 446	4 421	4 489	4 509	4 524	4 530	4 544	4 552
Canada	16 396	16 769	17 010	16 728	16 964	17 221	17 438	17 691	17 802	17 947
Chile	6 158	6 449	6 641	6 592	7 131	7 487	7 626	7 786	7 903	8 028
Czech Republic	4 811	4 908	4 986	4 920	4 870	4 888	4 872	4 920	4 957	5 028
Denmark	2 805	2 804	2 853	2 771	2 706	2 703	2 689	2 688	2 714	2 752
Estonia	647	654	653	591	565	601	613	619	622	638
Finland	2 434	2 483	2 522	2 449	2 438	2 464	2 474	2 448	2 439	2 428
France	25 758	26 120	26 249	25 963	26 004	26 213	26 304	26 353	26 459	..
Germany	36 949	37 763	38 345	38 279	38 549	38 598	38 931	39 343	39 691	40 024
Greece	4 532	4 572	4 637	4 585	4 437	4 124	3 730	3 535	3 539	3 626
Hungary	3 885	3 866	3 814	3 720	3 706	3 741	3 810	3 874	4 083	4 194
Iceland	170	177	179	168	167	167	169	175	178	184
Ireland	2 028	2 129	2 140	1 968	1 886	1 853	1 829	1 863	1 895	1 954
Israel[1]	2 581	2 692	2 784	2 841	2 938	3 025 |	3 359	3 450	3 556	3 644
Italy	22 509	22 646	22 848	22 450	22 269	22 359	22 300	21 949	22 042	22 216
Japan	63 890	64 270	64 090	63 140 |	62 980	62 890	62 700	63 110	63 510	63 760
Korea	23 151	23 433	23 577	23 506	23 829	24 244	24 681	25 066	25 599	25 936
Latvia	1 031	1 057	1 055	909	851	862	876	894	885	896
Luxembourg	319	333	349	352	360	370	379	387	396	406
Mexico	41 867	42 567	43 538	43 063 |	46 598	46 892	49 003	49 296	49 302	50 336
Netherlands	8 261	8 464	8 593	8 596	8 370	8 291	8 345	8 285	8 236	8 319
New Zealand	2 132	2 168	2 176	2 147	2 157	2 188	2 183	2 227	2 305	2 357
Norway	2 345	2 428	2 506	2 492	2 494	2 532	2 582	2 597	2 620	2 635
Poland	14 594	15 241	15 800	15 868	15 473	15 562	15 591	15 568	15 862	16 084
Portugal	5 051	5 059	5 087	4 940	4 874 |	4 709	4 517	4 404	4 475	4 520
Slovak Republic	2 301	2 357	2 434	2 366	2 318	2 315	2 329	2 329	2 363	2 424
Slovenia	961	985	996	981	966	936	924	906	917	917
Spain	19 853	20 491	20 373	19 000	18 619	18 321	17 536	17 052	17 249	17 776
Sweden	4 341	4 541	4 593	4 499	4 524	4 626	4 657	4 705	4 772	4 837
Switzerland	4 299	4 410	4 516	4 540	4 555	4 662	4 732	4 800	4 887	4 963
Turkey	20 423	20 738	21 194	21 277	22 594	24 110	24 821	25 524 |	25 933	26 621
United Kingdom	28 892	29 106	29 470	28 855	28 944	29 227	29 439	29 725	30 482	30 815
United States	144 427	146 047	145 363	139 878	139 064	139 869	142 469	143 929	146 305	148 833
OECD-Total	**538 005**	**546 454**	**550 528**	**539 626 |**	**543 714 |**	**547 818 |**	**553 852**	**557 573 |**	**564 155**	..
G7	338 822	342 721	343 375	335 293 |	334 774	336 377	339 581	342 100	346 292	..
Euro area	142 543	145 354	146 759	143 820	142 198	142 296	141 457	140 663	142 078	143 559
European Union[2]	216 156	220 363	222 876	218 952	216 121	216 219	215 811	215 415	218 334	220 845
Brazil	87 607	88 990	91 814	92 226	..	93 501	94 940	95 533	98 283	..
Colombia	16 895	17 106	17 442	18 420	19 213	20 020	20 696	21 048	21 503	22 017
Russian Federation	69 169	70 770	71 003	69 410	69 934	70 857	71 545	71 391	71 539	72 324

Disclaimer: http://oe.cd/disclaimer

1. Information on data for Israel: http://oe.cd/israel-disclaimer.
2. European Union refer to European Union with 28 countries.

Table 6. Civilian employment, index

2010=100

	2006	2007	2008	2009	2010	2011	2012	2013	2014	2015
Australia	91.9	94.7	97.4	98.0	100.0	101.7	103.0	103.9	104.6	106.6
Austria	95.3	97.7	99.4	99.1	100.0	100.9	101.7	102.2	102.4	103.3
Belgium	95.0	97.6	99.0	98.5	100.0	100.5	100.8	100.9	101.2	101.4
Canada	96.7	98.9	100.3	98.6	100.0	101.5	102.8	104.3	104.9	105.8
Chile	86.4	90.4	93.1	92.4	100.0	105.0	106.9	109.2	110.8	112.6
Czech Republic	98.8	100.8	102.4	101.0	100.0	100.4	100.0	101.0	101.8	103.2
Denmark	103.7	103.6	105.4	102.4	100.0	99.9	99.4	99.3	100.3	101.7
Estonia	114.6	115.8	115.6	104.7	100.0	106.4	108.5	109.7	110.2	112.9
Finland	99.9	101.9	103.5	100.5	100.0	101.1	101.5	100.4	100.1	99.6
France	99.1	100.4	100.9	99.8	100.0	100.8	101.2	101.3	101.8	..
Germany	95.8	98.0	99.5	99.3	100.0	100.1	101.0	102.1	103.0	103.8
Greece	102.1	103.1	104.5	103.3	100.0	93.0	84.1	79.7	79.8	81.7
Hungary	104.8	104.3	102.9	100.4	100.0	100.9	102.8	104.5	110.1	113.2
Iceland	101.4	106.0	106.8	100.3	100.0	100.1	101.2	104.6	106.3	109.9
Ireland	107.6	112.9	113.5	104.4	100.0	98.3	97.0	98.8	100.5	103.6
Israel[1]	87.8	91.6	94.8	96.7	100.0	102.9 |	114.3	117.4	121.0	124.0
Italy	101.1	101.7	102.6	100.8	100.0	100.4	100.1	98.6	99.0	99.8
Japan	101.4	102.0	101.8	100.3 |	100.0	99.9	99.6	100.2	100.8	101.2
Korea	97.2	98.3	98.9	98.6	100.0	101.7	103.6	105.2	107.4	108.8
Latvia	121.2	124.3	124.0	106.8	100.0	101.3	102.9	105.1	104.0	105.3
Luxembourg	88.6	92.6	97.0	97.9	100.0	102.9	105.3	107.5	110.0	112.8
Mexico	89.8	91.4	93.4	92.4 |	100.0	100.6	105.2	105.8	105.8	108.0
Netherlands	98.7	101.1	102.7	102.7	100.0	99.1	99.7	99.0	98.4	99.4
New Zealand	98.8	100.5	100.9	99.5	100.0	101.4	101.2	103.2	106.9	109.3
Norway	94.0	97.4	100.5	99.9	100.0	101.5	103.5	104.1	105.1	105.7
Poland	94.3	98.5	102.1	102.6	100.0	100.6	100.8	100.6	102.5	103.9
Portugal	103.6	103.8	104.4	101.4	100.0 |	96.6	92.7	90.4	91.8	92.8
Slovak Republic	99.3	101.7	105.0	102.1	100.0	99.9	100.5	100.5	102.0	104.6
Slovenia	99.5	102.0	103.1	101.5	100.0	96.9	95.6	93.8	94.9	95.0
Spain	106.6	110.1	109.4	102.0	100.0	98.4	94.2	91.6	92.6	95.5
Sweden	96.0	100.4	101.5	99.5	100.0	102.3	102.9	104.0	105.5	106.9
Switzerland	94.4	96.8	99.1	99.7	100.0	102.4	103.9	105.4	107.3	109.0
Turkey	90.4	91.8	93.8	94.2	100.0	106.7	109.9	113.0 |	114.8	117.8
United Kingdom	99.8	100.6	101.8	99.7	100.0	101.0	101.7	102.7	105.3	106.5
United States	103.9	105.0	104.5	100.6	100.0	100.6	102.4	103.5	105.2	107.0
OECD-Total	**99.0**	**100.5**	**101.3**	**99.2 |**	**100.0 |**	**100.8 |**	**101.9**	**102.5 |**	**103.8**	..
G7	101.2	102.4	102.6	100.2 |	100.0	100.5	101.4	102.2	103.4	..
Euro area	100.2	102.2	103.2	101.1	100.0	100.1	99.5	98.9	99.9	101.0
European Union[2]	100.0	102.0	103.1	101.3	100.0	100.0	99.9	99.7	101.0	102.2
Brazil	..	..	..	..	..	..	..	..	..	..
Colombia	87.9	89.0	90.8	95.9	100.0	104.2	107.7	109.6	111.9	114.6
Russian Federation	98.9	101.2	101.5	99.3	100.0	101.3	102.3	102.1	102.3	103.4

Disclaimer: http://oe.cd/disclaimer

1. Information on data for Israel: http://oe.cd/israel-disclaimer.
2. European Union refer to European Union with 28 countries.

Table 7. Female civilian employment, thousands

	2006	2007	2008	2009	2010	2011	2012	2013	2014	2015
Australia	4 565	4 702	4 851	4 926	5 001	5 106	5 184	5 249	5 297	5 422
Austria	1 741	1 785	1 830	1 848	1 868	1 890	1 913	1 924	1 937	1 954
Belgium	1 872	1 937	1 985	1 991	2 031	2 047	2 058	2 080	2 108	2 118
Canada	7 709	7 930	8 045	8 024	8 113	8 199	8 315	8 445	8 474	8 524
Chile	2 160	2 301	2 421	2 453	2 769	2 967	3 053	3 142	3 236	3 277
Czech Republic	2 085	2 115	2 138	2 110	2 086	2 108	2 109	2 142	2 155	2 203
Denmark	1 309	1 312	1 336	1 316	1 292	1 282	1 276	1 278	1 283	1 291
Estonia	321	322	321	302	290	300	305	306	304	313
Finland	1 177	1 202	1 216	1 202	1 188	1 196	1 206	1 195	1 193	1 188
France	12 153	12 394	12 557	12 526	12 568	12 650	12 693	12 724	12 800	..
Germany	16 822	17 230	17 497	17 644	17 834	17 971	18 086	18 367	18 548	18 733
Greece	1 768	1 795	1 834	1 846	1 813	1 688	1 543	1 459	1 477	1 538
Hungary	1 782	1 767	1 749	1 717	1 734	1 735	1 775	1 786	1 878	1 924
Iceland	78	81	81	80	80	80	81	84	85	88
Ireland	860	916	938	902	878	868	859	864	870	894
Israel[1]	1 196	1 248	1 293	1 339	1 387	1 421 |	1 571	1 614	1 675	1 715
Italy	8 998	9 077	9 264	9 151	9 146	9 254	9 366	9 268	9 328	9 376
Japan	26 540	26 650	26 640	26 490 |	26 560	26 530	26 540	27 010	27 290	27 540
Korea	9 706	9 826	9 874	9 772	9 914	10 091	10 294	10 494	10 761	10 965
Latvia	505	517	524	474	448	445	447	453	446	452
Luxembourg	139 e	148 e	151 e	152 e	156 e	161 e	..	..	..	..
Mexico	15 508	15 977	16 368	16 163 |	17 540	17 575	18 779	18 962	18 711	19 027
Netherlands	3 709	3 832	3 917	3 948	3 844	3 816	3 845	3 827	3 776	3 836
New Zealand	986	1 008	1 020	1 011	1 013	1 032	1 034	1 055	1 090	1 113
Norway	1 110	1 153	1 191	1 190	1 185	1 203	1 223	1 230	1 242	1 246
Poland	6 513	6 838	7 082	7 147	6 908	6 914	6 940	6 927	7 084	7 217
Portugal	2 352	2 362	2 389	2 354	2 326 |	2 250	2 187	2 139	2 178	2 212
Slovak Republic	1 010	1 036	1 070	1 039	1 033	1 023	1 026	1 034	1 047	1 075
Slovenia	438	446	453	450	443	430	424	411	417	417
Spain	8 122	8 503	8 656	8 363	8 290	8 257	8 014	7 816	7 888	8 096
Sweden	2 067	2 150	2 171	2 140	2 130	2 188	2 215	2 237	2 270	2 307
Switzerland	1 917	1 963	2 033	2 057	2 048	2 088	2 125	2 174	2 224	2 270
Turkey	5 258	5 356	5 596	5 871	6 425	6 973	7 309	7 641 |	7 689	8 058
United Kingdom	13 408	13 432	13 652	13 518	13 597	13 662	13 747	13 950	14 301	14 477
United States	66 926	67 792	67 876	66 208	65 705	65 579	66 914	67 577	68 613	69 703
OECD-Total	**232 808 e**	**237 103 e**	**240 018 e**	**237 725 e**	**239 642 e**	**240 978 e**	..	..	..	..
G7	152 555	154 505	155 530	153 562 |	153 522	153 844	155 661	157 341	159 353	..
Euro area	62 478	64 057	65 161	64 733	64 366	64 662	64 606	64 522	65 312	66 040
European Union[2]	96 094	98 238	99 837	99 205	98 157	98 466	98 621	98 746	100 223	101 415
Brazil	37 411	37 884	39 154	39 504	..	39 637	40 434	40 851	42 558	..
Colombia	6 533	6 637	6 807	7 326	7 760	8 144	8 547	8 742	8 962	9 220
Russian Federation	34 362	35 073	34 901	34 339	34 367	34 824	35 075	34 913	34 934	35 187

Disclaimer: http://oe.cd/disclaimer

1. Information on data for Israel: http://oe.cd/israel-disclaimer.
2. European Union refer to European Union with 28 countries.

Table 8. Female civilian employment as a percentage of civilian employment

Percentage

	2006	2007	2008	2009	2010	2011	2012	2013	2014	2015
Australia	45.1	45.1	45.2	45.6	45.4	45.5	45.7	45.8	45.9	46.1
Austria	45.6	45.6	46.0	46.6	46.6	46.7	46.9	47.0	47.2	47.2
Belgium	43.9	44.2	44.7	45.0	45.2	45.4	45.5	45.9	46.4	46.5
Canada	47.0	47.3	47.3	48.0	47.8	47.6	47.7	47.7	47.6	47.5
Chile	35.1	35.7	36.5	37.2	38.8	39.6	40.0	40.4	40.9	40.8
Czech Republic	43.3	43.1	42.9	42.9	42.8	43.1	43.3	43.5	43.5	43.8
Denmark	46.7	46.8	46.8	47.5	47.7	47.4	47.5	47.5	47.3	46.9
Estonia	49.6	49.3	49.2	51.1	51.4	49.9	49.8	49.5	48.9	49.0
Finland	48.4	48.4	48.2	49.1	48.7	48.5	48.7	48.8	48.9	48.9
France	47.2	47.4	47.8	48.2	48.3	48.3	48.3	48.3	48.4	..
Germany	45.5	45.6	45.6	46.1	46.3	46.6	46.5	46.7	46.7	46.8
Greece	39.0	39.3	39.6	40.3	40.9	40.9	41.4	41.3	41.7	42.4
Hungary	45.9	45.7	45.9	46.2	46.8	46.4	46.6	46.1	46.0	45.9
Iceland	45.7	45.5	45.6	47.4	47.9	48.0	48.0	47.9	47.8	47.7
Ireland	42.4	43.0	43.8	45.8	46.5	46.8	46.9	46.4	45.9	45.7
Israel[1]	46.3	46.3	46.4	47.1	47.2	47.0 |	46.8	46.8	47.1	47.1
Italy	40.0	40.1	40.5	40.8	41.1	41.4	42.0	42.2	42.3	42.2
Japan	41.5	41.5	41.6	42.0 |	42.2	42.2	42.3	42.8	43.0	43.2
Korea	41.9	41.9	41.9	41.6	41.6	41.6	41.7	41.9	42.0	42.3
Latvia	49.0	48.9	49.6	52.1	52.7	51.7	51.1	50.7	50.4	50.5
Luxembourg	43.7 e	44.5 e	43.4 e	43.2 e	43.4 e	43.4 e	..	..	..	..
Mexico	37.0	37.5	37.6	37.5 |	37.6	37.5	38.3	38.5	38.0	37.8
Netherlands	44.9	45.3	45.6	45.9	45.9	46.0	46.1	46.2	45.9	46.1
New Zealand	46.2	46.5	46.9	47.1	47.0	47.2	47.4	47.4	47.3	47.2
Norway	47.3	47.5	47.5	47.8	47.5	47.5	47.4	47.4	47.4	47.3
Poland	44.6	44.9	44.8	45.0	44.6	44.4	44.5	44.5	44.7	44.9
Portugal	46.6	46.7	47.0	47.6	47.7 |	47.8	48.4	48.6	48.7	48.9
Slovak Republic	43.9	43.9	44.0	43.9	44.6	44.2	44.0	44.4	44.3	44.3
Slovenia	45.5	45.2	45.5	45.9	45.8	45.9	45.9	45.4	45.5	45.4
Spain	40.9	41.5	42.5	44.0	44.5	45.1	45.7	45.8	45.7	45.5
Sweden	47.6	47.3	47.3	47.6	47.1	47.3	47.6	47.6	47.6	47.7
Switzerland	44.6	44.5	45.0	45.3	45.0	44.8	44.9	45.3	45.5	45.7
Turkey	25.7	25.8	26.4	27.6	28.4	28.9	29.4	29.9 |	29.6	30.3
United Kingdom	46.4	46.1	46.3	46.8	47.0	46.7	46.7	46.9	46.9	47.0
United States	46.3	46.4	46.7	47.3	47.2	46.9	47.0	47.0	46.9	46.8
OECD-Total	**43.3 e**	**43.4 e**	**43.6 e**	**44.1 e**	**44.1 e**	**44.0 e**	..	..	..	..
G7	45.0	45.1	45.3	45.8 |	45.9	45.7	45.8	46.0	46.0	..
Euro area	43.8	44.1	44.4	45.0	45.3	45.4	45.7	45.9	46.0	46.0
European Union[2]	44.5	44.6	44.8	45.3	45.4	45.5	45.7	45.8	45.9	45.9
Brazil	42.7	42.6	42.6	42.8	..	42.4	42.6	42.8	43.3	..
Colombia	38.7	38.8	39.0	39.8	40.4	40.7	41.3	41.5	41.7	41.9
Russian Federation	49.7	49.6	49.2	49.5	49.1	49.1	49.0	48.9	48.8	48.7

Disclaimer: http://oe.cd/disclaimer

1. Information on data for Israel: http://oe.cd/israel-disclaimer.
2. European Union refer to European Union with 28 countries.

Table 9. Male civilian employment, thousands

	2006	2007	2008	2009	2010	2011	2012	2013	2014	2015
Australia	5 560	5 732	5 880	5 879	6 021	6 109	6 164	6 202	6 235	6 329
Austria	2 075	2 127	2 152	2 120	2 137	2 153	2 162	2 170	2 164	2 184
Belgium	2 392	2 444	2 461	2 429	2 458	2 462	2 466	2 451	2 435	2 434
Canada	8 687	8 839	8 965	8 703	8 852	9 023	9 123	9 246	9 328	9 423
Chile	3 998	4 147	4 221	4 139	4 361	4 520	4 573	4 645	4 667	4 751
Czech Republic	2 727	2 793	2 848	2 810	2 784	2 780	2 762	2 779	2 801	2 824
Denmark	1 496	1 492	1 517	1 454	1 415	1 421	1 413	1 410	1 433	1 461
Estonia	326	332	332	289	275	301	307	313	318	325
Finland	1 257	1 281	1 306	1 247	1 250	1 268	1 268	1 253	1 246	1 240
France	13 605	13 726	13 692	13 437	13 436	13 563	13 611	13 629	13 660	..
Germany	20 127	20 534	20 849	20 636	20 716	20 627	20 846	20 976	21 143	21 291
Greece	2 763	2 778	2 803	2 739	2 623	2 436	2 187	2 076	2 062	2 088
Hungary	2 103	2 099	2 065	2 002	1 972	2 005	2 035	2 088	2 205	2 270
Iceland	92	97	97	88	87	87	88	91	93	96
Ireland	1 168	1 213	1 202	1 066	1 008	986	971	1 000	1 025	1 061
Israel[1]	1 385	1 444	1 491	1 502	1 552	1 604 |	1 788	1 835	1 880	1 928
Italy	13 511	13 569	13 584	13 299	13 124	13 105	12 934	12 680	12 714	12 840
Japan	37 350	37 630	37 450	36 660 |	36 430	36 360	36 160	36 100	36 210	36 220
Korea	13 444	13 607	13 703	13 734	13 915	14 153	14 387	14 573	14 839	14 971
Latvia	526	540	531	435	403	416	428	441	439	444
Luxembourg	180 e	185 e	198 e	200 e	204 e	210 e	..	..	..	..
Mexico	26 359	26 590	27 170	26 900 |	29 057	29 316	30 224	30 334	30 591	31 309
Netherlands	4 552	4 631	4 676	4 648	4 526	4 475	4 501	4 459	4 460	4 482
New Zealand	1 146	1 161	1 156	1 136	1 144	1 156	1 149	1 172	1 216	1 244
Norway	1 235	1 275	1 316	1 302	1 309	1 329	1 359	1 367	1 378	1 390
Poland	8 081	8 403	8 718	8 722	8 566	8 648	8 651	8 641	8 778	8 867
Portugal	2 699	2 697	2 698	2 587	2 548 |	2 459	2 330	2 265	2 297	2 309
Slovak Republic	1 291	1 322	1 364	1 326	1 285	1 292	1 304	1 295	1 316	1 349
Slovenia	524	540	543	531	524	506	500	495	499	501
Spain	11 731	11 988	11 717	10 636	10 329	10 064	9 521	9 236	9 360	9 681
Sweden	2 273	2 390	2 422	2 359	2 394	2 438	2 442	2 468	2 503	2 530
Switzerland	2 382	2 446	2 483	2 483	2 507	2 574	2 607	2 625	2 663	2 693
Turkey	15 165	15 382	15 598	15 406	16 170	17 137	17 512	17 883 |	18 244	18 562
United Kingdom	15 484	15 674	15 818	15 336	15 347	15 565	15 692	15 775	16 182	16 338
United States	77 502	78 254	77 486	73 670	73 359	74 290	75 555	76 353	77 692	79 131
OECD-Total	**305 197 e**	**309 363 e**	**310 513 e**	**301 913 e**	**304 085 e**	**306 839 e**	..	..	..	..
G7	186 267	188 227	187 845	181 742 |	181 263	182 533	183 921	184 760	186 929	..
Euro area	80 064	81 297	81 597	79 087	77 832	77 634	76 851	76 141	76 766	77 519
European Union[2]	120 061	122 125	123 039	119 748	117 964	117 753	117 190	116 669	118 111	119 431
Brazil	50 196	51 105	52 660	52 722	..	53 864	54 506	54 682	55 725	..
Colombia	10 362	10 469	10 635	11 094	11 453	11 875	12 149	12 306	12 541	12 798
Russian Federation	34 807	35 698	36 103	35 071	35 566	36 032	36 470	36 478	36 605	37 137

Disclaimer: http://oe.cd/disclaimer

1. Information on data for Israel: http://oe.cd/israel-disclaimer.
2. European Union refer to European Union with 28 countries.

Table 10. Male civilian employment as a percentage of civilian employment

Percentage

	2006	2007	2008	2009	2010	2011	2012	2013	2014	2015
Australia	54.9	54.9	54.8	54.4	54.6	54.5	54.3	54.2	54.1	53.9
Austria	54.4	54.4	54.0	53.4	53.4	53.3	53.1	53.0	52.8	52.8
Belgium	56.1	55.8	55.3	55.0	54.8	54.6	54.5	54.1	53.6	53.5
Canada	53.0	52.7	52.7	52.0	52.2	52.4	52.3	52.3	52.4	52.5
Chile	64.9	64.3	63.5	62.8	61.2	60.4	60.0	59.6	59.1	59.2
Czech Republic	56.7	56.9	57.1	57.1	57.2	56.9	56.7	56.5	56.5	56.2
Denmark	53.3	53.2	53.2	52.5	52.3	52.6	52.5	52.5	52.8	53.1
Estonia	50.4	50.7	50.8	48.9	48.6	50.1	50.2	50.5	51.1	51.0
Finland	51.6	51.6	51.8	50.9	51.3	51.5	51.3	51.2	51.1	51.1
France	52.8	52.6	52.2	51.8	51.7	51.7	51.7	51.7	51.6	..
Germany	54.5	54.4	54.4	53.9	53.7	53.4	53.5	53.3	53.3	53.2
Greece	61.0	60.7	60.4	59.7	59.1	59.1	58.6	58.7	58.3	57.6
Hungary	54.1	54.3	54.1	53.8	53.2	53.6	53.4	53.9	54.0	54.1
Iceland	54.3	54.5	54.4	52.6	52.1	52.0	52.0	52.1	52.2	52.3
Ireland	57.6	57.0	56.2	54.2	53.5	53.2	53.1	53.6	54.1	54.3
Israel[1]	53.7	53.7	53.6	52.9	52.8	53.0 |	53.2	53.2	52.9	52.9
Italy	60.0	59.9	59.5	59.2	58.9	58.6	58.0	57.8	57.7	57.8
Japan	58.5	58.5	58.4	58.1 |	57.8	57.8	57.7	57.2	57.0	56.8
Korea	58.1	58.1	58.1	58.4	58.4	58.4	58.3	58.1	58.0	57.7
Latvia	51.0	51.1	50.4	47.9	47.3	48.3	48.9	49.3	49.6	49.5
Luxembourg	56.6 e	55.7 e	56.8 e	56.9 e	56.6 e	56.6 e	..	..	..	..
Mexico	63.0	62.5	62.4	62.5 |	62.4	62.5	61.7	61.5	62.0	62.2
Netherlands	55.1	54.7	54.4	54.1	54.1	54.0	53.9	53.8	54.1	53.9
New Zealand	53.8	53.6	53.1	52.9	53.0	52.8	52.6	52.6	52.8	52.8
Norway	52.7	52.5	52.5	52.2	52.5	52.5	52.6	52.6	52.6	52.8
Poland	55.4	55.1	55.2	55.0	55.4	55.6	55.5	55.5	55.3	55.1
Portugal	53.4	53.3	53.0	52.4	52.3 |	52.2	51.6	51.4	51.3	51.1
Slovak Republic	56.1	56.1	56.0	56.1	55.4	55.8	56.0	55.6	55.7	55.7
Slovenia	54.5	54.8	54.5	54.1	54.2	54.1	54.1	54.6	54.5	54.6
Spain	59.1	58.5	57.5	56.0	55.5	54.9	54.3	54.2	54.3	54.5
Sweden	52.4	52.6	52.7	52.4	52.9	52.7	52.4	52.4	52.4	52.3
Switzerland	55.4	55.5	55.0	54.7	55.0	55.2	55.1	54.7	54.5	54.3
Turkey	74.3	74.2	73.6	72.4	71.6	71.1	70.6	70.1 |	70.4	69.7
United Kingdom	53.6	53.9	53.7	53.2	53.0	53.3	53.3	53.1	53.1	53.0
United States	53.7	53.6	53.3	52.7	52.8	53.1	53.0	53.0	53.1	53.2
OECD-Total	**56.7 e**	**56.6 e**	**56.4 e**	**55.9 e**	**55.9 e**	**56.0 e**	..	..	..	..
G7	55.0	54.9	54.7	54.2 |	54.1	54.3	54.2	54.0	54.0	..
Euro area	56.2	55.9	55.6	55.0	54.7	54.6	54.3	54.1	54.0	54.0
European Union[2]	55.5	55.4	55.2	54.7	54.6	54.5	54.3	54.2	54.1	54.1
Brazil	57.3	57.4	57.4	57.2	..	57.6	57.4	57.2	56.7	..
Colombia	61.3	61.2	61.0	60.2	59.6	59.3	58.7	58.5	58.3	58.1
Russian Federation	50.3	50.4	50.8	50.5	50.9	50.9	51.0	51.1	51.2	51.3

Disclaimer: http://oe.cd/disclaimer

1. Information on data for Israel: http://oe.cd/israel-disclaimer.
2. European Union refer to European Union with 28 countries.

Table 11. Civilian employment in agriculture, thousands

	2006	2007	2008	2009	2010	2011	2012	2013	2014	2015
Australia	344	346	345	348	355	315	317	299	323	311
Austria	188	206	210	212	209	200	191	188	199	188
Belgium	83	81	69	66	61	59	53	62	55	54
Canada	435	419	406	395	379	376	375	382	370	360
Chile	770	774	764	737	756	768	761 |	728	727	737
Czech Republic	174	169	159	154	151	146	149	150	137	147
Denmark	..	..	..	72	66	65	70	68	67	69
Estonia	32	31	26	24	24	27	28	27	24	25
Finland	114	113	114	113	108	104	103	101	104	103
France	737	711	689	674	662	657	656	656	..	..
Germany	843	858	871 |	647	633	638	611	572	570	560
Greece	536	522	516	526	547	504	484	481	476	472
Hungary	191	183	174	175	173	185	193	185	190	203
Iceland	11	11 |	8	9	10	10	10	8	8	8
Ireland	109	109	116	98	85	86	87	103	110	113
Israel[1]	46	43	48	48	48	43	51 |	43	40	37
Italy	982	923	895	838	849	832	833	799	812	843
Japan	2 720	2 720	2 680	2 620 |	2 520	2 230	2 400	2 330	2 300	2 280
Korea	1 781	1 723	1 686	1 648	1 567	1 542	1 528	1 520	1 452	1 345
Latvia	..	108	84	80	73	77	73	72	66	71
Luxembourg	5	5	4	4	4	5	5	5	5	5
Mexico	5 905	5 655	5 652	5 558	6 417	6 246	6 573	6 594	6 680	6 773
Netherlands	258	..	224	218	233	206	205	159	174	178
New Zealand	153	155	152	147	145	151	147	143	143	143
Norway	77	69	70	67	63	60	57	57	59	53
Poland	2 304	2 247	2 206	2 107	2 050	2 045	1 960	1 867	1 820	1 849
Portugal	604	601	596	569	549 |	484	491	453	389	343
Slovak Republic	101	99	98	85	75	71	75	77	83	77
Slovenia	92	96	85	89	85	80	77	77	88	64
Spain	944	926	879	788	786	755	743	737	736	737
Sweden	86	102	101	98	95	92	96	95	95	99
Switzerland	..	..	..	..	156	165	167	170	173	161
Turkey	4 908	4 866	5 016	5 240	5 683	6 143	6 097	6 015 |	5 470	5 483
United Kingdom	290	299	325 |	311	341	342	353	308	395	340
United States	2 206	2 095	2 168	2 103	2 206	2 254	2 186	2 130	2 237	2 422
OECD-Total	**..**	**..**	**..**	**26 867 e**	**28 163 |**	**27 960**	**28 207 |**	**27 659 |**	**..**	**..**
G7	8 214	8 025	8 033 |	7 589 |	7 591	7 329	7 414	7 176	..	..
Euro area	6 183	5 990	5 336	5 245	5 181	4 989	4 929	4 822	4 774	4 675
European Union[2]	12 528	12 214	11 522	11 322	11 184	10 770	10 682	10 363	10 264	9 934
Brazil	16 531	15 940	15 694	15 393	..	14 323	13 569	13 568	14 025	..
Colombia	3 226	3 142	3 176	3 440	3 561	3 634	3 622	3 549	3 495	3 544
Russian Federation	6 831	6 268	6 058	5 739	5 418	5 446	5 242	4 992	4 811	..

Disclaimer: http://oe.cd/disclaimer

1. Information on data for Israel: http://oe.cd/israel-disclaimer.
2. European Union refer to European Union with 28 countries.

Table 12. Civilian employment in agriculture, index

2010=100

	2006	2007	2008	2009	2010	2011	2012	2013	2014	2015
Australia	96.9	97.3	97.1	98.1	100.0	88.8	89.2	84.2	91.0	87.7
Austria	89.9	98.2	100.2	101.2	100.0	95.6	91.2	89.7	95.0	89.8
Belgium	136.6	133.8	113.8	108.3	100.0	96.6	87.4	101.5	91.2	88.2
Canada	114.9	110.6	107.0	104.3	100.0	99.1	98.9	100.8	97.7	95.0
Chile	101.8	102.3	101.1	97.4	100.0	101.6	100.7 |	96.3	96.2	97.5
Czech Republic	115.2	111.7	105.0	101.7	100.0	96.4	98.6	98.9	90.4	97.5
Denmark	..	..	..	109.2	100.0	98.9	106.3	104.0	102.6	104.6
Estonia	133.5	128.9	106.7	100.4	100.0	111.3	115.5	110.9	100.8	104.6
Finland	105.6	104.6	105.6	104.6	100.0	96.3	95.4	93.5	96.3	95.4
France	111.2	107.4	104.0	101.8	100.0	99.2	99.0	99.0	..	..
Germany	133.2	135.5	137.6 |	102.2	100.0	100.8	96.5	90.4	90.0	88.5
Greece	98.1	95.6	94.4	96.2	100.0	92.1	88.6	88.0	87.1	86.4
Hungary	110.5	105.9	100.7	101.2	100.0	106.8	111.5	106.8	109.7	117.6
Iceland	108.4	106.4 |	84.1	88.5	100.0	101.9	97.6	81.2	81.2	78.8
Ireland	128.1	127.7	136.3	114.6	100.0	100.7	102.4	121.5	129.0	132.2
Israel[1]	95.2	90.8	100.3	100.3	100.0	89.0	107.7 |	90.1	83.7	78.1
Italy	115.7	108.7	105.4	98.7	100.0	98.0	98.2	94.1	95.6	99.3
Japan	107.9	107.9	106.3	104.0 |	100.0	88.5	95.2	92.5	91.3	90.5
Korea	113.7	110.0	107.6	105.2	100.0	98.4	97.5	97.0	92.7	85.9
Latvia	..	146.7	114.5	108.5	100.0	104.5	100.0	98.1	90.5	97.0
Luxembourg	111.4	118.2	97.7	97.7	100.0	102.3	102.3	104.5	104.5	104.5
Mexico	92.0	88.1	88.1	86.6	100.0	97.3	102.4	102.8	104.1	105.5
Netherlands	110.9	..	96.1	93.8	100.0	88.6	88.2	68.4	74.8	76.5
New Zealand	105.5	106.9	104.8	101.4	100.0	104.1	101.4	98.6	98.6	98.6
Norway	122.2	109.5	111.1	106.3	100.0	95.2	90.5	90.5	93.7	84.1
Poland	112.4	109.6	107.6	102.8	100.0	99.8	95.6	91.1	88.8	90.2
Portugal	110.1	109.6	108.6	103.7	100.0 |	88.2	89.6	82.6	70.9	62.4
Slovak Republic	134.4	132.4	130.7	113.2	100.0	95.1	100.5	102.8	110.3	102.8
Slovenia	107.9	113.2	100.5	105.0	100.0	94.5	90.9	90.4	103.5	75.6
Spain	120.1	117.7	111.8	100.3	100.0	96.1	94.6	93.7	93.6	93.7
Sweden	90.7	107.4	106.3	103.2	100.0	97.2	101.3	100.4	99.5	104.0
Switzerland	..	..	..	..	100.0	105.8	107.1	109.0	110.9	103.2
Turkey	86.4	85.6	88.3	92.2	100.0	108.1	107.3	105.8 |	96.3	96.5
United Kingdom	85.0	87.6	95.2 |	91.2	100.0	100.3	103.5	90.2	115.7	99.7
United States	100.0	95.0	98.3	95.3	100.0	102.2	99.1	96.5	101.4	109.8
OECD-Total	**..**	**..**	**..**	**95.4 e**	**100.0 |**	**99.3**	**100.2 |**	**98.2 |**	**..**	**..**
G7	108.2	105.7	105.8 |	100.0 |	100.0	96.6	97.7	94.5	..	..
Euro area	119.3	115.6	103.0	101.2	100.0	96.3	95.1	93.1	92.2	90.2
European Union[2]	112.0	109.2	103.0	101.2	100.0	96.3	95.5	92.7	91.8	88.8
Brazil	..	..	..	..	..	..	..	..	..	..
Colombia	90.6	88.2	89.2	96.6	100.0	102.0	101.7	99.7	98.1	99.5
Russian Federation	126.1	115.7	111.8	105.9	100.0	100.5	96.7	92.1	88.8	..

Disclaimer: http://oe.cd/disclaimer

1. Information on data for Israel: http://oe.cd/israel-disclaimer.
2. European Union refer to European Union with 28 countries.

Table 13. Civilian employment in industry, thousands

	2006	2007	2008	2009	2010	2011	2012	2013	2014	2015
Australia	2 219	2 280	2 396	2 353	2 389	2 408	2 432	2 413	2 428	2 372
Austria	1 085	1 087	1 048	994	1 001	1 055	1 065	1 063	1 059	1 069
Belgium	1 053	1 071	1 097	1 038	1 049	1 048	984	983	972	976
Canada	3 526	3 538	3 561	3 312	3 336	3 415	3 488	3 518	3 516	3 500
Chile	1 456	1 533	1 587	1 531	1 637	1 750	1 817 |	1 886	1 883	1 904
Czech Republic	1 929	1 976	2 027	1 903	1 856	1 883	1 864	1 852	1 892	1 917
Denmark	654	658	..	..	..	..	529	522	521	529
Estonia	217	230	231	186	172	196	191	188	188	196
Finland	627	640	644	586	567	565	563	559	533	526
France	5 001 e	5 019 e	5 004 e	4 783 e	4 665 e	4 669 e	..	..	..	..
Germany	11 022	11 357	11 485 |	11 078	10 990	10 952	11 028	10 976	11 181	11 130
Greece	981	1 011	1 031	966	883	729	615	552	532	539
Hungary	1 270	1 281	1 247	1 167	1 147	1 161	1 141	1 165	1 249	1 273
Iceland	36	37 |	39	32	30	30	31	32	33	33
Ireland	546	576	538	421	371	346	331	341	342	372
Israel[1]	548	582	597	570	587	595	585 |	609	622	634
Italy	6 927	7 003	6 955	6 637	6 445	6 393	6 224	6 002	5 993	5 976
Japan	17 890	17 870	17 460	16 910 |	16 440	15 570	16 260	16 290	16 370	16 260
Korea	6 043	6 027	5 954	5 747	5 945	6 005	6 041	6 117	6 309	6 503
Latvia	282	302	310	221	196	..	205	214	211	212
Luxembourg	74	75	78	76	77	78	78	77	77	78
Mexico	10 813	11 022	11 219	10 446	11 172	11 449	11 559	11 770	12 134	12 543
Netherlands	1 595	1 569	1 514	1 426	1 335	1 270	1 292	1 254	1 232	1 261
New Zealand	479	478	473	451	450	444	439	449	478	517
Norway	490	513	529	504	492	512	520	524	535	528
Poland	4 373	4 682	5 036	4 934	4 812	4 933	4 740	4 752	4 836	4 897
Portugal	1 577	1 578	1 521	1 381	1 335 |	1 273	1 143	1 050	1 074	1 107
Slovak Republic	893	928	961	897	860	868	874	835	838	875
Slovenia	340	343	348	323	314	295	285	280	282	290
Spain	5 835	5 959	5 630	4 697	4 302	4 009	3 645	3 385	3 373	3 556
Sweden	957	982	994	904	899	918	911	898	885	882
Switzerland	..	..	..	..	1 026	1 051	1 054	1 042	1 057	1 064
Turkey	5 465	5 544	5 682	5 385	5 926	6 380	6 459	6 737 |	..	..
United Kingdom	6 559	6 660	6 406 |	5 644	5 544	5 586	5 623	5 551	5 724	5 758
United States	28 812	28 895	27 697	24 611	23 888	24 193	24 608	25 206	26 001	26 191
OECD-Total	**131 573 e**	**133 305 e**	..	..	..	..	..	..	..	..
G7	79 737 e	80 342 e	78 568 e	72 975 e	71 308 e	70 778 e	..	..	..	..
Euro area	39 463	40 110	39 671	37 144	35 712	35 335	34 506	33 593	33 643	33 868
European Union[2]	59 115	60 436	60 814	56 706	54 327	53 993	53 060	52 102	52 601	52 909
Brazil	18 934	19 738	21 001	20 612	..	20 506	21 700	21 754	22 036	..
Colombia	3 343	3 454	3 482	3 648	3 811	4 102	4 242	4 085	4 224	4 302
Russian Federation	20 232	20 635	20 569	19 109	19 402	19 452	19 867	19 794	19 685	19 658

Disclaimer: http://oe.cd/disclaimer

1. Information on data for Israel: http://oe.cd/israel-disclaimer.
2. European Union refer to European Union with 28 countries.

Table 14. Civilian employment in industry, index

2010=100

	2006	2007	2008	2009	2010	2011	2012	2013	2014	2015
Australia	92.9	95.4	100.3	98.5	100.0	100.8	101.8	101.0	101.6	99.3
Austria	108.5	108.6	104.7	99.4	100.0	105.4	106.5	106.3	105.9	106.8
Belgium	100.3	102.0	104.5	98.9	100.0	99.9	93.8	93.7	92.6	93.0
Canada	105.7	106.0	106.7	99.3	100.0	102.3	104.5	105.4	105.4	104.9
Chile	88.9	93.6	97.0	93.5	100.0	106.9	111.0 |	115.2	115.0	116.3
Czech Republic	104.0	106.5	109.2	102.6	100.0	101.5	100.5	99.8	102.0	103.3
Denmark	..	..	..	..	..	..	..	..	..	..
Estonia	126.2	133.8	134.3	108.4	100.0	113.8	111.2	109.3	109.4	114.1
Finland	110.6	112.9	113.6	103.4	100.0	99.6	99.3	98.6	94.0	92.8
France	107.2 e	107.6 e	107.3 e	102.5 e	100.0 e	100.1 e	..	..	..	..
Germany	100.3	103.3	104.5 |	100.8	100.0	99.7	100.3	99.9	101.7	101.3
Greece	111.1	114.5	116.8	109.3	100.0	82.6	69.6	62.5	60.2	61.0
Hungary	110.7	111.7	108.7	101.8	100.0	101.2	99.4	101.6	108.9	111.0
Iceland	120.0	121.0 |	129.1	106.0	100.0	100.1	101.3	107.4	108.1	108.1
Ireland	146.9	155.0	144.8	113.4	100.0	93.2	89.2	91.9	92.1	100.1
Israel[1]	93.3	99.0	101.7	97.1	100.0	101.4	99.7 |	103.7	105.9	108.0
Italy	107.5	108.7	107.9	103.0	100.0	99.2	96.6	93.1	93.0	92.7
Japan	108.8	108.7	106.2	102.9 |	100.0	94.7	98.9	99.1	99.6	98.9
Korea	101.7	101.4	100.1	96.7	100.0	101.0	101.6	102.9	106.1	109.4
Latvia	143.7	154.1	158.0	112.7	100.0	..	104.7	108.9	107.5	108.0
Luxembourg	96.6	98.6	101.3	99.9	100.0	101.6	102.0	100.4	100.8	102.2
Mexico	96.8	98.7	100.4	93.5	100.0	102.5	103.5	105.4	108.6	112.3
Netherlands	119.5	117.5	113.4	106.8	100.0	95.2	96.8	94.0	92.3	94.4
New Zealand	106.4	106.2	105.1	100.2	100.0	98.7	97.6	99.8	106.2	114.9
Norway	99.6	104.3	107.5	102.4	100.0	104.1	105.7	106.5	108.7	107.3
Poland	90.9	97.3	104.7	102.5	100.0	102.5	98.5	98.8	100.5	101.8
Portugal	118.1	118.2	113.9	103.5	100.0 |	95.3	85.6	78.6	80.4	83.0
Slovak Republic	103.8	107.9	111.7	104.3	100.0	100.9	101.6	97.0	97.3	101.7
Slovenia	108.3	109.5	111.1	103.2	100.0	94.1	90.8	89.2	89.9	92.5
Spain	135.6	138.5	130.9	109.2	100.0	93.2	84.7	78.7	78.4	82.7
Sweden	106.5	109.3	110.6	100.6	100.0	102.2	101.4	99.9	98.4	98.1
Switzerland	..	..	..	..	100.0	102.4	102.7	101.6	103.0	103.7
Turkey	92.2	93.6	95.9	90.9	100.0	107.7	109.0	113.7 |	..	..
United Kingdom	118.3	120.1	115.5 |	101.8	100.0	100.8	101.4	100.1	103.2	103.9
United States	120.6	121.0	115.9	103.0	100.0	101.3	103.0	105.5	108.8	109.6
OECD-Total	..	..	..	..	..	..	..	..	..	..
G7	111.8 e	112.7 e	110.2 e	102.3 e	100.0 e	99.3 e	..	..	..	..
Euro area	110.5	112.3	111.1	104.0	100.0	98.9	96.6	94.1	94.2	94.8
European Union[2]	108.8	111.2	111.9	104.4	100.0	99.4	97.7	95.9	96.8	97.4
Brazil	..	..	..	..	..	..	..	..	..	..
Colombia	87.7	90.6	91.4	95.7	100.0	107.6	111.3	107.2	110.8	112.9
Russian Federation	104.3	106.4	106.0	98.5	100.0	100.3	102.4	102.0	101.5	101.3

Disclaimer: http://oe.cd/disclaimer

1. Information on data for Israel: http://oe.cd/israel-disclaimer.
2. European Union refer to European Union with 28 countries.

Table 15. Civilian employment in services, thousands

	2006	2007	2008	2009	2010	2011	2012	2013	2014	2015
Australia	7 561	7 809	7 991	8 104	8 278	8 492	8 599	8 739	8 781	9 068
Austria	2 542	2 620	2 724	2 762	2 796	2 789	2 819	2 843	2 844	2 881
Belgium	3 129	3 229	3 280	3 317	3 379	3 403	3 487	3 485	3 516	3 522
Canada	12 435	12 812	13 044	13 020	13 249	13 431	13 575	13 791	13 916	14 087
Chile	3 932	4 142	4 290	4 324	4 737	4 969	5 047 |	5 172	5 293	5 387
Czech Republic	2 708	2 763	2 800	2 863	2 864	2 860	2 858	2 919	2 928	2 963
Denmark	..	..	..	..	..	..	2 090	2 097	2 126	2 154
Estonia	399	393	397	381	369	379	394	405	410	417
Finland	1 693	1 730	1 764	1 750	1 763	1 795	1 808	1 788	1 802	1 799
France	20 021 e	20 390 e	20 557 e	20 506 e	20 676 e	20 887 e	..	..	..	..
Germany	25 084	25 548	25 989 |	26 554	26 926	27 008	27 292	27 795	27 940	28 334
Greece	3 015	3 039	3 090	3 093	3 007	2 891	2 631	2 502	2 531	2 614
Hungary	2 424	2 401	2 393	2 377	2 386	2 395	2 476	2 525	2 644	2 718
Iceland	123	130 |	131	127	127	127	129	134	137	143
Ireland	1 374	1 445	1 487	1 450	1 430	1 422	1 411	1 419	1 443	1 470
Israel[1]	1 988	2 067	2 139	2 223	2 303	2 387 |	2 722 |	2 797	2 894	2 973
Italy	14 600	14 720	14 998	14 976	14 975	15 134	15 242	15 148	15 237	15 397
Japan	43 280	43 680	43 950	43 610 |	44 020	45 090	44 040	44 490	44 840	45 220
Korea	15 327	15 683	15 938	16 110	16 317	16 697	17 111	17 430	17 838	18 088
Latvia	..	648	661	608	581	..	597	608	608	613
Luxembourg	240	252	267	272	279	288	296	305	314	323
Mexico	25 149	25 890	26 667	27 059 |	29 008	29 197	30 871	30 932	30 488	31 020
Netherlands	6 408	..	6 855	6 952	6 803	6 815	6 848	6 872	6 830	6 880
New Zealand	1 500	1 535	1 551	1 549	1 562	1 593	1 597	1 635	1 684	1 697
Norway	1 778	1 846	1 907	1 921	1 939	1 960	2 005	2 016	2 026	2 054
Poland	7 917	8 312	8 558	8 827	8 611	8 584	8 891	8 949	9 206	9 338
Portugal	2 870	2 879	2 970	2 990	2 990 |	2 952	2 882	2 901	3 013	3 071
Slovak Republic	1 308	1 330	1 375	1 384	1 382	1 376	1 380	1 418	1 443	1 472
Slovenia	530	546	563	568	568	561	562	550	547	563
Spain	13 073	13 606	13 864	13 514	13 531	13 557	13 147	12 930	13 139	13 484
Sweden	3 298	3 457	3 498	3 497	3 530	3 615	3 650	3 711	3 793	3 857
Switzerland	..	..	..	..	3 373	3 446	3 511	3 588	3 657	3 738
Turkey	10 050	10 328	10 496	10 652	10 985	11 587	12 265	12 772 |	..	..
United Kingdom	22 042	22 147	22 739 |	22 900	23 058	23 299	23 463	23 866	24 364	24 716
United States	113 409	115 058	115 498	113 163	112 970	113 422	115 675	116 594	118 067	120 220
OECD-Total	..	..	..	..	..	..	..	..	..	..
G7	250 871 e	254 355 e	256 774 e	254 729 e	255 875 e	258 270 e	..	..	..	..
Euro area	96 897	99 254	101 752	101 431	101 304	101 972	102 022	102 248	103 661	105 016
European Union[2]	144 512	147 714	150 540	150 924	150 610	151 456	152 069	152 950	155 470	158 002
Brazil	52 143	53 312	55 119	56 221	..	58 671	59 671	60 211	62 221	..
Colombia	10 326	10 510	10 783	11 332	11 841	12 284	12 832	13 414	13 784	14 172
Russian Federation	42 106	43 867	44 375	44 562	45 114	45 959	46 437	46 605	47 044	..

Disclaimer: http://oe.cd/disclaimer

1. Information on data for Israel: http://oe.cd/israel-disclaimer.
2. European Union refer to European Union with 28 countries.

Table 16. Civilian employment in services, index

2010=100

	2006	2007	2008	2009	2010	2011	2012	2013	2014	2015
Australia	91.3	94.3	96.5	97.9	100.0	102.6	103.9	105.6	106.1	109.5
Austria	90.9	93.7	97.4	98.8	100.0	99.8	100.8	101.7	101.7	103.1
Belgium	92.6	95.6	97.1	98.2	100.0	100.7	103.2	103.2	104.1	104.3
Canada	93.9	96.7	98.4	98.3	100.0	101.4	102.5	104.1	105.0	106.3
Chile	83.0	87.4	90.6	91.3	100.0	104.9	106.5 |	109.2	111.7	113.7
Czech Republic	94.6	96.5	97.8	100.0	100.0	99.9	99.8	101.9	102.2	103.5
Denmark	..	..	..	..	..	..	..	..	..	..
Estonia	108.0	106.6	107.5	103.2	100.0	102.7	106.8	109.7	111.2	113.0
Finland	96.1	98.2	100.1	99.3	100.0	101.8	102.6	101.4	102.2	102.1
France	96.8 e	98.6 e	99.4 e	99.2 e	100.0 e	101.0 e	..	..	..	..
Germany	93.2	94.9	96.5 |	98.6	100.0	100.3	101.4	103.2	103.8	105.2
Greece	100.3	101.1	102.8	102.9	100.0	96.2	87.5	83.2	84.2	86.9
Hungary	101.6	100.6	100.3	99.6	100.0	100.3	103.8	105.8	110.8	113.9
Iceland	96.4	102.4 |	103.2	99.9	100.0	100.0	101.5	105.8	107.8	112.7
Ireland	96.1	101.1	104.0	101.4	100.0	99.5	98.7	99.2	101.0	102.8
Israel[1]	86.3	89.7	92.9	96.5	100.0	103.6 |	118.2 |	121.5	125.6	129.1
Italy	97.5	98.3	100.1	100.0	100.0	101.1	101.8	101.2	101.7	102.8
Japan	98.3	99.2	99.8	99.1 |	100.0	102.4	100.0	101.1	101.9	102.7
Korea	93.9	96.1	97.7	98.7	100.0	102.3	104.9	106.8	109.3	110.9
Latvia	..	111.4	113.7	104.6	100.0	..	102.7	104.7	104.5	105.5
Luxembourg	86.1	90.5	95.8	97.4	100.0	103.3	106.2	109.5	112.6	115.8
Mexico	86.7	89.3	91.9	93.3 |	100.0	100.6	106.4	106.6	105.1	106.9
Netherlands	94.2	..	100.8	102.2	100.0	100.2	100.7	101.0	100.4	101.1
New Zealand	96.0	98.3	99.3	99.2	100.0	102.0	102.2	104.7	107.8	108.6
Norway	91.7	95.2	98.3	99.1	100.0	101.1	103.4	104.0	104.5	105.9
Poland	91.9	96.5	99.4	102.5	100.0	99.7	103.3	103.9	106.9	108.4
Portugal	96.0	96.3	99.3	100.0	100.0 |	98.7	96.4	97.0	100.8	102.7
Slovak Republic	94.6	96.2	99.5	100.1	100.0	99.6	99.8	102.6	104.4	106.5
Slovenia	93.4	96.2	99.1	100.1	100.0	98.8	99.0	96.8	96.4	99.2
Spain	96.6	100.6	102.5	99.9	100.0	100.2	97.2	95.6	97.1	99.6
Sweden	93.4	97.9	99.1	99.1	100.0	102.4	103.4	105.1	107.5	109.2
Switzerland	..	..	..	..	100.0	102.2	104.1	106.4	108.4	110.8
Turkey	91.5	94.0	95.5	97.0	100.0	105.5	111.7	116.3 |	..	..
United Kingdom	95.6	96.0	98.6 |	99.3	100.0	101.0	101.8	103.5	105.7	107.2
United States	100.4	101.8	102.2	100.2	100.0	100.4	102.4	103.2	104.5	106.4
OECD-Total	..	..	..	..	..	..	..	..	..	..
G7	98.0 e	99.4 e	100.4 e	99.6 e	100.0 e	100.9 e	..	..	..	..
Euro area	95.6	98.0	100.4	100.1	100.0	100.7	100.7	100.9	102.3	103.7
European Union[2]	96.0	98.1	100.0	100.2	100.0	100.6	101.0	101.6	103.2	104.9
Brazil	..	..	..	..	..	..	..	..	..	..
Colombia	87.2	88.8	91.1	95.7	100.0	103.7	108.4	113.3	116.4	119.7
Russian Federation	93.3	97.2	98.4	98.8	100.0	101.9	102.9	103.3	104.3	..

Disclaimer: http://oe.cd/disclaimer

1. Information on data for Israel: http://oe.cd/israel-disclaimer.
2. European Union refer to European Union with 28 countries.

Table 17. Civilian employment by sector: agriculture as a percentage of civilian employment

Percentage

	2006	2007	2008	2009	2010	2011	2012	2013	2014	2015
Australia	3.4	3.3	3.2	3.2	3.2	2.8	2.8	2.6	2.8	2.6
Austria	4.9	5.3	5.3	5.3	5.2	4.9	4.7	4.6	4.8	4.5
Belgium	1.9	1.9	1.6	1.5	1.4	1.3	1.2	1.4	1.2	1.2
Canada	2.7	2.5	2.4	2.4	2.2	2.2	2.1	2.2	2.1	2.0
Chile	12.5	12.0	11.5	11.2	10.6	10.3	10.0 |	9.4	9.2	9.2
Czech Republic	3.6	3.4	3.2	3.1	3.1	3.0	3.1	3.0	2.8	2.9
Denmark	..	..	..	2.6	2.4	2.4	2.6	2.5	2.5	2.5
Estonia	4.9	4.7	3.9	4.1	4.2	4.4	4.5	4.3	3.9	3.9
Finland	4.7	4.6	4.5	4.6	4.4	4.2	4.2	4.1	4.3	4.2
France	2.9	2.7	2.6	2.6	2.5	2.5	2.5	2.5	..	..
Germany	2.3	2.3	2.3 |	1.7	1.6	1.7	1.6	1.5	1.4	1.4
Greece	11.8	11.4	11.1	11.5	12.3	12.2	13.0	13.6	13.4	13.0
Hungary	4.9	4.7	4.6	4.7	4.7	4.9	5.1	4.8	4.6	4.8
Iceland	6.3	5.9 |	4.7	5.2	5.9	6.0	5.7	4.6	4.5	4.2
Ireland	5.4	5.1	5.4	5.0	4.5	4.6	4.8	5.5	5.8	5.8
Israel[1]	1.8	1.6	1.7	1.7	1.6	1.4 |	1.5 |	1.2	1.1	1.0
Italy	4.4	4.1	3.9	3.7	3.8	3.7	3.7	3.6	3.7	3.8
Japan	4.3	4.2	4.2	4.1 |	4.0	3.5	3.8	3.7	3.6	3.6
Korea	7.7	7.4	7.2	7.0	6.6	6.4	6.2	6.1	5.7	5.2
Latvia	..	10.2	8.0	8.8	8.6	8.9	8.4	8.0	7.5	7.9
Luxembourg	1.5	1.6	1.2	1.2	1.2	1.2	1.2	1.2	1.2	1.1
Mexico	14.1	13.3	13.0	12.9 |	13.8	13.3	13.4	13.4	13.5	13.5
Netherlands	3.1	..	2.6	2.5	2.8	2.5	2.5	1.9	2.1	2.1
New Zealand	7.2	7.1	7.0	6.8	6.7	6.9	6.7	6.4	6.2	6.1
Norway	3.3	2.8	2.8	2.7	2.5	2.4	2.2	2.2	2.3	2.0
Poland	15.8	14.7	14.0	13.3	13.2	13.1	12.6	12.0	11.5	11.5
Portugal	12.0	11.9	11.7	11.5	11.3 |	10.3	10.9	10.3	8.7	7.6
Slovak Republic	4.4	4.2	4.0	3.6	3.2	3.1	3.2	3.3	3.5	3.2
Slovenia	9.5	9.7	8.6	9.1	8.8	8.6	8.3	8.5	9.6	7.0
Spain	4.8	4.5	4.3	4.1	4.2	4.1	4.2	4.3	4.3	4.1
Sweden	2.0	2.2	2.2	2.2	2.1	2.0	2.1	2.0	2.0	2.0
Switzerland	..	..	..	..	3.4	3.5	3.5	3.5	3.5	3.2
Turkey	24.0	23.5	23.7	24.6	25.2	25.5	24.6	23.6 |	21.1	20.6
United Kingdom	1.0	1.0	1.1 |	1.1	1.2	1.2	1.2	1.0	1.3	1.1
United States	1.5	1.4	1.5	1.5	1.6	1.6	1.5	1.5	1.5	1.6
OECD-Total	..	..	..	**5.0 e**	**5.2 |**	**5.1 |**	**5.1 |**	**5.0 |**	..	..
G7	2.4	2.3	2.3 |	2.3 |	2.3	2.2	2.2	2.1	..	..
Euro area	4.3	4.1	3.6	3.6	3.6	3.5	3.5	3.4	3.4	3.3
European Union[2]	5.8	5.5	5.2	5.2	5.2	5.0	4.9	4.8	4.7	4.5
Brazil	18.9	17.9	17.1	16.7	..	15.3	14.3	14.2	14.3	..
Colombia	19.1	18.4	18.2	18.7	18.5	18.2	17.5	16.9	16.3	16.1
Russian Federation	9.9	8.9	8.5	8.3	7.7	7.7	7.3	7.0	6.7	..

Disclaimer: http://oe.cd/disclaimer

1. Information on data for Israel: http://oe.cd/israel-disclaimer.
2. European Union refer to European Union with 28 countries.

Table 18. Civilian employment by sector: industry as a percentage of civilian employment

Percentage

	2006	2007	2008	2009	2010	2011	2012	2013	2014	2015
Australia	21.9	21.9	22.3	21.8	21.7	21.5	21.4	21.1	21.1	20.2
Austria	28.4	27.8	26.3	25.1	25.0	26.1	26.1	26.0	25.8	25.8
Belgium	24.7	24.4	24.7	23.5	23.4	23.2	21.8	21.7	21.4	21.4
Canada	21.5	21.1	20.9	19.8	19.7	19.8	20.0	19.9	19.8	19.5
Chile	23.6	23.8	23.9	23.2	23.0	23.4	23.8 |	24.2	23.8	23.7
Czech Republic	40.1	40.3	40.7	38.7	38.1	38.5	38.3	37.6	38.2	38.1
Denmark	23.3	23.5	..	..	..	..	19.7	19.4	19.2	19.2
Estonia	33.5	35.2	35.4	31.5	30.4	32.5	31.2	30.3	30.2	30.7
Finland	25.8	25.8	25.5	23.9	23.3	22.9	22.8	22.8	21.9	21.7
France	19.4 e	19.2 e	19.1 e	18.4 e	17.9 e	17.8 e	..	..	..	..
Germany	29.8	30.1	30.0 |	28.9	28.5	28.4	28.3	27.9	28.2	27.8
Greece	21.6	22.1	22.2	21.1	19.9	17.7	16.5	15.6	15.0	14.9
Hungary	32.7	33.1	32.7	31.4	31.0	31.0	29.9	30.1	30.6	30.4
Iceland	21.4	20.7 |	21.9	19.1	18.1	18.1	18.1	18.6	18.4	17.8
Ireland	26.9	27.0	25.1	21.4	19.7	18.7	18.1	18.3	18.0	19.0
Israel[1]	21.2	21.6	21.5	20.1	20.0	19.7 |	17.4 |	17.7	17.5	17.4
Italy	30.8	30.9	30.4	29.6	28.9	28.6	27.9	27.3	27.2	26.9
Japan	28.0	27.8	27.2	26.8 |	26.1	24.8	25.9	25.8	25.8	25.5
Korea	26.1	25.7	25.3	24.4	24.9	24.8	24.5	24.4	24.6	25.1
Latvia	27.3	28.6	29.4	24.3	23.1	..	23.5	23.9	23.8	23.6
Luxembourg	23.2	22.6	22.2	21.7	21.3	21.0	20.6	19.9	19.5	19.3
Mexico	25.8	25.9	25.8	24.3 |	24.0	24.4	23.6	23.9	24.6	24.9
Netherlands	19.3	18.5	17.6	16.6	15.9	15.3	15.5	15.1	15.0	15.2
New Zealand	22.5	22.0	21.7	21.0	20.9	20.3	20.1	20.2	20.7	21.9
Norway	20.9	21.1	21.1	20.2	19.7	20.2	20.1	20.2	20.4	20.0
Poland	30.0	30.7	31.9	31.1	31.1	31.7	30.4	30.5	30.5	30.4
Portugal	31.2	31.2	29.9	28.0	27.4 |	27.0	25.3	23.8	24.0	24.5
Slovak Republic	38.8	39.4	39.5	37.9	37.1	37.5	37.5	35.8	35.4	36.1
Slovenia	35.3	34.8	35.0	33.0	32.5	31.5	30.8	30.9	30.8	31.6
Spain	29.4	29.1	27.6	24.7	23.1	21.9	20.8	19.9	19.6	20.0
Sweden	22.0	21.6	21.6	20.1	19.9	19.9	19.6	19.1	18.5	18.2
Switzerland	..	..	..	..	22.5	22.5	22.3	21.7	21.6	21.4
Turkey	26.8	26.7	26.8	25.3	26.2	26.5	26.0	26.4 |	..	..
United Kingdom	22.7	22.9	21.7 |	19.6	19.2	19.1	19.1	18.7	18.8	18.7
United States	19.9	19.8	19.1	17.6	17.2	17.3	17.3	17.5	17.8	17.6
OECD-Total	**24.5 e**	**24.4 e**	..	..	..	..	..	..	..	..
G7	23.5 e	23.4 e	22.9 e	21.8 e	21.3 e	21.0 e	..	..	..	..
Euro area	27.7	27.6	27.0	25.8	25.1	24.8	24.4	23.9	23.7	23.6
European Union[2]	27.3	27.4	27.3	25.9	25.1	25.0	24.6	24.2	24.1	24.0
Brazil	21.6	22.2	22.9	22.3	..	21.9	22.9	22.8	22.4	..
Colombia	19.8	20.2	20.0	19.8	19.8	20.5	20.5	19.4	19.6	19.5
Russian Federation	29.3	29.2	29.0	27.5	27.7	27.5	27.8	27.7	27.5	27.2

Disclaimer: http://oe.cd/disclaimer

1. Information on data for Israel: http://oe.cd/israel-disclaimer.
2. European Union refer to European Union with 28 countries.

Table 19. Civilian employment by sector: services as a percentage of civilian employment

Percentage

	2006	2007	2008	2009	2010	2011	2012	2013	2014	2015
Australia	74.7	74.8	74.5	75.0	75.1	75.7	75.8	76.3	76.1	77.2
Austria	66.6	67.0	68.4	69.6	69.8	69.0	69.2	69.4	69.3	69.6
Belgium	73.4	73.7	73.8	75.0	75.3	75.5	77.1	76.9	77.4	77.4
Canada	75.8	76.4	76.7	77.8	78.1	78.0	77.8	78.0	78.2	78.5
Chile	63.9	64.2	64.6	65.6	66.4	66.4	66.2 |	66.4	67.0	67.1
Czech Republic	56.3	56.3	56.2	58.2	58.8	58.5	58.7	59.3	59.1	58.9
Denmark	..	..	..	..	..	..	77.7	78.0	78.3	78.3
Estonia	61.6	60.1	60.7	64.4	65.3	63.0	64.3	65.4	65.9	65.3
Finland	69.6	69.7	69.9	71.5	72.3	72.8	73.1	73.0	73.9	74.1
France	77.7 e	78.1 e	78.3 e	79.0 e	79.5 e	79.7 e	..	..	..	..
Germany	67.9	67.7	67.8 |	69.4	69.8	70.0	70.1	70.6	70.4	70.8
Greece	66.5	66.5	66.6	67.5	67.8	70.1	70.5	70.8	71.5	72.1
Hungary	62.4	62.1	62.7	63.9	64.4	64.0	65.0	65.2	64.8	64.8
Iceland	72.3	73.4 |	73.5	75.7	76.0	75.9	76.2	76.8	77.1	78.0
Ireland	67.7	67.9	69.5	73.6	75.8	76.7	77.1	76.1	76.2	75.2
Israel[1]	77.0	76.8	76.8	78.2	78.4	78.9 |	81.0 |	81.1	81.4	81.6
Italy	64.9	65.0	65.6	66.7	67.2	67.7	68.4	69.0	69.1	69.3
Japan	67.7	68.0	68.6	69.1 |	69.9	71.7	70.2	70.5	70.6	70.9
Korea	66.2	66.9	67.6	68.5	68.5	68.9	69.3	69.5	69.7	69.7
Latvia	..	61.2	62.7	66.9	68.3	..	68.2	68.1	68.7	68.4
Luxembourg	75.3	75.8	76.5	77.1	77.5	77.8	78.2	78.9	79.3	79.6
Mexico	60.1	60.8	61.3	62.8 |	62.3	62.3	63.0	62.7	61.8	61.6
Netherlands	77.6	..	79.8	80.9	81.3	82.2	82.1	82.9	82.9	82.7
New Zealand	70.4	70.8	71.3	72.1	72.4	72.8	73.2	73.4	73.1	72.0
Norway	75.8	76.0	76.1	77.1	77.7	77.4	77.7	77.6	77.3	78.0
Poland	54.2	54.5	54.2	55.6	55.7	55.2	57.0	57.5	58.0	58.1
Portugal	56.8	56.9	58.4	60.5	61.4 |	62.7	63.8	65.9	67.3	67.9
Slovak Republic	56.8	56.4	56.5	58.5	59.6	59.4	59.2	60.9	61.1	60.7
Slovenia	55.2	55.4	56.5	57.9	58.8	59.9	60.8	60.7	59.7	61.4
Spain	65.9	66.4	68.1	71.1	72.7	74.0	75.0	75.8	76.2	75.9
Sweden	76.0	76.1	76.2	77.7	78.0	78.2	78.4	78.9	79.5	79.7
Switzerland	..	..	..	..	74.0	73.9	74.2	74.7	74.8	75.3
Turkey	49.2	49.8	49.5	50.1	48.6	48.1	49.4	50.0 |	..	..
United Kingdom	76.3	76.1	77.2 |	79.4	79.7	79.7	79.7	80.3	79.9	80.2
United States	78.5	78.8	79.5	80.9	81.2	81.1	81.2	81.0	80.7	80.8
OECD-Total	..	..	..	..	..	..	..	..	..	..
G7	74.0 e	74.2 e	74.8 e	76.0 e	76.4 e	76.8 e	..	..	..	..
Euro area	68.0	68.3	69.3	70.5	71.2	71.7	72.1	72.7	73.0	73.2
European Union[2]	66.9	67.0	67.5	68.9	69.7	70.0	70.5	71.0	71.2	71.5
Brazil	59.5	59.9	60.0	61.0	..	62.7	62.9	63.0	63.3	..
Colombia	61.1	61.4	61.8	61.5	61.6	61.4	62.0	63.7	64.1	64.4
Russian Federation	60.9	62.0	62.5	64.2	64.5	64.9	64.9	65.3	65.8	..

Disclaimer: http://oe.cd/disclaimer

1. Information on data for Israel: http://oe.cd/israel-disclaimer.
2. European Union refer to European Union with 28 countries.

Table 20. Self-employment, thousands

	2006	2007	2008	2009	2010	2011	2012	2013	2014	2015
Australia[1]	1 224	1 220	1 231	1 245	1 269	1 242	1 179	1 158	1 176	1 212
Austria	499	537	541	543	555	538	534	542	547	539
Belgium	643	649	632	654	645	645	649	683	664	691
Canada[1]	1 506	1 561	1 566	1 595	1 575	1 555	1 550	1 562	1 559	1 548
Chile	1 787	1 809	1 783	1 824	1 889	1 975	1 912	1 980	2 045	2 059
Czech Republic	779	796	806	827	866	884	901	882	895	874
Denmark	254	253	252	259	246	246	245	242	241	238
Estonia	53	60	52	50	48	53	55	57	57	60
Finland	314	314	324	334	328	331	337	330	343	346
France	2 325	2 346	2 363	2 378	2 443	2 540	..	..	..	..
Germany	4 513	4 556	4 492	4 459	4 478	4 525	4 525	4 423	4 366	4 320
Greece	1 628	1 625	1 609	1 607	1 559	1 488	1 363	1 304	1 254	1 276
Hungary	500	486	470	473	460	457	449	439	449	457
Iceland	25	24	23	20	21	21	21	22	22	23
Ireland	329	356	368	345	323	307	305	319	330	343
Israel[2]	339	341	353	366	375	383	426	434	445	460
Italy	6 010	5 981	5 877	5 668	5 694	5 658	5 621	5 508	5 499	5 477
Japan	8 800	8 580	8 310	7 960 |	7 680	7 090	7 390	7 280	7 240	7 050
Korea	7 600	7 463	7 371	7 052	6 858	6 847	6 969	6 872	6 857	6 707
Latvia	120	116	108	105	98	98	100	103	102	113
Luxembourg	20	20	20	20	21	21	23	24	24	25
Mexico	14 427	14 617	14 775	14 550	16 160	15 796	16 511	16 263	15 808	16 167
Netherlands	1 053	1 113	1 131	1 162	1 257	1 256	1 282	1 330	1 369	1 401
New Zealand	377	373	376	353	350	366	363	343	352	348
Norway	199	194	196	202	193	178	179	181	189	185
Poland	3 565	3 575	3 621	3 608	3 556	3 559	3 491	3 399	3 387	3 415
Portugal	1 227	1 237	1 242	1 193	1 132 |	1 021	1 004	972	888	838
Slovak Republic	289	304	335	371	370	369	360	362	364	367
Slovenia	156	157	141	159	167	157	150	153	170	151
Spain	3 531	3 603	3 596	3 215	3 123	3 019	3 051	3 061	3 051	3 087
Sweden	433	481	478	481	495	482	487	498	493	496
Switzerland	478	508	499	482	480	490	489	498	489	446
Turkey	8 395	8 204	8 257	8 507	8 833	9 234	9 201	9 171 |	8 806	8 794
United Kingdom	3 781	3 877	3 942	3 910	4 010	4 077	4 313	4 297	4 706	4 602
United States[1]	10 691	10 544	10 202	9 922	9 798	9 555	9 639	9 509	9 444	9 609
OECD-Total	**87 869**	**87 879**	**87 341**	**85 900 |**	**87 355 |**	**86 463**	..	..	..	..
G7	37 626	37 444	36 752	35 893 |	35 677	35 000	..	..	..	..
Euro area	23 613	23 763	23 475	22 951	22 901	22 683	22 528	22 319	22 357	22 326
European Union[3]	36 945	37 191	36 879	36 352	36 416	36 001	35 946	35 583	35 872	35 562
Brazil	31 373	30 916	31 022	30 693	..	29 561	29 643	29 761	31 721	..
Colombia	8 005	7 879	8 838	9 728	10 319	10 841	11 064	11 069	11 130	11 298
Russian Federation	5 208	5 178	5 189	5 145	4 776	5 029	4 948	5 195	5 161	5 214

Disclaimer: http://oe.cd/disclaimer

1. It should be noted that in the case of Australia, Canada and United States self-employed data excludes "incorporated self-employed".
2. Information on data for Israel: http://oe.cd/israel-disclaimer.
3. European Union refer to European Union with 28 countries.

Table 21. Self-employment as a percentage of civilian employment

Percentage

	2006	2007	2008	2009	2010	2011	2012	2013	2014	2015
Australia[1]	12.1	11.7	11.5	11.5	11.5	11.1	10.4	10.1	10.2	10.3
Austria	13.1	13.7	13.6	13.7	13.9	13.3	13.1	13.2	13.3	13.0
Belgium	15.1	14.8	14.2	14.8	14.4	14.3	14.3	15.1	14.6	15.2
Canada[1]	9.2	9.3	9.2	9.5	9.3	9.0	8.9	8.8	8.8	8.6
Chile	29.0	28.1	26.8	27.7	26.5	26.4	25.1	25.4	25.9	25.6
Czech Republic	16.2	16.2	16.2	16.8	17.8	18.1	18.5	17.9	18.1	17.4
Denmark	9.1	9.0	8.8	9.3	9.1	9.1	9.1	9.0	8.9	8.7
Estonia	8.2	9.2	7.9	8.4	8.5	8.8	8.9	9.2	9.1	9.4
Finland	12.9	12.6	12.8	13.6	13.5	13.4	13.6	13.5	14.1	14.3
France	9.0	9.0	9.0	9.2	9.4	9.7	..	..	..	..
Germany	12.2	12.1	11.7	11.6	11.6	11.7	11.6	11.2	11.0	10.8
Greece	35.9	35.5	34.7	35.1	35.1	36.1	36.6	36.9	35.4	35.2
Hungary	12.9	12.6	12.3	12.7	12.4	12.2	11.8	11.3	11.0	10.9
Iceland	14.9	13.8	12.7	12.0	12.7	12.6	12.5	12.7	12.5	12.5
Ireland	16.2	16.7	17.2	17.5	17.1	16.6	16.7	17.1	17.4	17.6
Israel[2]	13.1	12.7	12.7	12.9	12.8	12.6 |	12.7	12.6	12.5	12.6
Italy	26.7	26.4	25.7	25.2	25.6	25.3	25.2	25.1	24.9	24.7
Japan	13.8	13.3	13.0	12.6 |	12.2	11.3	11.8	11.5	11.4	11.1
Korea	32.8	31.8	31.3	30.0	28.8	28.2	28.2	27.4	26.8	25.9
Latvia	11.7	11.0	10.2	11.5	11.5	11.3	11.4	11.5	11.5	12.6
Luxembourg	6.2	6.0	5.8	5.8	5.8	5.6	6.1	6.2	6.2	6.1
Mexico	34.5	34.3	33.9	33.8 |	34.7	33.7	33.7	33.0	32.1	32.1
Netherlands	12.7	13.1	13.2	13.5	15.0	15.2	15.4	16.1	16.6	16.8
New Zealand	17.7	17.2	17.3	16.4	16.2	16.7	16.6	15.4	15.3	14.8
Norway	8.5	8.0	7.8	8.1	7.7	7.0	6.9	7.0	7.2	7.0
Poland	24.4	23.5	22.9	22.7	23.0	22.9	22.4	21.8	21.4	21.2
Portugal	24.3	24.5	24.4	24.2	23.2 |	21.7	22.2	22.1	19.9	18.5
Slovak Republic	12.6	12.9	13.8	15.7	16.0	15.9	15.5	15.6	15.4	15.2
Slovenia	16.2	15.9	14.1	16.2	17.3	16.8	16.2	16.9	18.6	16.5
Spain	17.8	17.6	17.7	16.9	16.8	16.5	17.4	17.9	17.7	17.4
Sweden	10.0	10.6	10.4	10.7	11.0	10.4	10.5	10.6	10.3	10.3
Switzerland	11.1	11.5	11.0	10.6	10.5	10.5	10.3	10.4	10.0	9.0
Turkey	41.1	39.6	39.0	40.0	39.1	38.3	37.1	35.9 |	34.0	33.0
United Kingdom	13.1	13.3	13.4	13.6	13.9	13.9	14.6	14.5	15.4	14.9
United States[1]	7.4	7.2	7.0	7.1	7.0	6.8	6.8	6.6	6.5	6.5
OECD-Total	**16.3**	**16.1**	**15.9**	**15.9 |**	**16.1 |**	**15.8 |**	..	..	..	..
G7	11.1	10.9	10.7	10.7 |	10.7	10.4	..	..	..	..
Euro area	16.6	16.3	16.0	16.0	16.1	15.9	15.9	15.9	15.7	15.6
European Union[3]	17.1	16.9	16.5	16.6	16.8	16.7	16.7	16.5	16.4	16.1
Brazil	35.8	34.7	33.8	33.3	..	31.6	31.2	31.2	32.3	..
Colombia	47.4	46.1	50.7	52.8	53.7	54.2	53.5	52.6	51.8	51.3
Russian Federation	7.5	7.3	7.3	7.4	6.8	7.1	6.9	7.3	7.2	7.2

Disclaimer: http://oe.cd/disclaimer

1. It should be noted that in the case of Australia, Canada and United States self-employed data excludes "incorporated self-employed".
2. Information on data for Israel: http://oe.cd/israel-disclaimer.
3. European Union refer to European Union with 28 countries.

Table 22. Female self-employment as a percentage of female civilian employment

Percentage

	2006	2007	2008	2009	2010	2011	2012	2013	2014	2015
Australia	9.1	8.8	8.7	8.7	8.8	8.5	8.2	7.9	8.0	8.2
Austria	10.5	11.5	11.1	11.2	11.2	10.7	10.5	10.6	10.5	10.4
Belgium	11.8	11.5	10.8	11.3	10.8	10.5	10.5	10.7	10.9	11.1
Canada	7.9	8.0	7.9	8.4	8.2	8.0	8.0	8.1	8.0	8.0
Chile	25.6	25.0	24.4	25.2	24.9	26.0	24.8	25.1	25.6	25.2
Czech Republic	10.9	10.6	10.6	11.4	12.2	12.9	13.5	13.5	12.9	12.8
Denmark	5.8	5.3	5.0	5.4	5.6	5.4	5.6	..	..	5.4
Estonia	4.8	5.5	5.0	5.3	5.4	5.2	5.1	5.9	5.7	6.6
Finland	8.4	8.2	8.6	9.1	9.0	8.8	8.9	8.8	9.4	9.4
France	6.9	6.8	6.8	6.8	7.0	7.2	7.5	7.7	7.9	..
Germany	9.3	9.2	8.9	8.5	8.4	8.5	8.4	8.1	8.0	7.8
Greece	31.7	30.8	30.6	30.5	30.7	31.5	31.1	31.9	29.8	29.6
Hungary	9.1	9.2	8.6	9.2	9.0	8.6	8.7	8.2	7.8	8.0
Iceland	7.9	7.9	7.4	7.0	8.6	8.7	8.8	8.4	7.8	7.7
Ireland	6.7	7.2	7.5	7.3	7.7	7.4	7.5	8.1	7.9	8.3
Israel[1]	8.6	8.2	8.0	8.2	8.0	8.3 |	8.7	9.0	9.1	9.0
Italy	20.4	20.0	19.3	18.5	18.5	18.3	18.3	18.3	18.5	18.3
Japan	13.6	13.1	12.4	11.9 |	11.3	10.4	10.7	10.4	10.2	9.7
Korea	32.3	31.2	30.4	28.8	27.1	26.4	26.0	25.3	24.6	23.6
Latvia	8.4	7.1	6.3	7.3	8.0	8.0	8.2	8.7	8.2	8.9
Luxembourg	4.9 e	4.6 e	4.7 e	4.6 e	4.6 e	4.5 e	..	..	..	..
Mexico	34.6	34.7	34.7	34.4 |	35.5	34.7	35.1	33.8	32.7	32.8
Netherlands	9.9	10.0	10.1	10.5	11.5	11.6	11.7	12.2	12.7	13.4
New Zealand	12.6	12.6	12.5	11.9	11.8	12.7	12.4	11.7	11.8	11.5
Norway	4.9	4.7	4.5	4.9	4.4	4.1	4.1	4.4	4.3	4.6
Poland	21.8	20.9	20.4	20.1	20.1	19.8	19.2	18.4	17.7	17.6
Portugal	22.6	22.4	22.6	21.5	20.4 |	17.3	17.7	17.5	14.9	13.9
Slovak Republic	7.3	7.3	7.8	9.8	9.4	9.7	9.9	9.8	9.9	10.3
Slovenia	13.3	13.2	11.3	12.8	14.0	13.4	12.8	13.6	16.0	13.5
Spain	13.6	13.3	13.2	12.6	12.3	12.2	12.7	13.1	13.0	12.8
Sweden	5.4	5.8	5.9	6.2	6.4	6.0	5.9	6.2	6.2	6.2
Switzerland	10.6	11.3	10.4	10.2	10.0	10.4	10.3	10.2	10.0	9.3
Turkey	49.2	47.6	46.8	48.9	49.3	48.4	45.7	43.4 |	39.8	38.3
United Kingdom	8.0	8.1	8.2	8.5	8.9	9.0	9.6	9.6	10.6	10.2
United States	6.0	5.8	5.6	5.7	5.6	5.5	5.6	5.6	5.4	5.3
OECD-Total	**13.5 e**	**13.3 e**	**13.0 e**	**13.0 e**	**13.2 e**	**13.0 e**	..	..	..	..
G7	8.9	8.7	8.4	8.3 |	8.2	8.1	8.2	8.1	8.1	..
Euro area	12.5	12.2	11.9	11.6	11.7	11.5	11.5	11.4	11.4	11.3
European Union[2]	13.1	12.9	12.6	12.5	12.6	12.4	12.4	12.3	12.2	12.0
Brazil	33.5	32.4	31.6	30.6	..	27.5	27.1	26.8	28.3	..
Colombia	46.2	44.8	48.6	51.3	52.5	53.7	53.5	52.1	50.7	50.0
Russian Federation	6.9	6.6	6.6	6.7	6.0	6.3	6.0	6.4	6.3	6.3

Disclaimer: http://oe.cd/disclaimer

1. Information on data for Israel: http://oe.cd/israel-disclaimer.
2. European Union refer to European Union with 28 countries.

Table 23. Male self-employment as a percentage of male civilian employment

Percentage

	2006	2007	2008	2009	2010	2011	2012	2013	2014	2015
Australia	14.6	14.1	13.7	13.9	13.8	13.2	12.2	12.0	12.1	12.1
Austria	15.2	15.6	15.7	15.9	16.2	15.6	15.4	15.6	15.8	15.4
Belgium	17.6	17.4	17.0	17.7	17.3	17.5	17.6	18.8	17.9	18.7
Canada	10.3	10.4	10.3	10.6	10.3	10.0	9.7	9.5	9.4	9.2
Chile	30.9	29.8	28.2	29.1	27.5	26.6	25.3	25.7	26.0	25.9
Czech Republic	20.3	20.5	20.3	20.9	22.0	22.0	22.3	21.3	22.1	21.0
Denmark	..	12.3	12.2	..	12.3	..	..	12.1	..	..
Estonia	11.6	12.8	10.7	11.7	11.9	12.3	12.6	12.4	12.5	12.1
Finland	17.1	16.8	16.8	18.0	17.7	17.7	18.2	18.0	18.5	18.9
France	10.9	10.9	11.1	11.3	11.6	12.0	12.4	12.8	13.1	..
Germany	14.7	14.4	14.1	14.4	14.4	14.5	14.4	14.0	13.6	13.5
Greece	38.7	38.6	37.4	38.2	38.2	39.3	40.4	40.4	39.4	39.3
Hungary	16.0	15.4	15.5	15.7	15.4	15.4	14.5	14.0	13.7	13.3
Iceland	20.7	18.8	17.1	16.6	16.5	16.2	15.9	16.7	16.8	16.8
Ireland	23.2	23.9	24.7	26.2	25.3	24.6	24.8	24.9	25.5	25.4
Israel[1]	17.1	16.5	16.7	17.0	17.0	16.5 |	16.2	15.8	15.6	15.9
Italy	30.9	30.7	30.1	29.9	30.5	30.3	30.2	30.1	29.7	29.3
Japan	13.8	13.5	13.3	13.1 |	12.8	11.9	12.6	12.4	12.3	12.1
Korea	33.2	32.3	31.9	30.8	30.0	29.6	29.8	29.0	28.4	27.5
Latvia	11.7	11.3	11.4	12.9	12.4	12.6	12.8	12.8	13.3	14.8
Luxembourg	7.2 e	7.0 e	6.7 e	6.7 e	6.7 e	6.5 e	..	..	..	..
Mexico	34.4	34.1	33.5	33.4 |	34.2	33.1	32.8	32.5	31.7	31.7
Netherlands	15.1	15.7	15.8	16.1	18.0	18.2	18.5	19.3	20.0	19.8
New Zealand	22.1	21.2	21.5	20.5	20.1	20.5	20.4	18.8	18.3	17.7
Norway	11.7	11.1	10.9	11.1	10.8	9.7	9.4	9.3	9.8	9.1
Poland	26.6	25.5	25.0	24.9	25.3	25.3	25.0	24.5	24.3	24.2
Portugal	25.8	26.3	26.0	26.6	25.8 |	25.7	26.5	26.4	24.6	23.0
Slovak Republic	16.7	17.2	18.4	20.3	21.3	20.8	19.8	20.2	19.7	19.0
Slovenia	18.6	18.1	16.5	19.0	20.0	19.7	19.2	19.6	20.7	19.0
Spain	20.7	20.6	21.0	20.3	20.4	20.0	21.3	22.1	21.7	21.2
Sweden	14.2	14.9	14.5	14.7	15.0	14.4	14.6	14.5	14.1	13.9
Switzerland	11.5	11.7	11.6	10.9	11.0	10.6	10.4	10.5	10.0	8.7
Turkey	38.3	36.8	36.1	36.6	35.1	34.2	33.5	32.7 |	31.5	30.7
United Kingdom	17.5	17.8	17.8	18.0	18.3	18.3	19.1	18.7	19.7	19.1
United States	8.6	8.4	8.3	8.4	8.3	8.0	7.8	7.5	7.4	7.5
OECD-Total	..	**18.2 e**	**18.0 e**	..	**18.3 e**	..	..	..	..	..
G7	12.9	12.8	12.6	12.7 |	12.7	12.4	12.4	12.2	12.2	..
Euro area	19.8	19.6	19.3	19.5	19.8	19.7	19.7	19.6	19.4	19.1
European Union[2]	20.3	20.1	19.8	20.0	20.4	20.2	20.2	20.1	20.0	19.6
Brazil	37.5	36.5	35.4	35.3	..	34.6	34.3	34.4	35.3	..
Colombia	48.1	46.8	52.0	53.8	54.5	54.4	53.4	52.9	52.5	52.3
Russian Federation	8.2	8.0	8.0	8.2	7.7	7.9	7.8	8.1	8.1	8.1

Disclaimer: http://oe.cd/disclaimer

1. Information on data for Israel: http://oe.cd/israel-disclaimer.
2. European Union refer to European Union with 28 countries.

Table 24. Part-time employment as a percentage of employment

Percentage

	2006	2007	2008	2009	2010	2011	2012	2013	2014	2015
Australia	23.9	23.7	23.8	24.6	24.8	24.7	24.6	24.9	25.2	25.2
Austria	17.0	17.3	17.8	18.7	19.2	19.0	19.4	19.9	20.9	21.0
Belgium	18.7	18.1	18.3	18.2	18.3	18.8	18.7	18.2	18.1	18.2
Canada	18.2	18.3	18.6	19.3	19.6	19.3	19.0	19.1	19.3	18.9
Chile	7.7	8.0	9.1	10.5	17.4	17.2	16.7	16.5	17.0	16.8
Czech Republic	3.3	3.5	3.5	3.9	4.3	3.9	4.3	4.9	4.8	4.7
Denmark	17.9	17.3	17.8	18.8	19.2	19.2	19.4	19.2	19.7	20.0
Estonia	6.8	6.8	6.3	8.5	8.8	8.9	8.2	8.0	7.6	8.6
Finland	11.4	11.7	11.5	12.2	12.5	12.7	13.0	13.0	13.3	13.4
France	13.2	13.3	13.0	13.5	13.7	13.7	13.9	14.0	14.3	14.4
Germany	21.8	22.0	21.8	21.9	21.8	22.3	22.2	22.6	22.3	22.4
Greece	7.4	7.7	7.9	8.5	8.9	9.1	9.8	10.3	11.2	11.1
Hungary	2.9	3.1	3.4	3.8	4.0	5.2	5.2	4.9	4.5	4.4
Iceland	16.0	15.9	15.1	17.5	18.4	17.0	17.3	17.4	16.7	17.2
Ireland	19.3	19.9	20.9	23.8	24.9	25.7	25.0	24.2	23.4	23.3
Israel[1]	16.6	16.1	16.0	16.1	15.2	14.9	16.1	15.9	16.0	15.9
Italy	15.0	15.3	16.0	15.9	16.4	16.7	17.8	18.5	18.8	18.7
Japan	18.0	18.9	19.6	20.3	20.2	20.6	20.5	21.9	22.7	22.7
Korea	8.8	8.9	9.3	9.9	10.7	13.5	10.2	11.1	10.5	10.6
Latvia	5.3	5.4	6.0	7.4	8.2	8.0	8.3	7.6	6.6	6.8
Luxembourg	12.7	13.1	13.4	16.4	15.8	16.0	15.5	15.3	15.5	14.9
Mexico	17.0	17.7	17.7	18.1	18.9	18.2	19.4	19.0	18.7	18.2
Netherlands	35.4	35.9	36.1	36.7	37.1	37.0	37.6	38.5	38.3	38.5
New Zealand	21.2	21.9	22.1	22.4	21.8	22.1	22.3	21.6	21.5	21.3
Norway	21.1	20.4	20.3	20.4	20.1	20.0	19.8	19.5	18.8	19.4
Poland	10.8	10.1	9.3	8.7	8.7	8.3	8.0	7.7	7.1	6.4
Portugal	9.4	10.0	9.9	9.8	9.6	11.7	12.5	12.0	11.0	10.5
Slovak Republic	2.4	2.4	2.6	2.9	3.7	4.0	3.8	4.3	4.9	5.7
Slovenia	7.8	7.8	7.5	8.3	9.4	8.6	7.9	8.6	9.6	9.2
Spain	10.7	10.5	10.9	11.6	12.2	12.7	13.6	14.7	14.7	14.5
Sweden	13.4	14.4	14.4	14.6	14.5	14.3	14.3	14.3	14.2	14.1
Switzerland	25.5	25.4	25.9	26.5	26.1	25.9	26.0	26.4	26.9	26.8
Turkey	7.6	8.1	8.5	11.1	11.5	11.7	11.8	12.3	10.6	9.9
United Kingdom	23.1	22.9	23.0	23.9	24.6	24.7	25.0	24.6	24.1	24.0
United States	..	..	..	..	..	..	..	..	..	..
OECD-Total	**15.2**	**15.4**	**15.6**	**16.4**	**16.7**	**16.8**	**16.9**	**17.1**	**17.0**	**16.8**
G7	..	..	..	..	..	..	..	..	..	..
Euro area	..	..	..	..	..	..	..	..	..	..
European Union	15.8	15.8	15.9	16.3	16.6	16.9	17.2	17.5	17.3	17.2
Brazil	19.2	18.3	18.0	17.8	..	16.0	16.2	16.4	17.1	..
Colombia	..	14.5	14.0	15.1	16.3	16.9	18.0	17.8	16.5	..
Russian Federation	5.3	5.1	5.0	4.7	4.3	4.1	4.1	4.3	4.0	4.2

Disclaimer: http://oe.cd/disclaimer

1. Information on data for Israel: http://oe.cd/israel-disclaimer.

Table 25. Female share of part-time employment

Percentage

	2006	2007	2008	2009	2010	2011	2012	2013	2014	2015
Australia	72.0	71.5	71.7	70.8	70.4	70.8	71.1	70.3	69.9	69.5
Austria	83.6	82.4	80.5	80.4	80.0	80.5	80.6	78.9	78.6	78.4
Belgium	81.8	80.7	81.3	80.6	80.4	79.9	79.8	80.8	79.1	78.9
Canada	68.1	68.0	67.7	67.6	67.6	66.6	67.3	66.7	66.6	66.4
Chile	55.6	56.9	56.4	56.0	58.1	58.7	59.2	59.2	60.2	59.4
Czech Republic	72.8	72.3	72.1	68.7	69.2	72.9	69.7	71.2	70.5	69.5
Denmark	64.3	63.3	61.3	62.0	63.2	62.1	60.9	61.1	61.0	60.3
Estonia	75.1	73.2	70.4	67.6	67.9	71.7	71.7	69.3	66.1	69.8
Finland	62.9	63.7	63.0	63.6	62.2	61.0	61.7	62.2	61.4	59.5
France	79.8	80.5	79.9	79.9	78.1	77.4	77.5	77.0	75.6	75.2
Germany	80.9	80.7	80.3	80.4	80.9	79.7	79.2	78.6	78.1	77.9
Greece	67.0	67.7	67.7	68.0	66.3	63.4	63.7	62.3	60.8	61.9
Hungary	70.6	68.6	64.7	64.5	65.7	61.2	64.9	62.5	62.8	63.6
Iceland	74.2	72.7	71.2	70.0	67.6	68.0	65.8	67.5	66.2	65.6
Ireland	79.4	79.8	78.7	76.2	75.1	74.5	73.3	71.9	72.2	72.1
Israel[1]	73.9	73.3	72.3	72.6	72.9	71.7	67.9	68.5	68.6	68.3
Italy	77.8	78.2	77.1	77.7	77.1	76.9	75.3	74.1	73.4	73.5
Japan	72.4	71.5	70.4	69.9	70.3	71.0	70.8	70.3	69.8	69.8
Korea	58.5	58.9	59.0	59.3	60.3	56.6	61.0	60.5	62.2	62.6
Latvia	67.7	67.5	68.0	64.3	64.9	63.6	65.6	65.5	69.2	69.7
Luxembourg	93.1	93.9	92.6	81.2	83.7	82.2	80.5	80.3	80.1	80.8
Mexico	60.6	60.0	58.9	58.1	57.7	57.1	56.8	57.6	56.8	57.3
Netherlands	75.9	75.5	75.6	75.0	75.0	75.4	74.5	73.3	72.6	72.7
New Zealand	74.7	73.2	72.9	72.2	72.5	73.4	74.0	73.2	72.0	72.3
Norway	73.5	72.9	71.7	70.8	70.3	71.1	69.4	69.4	69.8	67.1
Poland	67.0	67.0	68.1	68.4	66.9	66.9	67.6	67.9	67.1	67.0
Portugal	66.3	66.7	68.4	67.9	65.8	59.8	58.6	58.0	57.9	59.3
Slovak Republic	70.0	74.0	67.1	59.0	58.6	61.6	59.4	58.0	58.2	59.9
Slovenia	57.1	56.2	58.3	57.3	58.5	58.0	59.5	59.1	59.5	59.8
Spain	79.0	80.0	80.2	78.8	77.9	76.4	76.0	73.4	74.0	73.3
Sweden	67.3	65.0	64.6	64.2	63.0	62.7	62.0	61.2	61.1	60.7
Switzerland	81.2	81.3	81.2	81.2	80.4	80.2	80.0	80.0	78.5	78.3
Turkey	58.5	59.6	58.7	58.4	58.0	60.0	60.0	59.9	57.7	58.2
United Kingdom	77.6	77.2	76.2	76.0	75.0	74.8	73.9	73.8	74.2	73.7
United States	..	..	..	..	..	..	..	..	..	..
OECD-Total	**71.7**	**71.5**	**70.8**	**70.2**	**69.9**	**69.4**	**69.3**	**68.9**	**68.8**	**68.7**
G7	..	..	..	..	..	..	..	..	..	..
Euro area	..	..	..	..	..	..	..	..	..	..
European Union	77.2	77.2	76.7	76.5	75.9	75.4	74.8	74.2	73.8	73.6
Brazil	68.0	67.6	67.8	67.5	..	65.1	64.4	64.2	64.8	..
Colombia	..	61.3	64.6	65.7	65.5	66.0	65.9	66.5	67.5	..
Russian Federation	64.3	64.8	64.5	65.2	64.3	65.4	64.5	65.5	65.1	64.9

Disclaimer: http://oe.cd/disclaimer

1. Information on data for Israel: http://oe.cd/israel-disclaimer.

Table 26. Female part-time employment as a percentage of female employment

Percentage

	2006	2007	2008	2009	2010	2011	2012	2013	2014	2015
Australia	38.3	37.7	37.7	38.2	38.6	38.4	38.2	38.1	38.4	38.0
Austria	31.2	31.4	31.3	32.4	33.0	32.8	33.5	33.4	34.9	35.0
Belgium	33.8	32.2	32.5	31.8	31.7	32.4	32.1	31.4	30.5	30.2
Canada	26.4	26.3	26.6	27.2	27.7	27.0	26.7	26.7	27.0	26.4
Chile	13.3	13.9	15.2	17.0	25.7	25.5	24.6	24.3	25.0	24.5
Czech Republic	5.6	5.9	5.8	6.2	7.0	6.6	7.0	8.0	7.7	7.4
Denmark	24.6	23.4	23.3	24.5	25.4	25.2	24.9	24.7	25.4	25.8
Estonia	10.3	10.1	9.0	11.3	11.7	12.9	11.9	11.3	10.3	12.2
Finland	14.9	15.5	15.1	15.9	16.0	16.0	16.5	16.7	16.8	16.4
France	22.6	22.8	22.1	22.7	22.5	22.3	22.6	22.5	22.5	22.3
Germany	39.0	39.1	38.5	38.3	38.2	38.3	38.0	38.1	37.5	37.4
Greece	12.8	13.3	13.6	14.4	14.5	14.0	15.1	15.6	16.2	16.3
Hungary	4.4	4.5	4.6	5.2	5.4	6.7	7.0	6.5	6.0	6.0
Iceland	26.0	25.4	23.6	25.8	25.9	24.1	23.7	24.6	23.2	23.7
Ireland	34.3	35.0	35.5	37.4	38.2	39.1	37.5	36.2	35.4	35.4
Israel[1]	26.2	25.3	24.5	24.5	23.3	22.5	23.6	23.4	23.5	23.3
Italy	29.3	29.8	30.5	30.5	31.0	31.2	32.2	32.8	32.9	32.8
Japan	31.3	32.6	33.2	33.8	33.9	34.8	34.5	36.2	37.2	36.9
Korea	12.3	12.5	13.2	14.2	15.5	18.5	15.0	16.2	15.6	15.9
Latvia	7.3	7.4	8.2	9.0	10.0	9.8	10.7	9.9	9.0	9.4
Luxembourg	27.2	27.6	28.9	31.1	30.4	30.2	28.1	27.7	27.7	26.7
Mexico	27.8	28.2	27.8	28.0	28.8	27.7	28.7	28.4	27.9	27.5
Netherlands	59.8	59.9	59.8	59.9	60.6	60.6	60.9	61.1	60.6	60.7
New Zealand	34.3	34.5	34.4	34.3	33.7	34.4	35.0	33.5	32.7	32.7
Norway	32.9	31.6	30.8	30.4	29.8	30.0	29.1	28.8	27.7	27.6
Poland	16.3	15.0	14.1	13.1	13.1	12.5	12.2	11.8	10.7	9.6
Portugal	13.5	14.4	14.5	14.0	13.2	14.5	14.9	14.1	12.9	12.6
Slovak Republic	3.8	4.0	4.0	4.0	4.8	5.6	5.1	5.6	6.4	7.8
Slovenia	9.8	9.7	9.6	10.4	12.1	10.9	10.3	11.2	12.5	12.1
Spain	20.4	20.1	20.4	20.7	21.2	21.4	22.4	23.4	23.6	23.1
Sweden	19.0	19.7	19.6	19.8	19.4	19.0	18.6	18.4	18.3	18.0
Switzerland	45.7	45.6	45.9	46.7	46.1	45.5	45.6	45.7	45.6	45.0
Turkey	17.3	18.6	19.0	23.5	23.4	24.3	24.2	24.5	20.6	19.0
United Kingdom	38.5	38.2	37.7	38.7	39.3	39.3	39.4	38.7	38.1	37.7
United States	..	..	..	..	..	..	..	..	..	..
OECD-Total	**25.1**	**25.3**	**25.3**	**26.1**	**26.3**	**26.4**	**26.4**	**26.5**	**26.3**	**25.9**
G7	..	..	..	..	..	..	..	..	..	..
Euro area	..	..	..	..	..	..	..	..	..	..
European Union[2]	27.4	27.3	27.1	27.4	27.7	27.8	28.1	28.1	27.7	27.5
Brazil	30.6	29.1	28.7	28.1	..	24.6	24.6	24.7	25.6	..
Colombia	..	22.8	23.1	24.8	26.3	27.3	28.6	28.4	26.6	..
Russian Federation	6.9	6.6	6.5	6.2	5.6	5.4	5.4	5.8	5.3	5.6

Disclaimer: http://oe.cd/disclaimer

1. Information on data for Israel: http://oe.cd/israel-disclaimer.
2. European Union refer to European Union with 28 countries.

Table 27. Male part-time employment as a percentage of male employment

Percentage

	2006	2007	2008	2009	2010	2011	2012	2013	2014	2015
Australia	12.2	12.3	12.3	13.2	13.5	13.2	13.1	13.6	14.0	14.2
Austria	5.1	5.6	6.4	6.8	7.2	7.0	7.1	7.9	8.5	8.6
Belgium	6.2	6.4	6.3	6.6	6.7	7.0	7.1	6.6	7.2	7.3
Canada	10.9	11.1	11.4	12.0	12.1	12.3	11.9	12.2	12.3	12.1
Chile	5.0	5.2	6.0	7.1	12.0	11.8	11.3	11.3	11.5	11.5
Czech Republic	1.6	1.7	1.7	2.1	2.3	1.9	2.3	2.5	2.5	2.5
Denmark	12.0	11.9	13.0	13.6	13.5	13.8	14.4	14.2	14.6	15.0
Estonia	3.3	3.6	3.6	5.6	5.8	5.0	4.6	4.9	5.0	5.1
Finland	8.1	8.2	8.2	8.7	9.2	9.6	9.7	9.6	10.0	10.6
France	5.0	4.9	4.9	5.1	5.7	5.9	6.0	6.2	6.7	6.9
Germany	7.6	7.8	7.9	7.9	7.8	8.4	8.6	9.0	9.1	9.3
Greece	4.0	4.1	4.2	4.6	5.1	5.6	6.1	6.6	7.5	7.3
Hungary	1.6	1.8	2.3	2.6	2.6	3.9	3.5	3.5	3.2	3.0
Iceland	7.6	8.0	8.0	10.0	11.4	10.4	11.4	10.9	10.8	11.3
Ireland	7.2	7.4	8.3	11.0	12.1	12.8	13.1	13.1	12.5	12.3
Israel[1]	8.2	8.1	8.4	8.4	7.9	8.0	9.6	9.4	9.4	9.4
Italy	5.5	5.5	6.1	6.0	6.3	6.5	7.5	8.3	8.6	8.5
Japan	8.5	9.2	9.9	10.5	10.4	10.3	10.3	11.3	12.0	12.0
Korea	6.3	6.3	6.5	6.9	7.2	10.0	6.8	7.5	6.8	6.9
Latvia	3.4	3.4	3.8	5.5	6.1	6.1	5.9	5.4	4.1	4.2
Luxembourg	1.5	1.4	1.7	5.4	4.6	5.0	5.4	5.4	5.6	5.2
Mexico	10.7	11.3	11.7	12.1	12.8	12.5	13.6	13.1	13.0	12.5
Netherlands	15.5	16.1	16.2	17.0	17.2	16.9	17.8	19.2	19.4	19.5
New Zealand	9.9	11.0	11.2	11.8	11.3	11.1	11.0	11.0	11.4	11.2
Norway	10.6	10.5	10.9	11.3	11.4	11.0	11.5	11.3	10.8	12.1
Poland	6.5	6.0	5.3	5.0	5.2	5.0	4.7	4.5	4.2	3.8
Portugal	5.9	6.3	5.9	6.0	6.3	9.1	10.1	9.9	9.1	8.5
Slovak Republic	1.3	1.1	1.5	2.1	2.7	2.7	2.7	3.3	3.7	4.1
Slovenia	6.1	6.3	5.7	6.6	7.2	6.7	5.9	6.4	7.1	6.7
Spain	3.8	3.6	3.8	4.4	4.9	5.4	6.0	7.3	7.1	7.2
Sweden	8.4	9.5	9.6	10.0	10.1	10.1	10.3	10.6	10.5	10.6
Switzerland	8.8	8.7	9.0	9.2	9.4	9.4	9.6	9.8	10.8	10.9
Turkey	4.2	4.4	4.8	6.4	6.7	6.6	6.7	7.0	6.4	5.9
United Kingdom	9.7	9.7	10.2	10.8	11.6	11.7	12.3	12.2	11.7	11.9
United States	..	..	..	..	..	..	..	..	..	..
OECD-Total	**7.6**	**7.8**	**8.1**	**8.8**	**9.0**	**9.2**	**9.3**	**9.6**	**9.6**	**9.5**
G7	..	..	..	..	..	..	..	..	..	..
Euro area	..	..	..	..	..	..	..	..	..	..
European Union[2]	6.5	6.5	6.7	7.0	7.4	7.6	8.0	8.4	8.4	8.5
Brazil	10.7	10.3	10.1	10.1	..	9.7	10.0	10.2	10.6	..
Colombia	..	9.2	8.1	8.6	9.4	9.7	10.4	10.2	9.2	..
Russian Federation	3.8	3.5	3.5	3.3	3.0	2.8	2.9	2.9	2.7	2.9

Disclaimer: http://oe.cd/disclaimer

1. Information on data for Israel: http://oe.cd/israel-disclaimer.
2. European Union refer to European Union with 28 countries.

Table 28. Unemployment, thousands

	2006	2007	2008	2009	2010	2011	2012	2013	2014	2015
Australia	508	478	474	636	606	600	625	686	746	758
Austria	212	200	172	223	203	194	209	231	245	252
Belgium	383	353	334	380	406	347	369	417	423	422
Canada	1 106	1 077	1 112	1 523	1 486	1 399	1 372	1 347	1 322	1 331
Chile	513	496	562	707	632	574	524	491	540	532
Czech Republic	371	276	230	352	384	354	367	369	324	268
Denmark	114	111	101	177	218	221	219	202	192	181
Estonia	41	32	38	93	114	85	69	59	50	42
Finland	204	183	172	221	224	209	207	219	232	252
France	2 321	2 122	1 971	2 458	2 505	2 489	2 674	2 824	2 838	..
Germany	4 257	3 601	3 136	3 228	2 946	2 399	2 222	2 179	2 088	1 947
Greece	441	409	367	456	605	816	1 163	1 328	1 280	1 180
Hungary	318	312	326	418	469	466	473	441	343	308
Iceland	5	4	6	13	14	13	11	10	9	8
Ireland	99	108	131	275	305	317	323	301	255	211
Israel[1]	236	212	180	232	209	180 |	247	228	223	202
Italy	1 654	1 481	1 664	1 907	2 056	2 061	2 691	3 069	3 236	3 033
Japan	2 750	2 570	2 650	3 360 |	3 340	3 020	2 850	2 650	2 360	2 220
Korea	827	783	769	889	920	855	820	807	937	976
Latvia	78	68	89	193	206	167	155	120	108	98
Luxembourg	9	9	9	12	14	14	15	17	18	18
Mexico	1 367	1 496	1 584	2 352 |	2 536	2 591	2 474	2 600	2 535	2 288
Netherlands	336	278	243	304	390	434	516	647	660	614
New Zealand	85	82	95	140	151	152	163	148	141	144
Norway	84	63	67	82	94	86	86	95	96	121
Poland	2 344	1 619	1 211	1 411	1 650	1 659	1 749	1 793	1 567	1 304
Portugal	421	441	418	517	591 |	688	836	855	726	647
Slovak Republic	353	292	258	324	389	365	378	386	359	314
Slovenia	61	50	46	61	75	83	90	102	99	91
Spain	1 839	1 845	2 594	4 151	4 639	5 011	5 810	6 050	5 610	5 055
Sweden	330	298	305	408	425	390	403	411	411	386
Switzerland	170	157	150	193	204	184	193	205	215	219
Turkey	2 328	2 376	2 611	3 471	3 046	2 615	2 518	2 747 |	2 853	3 057
United Kingdom	1 648	1 623	1 646	2 413	2 451	2 501	2 542	2 485	2 031	1 815
United States	7 001	7 078	8 924	14 265	14 825	13 747	12 506	11 460	9 616	8 296
OECD-Total	**34 815**	**32 581**	**34 644**	**47 845 |**	**49 325 |**	**47 283 |**	**47 866**	**47 979 |**	**44 685**	..
G7	20 738	19 552	21 104	29 153 |	29 608	27 616	26 856	26 013	23 491	..
Euro area	12 820	11 573	11 790	15 069	15 906	16 017	18 015	19 055	18 641	17 450
European Union[2]	19 179	16 886	16 660	21 303	22 739	22 957	25 095	26 117	24 815	22 884
Brazil	8 036	7 839	7 010	8 325	..	6 718	6 244	6 637	7 254	..
Colombia	2 311	2 152	2 214	2 515	2 564	2 426	2 394	2 243	2 151	2 156
Russian Federation	5 250	4 519	4 697	6 284	5 544	4 922	4 131	4 137	3 889	4 264

Disclaimer: http://oe.cd/disclaimer

1. Information on data for Israel: http://oe.cd/israel-disclaimer.
2. European Union refer to European Union with 28 countries.

Table 29. Unemployment as a percentage of civilian labour force

Percentage

	2006	2007	2008	2009	2010	2011	2012	2013	2014	2015
Australia	4.8	4.4	4.2	5.6	5.2	5.1	5.2	5.7	6.1	6.1
Austria	5.3	4.9	4.1	5.3	4.8	4.6	4.9	5.3	5.6	5.7
Belgium	8.2	7.5	7.0	7.9	8.3	7.1	7.5	8.4	8.5	8.5
Canada	6.3	6.0	6.1	8.3	8.1	7.5	7.3	7.1	6.9	6.9
Chile	7.7	7.1	7.8	9.7	8.1	7.1	6.4	5.9	6.4	6.2
Czech Republic	7.2	5.3	4.4	6.7	7.3	6.7	7.0	7.0	6.1	5.1
Denmark	3.9	3.8	3.4	6.0	7.5	7.6	7.5	7.0	6.6	6.2
Estonia	6.0	4.6	5.5	13.6	16.8	12.4	10.1	8.7	7.4	6.2
Finland	7.7	6.9	6.4	8.3	8.4	7.8	7.7	8.2	8.7	9.4
France	8.3	7.5	7.0	8.6	8.8	8.7	9.2	9.7	9.7	..
Germany	10.3	8.7	7.6	7.8	7.1	5.9	5.4	5.2	5.0	4.6
Greece	8.9	8.2	7.3	9.0	12.0	16.5	23.8	27.3	26.6	24.6
Hungary	7.6	7.5	7.9	10.1	11.2	11.1	11.0	10.2	7.8	6.8
Iceland	2.9	2.3	3.0	7.2	7.6	7.1	6.0	5.4	5.0	4.0
Ireland	4.7	4.8	5.8	12.3	13.9	14.6	15.0	13.9	11.8	9.8
Israel[1]	8.4	7.3	6.1	7.5	6.6	5.6 |	6.9	6.2	5.9	5.3
Italy	6.8	6.1	6.8	7.8	8.5	8.4	10.8	12.3	12.8	12.0
Japan	4.1	3.8	4.0	5.1 |	5.0	4.6	4.3	4.0	3.6	3.4
Korea	3.5	3.2	3.2	3.6	3.7	3.4	3.2	3.1	3.5	3.6
Latvia	7.0	6.1	7.7	17.5	19.5	16.2	15.0	11.9	10.8	9.9
Luxembourg	4.2	4.2	4.2	5.4	5.8	5.7	6.1	6.9	7.1	6.8
Mexico	3.2	3.4	3.5	5.2 |	5.2	5.2	4.8	5.0	4.9	4.3
Netherlands	3.9	3.2	2.8	3.4	4.5	5.0	5.8	7.2	7.4	6.9
New Zealand	3.8	3.6	4.2	6.1	6.5	6.5	6.9	6.2	5.8	5.8
Norway	3.5	2.5	2.6	3.2	3.6	3.3	3.2	3.5	3.5	4.4
Poland	13.8	9.6	7.1	8.2	9.6	9.6	10.1	10.3	9.0	7.5
Portugal	7.7	8.0	7.6	9.5	10.8 |	12.8	15.6	16.3	14.0	12.5
Slovak Republic	13.3	11.0	9.6	12.1	14.4	13.6	13.9	14.2	13.2	11.5
Slovenia	5.9	4.8	4.4	5.9	7.2	8.2	8.8	10.1	9.7	9.0
Spain	8.5	8.3	11.3	17.9	19.9	21.5	24.9	26.2	24.5	22.1
Sweden	7.1	6.2	6.2	8.3	8.6	7.8	8.0	8.0	7.9	7.4
Switzerland	3.8	3.4	3.2	4.1	4.3	3.8	3.9	4.1	4.2	4.2
Turkey	10.2	10.3	11.0	14.0	11.9	9.8	9.2	9.7 |	9.9	10.3
United Kingdom	5.4	5.3	5.3	7.7	7.8	7.9	7.9	7.7	6.2	5.6
United States	4.6	4.6	5.8	9.3	9.6	8.9	8.1	7.4	6.2	5.3
OECD-Total	**6.1**	**5.6**	**5.9**	**8.1 |**	**8.3 |**	**7.9 |**	**8.0**	**7.9 |**	**7.3**	..
G7	5.8	5.4	5.8	8.0 |	8.1	7.6	7.3	7.1	6.4	..
Euro area	8.3	7.4	7.4	9.5	10.1	10.1	11.3	11.9	11.6	10.8
European Union[2]	8.1	7.1	7.0	8.9	9.5	9.6	10.4	10.8	10.2	9.4
Brazil	8.4	8.1	7.1	8.3	..	6.7	6.2	6.5	6.9	..
Colombia	12.0	11.2	11.3	12.0	11.8	10.8	10.4	9.6	9.1	8.9
Russian Federation	7.1	6.0	6.2	8.3	7.3	6.5	5.5	5.5	5.2	5.6

Disclaimer: http://oe.cd/disclaimer

1. Information on data for Israel: http://oe.cd/israel-disclaimer.
2. European Union refer to European Union with 28 countries.

Table 30. Duration of unemployment: less than one month

Thousands of persons

	2006	2007	2008	2009	2010	2011	2012	2013	2014	2015
Australia	139.6	142.0	143.6	159.7	151.1	151.5	151.4	153.1	172.6	149.9
Austria	21.6	21.9	20.0	25.4	19.0	21.1	20.3	20.8	23.3	22.3
Belgium	23.8	21.2	24.0	27.4	21.7	15.7	17.5	14.0	15.4	14.2
Canada	318.8	310.4	327.7	361.4	329.8	325.8	324.5	310.8	307.2	312.9
Chile	..	..	..	..	..	..	..	..	..	..
Czech Republic	17.7	17.0	15.4	28.5	24.7	25.6	22.9	24.0	24.3	19.1
Denmark	28.9	32.3	35.1	40.1	37.0	36.6	34.3	35.5	34.5	32.4
Estonia	4.2	4.7	7.0	10.5	8.1	7.9	6.2	4.3	5.0	4.4
Finland	20.1	25.3	25.5	27.9	27.2	28.0	26.5	26.6	26.7	29.4
France	301.0	287.5	277.8	311.0	301.4	293.9	326.6	136.9	139.0	131.8
Germany	243.3	224.0	209.7	246.7	215.2	219.5	219.1	203.0	205.4	200.4
Greece	17.3	23.5	25.6	34.8	40.9	44.6	47.8	41.3	31.9	34.0
Hungary	14.6	15.0	15.2	19.9	17.7	30.0	40.5	51.1	38.6	34.1
Iceland	2.1	1.7	2.0	2.4	2.0	2.1	2.1	2.0	2.3	2.1
Ireland	21.9	9.4	12.3	19.8	13.2	13.3	12.5	12.2	10.8	9.6
Israel[1]	44.1	45.6	37.4	45.1	43.9	37.9	66.4	56.7	57.1	50.5
Italy	116.7	121.8	140.4	140.0	141.2	130.4	139.7	144.3	139.4	167.3
Japan	410.0	390.0	380.0	440.0	320.0	300.0	340.0	290.0	280.0	270.0
Korea	..	..	..	..	..	..	..	..	..	..
Latvia	17.5	24.1	22.0	12.9	8.2	8.5	8.7	9.4	7.1	6.5
Luxembourg	0.6	0.6	1.2	0.7	1.3	0.9	1.0	0.8	1.4	2.6
Mexico	656.6	734.9	774.1	1 025.1	1 017.3	1 106.7	990.1	1 088.4	1 118.7	980.2
Netherlands	11.5	13.5	15.8	22.5	26.1	28.3	39.7	42.7	40.0	35.5
New Zealand	24.8	27.5	31.1	36.6	32.2	35.6	37.0	31.5	31.1	33.7
Norway	20.7	19.2	24.8	22.8	23.9	21.5	21.3	23.4	23.2	25.3
Poland	165.1	132.6	185.5	199.7	218.1	195.9	192.9	195.6	183.4	149.5
Portugal	24.9	27.8	29.3	33.0	30.6	34.4	33.6	27.2	27.6	26.4
Slovak Republic	14.8	16.3	19.4	36.8	25.8	21.4	25.1	23.9	23.0	31.1
Slovenia	2.0	2.5	2.9	3.6	3.0	3.1	3.5	3.1	2.1	3.4
Spain	332.7	343.9	416.2	396.7	348.4	369.1	365.6	348.8	331.3	329.1
Sweden	..	86.9	99.1	99.7	95.7	89.9	93.2	93.5	99.8	93.2
Switzerland	14.8	12.1	16.6	18.9	17.4	19.6	21.9	17.1	21.1	18.7
Turkey	48.0	65.0	85.0	102.0	124.0	115.0	99.0	118.0	142.0	159.0
United Kingdom	285.4	266.6	292.5	294.5	254.9	267.9	275.8	266.6	252.6	250.9
United States	2 615.0	2 540.0	2 932.0	3 165.0	2 771.0	2 678.0	2 644.0	2 583.0	2 470.0	2 397.0
OECD-Total	**5 980.1**	**6 006.9**	**6 646.2**	**7 411.3**	**6 712.3**	**6 679.5**	**6 650.7**	**6 399.8**	**6 288.0**	**6 026.6**
G7	..	..	..	..	..	..	..	..	..	..
Euro area	..	..	..	..	..	..	..	..	..	..
European Union	1 801.6	1 852.5	2 089.1	2 176.1	2 020.4	1 988.6	2 047.7	1 817.0	1 743.9	1 706.8
Brazil	..	..	..	..	..	..	..	..	..	..
Colombia	..	380.6	394.7	427.6	456.4	485.9	521.5	499.6	492.8	480.8
Russian Federation	539.9	492.1	611.4	794.7	625.4	521.9	472.9	494.3	479.3	491.7

Disclaimer: http://oe.cd/disclaimer

1. Information on data for Israel: http://oe.cd/israel-disclaimer.

Table 31. Duration of unemployment: more than 1 month and less than 3 months

Thousands of persons

	2006	2007	2008	2009	2010	2011	2012	2013	2014	2015
Australia	134.4	130.4	132.5	170.6	153.7	157.3	165.3	182.2	171.4	185.8
Austria	51.7	48.7	45.3	56.6	53.4	49.9	56.5	58.7	58.6	57.4
Belgium	56.1	56.4	57.6	63.6	63.0	56.9	65.8	72.3	63.5	68.1
Canada	415.1	410.0	419.9	572.7	524.7	492.4	493.6	485.9	479.9	492.1
Chile	..	..	..	..	..	..	..	..	..	..
Czech Republic	30.1	25.2	23.8	58.1	46.2	46.7	47.5	45.5	42.8	31.8
Denmark	24.4	28.1	26.1	49.6	50.7	48.5	44.8	43.4	42.0	38.6
Estonia	5.6	4.3	7.0	17.0	11.6	8.8	7.5	9.8	7.7	7.6
Finland	57.0	50.9	57.7	72.6	64.2	63.7	64.9	68.9	68.6	72.7
France	379.8	373.4	381.5	459.0	423.5	424.0	460.6	503.6	480.1	478.4
Germany	489.9	448.6	427.2	496.9	414.9	360.8	352.3	346.4	336.8	305.3
Greece	42.4	57.3	60.6	86.2	98.1	118.9	116.0	91.9	78.3	70.4
Hungary	34.3	35.9	37.5	48.8	44.6	50.2	42.9	33.7	29.8	30.5
Iceland	0.7	0.7	1.7	3.7	2.8	2.4	2.0	2.4	2.0	1.7
Ireland	9.2	25.0	36.8	51.9	35.4	30.2	30.5	28.2	25.4	21.6
Israel[1]	51.7	44.0	40.8	55.9	47.1	43.8	59.9	53.8	51.9	46.0
Italy	237.2	228.5	265.3	276.1	268.4	235.4	315.0	328.6	319.2	308.3
Japan	550.0	520.0	560.0	730.0	610.0	510.0	500.0	480.0	490.0	450.0
Korea	506.3	470.8	479.3	567.5	617.8	576.7	524.1	515.4	592.5	580.4
Latvia	25.3	24.6	38.4	32.8	18.5	16.6	19.4	14.1	13.7	11.8
Luxembourg	1.9	1.8	2.3	2.5	1.8	2.4	3.0	3.3	3.5	3.1
Mexico	410.1	467.3	481.4	773.6	836.3	871.2	873.2	866.3	833.7	806.8
Netherlands	66.7	61.0	60.6	81.1	97.1	103.4	115.6	123.4	113.1	108.1
New Zealand	21.2	19.8	26.7	37.4	39.7	37.7	37.4	33.7	31.9	31.9
Norway	19.9	15.2	18.0	22.1	22.6	20.3	21.7	23.8	22.2	28.0
Poland	237.2	199.5	225.6	290.1	317.0	285.3	283.0	274.8	248.1	149.6
Portugal	53.2	61.5	63.7	76.3	66.7	104.4	115.0	97.0	84.9	89.3
Slovak Republic	18.4	15.8	15.4	33.0	24.9	23.2	24.8	22.6	22.1	23.7
Slovenia	8.2	8.7	8.7	13.6	10.3	13.6	13.5	12.5	12.0	11.9
Spain	514.5	525.8	770.1	901.4	818.0	813.0	873.3	804.5	754.0	730.7
Sweden	..	70.5	69.4	98.5	91.8	88.6	89.4	89.2	87.9	80.6
Switzerland	25.1	23.5	23.9	35.4	36.3	30.7	36.1	40.2	36.3	40.3
Turkey	543.0	620.0	716.0	870.0	800.0	765.0	747.0	808.0	1 054.0	1 105.0
United Kingdom	393.2	408.7	433.5	530.9	483.0	506.6	473.3	470.4	391.3	388.3
United States	2 120.0	2 231.0	2 806.0	3 828.0	3 268.0	2 994.0	2 867.0	2 759.0	2 431.0	2 304.0
OECD-Total	**7 533.8**	**7 712.9**	**8 820.6**	**11 463.5**	**10 462.1**	**9 952.4**	**9 942.0**	**9 793.5**	**9 480.1**	**9 159.7**
G7	..	..	..	..	..	..	..	..	..	..
Euro area	..	..	..	..	..	..	..	..	..	..
European Union	2 887.7	2 897.8	3 261.6	3 999.8	3 702.9	3 656.9	3 825.1	3 766.8	3 492.5	3 269.8
Brazil	..	..	..	..	..	..	..	..	..	..
Colombia	..	671.2	700.2	793.8	797.5	783.4	793.0	754.0	722.6	763.5
Russian Federation	800.6	753.6	916.0	1 390.2	1 036.3	956.2	883.9	893.4	852.3	969.8

Disclaimer: http://oe.cd/disclaimer

1. Information on data for Israel: http://oe.cd/israel-disclaimer.

Table 32. Duration of unemployment: more than 3 months and less than 6 months

Thousands of persons

	2006	2007	2008	2009	2010	2011	2012	2013	2014	2015
Australia	77.7	76.0	71.8	115.5	99.3	96.8	101.6	116.2	118.9	126.7
Austria	43.7	40.7	33.4	51.7	42.9	39.2	41.6	50.6	49.0	48.0
Belgium	53.3	45.5	46.9	60.0	52.6	51.9	60.8	64.3	64.5	60.9
Canada	146.8	149.9	151.0	265.6	241.8	210.8	211.3	205.5	201.3	204.9
Chile	..	..	..	..	..	..	..	..	..	..
Czech Republic	45.0	36.4	31.2	71.9	59.4	57.8	59.7	57.7	49.4	39.0
Denmark	21.1	18.1	17.8	41.9	46.0	43.1	41.8	38.5	36.8	32.7
Estonia	5.9	4.1	5.9	20.6	18.0	9.0	8.4	10.0	7.0	7.7
Finland	40.7	36.3	33.3	49.5	43.0	40.5	38.9	42.8	47.2	47.9
France	235.6	231.5	224.6	312.9	275.9	273.8	293.8	493.6	494.7	492.2
Germany	472.3	404.5	398.8	476.0	401.8	311.1	314.4	312.3	293.9	278.7
Greece	65.9	62.5	57.1	80.6	100.8	127.4	139.6	122.2	96.1	86.7
Hungary	51.6	45.6	47.9	70.6	64.1	65.9	62.9	50.2	40.2	38.2
Iceland	0.3	0.2	0.5	3.2	2.3	2.2	1.8	1.6	1.7	1.1
Ireland	15.7	19.6	29.1	52.0	41.2	34.2	33.1	29.5	26.6	24.5
Israel[1]	36.4	30.5	27.8	41.1	31.6	29.1	38.5	33.9	32.3	29.0
Italy	235.5	220.9	254.4	310.1	311.6	307.4	377.4	396.1	381.5	356.6
Japan	440.0	370.0	430.0	580.0	500.0	410.0	420.0	360.0	330.0	340.0
Korea	227.5	220.6	215.7	241.3	237.9	220.0	225.9	227.3	273.7	298.3
Latvia	34.0	28.7	42.4	44.9	35.8	22.3	21.9	17.7	19.2	17.3
Luxembourg	2.3	2.0	2.0	2.8	2.3	2.2	2.3	3.5	3.1	3.6
Mexico	175.3	188.0	224.1	402.3	416.1	387.3	390.9	382.1	372.1	271.8
Netherlands	53.1	45.4	42.1	65.9	74.2	78.8	90.8	118.7	109.5	96.4
New Zealand	10.9	9.7	11.0	22.8	26.8	25.5	24.3	22.9	20.3	19.3
Norway	10.9	8.8	9.0	14.0	15.4	14.0	14.1	15.7	15.9	22.3
Poland	321.0	245.7	234.7	291.1	347.7	313.1	314.1	312.9	262.4	251.1
Portugal	56.2	64.1	57.7	77.5	76.4	103.2	121.6	104.7	77.1	75.8
Slovak Republic	22.3	19.5	20.4	37.9	36.9	31.4	31.8	30.6	26.7	26.5
Slovenia	9.4	8.0	7.8	13.0	14.3	14.2	13.6	14.9	13.8	12.5
Spain	331.6	333.6	533.9	919.9	797.0	811.5	890.4	841.8	719.5	657.7
Sweden	..	48.7	46.6	76.7	70.3	60.3	62.1	63.7	61.2	54.1
Switzerland	28.9	31.0	32.4	39.6	35.2	28.1	34.4	35.8	32.7	36.1
Turkey	545.0	591.0	697.0	938.0	732.0	616.0	651.0	719.0	694.0	709.0
United Kingdom	306.2	296.7	318.4	478.3	425.2	454.7	424.7	398.2	309.2	288.9
United States	1 033.0	1 062.0	1 426.0	2 776.0	2 372.0	2 063.0	1 861.0	1 805.0	1 497.0	1 265.0
OECD-Total	**5 154.8**	**4 996.0**	**5 782.8**	**9 044.8**	**8 047.8**	**7 355.5**	**7 420.5**	**7 499.5**	**6 778.5**	**6 320.5**
G7	..	..	..	..	..	..	..	..	..	..
Euro area	..	..	..	..	..	..	..	..	..	..
European Union	2 589.1	2 408.0	2 634.2	3 860.0	3 564.6	3 463.4	3 660.1	3 789.0	3 404.4	3 189.7
Brazil	..	..	..	..	..	..	..	..	..	..
Colombia	..	346.7	393.9	442.6	447.0	402.6	392.1	364.9	336.9	336.8
Russian Federation	718.1	621.8	707.5	1 277.6	1 250.9	839.4	773.6	688.8	660.0	759.1

Disclaimer: http://oe.cd/disclaimer

1. Information on data for Israel: http://oe.cd/israel-disclaimer.

Table 33. Duration of unemployment: more than 6 months and less than 1 year

Thousands of persons

	2006	2007	2008	2009	2010	2011	2012	2013	2014	2015
Australia	64.7	55.7	55.8	96.8	89.0	81.1	88.2	103.5	121.3	117.1
Austria	35.5	34.5	31.4	41.0	36.4	32.8	38.5	44.3	47.4	50.5
Belgium	53.4	51.6	45.8	60.6	70.1	54.6	59.6	73.9	68.4	60.2
Canada	76.2	74.7	80.1	148.1	158.2	132.0	114.8	120.8	118.5	120.3
Chile	..	..	..	..	..	..	..	..	..	..
Czech Republic	73.6	50.3	44.1	83.6	88.3	76.4	74.1	75.9	63.0	48.6
Denmark	15.4	14.2	8.6	28.6	40.4	39.3	36.6	33.3	29.9	28.4
Estonia	5.4	2.8	6.1	19.6	24.7	10.5	8.9	8.4	7.5	6.3
Finland	29.1	27.0	22.7	33.0	35.2	27.0	29.4	32.0	33.5	36.1
France	424.1	370.6	342.0	500.4	489.2	461.2	508.9	536.3	560.2	581.5
Germany	623.9	469.3	433.7	518.1	454.1	350.3	321.2	337.3	317.1	298.4
Greece	79.9	67.1	61.8	87.4	114.3	155.9	185.6	182.3	131.3	130.6
Hungary	70.5	67.3	71.2	101.2	107.0	92.4	106.5	86.4	66.8	61.3
Iceland	0.2	0.1	0.2	2.2	2.6	1.5	1.3	1.1	1.6	0.8
Ireland	17.4	18.6	26.9	64.5	62.9	49.6	43.8	39.9	34.5	28.6
Israel[1]	32.5	27.2	22.1	32.5	28.3	21.3	32.2	28.0	24.9	23.2
Italy	225.6	196.8	232.0	321.8	327.6	305.3	413.8	438.9	395.7	396.9
Japan	410.0	400.0	350.0	580.0	580.0	440.0	450.0	380.0	330.0	320.0
Korea	84.6	87.4	71.2	75.4	61.0	54.9	67.4	60.9	68.1	93.8
Latvia	26.2	21.7	31.2	52.2	50.6	28.4	24.3	20.3	20.9	17.6
Luxembourg	2.0	1.8	1.8	3.0	1.6	2.8	2.6	2.7	3.0	3.9
Mexico	34.6	31.4	25.9	66.0	91.4	52.9	53.5	74.2	51.1	50.8
Netherlands	56.3	44.6	36.0	55.6	80.0	71.7	87.5	120.7	125.4	98.0
New Zealand	9.5	7.6	8.6	21.4	26.5	27.9	27.8	25.9	23.1	24.2
Norway	14.2	9.9	7.9	13.7	19.7	17.3	16.1	17.3	18.2	22.5
Poland	438.3	298.4	213.6	274.6	346.4	340.1	350.9	355.0	305.5	241.0
Portugal	73.9	78.7	67.9	100.2	107.1	113.3	157.5	144.1	103.3	83.9
Slovak Republic	39.5	33.6	32.3	51.5	70.6	55.2	55.2	51.9	47.3	37.2
Slovenia	11.2	7.8	6.9	12.5	15.1	15.6	16.1	19.4	16.7	15.2
Spain	263.3	266.0	408.5	946.8	976.8	933.9	1 103.3	1 049.4	840.5	729.4
Sweden	..	39.6	37.6	64.7	69.8	55.3	56.6	58.7	55.2	50.4
Switzerland	32.4	24.2	21.7	32.3	45.7	32.3	30.2	40.7	41.5	36.9
Turkey	362.0	380.0	411.0	682.0	520.0	428.0	393.0	432.0	374.0	438.0
United Kingdom	283.6	262.1	282.2	478.0	489.1	467.9	473.7	416.6	323.2	273.4
United States	534.0	538.0	813.0	2 176.0	2 118.0	1 709.0	1 472.0	1 339.0	1 005.0	781.0
OECD-Total	**4 502.9**	**4 060.6**	**4 311.9**	**7 825.2**	**7 797.9**	**6 737.7**	**6 901.1**	**6 751.0**	**5 773.3**	**5 305.8**
G7	..	..	..	..	..	..	..	..	..	..
Euro area	..	..	..	..	..	..	..	..	..	..
European Union	3 047.9	2 604.0	2 605.3	4 163.6	4 388.3	4 017.0	4 418.7	4 405.5	3 877.3	3 522.7
Brazil	..	..	..	..	..	..	..	..	..	..
Colombia	..	302.8	335.7	392.5	367.5	318.2	293.9	273.5	258.8	252.4
Russian Federation	971.3	814.4	809.0	1 015.6	966.3	986.8	724.1	779.1	805.9	879.1

Disclaimer: http://oe.cd/disclaimer

1. Information on data for Israel: http://oe.cd/israel-disclaimer.

Table 34. Duration of unemployment: 1 year and over

Thousands of persons

	2006	2007	2008	2009	2010	2011	2012	2013	2014	2015
Australia	92.1	73.4	70.8	93.7	112.8	113.6	118.6	131.5	161.4	178.1
Austria	59.2	54.6	41.8	48.3	51.8	50.9	52.0	56.9	66.6	73.6
Belgium	195.8	177.3	158.0	167.7	197.5	167.4	164.6	191.6	211.2	218.0
Canada	91.5	76.3	76.7	116.6	172.7	182.8	166.5	165.7	163.5	147.8
Chile	..	..	..	..	..	..	..	..	..	..
Czech Republic	205.0	147.5	115.4	109.6	167.2	146.8	156.7	165.8	144.1	129.5
Denmark	23.6	17.8	13.7	16.8	44.1	53.9	61.3	51.5	48.2	48.6
Estonia	19.9	15.7	11.8	25.4	51.6	48.6	37.4	26.1	22.5	16.2
Finland	48.5	41.6	30.9	36.5	52.4	46.6	44.2	45.8	52.8	62.3
France	951.8	831.3	721.6	847.6	988.2	1 013.5	1 058.0	1 134.9	1 328.4	1 340.3
Germany	2 364.7	2 015.2	1 625.1	1 449.8	1 332.4	1 140.6	1 002.2	967.4	918.5	850.0
Greece	242.6	207.8	182.7	195.5	285.0	434.9	706.1	892.6	936.1	874.7
Hungary	147.3	148.2	154.5	177.3	236.0	227.4	220.3	219.6	167.9	143.8
Iceland	0.3	0.2	0.2	0.8	2.6	3.2	2.8	2.0	1.2	1.1
Ireland	29.6	31.2	38.0	77.2	147.4	185.7	193.3	169.0	141.3	114.4
Israel[1]	61.9	48.8	37.6	44.4	43.5	33.5	30.1	25.2	19.8	19.2
Italy	801.0	694.6	751.6	843.6	986.5	1 058.8	1 414.1	1 729.3	1 965.6	1 763.2
Japan	890.0	790.0	860.0	930.0	1 210.0	1 080.0	1 070.0	1 060.0	860.0	760.0
Korea	8.9	4.4	3.4	4.5	3.0	3.3	2.4	3.2	2.1	3.6
Latvia	52.8	36.8	42.3	49.7	92.6	90.7	80.7	57.9	46.1	44.4
Luxembourg	2.9	2.5	3.5	2.7	2.9	3.3	3.9	4.5	4.2	5.2
Mexico	26.4	32.9	21.7	40.1	48.9	46.9	42.6	35.3	29.7	25.0
Netherlands	141.5	106.9	81.1	74.2	105.6	140.2	168.3	224.4	257.6	261.1
New Zealand	5.5	4.1	3.5	8.1	12.2	12.4	19.4	15.8	16.8	16.6
Norway	11.1	5.1	3.8	6.0	8.5	9.6	6.9	8.1	10.6	13.0
Poland	1 182.3	742.3	351.4	355.9	421.1	524.2	608.1	654.4	567.5	511.9
Portugal	211.8	207.4	197.3	227.4	307.3	332.7	407.3	481.7	432.2	370.6
Slovak Republic	258.2	206.8	169.9	165.1	230.7	233.4	240.6	257.0	239.5	195.7
Slovenia	30.0	22.8	19.2	18.3	32.6	36.8	42.9	51.9	53.5	47.2
Spain	398.3	376.4	467.0	988.5	1 699.5	2 084.3	2 577.9	3 006.2	2 964.3	2 608.6
Sweden	..	36.0	34.7	49.7	68.4	65.5	64.1	62.5	61.5	59.4
Switzerland	64.8	62.6	49.4	54.4	66.7	70.3	67.0	66.6	79.8	83.0
Turkey	831.0	721.0	702.0	877.0	871.0	693.0	627.0	670.0	589.0	647.0
United Kingdom	365.2	384.9	422.7	578.9	797.4	853.4	876.5	878.6	709.6	531.5
United States	701.0	704.0	950.0	2 318.0	4 298.0	4 307.0	3 664.0	2 968.0	2 214.0	1 547.0
OECD-Total	**10 516.4**	**9 028.4**	**8 413.3**	**10 999.4**	**15 148.2**	**15 495.1**	**15 997.8**	**16 480.9**	**15 487.2**	**13 711.7**
G7	..	..	..	..	..	..	..	..	..	..
Euro area	..	..	..	..	..	..	..	..	..	..
European Union	8 523.6	7 131.1	6 122.0	6 979.7	8 934.3	9 708.9	10 990.9	12 182.0	12 129.0	11 016.5
Brazil	..	..	..	..	..	..	..	..	..	..
Colombia	..	232.4	206.9	265.3	279.1	231.0	209.3	179.3	182.0	152.4
Russian Federation	2 220.3	1 836.7	1 653.0	1 805.6	1 665.3	1 618.1	1 276.3	1 281.8	1 091.9	1 164.3

Disclaimer: http://oe.cd/disclaimer

1. Information on data for Israel: http://oe.cd/israel-disclaimer.

OECD Labour Force Statistics 2016
© OECD 2017

Country tables

AUSTRALIA

Table 1. Labour force

Annual average estimates

	2006	2007	2008	2009	2010	2011	2012	2013	2014	2015
Civilian labour force, thousands										
All persons	10 633	10 912	11 206	11 442	11 628	11 815	11 973	12 137	12 278	12 509
Males	5 832	5 974	6 123	6 234	6 343	6 424	6 498	6 577	6 633	6 738
Females	4 801	4 938	5 083	5 208	5 285	5 392	5 475	5 560	5 645	5 771
Unemployed, thousands										
All persons	508	478	474	636	606	600	625	686	746	758
Males	272	241	242	355	322	314	334	375	398	408
Females	236	236	232	281	284	286	291	311	348	350
Civilian employment, thousands										
All persons	10 124	10 434	10 731	10 806	11 022	11 215	11 347	11 451	11 532	11 751
Males	5 560	5 732	5 880	5 879	6 021	6 109	6 164	6 202	6 235	6 330
Females	4 565	4 702	4 851	4 926	5 001	5 106	5 184	5 249	5 297	5 421
Civilian employment (%)										
All persons	100.0	100.0	100.0	100.0	100.0	100.0	100.0	100.0	100.0	100.0
Males	54.9	54.9	54.8	54.4	54.6	54.5	54.3	54.2	54.1	53.9
Females	45.1	45.1	45.2	45.6	45.4	45.5	45.7	45.8	45.9	46.1
Unemployment rate (% of civilian labour force)										
All persons	4.8	4.4	4.2	5.6	5.2	5.1	5.2	5.7	6.1	6.1
Males	4.7	4.0	4.0	5.7	5.1	4.9	5.1	5.7	6.0	6.1
Females	4.9	4.8	4.6	5.4	5.4	5.3	5.3	5.6	6.2	6.1
CIVIL. EMPL. - PROFESSIONAL STATUS, thousands										
All activities	**10 124**	**10 434**	**10 731**	**10 806**	**11 022**	**11 215**	**11 347**	**11 451**	**11 532**	**11 746**
Employees	8 900	9 215	9 500	9 561	9 753	9 973	10 169	10 293	10 356	10 535
Employers and persons working on own account	1 192	1 191	1 205	1 218	1 240	1 217	1 155	1 132	1 149	1 185
Unpaid family workers	32	29	26	27	30	25	24	25	28	27
Employees as % of civilian employment	**87.9**	**88.3**	**88.5**	**88.5**	**88.5**	**88.9**	**89.6**	**89.9**	**89.8**	**89.7**
Part-time employment (%)										
Part-time as % of employment	23.9	23.7	23.8	24.6	24.8	24.7	24.6	24.9	25.2	25.2
Male share of part time employment	28.0	28.5	28.3	29.2	29.6	29.2	28.9	29.7	30.1	30.5
Female share of part time employment	72.0	71.5	71.7	70.8	70.4	70.8	71.1	70.3	69.9	69.5
Male part-time as % of male employment	12.2	12.3	12.3	13.2	13.5	13.2	13.1	13.6	14.0	14.2
Female part-time as % of female employment	38.3	37.7	37.7	38.2	38.6	38.4	38.2	38.1	38.4	38.0
Duration of unemployment (% of total unemployment)										
Less than one month	27.5	29.7	30.3	25.1	24.9	25.2	24.2	22.3	23.1	19.8
More than 1 month and less than 3 months	26.4	27.3	27.9	26.8	25.4	26.2	26.4	26.5	23.0	24.5
More than 3 months and less than 6 months	15.3	15.9	15.1	18.2	16.4	16.1	16.3	16.9	15.9	16.7
More than 6 months and less than 1 year	12.7	11.7	11.8	15.2	14.7	13.5	14.1	15.1	16.3	15.5
More than 1 year	18.1	15.4	14.9	14.7	18.6	18.9	19.0	19.1	21.7	23.5

Note: Detailed metadata: http://metalinks.oecd.org/lfs/20170518/daf7a, http://metalinks.oecd.org/lfs/20170518/87289, http://metalinks.oecd.org/lfs/20170518/9d0b4 and http://metalinks.oecd.org/lfs/20170518/e896a.

Disclaimer: http://oe.cd/disclaimer

AUSTRALIA

Table 2. Participation rates and unemployment rates by age and sex

Annual average estimates, percentage

	2006	2007	2008	2009	2010	2011	2012	2013	2014	2015
Participation rates										
Males										
15-19	58.4	58.0	58.5	55.7	54.6	53.5	52.9	51.8	51.8	51.8
20-24	85.4	85.2	84.8	84.1	83.4	82.8	82.3	81.6	80.6	82.3
25-34	91.6	92.2	92.4	91.1	91.3	91.8	91.0	91.1	90.7	91.0
35-44	91.1	91.5	91.7	91.3	91.4	91.4	91.4	91.0	91.0	91.2
45-54	88.3	88.6	88.7	88.6	88.8	88.4	88.0	88.2	87.7	88.6
55-59	76.2	77.1	76.4	78.3	80.2	80.7	80.0	80.8	80.3	80.5
60-64	56.0	56.4	57.8	59.4	61.5	61.8	62.6	62.5	63.1	64.1
15-24	72.1	71.8	72.0	70.4	69.6	68.8	68.2	67.4	66.9	67.9
25-54	90.3	90.8	90.9	90.4	90.6	90.6	90.1	90.1	89.9	90.3
55-64	67.3	67.7	67.6	69.3	71.2	71.7	71.8	72.1	72.2	72.8
65 and over	12.2	13.4	14.1	15.3	15.4	16.1	16.9	16.8	17.0	16.4
15-64	82.7	83.0	83.0	82.6	82.9	82.8	82.5	82.4	82.1	82.7
Females										
15-19	60.7	60.7	59.9	58.2	57.6	57.3	56.7	55.9	55.8	56.0
20-24	77.9	78.2	78.6	76.5	75.9	76.6	75.8	75.4	75.5	76.2
25-34	72.7	72.9	74.1	73.3	72.9	73.8	73.9	74.4	74.6	75.5
35-44	74.0	74.4	74.8	75.3	74.3	75.2	75.5	75.2	75.1	76.2
45-54	76.0	77.0	77.3	78.0	78.3	78.0	77.4	77.9	78.0	78.0
55-59	58.1	59.3	60.7	63.4	64.5	65.2	65.7	65.3	66.1	66.3
60-64	33.3	35.7	37.9	41.1	42.7	43.8	44.4	45.1	45.1	47.1
15-24	69.5	69.7	69.5	67.7	67.2	67.5	66.8	66.2	66.2	66.7
25-54	74.2	74.8	75.4	75.5	75.1	75.6	75.6	75.8	75.9	76.6
55-64	47.2	48.6	50.1	52.9	54.1	55.0	55.7	55.8	56.2	57.3
65 and over	4.3	5.0	5.4	6.0	6.8	7.0	7.8	8.0	8.3	8.5
15-64	68.9	69.4	70.0	70.1	70.0	70.5	70.4	70.5	70.5	71.2
All persons										
15-24	70.8	70.8	70.7	69.1	68.4	68.1	67.5	66.8	66.6	67.3
25-54	82.2	82.7	83.1	82.9	82.8	83.1	82.8	82.9	82.8	83.4
55-64	57.3	58.1	58.9	61.1	62.6	63.3	63.7	63.9	64.1	64.9
65 and over	7.8	8.8	9.4	10.2	10.8	11.2	12.0	12.1	12.3	12.2
15-64	75.8	76.2	76.5	76.4	76.4	76.6	76.4	76.4	76.3	77.0
Unemployment rates										
Males										
15-19	15.6	14.1	12.7	17.8	17.6	16.7	18.4	17.6	19.5	20.5
20-24	7.2	6.4	6.6	9.2	8.6	9.1	9.0	10.4	11.0	10.8
25-34	4.3	3.7	3.6	5.5	4.7	4.3	4.5	5.3	5.2	5.1
35-44	2.9	2.6	2.6	4.0	3.3	3.3	3.5	4.1	4.3	4.5
45-54	3.2	2.5	2.6	4.0	3.2	3.1	3.4	3.8	4.1	4.0
55-59	3.3	2.7	2.8	3.3	3.7	3.6	3.8	4.0	4.0	4.5
60-64	4.1	3.0	3.4	4.3	3.7	3.8	3.7	4.8	4.8	5.3
15-24	10.6	9.5	9.0	12.5	11.9	11.9	12.5	13.0	14.1	14.3
25-54	3.4	3.0	2.9	4.5	3.7	3.6	3.8	4.4	4.6	4.6
55-64	3.5	2.8	3.1	3.7	3.7	3.7	3.7	4.3	4.3	4.8
65 and over	1.4	1.2	0.9	1.4	1.7	1.2	1.9	1.7	2.6	1.6
15-64	4.8	4.1	4.0	5.8	5.2	5.0	5.3	5.9	6.1	6.2
Total	4.7	4.0	4.0	5.7	5.1	4.9	5.1	5.7	6.0	6.1
Females										
15-19	13.9	13.5	13.0	15.0	16.2	15.6	15.1	15.2	17.4	16.6
20-24	6.2	6.1	5.5	7.1	7.6	7.5	8.2	8.8	9.2	8.9
25-34	4.8	4.6	4.5	5.4	5.4	4.9	5.1	5.4	5.6	5.8
35-44	4.2	3.9	4.0	4.7	4.3	4.6	4.4	4.7	5.4	5.5
45-54	3.1	3.2	3.3	3.6	3.5	3.6	3.5	3.9	4.3	4.4
55-59	3.0	2.7	1.8	3.1	2.5	3.1	3.3	3.1	3.7	3.5
60-64	2.4	2.5	2.4	2.4	2.8	2.5	2.8	3.2	4.0	3.6
15-24	9.5	9.2	8.6	10.4	11.1	10.8	11.0	11.3	12.5	11.9
25-54	4.0	3.9	3.9	4.6	4.4	4.4	4.4	4.7	5.1	5.2
55-64	2.8	2.6	2.0	2.9	2.6	2.9	3.1	3.2	3.8	3.5
65 and over	1.2	1.1	1.2	1.0	1.2	1.1	1.2	1.2	1.6	1.4
15-64	5.0	4.8	4.6	5.5	5.5	5.4	5.4	5.7	6.3	6.2
Total	4.9	4.8	4.6	5.4	5.4	5.3	5.3	5.6	6.2	6.1
All persons										
15-24	10.0	9.4	8.8	11.5	11.6	11.4	11.7	12.2	13.3	13.1
25-54	3.7	3.4	3.4	4.5	4.0	3.9	4.1	4.6	4.8	4.9
55-64	3.2	2.7	2.6	3.3	3.2	3.3	3.5	3.8	4.1	4.3
65 and over	1.3	1.2	1.0	1.3	1.5	1.1	1.6	1.5	2.2	1.5
15-64	4.9	4.4	4.3	5.7	5.3	5.2	5.3	5.8	6.2	6.2

Note: Detailed metadata at:http://metalinks.oecd.org/lfs/20170518/6f97b
Disclaimer: http://oe.cd/disclaimer

AUSTRALIA

Table 3. Civilian employment and employees: breakdown by activity - ISIC Rev. 3

Annual average estimates

		2006	2007	2008	2009	2010	2011	2012	2013	2014	2015
	CIVILIAN EMPLOYMENT										
	By activity, thousands										
A-X	**All activities**	**10 220 |**	**10 549**	**10 840**	**10 921**	**11 157**	**11 353**	**11 470**	**..**	**..**	**..**
A	Agriculture, hunting and forestry	341 |	341	347	356	360	317	324	..	..	..
B	Fishing	10 |	11	11	8	11	10	9	..	..	..
C	Mining and quarrying	117 |	120	135	141	168	200	242	..	..	..
D	Manufacturing	1 075 |	1 096	1 112	1 062	1 038	1 010	1 013	..	..	..
E	Electricity, gas and water supply	85 |	87	100	109	113	118	126	..	..	..
F	Construction	915 |	951	998	996	1 017	1 033	1 000	..	..	..
G	Wholesale, retail trade: vehicle repair, household gds	1 786 |	1 831	1 867	1 842	1 856	1 871	1 845	..	..	..
H	Hotels and restaurants	667 |	707	716	738	751	781	769	..	..	..
I	Transport, storage and communication	641 |	680	701	717	706	713	699	..	..	..
J	Financial intermediation	387 |	408	405	398	396	422	424	..	..	..
K	Real estate, renting and business activities	1 280 |	1 296	1 337	1 314	1 405	1 439	1 489	..	..	..
L	Public adm., defence; social sec., excl. armed forces	626 |	643	650	675	695	721	707	..	..	..
M	Education	742 |	774	814	817	851	856	887	..	..	..
N	Health and social work	1 078 |	1 101	1 138	1 218	1 269	1 336	1 384	..	..	..
O	Other community, social, personal service activities	471 |	502	507	526	518	523	547	..	..	..
P	Private households with employed persons	1 |	2	2	5	4	3	5	..	..	..
Q	Extra-territorial organisations and bodies	0 |	0	0	0	0	0	0	..	..	..
X	Not classifiable by economic activities	0 |	0	0	0	0	0	0	..	..	..
	By sector, thousands										
A-B	Agriculture	351 |	353	359	364	371	327	333	..	..	..
C-F	Industry	2 192 |	2 253	2 344	2 308	2 336	2 360	2 380	..	..	..
G-Q	Services	7 678 |	7 943	8 137	8 249	8 450	8 666	8 756	..	..	..
	By sector, percentages										
A-B	Agriculture	3.4 |	3.3	3.3	3.3	3.3	2.9	2.9	..	..	..
C-F	Industry	21.4 |	21.4	21.6	21.1	20.9	20.8	20.8	..	..	..
G-Q	Services	75.1 |	75.3	75.1	75.5	75.7	76.3	76.3	..	..	..
	EMPLOYEES										
	By activity, thousands										
A-X	**All activities**	**8 945**	**9 285**	**9 564**	**9 630**	**9 837**	**10 064**	**10 248**	**..**	**..**	**..**
A	Agriculture, hunting and forestry	169	168	170	176	182	180	191	..	..	..
B	Fishing	6	8	7	6	7	7	6	..	..	..
C	Mining and quarrying	115	118	134	140	167	198	241	..	..	..
D	Manufacturing	999	1 026	1 039	991	967	940	948	..	..	..
E	Electricity, gas and water supply	83	85	99	108	111	117	124	..	..	..
F	Construction	630	681	712	707	737	751	747	..	..	..
G	Wholesale, retail trade: vehicle repair, household gds	1 613	1 651	1 687	1 676	1 689	1 713	1 695	..	..	..
H	Hotels and restaurants	610	649	664	692	692	720	714	..	..	..
I	Transport, storage and communication	564	597	621	627	618	635	624	..	..	..
J	Financial intermediation	368	390	385	383	380	402	408	..	..	..
K	Real estate, renting and business activities	1 068	1 080	1 133	1 093	1 164	1 190	1 246	..	..	..
L	Public adm., defence; social sec., excl. armed forces	617	638	645	669	691	715	703	..	..	..
M	Education	709	739	775	775	810	810	843	..	..	..
N	Health and social work	1 016	1 041	1 071	1 148	1 188	1 261	1 307	..	..	..
O	Other community, social, personal service activities	377	413	419	433	430	424	445	..	..	..
P	Private households with employed persons	1	2	2	5	4	3	5	..	..	..
Q	Extra-territorial organisations and bodies	0	0	0	0	0	0	0	..	..	..
X	Not classifiable by economic activities	0	0	0	0	0	0	0	..	..	..
	By sector, thousands										
A-B	Agriculture	175	176	177	182	189	187	197	..	..	..
C-F	Industry	1 827	1 909	1 983	1 946	1 981	2 005	2 060	..	..	..
G-Q	Services	6 943	7 200	7 404	7 501	7 666	7 873	7 990	..	..	..
	By sector, percentages										
A-B	Agriculture	2.0	1.9	1.9	1.9	1.9	1.9	1.9	..	..	..
C-F	Industry	20.4	20.6	20.7	20.2	20.1	19.9	20.1	..	..	..
G-Q	Services	77.6	77.5	77.4	77.9	77.9	78.2	78.0	..	..	..

Note: Detailed metadata:http://metalinks.oecd.org/lfs/20170518/87289

Disclaimer: http://oe.cd/disclaimer

AUSTRIA

Table 1. Labour force

Annual average estimates

	2006	2007	2008	2009	2010	2011	2012	2013	2014	2015
Civilian labour force, thousands										
All persons	4 028	4 113	4 154	4 192	4 209	4 237	4 284	4 326	4 347	4 390
Males	2 184	2 228	2 239	2 244	2 250	2 256	2 275	2 294	2 299	2 326
Females	1 844	1 885	1 914	1 947	1 959	1 981	2 009	2 032	2 048	2 064
Unemployed, thousands										
All persons	212	200	172	223	203	194	209	231	245	252
Males	108	100	88	124	113	103	113	124	135	142
Females	103	100	84	99	91	91	96	108	110	110
Civilian employment, thousands										
All persons	3 816	3 912	3 982	3 969	4 006	4 043	4 075	4 094	4 102	4 138
Males	2 075	2 127	2 152	2 120	2 137	2 153	2 162	2 170	2 164	2 184
Females	1 741	1 785	1 830	1 848	1 868	1 890	1 913	1 924	1 937	1 954
Civilian employment (%)										
All persons	100.0	100.0	100.0	100.0	100.0	100.0	100.0	100.0	100.0	100.0
Males	54.4	54.4	54.0	53.4	53.4	53.3	53.1	53.0	52.8	52.8
Females	45.6	45.6	46.0	46.6	46.6	46.7	46.9	47.0	47.2	47.2
Unemployment rate (% of civilian labour force)										
All persons	5.3	4.9	4.1	5.3	4.8	4.6	4.9	5.3	5.6	5.7
Males	5.0	4.5	3.9	5.5	5.0	4.6	5.0	5.4	5.9	6.1
Females	5.6	5.3	4.4	5.1	4.6	4.6	4.8	5.3	5.4	5.3
CIVIL. EMPL. - PROFESSIONAL STATUS, thousands										
All activities	**3 816**	**3 912**	**3 982**	**3 969**	**4 006**	**4 043**	**4 075**	**4 094**	**4 102**	**4 138**
Employees	3 317	3 375	3 441	3 426	3 451	3 505	3 541	3 552	3 555	3 599
Employers and persons working on own account	444	445	449	456	468	456	455	466	464	472
Unpaid family workers	55	92	92	87	87	82	79	76	83	67
Employees as % of civilian employment	**86.9**	**86.3**	**86.4**	**86.3**	**86.1**	**86.7**	**86.9**	**86.8**	**86.7**	**87.0**
Part-time employment (%)										
Part-time as % of employment	17.0	17.3	17.8	18.7	19.2	19.0	19.4	19.9	20.9	21.0
Male share of part time employment	16.4	17.6	19.5	19.6	20.0	19.5	19.4	21.1	21.4	21.6
Female share of part time employment	83.6	82.4	80.5	80.4	80.0	80.5	80.6	78.9	78.6	78.4
Male part-time as % of male employment	5.1	5.6	6.4	6.8	7.2	7.0	7.1	7.9	8.5	8.6
Female part-time as % of female employment	31.2	31.4	31.3	32.4	33.0	32.8	33.5	33.4	34.9	35.0
Duration of unemployment (% of total unemployment)										
Less than one month	10.2	10.9	11.6	11.4	9.4	10.9	9.7	9.0	9.5	8.9
More than 1 month and less than 3 months	24.4	24.3	26.3	25.4	26.2	25.7	27.1	25.4	23.9	22.8
More than 3 months and less than 6 months	20.6	20.3	19.4	23.2	21.1	20.2	19.9	21.9	20.0	19.1
More than 6 months and less than 1 year	16.8	17.2	18.3	18.4	17.9	16.9	18.4	19.2	19.3	20.0
More than 1 year	28.0	27.2	24.3	21.7	25.4	26.3	24.9	24.6	27.2	29.2

Note: Detailed metadata: http://metalinks.oecd.org/lfs/20170518/88fce, http://metalinks.oecd.org/lfs/20170518/87289, http://metalinks.oecd.org/lfs/20170518/f462c and http://metalinks.oecd.org/lfs/20170518/f3e3c.

Disclaimer: http://oe.cd/disclaimer

AUSTRIA

Table 2. Participation rates and unemployment rates by age and sex

Annual average estimates, percentage

	2006	2007	2008	2009	2010	2011	2012	2013	2014	2015
Participation rates										
Males										
15-19	47.3	48.2	48.0	48.4	48.3	48.1	47.0	45.8	44.4	41.6
20-24	75.8	77.1	77.5	77.1	76.5	78.4	77.9	76.9	74.7	76.7
25-34	92.2	92.9	92.3	92.1	91.0	91.2	91.8	91.3	91.0	91.1
35-44	94.7	95.0	94.8	94.6	94.1	94.5	94.5	94.1	93.8	93.8
45-54	89.0	89.4	88.9	89.0	90.5	90.2	90.7	91.0	89.9	90.3
55-59	65.3	66.6	70.1	71.0	71.7	73.1	74.0	75.0	76.9	77.2
60-64	19.2	25.3	26.9	27.9	29.1	25.9	27.8	31.6	32.1	32.3
15-24	61.8	62.9	62.9	62.9	62.6	63.6	63.1	62.3	60.7	60.7
25-54	92.2	92.5	92.1	91.9	91.9	92.0	92.3	92.1	91.5	91.6
55-64	44.1	47.6	49.9	50.5	51.4	50.4	52.2	55.1	56.8	57.4
65 and over	5.1	6.7	7.3	7.9	7.5	7.0	6.9	7.4	7.6	7.5
15-64	78.9	80.0	80.0	80.0	80.0	79.9	80.2	80.4	80.0	80.1
Females										
15-19	36.7	40.2	41.1	39.0	36.6	37.1	38.0	35.9	35.0	34.4
20-24	70.2	71.0	70.6	72.7	70.5	71.3	71.1	72.4	72.8	70.7
25-34	78.5	78.3	79.7	81.3	81.3	81.7	83.8	83.5	83.7	83.3
35-44	83.1	84.1	83.9	85.0	84.7	85.9	85.8	86.2	85.6	85.9
45-54	77.9	78.4	78.7	79.6	80.9	82.0	82.6	84.0	84.3	84.0
55-59	39.3	42.4	46.4	47.9	51.5	50.4	53.3	55.4	55.6	59.7
60-64	9.3	10.6	12.2	13.0	14.4	14.8	13.9	14.7	16.0	16.5
15-24	54.1	56.0	56.2	56.2	54.0	54.8	55.4	55.3	55.4	54.1
25-54	80.1	80.5	80.9	82.1	82.4	83.2	84.0	84.5	84.5	84.4
55-64	25.2	27.5	30.1	31.1	33.6	33.0	34.5	36.4	37.5	40.2
65 and over	2.1	2.8	3.0	3.3	3.5	3.4	3.5	3.4	3.5	3.6
15-64	66.0	67.1	67.8	68.7	68.9	69.3	70.0	70.7	70.8	70.9
All persons										
15-24	57.9	59.4	59.5	59.5	58.3	59.2	59.2	58.8	58.0	57.4
25-54	86.1	86.5	86.5	87.0	87.1	87.6	88.1	88.3	88.0	88.0
55-64	34.3	37.2	39.7	40.5	42.2	41.4	43.1	45.5	46.9	48.6
65 and over	3.3	4.5	4.8	5.2	5.2	5.0	4.9	5.1	5.3	5.3
15-64	72.4	73.5	73.9	74.3	74.4	74.6	75.1	75.5	75.4	75.5
Unemployment rates										
Males										
15-19	10.9	10.7	10.0	12.2	9.9	9.3	9.7	10.3	9.7	11.3
20-24	9.2	8.4	7.5	10.6	9.4	8.5	9.4	8.9	11.1	11.0
25-34	5.4	4.6	4.1	5.9	6.1	4.7	5.4	6.7	7.0	6.6
35-44	3.5	3.3	2.9	4.5	3.9	3.7	3.7	4.0	4.4	5.1
45-54	3.7	3.8	3.3	4.6	4.0	3.4	4.1	4.5	4.9	4.8
55-59	5.1	3.9	2.1	3.2	3.4	4.5	3.8	4.5	5.3	6.1
60-64	4.1	1.8	1.5	1.9	1.3	3.9	4.3	3.3	2.1	4.4
15-24	9.8	9.3	8.4	11.2	9.6	8.8	9.6	9.4	10.6	11.1
25-54	4.1	3.8	3.4	4.9	4.6	3.9	4.4	5.0	5.4	5.5
55-64	4.9	3.4	1.9	2.9	2.9	4.4	3.9	4.2	4.5	5.7
65 and over	0.6	0.3	0.3	0.4	0.4	0.3	0.3	0.1	0.9	0.2
15-64	5.0	4.6	4.0	5.6	5.1	4.6	5.0	5.5	5.9	6.2
Total	4.9	4.5	3.9	5.5	5.0	4.5	4.9	5.4	5.8	6.1
Females										
15-19	15.0	13.6	13.3	13.1	12.8	12.6	11.5	14.0	13.5	11.7
20-24	7.2	7.5	6.0	8.6	7.7	7.4	8.1	8.3	8.5	9.3
25-34	5.6	5.7	5.0	5.7	5.9	5.3	5.6	6.4	6.7	6.0
35-44	5.2	4.6	3.5	4.2	3.4	4.0	4.4	4.9	5.2	4.9
45-54	4.6	3.9	3.3	3.8	3.5	3.2	3.2	3.5	3.5	3.9
55-59	2.6	4.1	3.3	2.8	2.3	2.9	3.3	3.6	3.3	4.0
60-64	2.3	1.1	0.6	1.3	0.6	1.1	0.4	1.6	1.1	0.7
15-24	9.8	9.6	8.6	10.1	9.4	9.1	9.2	10.0	9.9	10.0
25-54	5.1	4.7	3.8	4.5	4.2	4.1	4.3	4.8	5.0	4.9
55-64	2.5	3.5	2.7	2.5	1.9	2.5	2.7	3.2	2.8	3.4
65 and over	0.3	0.6	0.1	0.4	0.2	0.9	0.5	0.6	0.6	0.7
15-64	5.6	5.4	4.5	5.2	4.7	4.6	4.8	5.4	5.5	5.4
Total	5.6	5.3	4.4	5.1	4.6	4.6	4.8	5.3	5.4	5.3
All persons										
15-24	9.8	9.4	8.5	10.7	9.5	8.9	9.4	9.7	10.3	10.6
25-54	4.6	4.2	3.6	4.7	4.4	4.0	4.3	4.9	5.2	5.2
55-64	4.0	3.4	2.2	2.7	2.5	3.6	3.4	3.8	3.8	4.7
65 and over	0.5	0.4	0.3	0.4	0.3	0.5	0.4	0.3	0.8	0.4
15-64	5.3	4.9	4.2	5.4	4.9	4.6	4.9	5.4	5.7	5.8

Note: Detailed metadata at:http://metalinks.oecd.org/lfs/20170518/6f97b
Disclaimer: http://oe.cd/disclaimer

Table 3. Civilian employment and employees: breakdown by activity - ISIC Rev. 4

Annual average estimates

		2006	2007	2008	2009	2010	2011	2012	2013	2014	2015
	CIVILIAN EMPLOYMENT										
	By activity, thousands										
A-U	**All activities**	**3 816.0**	**3 912.5**	**3 981.6**	**3 968.7**	**4 005.5**	**4 043.4**	**4 074.9**	**4 094.4**	**4 101.8**	**4 137.8**
A	Agriculture, hunting and forestry	188.2	205.7	209.8	211.9	209.4	200.1	191.0	187.8	198.9	188.0
B-F	**Industry**	**1 085.3**	**1 086.6**	**1 047.8**	**994.4**	**1 000.5**	**1 054.7**	**1 065.3**	**1 063.5**	**1 059.1**	**1 068.8**
B	Mining and quarrying	9.5	8.4	10.3	10.0	9.8	10.8	9.0	7.3	6.2	7.3
C	Manufacturing	703.2	693.7	627.2	595.4	612.1	642.0	645.0	642.8	643.4	662.8
D	Electricity, gas, steam, air cond. supply	27.2	26.3	22.7	23.9	26.1	30.8	26.9	28.4	31.3	30.4
E	Water supply, sewerage, waste mgt, remediation	17.5	21.6	19.8	19.0	17.9	16.9	15.9	20.6	20.7	20.5
F	Construction	327.8	336.6	367.7	346.1	334.5	354.2	368.4	364.3	357.4	347.9
G-U	**Services**	**2 542.5**	**2 620.2**	**2 724.1**	**2 762.3**	**2 795.6**	**2 788.6**	**2 818.6**	**2 843.1**	**2 843.8**	**2 881.0**
G	Wholesale, retail trade, vehicle, motorcycle repair	590.3	625.3	645.3	630.6	612.3	616.8	613.6	600.3	601.5	598.7
H	Transportation and storage	194.1	193.2	197.4	195.9	192.1	201.8	205.5	211.3	202.3	206.3
I	Accommodation and food service activities	235.2	247.0	243.4	249.3	246.2	243.7	257.8	240.5	235.2	238.8
J	Information and communication	94.8	92.0	95.1	104.7	107.6	100.1	103.2	112.7	120.6	117.0
K	Financial and insurance activities	131.3	133.3	141.2	141.1	144.9	148.1	144.2	144.3	137.2	134.3
L	Real estate activities	30.0	33.5	31.9	30.2	37.0	38.8	36.4	37.4	35.5	39.0
M	Professional, scientific and technical activities	176.1	180.4	208.5	207.5	213.6	211.1	223.9	234.6	235.5	234.0
N	Administrative and support service activities	120.0	126.1	132.0	136.2	137.1	142.5	132.7	135.6	138.6	134.7
O	Public administration, defence, social security	239.4	262.4	260.2	256.2	262.5	260.5	258.8	259.2	262.0	269.1
P	Education	226.5	216.8	231.0	248.1	257.0	254.6	259.0	275.5	281.4	283.5
Q	Human health and social work activities	336.6	335.0	351.9	379.1	388.8	382.1	388.9	400.3	404.5	420.6
R	Arts, entertainment and recreation	51.4	56.7	70.6	68.6	72.2	70.3	74.1	71.8	70.6	82.3
S	Other service activities	100.5	103.9	96.8	96.9	105.2	103.3	104.6	104.9	103.7	105.6
T	Households as employers and own-use activities	10.3	8.6	11.7	9.9	10.6	8.9	10.3	9.9	9.0	9.0
U	Activities of extraterritorial organizations, bodies	6.1	6.0	6.9	8.1	8.3	6.2	5.6	4.6	6.1	8.0
	EMPLOYEES										
	By activity, thousands										
A-U	**All activities**	**3 317.1**	**3 375.5**	**3 440.7**	**3 425.5**	**3 450.7**	**3 505.4**	**3 540.9**	**3 552.5**	**3 555.3**	**3 598.6**
A	Agriculture, hunting and forestry	25.3	28.7	28.8	32.8	33.8	26.9	26.8	25.9	28.3	30.4
B-F	**Industry**	**1 021.7**	**1 018.2**	**984.1**	**935.7**	**941.0**	**992.2**	**1 000.3**	**996.0**	**993.5**	**1 000.7**
B	Mining and quarrying	9.1	8.1	10.0	9.9	9.5	10.5	9.0	6.9	5.7	7.1
C	Manufacturing	668.2	656.6	596.5	569.3	587.4	614.0	616.6	612.7	617.0	635.6
D	Electricity, gas, steam, air cond. supply	27.0	25.7	22.2	23.6	25.8	30.3	25.9	27.6	30.2	30.1
E	Water supply, sewerage, waste mgt, remediation	17.0	20.8	18.8	18.7	17.0	16.4	15.4	19.7	19.9	20.1
F	Construction	300.4	307.0	336.6	314.2	301.2	321.0	333.3	329.1	320.7	307.9
G-U	**Services**	**2 270.2**	**2 328.5**	**2 427.7**	**2 457.1**	**2 475.9**	**2 486.2**	**2 513.8**	**2 530.6**	**2 533.5**	**2 567.5**
G	Wholesale, retail trade, vehicle, motorcycle repair	528.5	562.6	579.8	562.7	542.1	552.2	553.4	538.5	539.6	539.4
H	Transportation and storage	178.4	181.8	184.9	182.3	176.7	188.8	191.9	195.7	188.6	191.7
I	Accommodation and food service activities	190.4	195.4	194.4	207.7	203.7	202.3	209.8	199.8	194.3	201.6
J	Information and communication	79.2	78.1	80.2	89.2	90.1	82.7	86.5	96.0	103.4	98.0
K	Financial and insurance activities	124.3	127.6	134.0	131.1	135.9	138.1	135.3	136.9	129.5	125.4
L	Real estate activities	23.3	26.4	26.7	25.6	29.5	31.0	29.4	29.9	26.8	27.8
M	Professional, scientific and technical activities	125.0	128.7	151.8	150.9	152.4	154.0	163.4	170.8	170.7	170.8
N	Administrative and support service activities	108.6	111.1	120.4	120.5	122.9	126.6	120.0	124.6	126.7	121.7
O	Public administration, defence, social security	239.4	262.4	260.2	256.2	262.5	260.5	258.8	259.2	262.0	269.1
P	Education	219.0	207.3	220.3	239.0	246.5	246.3	250.5	263.7	272.3	273.0
Q	Human health and social work activities	311.2	305.8	324.9	348.7	356.5	349.3	358.5	362.7	367.7	384.0
R	Arts, entertainment and recreation	39.7	40.0	50.6	46.0	51.6	51.4	53.2	51.1	50.7	61.6
S	Other service activities	87.1	87.9	81.5	79.6	87.3	88.7	88.4	88.8	87.4	87.2
T	Households as employers and own-use activities	9.9	7.4	11.0	9.4	9.8	8.2	9.1	8.3	7.7	8.3
U	Activities of extraterritorial organizations, bodies	6.1	6.0	6.9	8.1	8.3	6.2	5.6	4.6	6.1	8.0

Note: Detailed metadata:http://metalinks.oecd.org/lfs/20170518/87289
Disclaimer: http://oe.cd/disclaimer

BELGIUM

Table 1. Labour force

Annual average estimates

	2006	2007	2008	2009	2010	2011	2012	2013	2014	2015
Civilian labour force, thousands										
All persons	4 647	4 733	4 780	4 800	4 895	4 856	4 893	4 947	4 967	4 974
Males	2 583	2 618	2 631	2 633	2 675	2 650	2 670	2 682	2 677	2 677
Females	2 065	2 115	2 148	2 167	2 220	2 206	2 223	2 265	2 290	2 297
Unemployed, thousands										
All persons	383	353	334	380	406	347	369	417	423	422
Males	191	174	170	204	217	188	204	232	242	244
Females	192	179	163	176	189	158	165	185	182	178
Civilian employment, thousands										
All persons	4 264	4 380	4 446	4 421	4 489	4 509	4 524	4 530	4 544	4 552
Males	2 392	2 444	2 461	2 429	2 458	2 462	2 466	2 451	2 435	2 434
Females	1 872	1 937	1 985	1 991	2 031	2 047	2 058	2 080	2 108	2 118
Civilian employment (%)										
All persons	100.0	100.0	100.0	100.0	100.0	100.0	100.0	100.0	100.0	100.0
Males	56.1	55.8	55.3	55.0	54.8	54.6	54.5	54.1	53.6	53.5
Females	43.9	44.2	44.7	45.0	45.2	45.4	45.5	45.9	46.4	46.5
Unemployment rate (% of civilian labour force)										
All persons	8.2	7.5	7.0	7.9	8.3	7.1	7.5	8.4	8.5	8.5
Males	7.4	6.7	6.5	7.7	8.1	7.1	7.7	8.6	9.0	9.1
Females	9.3	8.4	7.6	8.1	8.5	7.2	7.4	8.2	7.9	7.8
CIVIL. EMPL. - PROFESSIONAL STATUS, thousands										
All activities	**4 264**	**4 380**	**4 446**	**4 421**	**4 489**	**4 509**	**4 524**	**4 530**	**4 544**	**4 552**
Employees	3 621	3 731	3 813	3 766	3 844	3 864	3 875	3 847	3 880	3 861
Employers and persons working on own account	577	593	579	599	601	595	611	642	623	650
Unpaid family workers	66	57	54	55	44	50	38	41	41	41
Employees as % of civilian employment	**84.9**	**85.2**	**85.8**	**85.2**	**85.6**	**85.7**	**85.7**	**84.9**	**85.4**	**84.8**
Part-time employment (%)										
Part-time as % of employment	18.7	18.1	18.3	18.2	18.3	18.8	18.7	18.2	18.1	18.2
Male share of part time employment	18.2	19.3	18.7	19.4	19.6	20.1	20.2	19.2	20.9	21.1
Female share of part time employment	81.8	80.7	81.3	80.6	80.4	79.9	79.8	80.8	79.1	78.9
Male part-time as % of male employment	6.2	6.4	6.3	6.6	6.7	7.0	7.1	6.6	7.2	7.3
Female part-time as % of female employment	33.8	32.2	32.5	31.8	31.7	32.4	32.1	31.4	30.5	30.2
Duration of unemployment (% of total unemployment)										
Less than one month	6.2	6.0	7.2	7.2	5.4	4.5	4.7	3.4	3.6	3.4
More than 1 month and less than 3 months	14.7	16.0	17.3	16.8	15.6	16.4	17.9	17.4	15.0	16.2
More than 3 months and less than 6 months	13.9	12.9	14.1	15.8	13.0	15.0	16.5	15.4	15.2	14.4
More than 6 months and less than 1 year	14.0	14.7	13.8	16.0	17.3	15.8	16.2	17.8	16.2	14.3
More than 1 year	51.2	50.4	47.6	44.2	48.8	48.3	44.7	46.0	49.9	51.7

Note: Detailed metadata: http://metalinks.oecd.org/lfs/20170518/9b335, http://metalinks.oecd.org/lfs/20170518/87289, http://metalinks.oecd.org/lfs/20170518/54763 and http://metalinks.oecd.org/lfs/20170518/061c2.

Disclaimer: http://oe.cd/disclaimer

BELGIUM

Table 2. Participation rates and unemployment rates by age and sex

Annual average estimates, percentage

	2006	2007	2008	2009	2010	2011	2012	2013	2014	2015
Participation rates										
Males										
15-19	11.6	10.9	12.0	10.9	10.5	10.3	10.5	8.6	8.3	8.2
20-24	63.7	62.2	60.7	59.2	59.5	56.8	57.7	56.6	54.1	55.5
25-34	93.2	93.5	93.7	92.9	92.8	91.3	91.0	91.2	91.3	89.8
35-44	94.0	94.4	94.2	93.5	93.7	92.6	92.7	92.7	92.4	91.6
45-54	88.4	89.6	89.0	89.1	90.1	88.3	88.7	88.8	88.6	88.4
55-59	58.3	61.7	62.8	62.6	66.2	66.7	66.8	69.5	70.2	72.1
60-64	22.6	23.8	23.5	25.7	27.2	27.1	26.8	29.0	29.7	29.4
15-24	37.4	36.1	36.0	34.9	35.2	34.1	35.0	33.7	32.3	32.8
25-54	91.9	92.5	92.3	91.8	92.2	90.7	90.7	90.9	90.7	89.9
55-64	42.7	44.4	44.4	45.2	47.6	47.8	47.9	50.5	51.3	52.2
65 and over	2.7	3.0	2.9	3.1	3.2	3.4	4.0	3.6	3.8	4.2
15-64	73.4	73.6	73.3	72.8	73.4	72.3	72.5	72.7	72.4	72.2
Females										
15-19	7.3	8.0	7.2	7.9	7.5	8.8	6.4	6.1	6.6	5.9
20-24	56.2	55.1	54.3	51.5	51.0	49.2	47.3	48.0	47.2	46.3
25-34	84.1	83.2	84.7	84.2	84.0	81.4	82.2	81.2	82.6	81.2
35-44	80.3	81.2	82.1	81.9	84.0	81.7	81.4	82.8	82.9	82.5
45-54	67.2	70.2	70.9	72.3	73.8	73.6	74.3	75.6	76.6	77.1
55-59	36.2	40.8	42.4	43.8	45.7	48.7	51.0	55.1	56.2	59.5
60-64	10.3	12.1	11.8	13.6	15.0	16.0	17.2	18.7	19.6	20.7
15-24	31.9	31.6	30.8	29.9	29.8	29.8	27.9	28.2	28.1	27.1
25-54	77.0	78.0	79.0	79.2	80.4	78.7	79.1	79.7	80.6	80.2
55-64	24.6	27.5	27.9	29.3	30.9	33.0	34.9	37.8	39.0	41.2
65 and over	1.0	0.9	1.0	0.7	1.2	1.1	1.1	1.4	1.2	1.4
15-64	59.5	60.4	60.8	60.9	61.8	61.1	61.3	62.3	63.0	63.0
All persons										
15-24	34.7	33.9	33.4	32.4	32.5	32.0	31.5	31.0	30.2	30.0
25-54	84.5	85.3	85.7	85.6	86.3	84.7	85.0	85.3	85.6	85.1
55-64	33.6	35.9	36.1	37.2	39.2	40.3	41.4	44.1	45.1	46.6
65 and over	1.7	1.8	1.8	1.7	2.1	2.0	2.3	2.3	2.3	2.6
15-64	66.5	67.1	67.1	66.9	67.7	66.7	66.9	67.5	67.7	67.6
Unemployment rates										
Males										
15-19	26.4	27.5	24.4	26.6	34.1	30.1	31.8	38.3	31.5	31.8
20-24	17.4	15.2	15.9	20.5	20.4	16.8	18.5	22.8	22.9	22.7
25-34	8.2	8.3	7.4	9.4	9.7	8.8	9.6	10.0	11.0	10.6
35-44	6.0	5.3	5.3	6.2	6.4	5.9	6.4	7.2	8.0	7.7
45-54	5.4	4.4	4.4	4.8	5.8	4.7	4.9	5.7	5.8	6.4
55-59	4.4	4.0	4.1	5.5	4.4	4.4	4.3	6.0	6.2	7.0
60-64	3.5	2.3	2.1	3.9	3.8	2.4	3.3	4.1	3.9	4.6
15-24	18.8	17.1	17.3	21.5	22.4	18.7	20.4	24.7	24.0	23.8
25-54	6.5	5.9	5.7	6.7	7.2	6.4	6.9	7.5	8.2	8.2
55-64	4.2	3.6	3.6	5.0	4.2	3.9	4.1	5.5	5.6	6.3
65 and over	0.6	1.7	1.4	0.8	0.4	0.4	1.6	0.4	0.2	1.1
15-64	7.5	6.7	6.5	7.8	8.2	7.2	7.7	8.7	9.1	9.2
Total	7.4	6.7	6.5	7.7	8.1	7.1	7.7	8.6	9.0	9.1
Females										
15-19	32.7	32.9	27.4	29.9	36.6	26.7	24.1	27.7	36.4	28.2
20-24	21.3	19.1	17.6	21.4	20.4	17.4	18.2	21.9	20.6	19.1
25-34	10.0	9.3	8.7	9.3	9.9	8.5	9.3	9.6	9.3	9.8
35-44	7.6	6.7	5.8	6.1	6.9	5.6	5.9	7.0	6.6	6.4
45-54	6.6	6.1	5.3	5.2	5.6	5.0	4.7	5.1	5.0	5.4
55-59	5.8	5.3	5.7	5.6	5.7	4.5	5.0	5.8	5.6	5.1
60-64	5.0	5.5	5.2	4.0	3.9	3.4	5.2	3.6	3.5	3.5
15-24	22.6	20.9	18.7	22.5	22.4	18.7	18.9	22.5	22.3	20.0
25-54	8.1	7.4	6.6	6.9	7.5	6.3	6.6	7.2	7.0	7.1
55-64	5.7	5.3	5.6	5.2	5.2	4.2	5.1	5.3	5.1	4.7
65 and over	1.0	0.0	0.7	0.2	1.8	1.6	0.6	2.3	1.5	0.4
15-64	9.4	8.5	7.6	8.1	8.6	7.2	7.4	8.2	8.0	7.8
Total	9.3	8.4	7.6	8.1	8.5	7.2	7.4	8.2	7.9	7.8
All persons										
15-24	20.5	18.8	18.0	21.9	22.4	18.7	19.8	23.7	23.2	22.1
25-54	7.2	6.6	6.1	6.8	7.3	6.4	6.7	7.4	7.6	7.7
55-64	4.8	4.2	4.4	5.1	4.6	4.0	4.5	5.4	5.4	5.6
65 and over	0.8	1.2	1.2	0.7	0.9	0.8	1.4	1.0	0.6	0.9
15-64	8.3	7.5	7.0	8.0	8.4	7.2	7.6	8.5	8.6	8.6

Note: Detailed metadata at:http://metalinks.oecd.org/lfs/20170518/6f97b
Disclaimer: http://oe.cd/disclaimer

BELGIUM

Table 3. Civilian employment and employees: breakdown by activity - ISIC Rev. 4

Annual average estimates

		2006	2007	2008	2009	2010	2011	2012	2013	2014	2015
	CIVILIAN EMPLOYMENT										
	By activity, thousands										
A-U	**All activities**	**..**	**..**	**4 445.9**	**4 420.7**	**4 488.7**	**4 509.3**	**4 523.9**	**4 530.3**	**4 543.5**	**4 551.6**
A	Agriculture, hunting and forestry	..	..	69.0	65.7	60.7	58.6	53.0	61.6	55.3	53.6
B-F	**Industry**	**..**	**..**	**1 096.9**	**1 037.7**	**1 049.2**	**1 047.7**	**984.1**	**983.2**	**972.0**	**975.6**
B	Mining and quarrying	..	..	5.3	5.7	4.5	4.9	7.1	4.8	5.2	3.7
C	Manufacturing	..	..	710.3	656.1	652.9	641.4	594.9	588.9	581.5	589.3
D	Electricity, gas, steam, air cond. supply	..	..	32.4	29.4	30.8	29.2	26.4	27.2	24.7	22.7
E	Water supply, sewerage, waste mgt, remediation	..	..	26.7	30.3	38.3	34.6	30.9	32.7	35.6	36.7
F	Construction	..	..	322.3	316.3	322.7	337.5	324.9	329.6	325.1	323.2
G-U	**Services**	**..**	**..**	**3 279.9**	**3 317.3**	**3 378.8**	**3 403.0**	**3 486.8**	**3 485.5**	**3 516.2**	**3 522.5**
G	Wholesale, retail trade, vehicle, motorcycle repair	..	..	567.6	571.6	589.5	588.4	607.0	629.6	608.6	616.9
H	Transportation and storage	..	..	283.1	266.8	266.9	272.2	254.8	241.8	246.5	248.9
I	Accommodation and food service activities	..	..	143.0	142.7	143.0	149.5	154.0	145.3	154.5	155.6
J	Information and communication	..	..	129.7	140.4	152.8	138.0	150.4	141.4	144.1	141.8
K	Financial and insurance activities	..	..	175.9	157.6	158.0	161.0	157.0	158.2	153.4	148.6
L	Real estate activities	..	..	23.0	20.6	22.5	23.8	26.1	29.6	29.9	29.2
M	Professional, scientific and technical activities	..	..	198.8	208.3	197.2	210.5	212.3	222.7	232.7	234.2
N	Administrative and support service activities	..	..	168.5	177.5	174.9	187.3	233.9	257.7	264.7	260.0
O	Public administration, defence, social security	..	..	429.6	418.7	407.9	401.4	406.1	383.1	380.0	379.7
P	Education	..	..	378.0	393.3	414.2	412.9	411.0	398.6	432.3	422.4
Q	Human health and social work activities	..	..	567.3	590.2	608.2	614.1	657.0	634.0	652.9	668.0
R	Arts, entertainment and recreation	..	..	61.5	59.9	64.8	70.5	65.5	73.1	65.3	65.0
S	Other service activities	..	..	93.3	92.5	98.8	97.8	96.3	105.8	99.2	105.0
T	Households as employers and own-use activities	..	..	29.5	34.5	38.1	37.3	17.0	22.6	9.7	4.0
U	Activities of extraterritorial organizations, bodies	..	..	31.0	42.6	42.1	38.2	38.5	42.0	42.4	43.1
	EMPLOYEES										
	By activity, thousands										
A-U	**All activities**	**..**	**..**	**3 813.5**	**3 766.5**	**3 844.1**	**3 864.4**	**3 874.9**	**3 847.2**	**3 879.6**	**3 860.7**
A	Agriculture, hunting and forestry	..	..	17.4	19.2	14.3	14.6	14.9	12.8	12.9	10.2
B-F	**Industry**	**..**	**..**	**973.8**	**907.5**	**920.0**	**912.6**	**857.4**	**848.4**	**847.2**	**834.4**
B	Mining and quarrying	..	..	5.1	5.7	4.4	4.8	6.4	4.7	5.0	3.6
C	Manufacturing	..	..	668.2	612.9	612.4	602.1	556.8	552.5	544.0	548.9
D	Electricity, gas, steam, air cond. supply	..	..	31.7	28.6	30.3	28.4	26.0	26.1	24.4	21.7
E	Water supply, sewerage, waste mgt, remediation	..	..	26.0	29.0	37.4	34.2	29.4	32.1	34.1	35.0
F	Construction	..	..	242.8	231.3	235.4	243.1	238.7	232.9	239.7	225.1
G-U	**Services**	**..**	**..**	**2 822.2**	**2 839.8**	**2 909.7**	**2 937.2**	**3 002.5**	**2 986.0**	**3 019.5**	**3 016.1**
G	Wholesale, retail trade, vehicle, motorcycle repair	..	..	431.0	433.7	462.7	457.0	488.7	494.8	488.7	495.6
H	Transportation and storage	..	..	268.1	247.7	254.1	259.0	238.4	227.1	234.5	234.9
I	Accommodation and food service activities	..	..	97.7	91.6	89.9	100.3	97.6	98.0	104.1	97.5
J	Information and communication	..	..	110.4	120.4	129.8	115.2	123.8	114.9	118.7	113.9
K	Financial and insurance activities	..	..	156.9	141.8	140.3	141.5	140.5	141.0	135.7	135.0
L	Real estate activities	..	..	15.0	13.7	14.6	16.6	16.5	19.6	18.9	19.3
M	Professional, scientific and technical activities	..	..	124.3	128.4	123.5	133.8	129.5	135.6	137.6	140.8
N	Administrative and support service activities	..	..	151.5	158.0	152.0	167.6	211.6	235.1	236.5	237.5
O	Public administration, defence, social security	..	..	427.6	417.1	405.0	398.5	402.9	380.1	377.6	377.9
P	Education	..	..	372.8	389.7	408.8	409.1	405.5	392.1	425.2	414.8
Q	Human health and social work activities	..	..	497.0	515.1	531.5	543.1	575.7	557.1	573.3	583.0
R	Arts, entertainment and recreation	..	..	49.4	48.8	52.3	56.3	53.4	58.9	53.1	52.0
S	Other service activities	..	..	61.6	57.8	65.7	64.9	64.6	70.7	64.3	67.9
T	Households as employers and own-use activities	..	..	28.5	33.7	37.8	37.0	15.8	19.9	9.1	3.7
U	Activities of extraterritorial organizations, bodies	..	..	30.5	42.5	41.7	37.5	38.0	41.1	42.2	42.3

Note: Detailed metadata:http://metalinks.oecd.org/lfs/20170518/87289
Disclaimer: http://oe.cd/disclaimer

CANADA

Table 1. Labour force

Annual average estimates

	2006	2007	2008	2009	2010	2011	2012	2013	2014	2015
Civilian labour force, thousands										
All persons	17 502	17 847	18 122	18 250	18 451	18 620	18 810	19 038	19 125	19 278
Males	9 293	9 442	9 596	9 621	9 705	9 803	9 886	9 997	10 072	10 182
Females	8 209	8 405	8 527	8 629	8 746	8 817	8 924	9 041	9 053	9 096
Unemployed, thousands										
All persons	1 106	1 077	1 112	1 523	1 486	1 399	1 372	1 347	1 322	1 331
Males	606	602	630	918	853	781	763	750	744	760
Females	500	475	482	605	633	618	609	597	579	572
Civilian employment, thousands										
All persons	16 396	16 769	17 010	16 728	16 964	17 221	17 438	17 691	17 802	17 947
Males	8 687	8 839	8 965	8 703	8 852	9 023	9 123	9 246	9 328	9 423
Females	7 709	7 930	8 045	8 024	8 113	8 199	8 315	8 445	8 474	8 524
Civilian employment (%)										
All persons	100.0	100.0	100.0	100.0	100.0	100.0	100.0	100.0	100.0	100.0
Males	53.0	52.7	52.7	52.0	52.2	52.4	52.3	52.3	52.4	52.5
Females	47.0	47.3	47.3	48.0	47.8	47.6	47.7	47.7	47.6	47.5
Unemployment rate (% of civilian labour force)										
All persons	6.3	6.0	6.1	8.3	8.1	7.5	7.3	7.1	6.9	6.9
Males	6.5	6.4	6.6	9.5	8.8	8.0	7.7	7.5	7.4	7.5
Females	6.1	5.6	5.7	7.0	7.2	7.0	6.8	6.6	6.4	6.3
CIVIL. EMPL. - PROFESSIONAL STATUS, thousands										
All activities	**16 396**	**16 769**	**17 010**	**16 728**	**16 964**	**17 221**	**17 438**	**17 691**	**17 802**	**17 947**
Employees	14 890	15 209	15 444	15 133	15 390	15 666	15 888	16 129	16 243	16 399
Employers and persons working on own account	1 478	1 535	1 541	1 574	1 557	1 535	1 531	1 541	1 537	1 526
Unpaid family workers	29	25	25	21	18	21	19	22	22	22
Employees as % of civilian employment	**90.8**	**90.7**	**90.8**	**90.5**	**90.7**	**91.0**	**91.1**	**91.2**	**91.2**	**91.4**
Part-time employment (%)										
Part-time as % of employment	18.2	18.3	18.6	19.3	19.6	19.3	19.0	19.1	19.3	18.9
Male share of part time employment	31.9	32.0	32.3	32.4	32.4	33.4	32.7	33.3	33.4	33.6
Female share of part time employment	68.1	68.0	67.7	67.6	67.6	66.6	67.3	66.7	66.6	66.4
Male part-time as % of male employment	10.9	11.1	11.4	12.0	12.1	12.3	11.9	12.2	12.3	12.1
Female part-time as % of female employment	26.4	26.3	26.6	27.2	27.7	27.0	26.7	26.7	27.0	26.4
Duration of unemployment (% of total unemployment)										
Less than one month	30.4	30.4	31.0	24.7	23.1	24.2	24.8	24.1	24.2	24.5
More than 1 month and less than 3 months	39.6	40.1	39.8	39.1	36.8	36.6	37.7	37.7	37.8	38.5
More than 3 months and less than 6 months	14.0	14.7	14.3	18.1	16.9	15.7	16.1	15.9	15.8	16.0
More than 6 months and less than 1 year	7.3	7.3	7.6	10.1	11.1	9.8	8.8	9.4	9.3	9.4
More than 1 year	8.7	7.5	7.3	8.0	12.1	13.6	12.7	12.9	12.9	11.6

Note: Detailed metadata: http://metalinks.oecd.org/lfs/20170518/a40a4, http://metalinks.oecd.org/lfs/20170518/87289, http://metalinks.oecd.org/lfs/20170518/e5187 and http://metalinks.oecd.org/lfs/20170518/fd59a.

Disclaimer: http://oe.cd/disclaimer

CANADA

Table 2. Participation rates and unemployment rates by age and sex

Annual average estimates, percentage

	2006	2007	2008	2009	2010	2011	2012	2013	2014	2015
Participation rates										
Males										
15-19	52.4	54.1	54.7	51.6	49.5	49.6	48.5	48.3	47.9	48.5
20-24	79.9	80.7	81.0	79.2	78.6	79.1	77.3	77.9	77.7	77.3
25-34	91.3	91.8	91.6	90.7	90.7	90.5	91.1	90.4	90.1	90.8
35-44	92.6	92.4	93.1	92.1	91.9	92.0	92.7	92.6	92.3	92.7
45-54	89.3	89.3	89.9	89.7	89.4	89.6	89.0	89.3	89.3	89.4
55-59	76.1	77.5	76.9	76.2	77.2	77.2	78.2	77.7	78.2	79.7
60-64	53.2	53.9	54.8	56.8	57.2	57.6	57.2	59.5	59.5	60.2
15-24	66.2	67.4	67.9	65.4	64.2	64.6	63.3	63.8	63.8	64.1
25-54	91.1	91.1	91.5	90.8	90.6	90.7	90.8	90.7	90.5	90.9
55-64	66.2	67.0	66.8	67.3	68.0	68.1	68.5	69.4	69.7	70.7
65 and over	12.1	12.9	14.2	15.2	16.0	16.4	16.9	17.6	18.2	18.0
15-64	82.1	82.4	82.6	81.7	81.4	81.4	81.3	81.4	81.3	81.8
Females										
15-19	55.1	56.6	57.4	54.5	53.8	53.1	51.1	51.4	51.9	51.4
20-24	77.1	76.2	76.0	75.8	75.4	75.1	75.1	74.8	75.5	75.4
25-34	81.1	81.8	81.1	81.8	81.8	81.1	81.5	81.7	81.2	80.6
35-44	82.2	83.1	82.7	82.7	82.9	82.9	83.0	83.8	82.9	82.6
45-54	80.4	81.4	81.8	81.9	82.4	82.4	82.8	82.7	81.7	82.7
55-59	62.2	63.9	65.8	66.8	67.5	68.3	69.2	69.8	69.2	68.6
60-64	37.1	40.3	40.7	43.5	43.9	44.3	45.5	47.3	47.5	47.9
15-24	66.2	66.5	66.8	65.3	64.8	64.5	63.7	63.8	64.6	64.4
25-54	81.2	82.1	81.9	82.1	82.3	82.2	82.5	82.7	81.9	82.0
55-64	51.3	53.3	54.3	56.0	56.5	57.1	58.2	59.5	59.2	59.0
65 and over	5.2	5.6	6.7	6.7	7.4	8.0	8.7	9.1	9.4	9.5
15-64	73.3	74.2	74.2	74.2	74.3	74.1	74.3	74.7	74.2	74.2
All persons										
15-24	66.2	67.0	67.3	65.3	64.5	64.5	63.5	63.8	64.2	64.2
25-54	86.2	86.6	86.7	86.5	86.5	86.4	86.6	86.7	86.2	86.4
55-64	58.6	60.0	60.5	61.6	62.2	62.5	63.3	64.4	64.4	64.8
65 and over	8.3	8.9	10.1	10.5	11.3	11.8	12.4	13.0	13.4	13.4
15-64	77.7	78.3	78.4	78.0	77.8	77.8	77.8	78.0	77.8	78.0
Unemployment rates										
Males										
15-19	17.5	16.4	17.0	23.2	22.8	21.9	22.0	21.3	20.0	19.9
20-24	9.9	9.5	10.4	15.2	13.9	12.5	12.6	11.8	12.3	12.4
25-34	6.1	6.4	6.0	9.2	8.5	7.5	7.5	7.3	7.6	7.1
35-44	5.3	5.1	5.2	7.7	6.9	5.9	5.4	5.3	5.2	5.6
45-54	4.7	4.7	5.0	7.4	6.9	6.1	6.1	5.8	5.3	5.8
55-59	5.3	5.2	5.3	7.9	7.1	6.8	6.3	6.6	6.6	6.2
60-64	5.3	5.1	6.4	8.4	7.9	7.8	7.1	7.2	6.9	7.2
15-24	12.9	12.3	13.0	18.3	17.3	16.1	16.1	15.2	15.0	15.0
25-54	5.4	5.3	5.4	8.1	7.4	6.5	6.3	6.1	6.0	6.2
55-64	5.3	5.2	5.8	8.1	7.4	7.2	6.6	6.8	6.7	6.6
65 and over	4.6	3.6	2.8	4.8	5.0	4.9	4.7	4.7	4.8	4.9
15-64	6.6	6.5	6.7	9.7	8.9	8.1	7.8	7.6	7.5	7.6
Total	6.5	6.4	6.6	9.5	8.8	8.0	7.7	7.5	7.4	7.5
Females										
15-19	14.3	13.2	14.0	16.9	17.4	17.1	18.2	17.6	16.9	16.5
20-24	7.7	7.8	7.2	9.0	9.2	9.3	9.4	9.0	9.0	8.3
25-34	5.7	4.9	5.1	6.6	7.0	6.6	6.4	6.2	5.8	5.9
35-44	5.5	5.2	4.9	6.3	6.7	6.3	5.9	5.2	5.4	5.5
45-54	4.6	4.2	4.4	5.5	5.5	5.4	5.1	5.4	5.2	4.9
55-59	4.9	4.9	5.0	5.7	5.3	5.7	5.6	5.5	5.3	5.4
60-64	5.4	4.9	4.8	5.6	6.2	6.5	5.9	6.2	5.8	5.4
15-24	10.4	10.1	10.1	12.3	12.5	12.4	12.7	12.2	11.9	11.3
25-54	5.2	4.8	4.8	6.1	6.4	6.0	5.8	5.6	5.5	5.4
55-64	5.1	4.9	4.9	5.6	5.6	6.0	5.7	5.8	5.5	5.4
65 and over	4.1	3.4	2.9	3.7	4.4	4.5	4.3	3.8	3.1	4.0
15-64	6.1	5.7	5.7	7.1	7.3	7.1	6.9	6.7	6.5	6.4
Total	6.1	5.7	5.7	7.0	7.2	7.0	6.8	6.6	6.4	6.3
All persons										
15-24	11.7	11.2	11.6	15.3	14.9	14.3	14.4	13.7	13.5	13.2
25-54	5.3	5.1	5.1	7.1	6.9	6.3	6.0	5.9	5.8	5.8
55-64	5.2	5.1	5.4	7.0	6.6	6.6	6.2	6.3	6.2	6.1
65 and over	4.4	3.6	2.9	4.4	4.8	4.8	4.6	4.4	4.1	4.5
15-64	6.4	6.1	6.2	8.4	8.1	7.6	7.4	7.2	7.0	7.0

Note: Detailed metadata at:http://metalinks.oecd.org/lfs/20170518/6f97b
Disclaimer: http://oe.cd/disclaimer

Table 3. Civilian employment and employees: breakdown by activity - ISIC Rev. 3

Annual average estimates

		2006	2007	2008	2009	2010	2011	2012	2013	2014	2015
	CIVILIAN EMPLOYMENT										
	By activity, thousands										
A-X	**All activities**	**16 396**	**16 769**	**17 010**	**16 728**	**16 964**	**17 221**	**17 438**	**17 691**	**17 802**	**17 947**
A	Agriculture, hunting and forestry	405	391	379	372	354	351	354	361	351	342
B	Fishing	30	28	26	24	25	24	21	21	19	18
C	Mining and quarrying	245	259	266	246	252	272	297	300	308	290
D	Manufacturing	2 102	2 026	1 927	1 745	1 711	1 722	1 747	1 723	1 711	1 712
E	Electricity, gas and water supply	122	138	146	144	141	137	133	135	137	137
F	Construction	1 057	1 116	1 222	1 177	1 232	1 284	1 312	1 360	1 361	1 361
G	Wholesale, retail trade: vehicle repair, household gds	2 882	2 930	2 955	2 919	2 948	2 952	2 943	2 985	3 018	3 005
H	Hotels and restaurants	1 018	1 072	1 089	1 076	1 098	1 141	1 170	1 170	1 208	1 211
I	Transport, storage and communication	1 174	1 202	1 215	1 180	1 170	1 212	1 217	1 224	1 231	1 243
J	Financial intermediation	731	745	762	753	765	747	756	767	780	791
K	Real estate, renting and business activities	2 048	2 124	2 177	2 138	2 212	2 280	2 267	2 352	2 362	2 427
L	Public adm., defence; social sec., excl. armed forces	832	863	908	915	918	917	921	915	907	905
M	Education	1 155	1 174	1 164	1 151	1 166	1 170	1 210	1 227	1 237	1 274
N	Health and social work	1 776	1 839	1 890	1 962	2 042	2 084	2 141	2 190	2 220	2 292
O	Other community, social, personal service activities	756	803	809	849	854	852	866	880	881	878
P	Private households with employed persons	59	59	73	75	75	71	82	78	70	59
Q	Extra-territorial organisations and bodies	3	3	2	3	2	3	4	4	4	3
X	Not classifiable by economic activities	0	0	0	0	0	0	0	0	0	0
	By sector, thousands										
A-B	Agriculture	435	419	406	395	379	376	375	382	370	360
C-F	Industry	3 526	3 538	3 561	3 312	3 336	3 415	3 488	3 518	3 516	3 500
G-Q	Services	12 434	12 812	13 044	13 020	13 249	13 431	13 575	13 791	13 916	14 087
	By sector, percentages										
A-B	Agriculture	2.7	2.5	2.4	2.4	2.2	2.2	2.1	2.2	2.1	2.0
C-F	Industry	21.5	21.1	20.9	19.8	19.7	19.8	20.0	19.9	19.8	19.5
G-Q	Services	75.8	76.4	76.7	77.8	78.1	78.0	77.8	78.0	78.2	78.5
	EMPLOYEES										
	By activity, thousands										
A-X	**All activities**	**14 890**	**15 209**	**15 444**	**15 133**	**15 390**	**15 666**	**15 888**	**16 129**	**16 243**	**16 399**
A	Agriculture, hunting and forestry	246	230	230	223	219	213	226	225	225	226
B	Fishing	17	16	15	14	14	15	12	13	12	12
C	Mining and quarrying	240	255	262	244	249	270	293	296	304	286
D	Manufacturing	2 071	1 990	1 893	1 711	1 680	1 694	1 722	1 700	1 684	1 688
E	Electricity, gas and water supply	122	138	146	144	141	137	133	135	137	137
F	Construction	873	932	1 016	969	1 030	1 083	1 105	1 157	1 161	1 159
G	Wholesale, retail trade: vehicle repair, household gds	2 693	2 744	2 781	2 740	2 776	2 788	2 775	2 835	2 863	2 858
H	Hotels and restaurants	980	1 033	1 049	1 041	1 060	1 110	1 139	1 133	1 170	1 172
I	Transport, storage and communication	1 085	1 104	1 118	1 088	1 078	1 121	1 127	1 126	1 131	1 144
J	Financial intermediation	691	700	722	707	719	704	707	727	734	744
K	Real estate, renting and business activities	1 665	1 725	1 762	1 714	1 783	1 839	1 832	1 917	1 927	1 992
L	Public adm., defence; social sec., excl. armed forces	832	863	908	915	918	917	921	915	907	905
M	Education	1 114	1 130	1 123	1 105	1 116	1 124	1 164	1 175	1 179	1 224
N	Health and social work	1 606	1 660	1 714	1 785	1 866	1 911	1 963	2 008	2 040	2 099
O	Other community, social, personal service activities	621	654	658	686	692	690	707	708	720	714
P	Private households with employed persons	31	33	45	45	46	48	57	56	48	38
Q	Extra-territorial organisations and bodies	3	3	2	3	2	3	4	4	4	3
X	Not classifiable by economic activities	0	0	0	0	0	0	0	0	0	0
	By sector, thousands										
A-B	Agriculture	263	246	245	237	233	228	239	238	237	238
C-F	Industry	3 306	3 314	3 318	3 068	3 100	3 183	3 253	3 288	3 285	3 270
G-Q	Services	11 322	11 648	11 882	11 828	12 057	12 254	12 396	12 603	12 721	12 892
	By sector, percentages										
A-B	Agriculture	1.8	1.6	1.6	1.6	1.5	1.5	1.5	1.5	1.5	1.4
C-F	Industry	22.2	21.8	21.5	20.3	20.1	20.3	20.5	20.4	20.2	19.9
G-Q	Services	76.0	76.6	76.9	78.2	78.3	78.2	78.0	78.1	78.3	78.6

Note: Detailed metadata:http://metalinks.oecd.org/lfs/20170518/87289
Disclaimer: http://oe.cd/disclaimer

CHILE

Table 1. Labour force

Annual average estimates

	2006	2007	2008	2009	2010	2011	2012	2013	2014	2015
Civilian labour force, thousands										
All persons	6 671	6 944	7 203	7 299	7 763	8 061	8 150	8 277	8 443	8 560
Males	4 286	4 426	4 528	4 553	4 698	4 812	4 835	4 903	4 967	5 042
Females	2 384	2 518	2 675	2 747	3 064	3 249	3 315	3 374	3 476	3 517
Unemployed, thousands										
All persons	513	496	562	707	632	574	524	491	540	532
Males	288	279	307	414	337	292	262	259	300	291
Females	225	217	254	293	295	281	262	232	240	240
Civilian employment, thousands										
All persons	6 158	6 449	6 641	6 592	7 131	7 487	7 626	7 786	7 903	8 028
Males	3 998	4 147	4 221	4 139	4 361	4 520	4 573	4 645	4 667	4 751
Females	2 160	2 301	2 421	2 453	2 769	2 967	3 053	3 142	3 236	3 277
Civilian employment (%)										
All persons	100.0	100.0	100.0	100.0	100.0	100.0	100.0	100.0	100.0	100.0
Males	64.9	64.3	63.5	62.8	61.2	60.4	60.0	59.6	59.1	59.2
Females	35.1	35.7	36.5	37.2	38.8	39.6	40.0	40.4	40.9	40.8
Unemployment rate (% of civilian labour force)										
All persons	7.7	7.1	7.8	9.7	8.1	7.1	6.4	5.9	6.4	6.2
Males	6.7	6.3	6.8	9.1	7.2	6.1	5.4	5.3	6.0	5.8
Females	9.4	8.6	9.5	10.7	9.6	8.7	7.9	6.9	6.9	6.8
CIVIL. EMPL. - PROFESSIONAL STATUS, thousands										
All activities	**6 158**	**6 449**	**6 641**	**6 592**	**7 131**	**7 487**	**7 626**	**7 786**	**7 903**	**8 028**
Employees	4 371	4 640	4 858	4 768	4 908	5 147	5 360	5 479	5 531	5 657
Employers and persons working on own account	1 664	1 693	1 671	1 715	1 784	1 873	1 814	1 873	1 939	1 963
Unpaid family workers	123	116	112	109	105	102	99	106	106	96
Employees as % of civilian employment	**71.0**	**71.9**	**73.2**	**72.3**	**68.8**	**68.7**	**70.3**	**70.4**	**70.0**	**70.5**
Part-time employment (%)										
Part-time as % of employment	7.7	8.0	9.1	10.5	17.4	17.2	16.7	16.5	17.0	16.8
Male share of part time employment	44.4	43.1	43.6	44.0	41.9	41.3	40.8	40.8	39.8	40.6
Female share of part time employment	55.6	56.9	56.4	56.0	58.1	58.7	59.2	59.2	60.2	59.4
Male part-time as % of male employment	5.0	5.2	6.0	7.1	12.0	11.8	11.3	11.3	11.5	11.5
Female part-time as % of female employment	13.3	13.9	15.2	17.0	25.7	25.5	24.6	24.3	25.0	24.5
Duration of unemployment (% of total unemployment)										
Less than one month	..	..	..	..	..	..	..	..	..	..
More than 1 month and less than 3 months	..	..	..	..	..	..	..	..	..	..
More than 3 months and less than 6 months	..	..	..	..	..	..	..	..	..	..
More than 6 months and less than 1 year	..	..	..	..	..	..	..	..	..	..
More than 1 year	..	..	..	..	..	..	..	..	..	..

Note: Detailed metadata: http://metalinks.oecd.org/lfs/20170518/07b97, http://metalinks.oecd.org/lfs/20170518/87289, http://metalinks.oecd.org/lfs/20170518/74017 and http://metalinks.oecd.org/lfs/20170518/b4262.

Disclaimer: http://oe.cd/disclaimer

CHILE

Table 2. Participation rates and unemployment rates by age and sex

Annual average estimates, percentage

	2006	2007	2008	2009	2010	2011	2012	2013	2014	2015
Participation rates										
Males										
15-19	17.2	18.0	18.8	17.2	23.4	23.8	21.8	19.9	18.5	18.7
20-24	65.0	65.1	67.7	64.5	67.1	66.2	64.2	63.0	64.2	63.7
25-34	92.2	91.5	91.5	91.2	90.3	91.2	89.4	89.4	88.5	88.5
35-44	96.2	96.4	96.3	95.5	94.4	94.1	94.3	94.5	94.1	93.9
45-54	93.6	93.7	93.8	93.9	92.7	93.3	93.6	93.0	92.6	93.1
55-59	85.5	86.6	87.3	87.1	87.5	87.7	89.5	89.7	88.2	89.2
60-64	71.8	72.8	74.3	74.9	75.6	77.2	79.7	80.6	82.5	81.1
15-24	38.9	39.0	41.5	39.7	43.8	44.3	42.1	41.1	40.8	40.8
25-54	94.0	93.9	93.9	93.6	92.5	92.9	92.5	92.3	91.7	91.8
55-64	79.1	80.2	81.2	81.5	82.2	82.9	85.0	85.7	85.8	85.6
65 and over	26.4	26.5	27.1	27.4	32.9	35.3	36.1	35.2	35.8	36.6
15-64	77.4	77.4	78.1	77.3	77.8	78.6	78.0	78.1	77.6	77.7
Females										
15-19	8.4	9.2	10.9	10.8	14.9	16.0	15.4	14.2	13.7	12.5
20-24	41.0	41.8	43.7	42.7	47.1	48.1	46.5	46.7	46.1	45.8
25-34	56.2	58.0	61.9	62.7	66.4	68.4	67.9	68.2	69.0	67.9
35-44	53.5	54.5	58.0	58.9	65.0	67.0	66.8	67.2	68.9	70.2
45-54	49.6	51.2	52.4	53.9	58.5	61.6	63.1	64.4	64.4	65.0
55-59	40.0	40.8	43.0	44.2	48.9	51.2	54.7	55.4	55.6	56.4
60-64	25.0	25.9	27.1	28.2	31.4	33.7	37.3	36.2	39.2	39.2
15-24	24.2	24.8	26.3	26.3	30.4	32.0	31.6	31.1	30.6	29.9
25-54	53.2	54.6	57.3	58.4	63.2	65.5	65.8	66.5	67.3	67.5
55-64	32.9	33.7	35.4	36.6	40.8	43.2	46.8	47.0	48.4	48.6
65 and over	7.5	8.0	8.1	7.6	10.1	12.1	11.8	12.7	13.4	13.3
15-64	43.3	44.4	46.6	47.4	51.8	53.9	54.6	54.9	55.7	55.8
All persons										
15-24	31.8	32.1	34.2	33.3	37.5	38.4	37.1	36.3	36.0	35.7
25-54	73.3	73.9	75.3	75.6	77.6	79.0	78.9	79.2	79.3	79.4
55-64	55.2	56.5	57.9	58.4	60.6	62.2	65.0	65.9	66.6	66.5
65 and over	15.9	16.1	16.5	16.4	20.2	22.6	23.0	22.9	23.5	23.8
15-64	60.3	60.8	62.3	62.3	64.8	66.2	66.3	66.4	66.6	66.8
Unemployment rates										
Males										
15-19	22.0	20.7	23.0	26.5	19.6	19.0	17.2	20.5	18.3	17.9
20-24	14.6	14.5	16.1	20.0	15.5	13.7	13.3	11.7	13.1	12.5
25-34	8.2	7.3	8.1	11.3	8.7	7.6	6.5	6.8	7.8	8.5
35-44	4.7	4.5	4.6	6.5	5.1	4.1	3.9	3.8	4.7	4.1
45-54	4.2	4.0	4.1	6.0	4.6	3.5	3.1	3.3	3.7	3.5
55-59	4.1	4.3	4.2	6.2	4.6	3.6	3.5	2.8	3.6	3.0
60-64	3.4	3.2	3.1	5.4	4.2	4.0	3.4	3.2	4.1	3.5
15-24	16.4	16.1	17.8	21.5	16.6	15.2	14.3	13.9	14.3	13.8
25-54	5.7	5.2	5.5	7.8	6.1	5.0	4.4	4.5	5.3	5.3
55-64	3.8	3.8	3.8	5.8	4.5	3.8	3.5	3.0	3.8	3.2
65 and over	2.3	1.5	1.8	2.7	3.1	2.8	2.3	2.1	3.2	2.5
15-64	6.9	6.5	7.0	9.4	7.4	6.3	5.7	5.5	6.3	6.1
Total	6.7	6.3	6.8	9.1	7.2	6.1	5.4	5.3	6.0	5.8
Females										
15-19	31.3	31.0	32.3	34.4	29.5	26.3	26.4	26.3	25.7	24.6
20-24	19.5	18.3	20.3	21.8	19.0	19.4	16.9	17.1	18.1	16.6
25-34	11.2	10.7	11.1	12.9	11.0	10.4	9.8	8.3	7.6	8.2
35-44	7.5	6.2	7.2	9.2	8.0	7.0	6.3	5.6	5.8	5.8
45-54	5.8	4.9	6.1	6.5	6.8	5.1	5.1	3.7	4.1	4.7
55-59	3.8	4.0	3.7	4.3	4.2	4.3	3.0	3.2	3.2	2.9
60-64	2.5	3.0	2.9	3.7	3.7	3.6	4.3	2.3	3.2	2.6
15-24	21.6	20.8	23.0	24.4	21.7	21.1	19.1	19.2	19.7	18.2
25-54	8.3	7.3	8.2	9.5	8.6	7.4	7.0	5.8	5.8	6.1
55-64	3.3	3.6	3.4	4.1	4.0	4.1	3.5	2.9	3.2	2.8
65 and over	1.6	1.0	2.6	1.9	1.8	2.0	2.3	1.7	2.3	2.9
15-64	9.6	8.8	9.7	10.9	9.9	8.9	8.1	7.1	7.1	7.0
Total	9.4	8.6	9.5	10.7	9.6	8.7	7.9	6.9	6.9	6.8
All persons										
15-24	18.3	17.8	19.7	22.6	18.6	17.5	16.3	16.1	16.5	15.5
25-54	6.7	6.0	6.6	8.5	7.1	6.0	5.5	5.1	5.5	5.7
55-64	3.7	3.8	3.7	5.3	4.3	3.9	3.5	2.9	3.6	3.1
65 and over	2.1	1.4	2.0	2.5	2.7	2.6	2.3	2.0	2.9	2.6
15-64	7.9	7.4	8.0	10.0	8.4	7.4	6.7	6.2	6.6	6.5

Note: Detailed metadata at:http://metalinks.oecd.org/lfs/20170518/6f97b
Disclaimer: http://oe.cd/disclaimer

Table 3. Civilian employment and employees: breakdown by activity - ISIC Rev. 3

Annual average estimates

		2006	2007	2008	2009	2010	2011	2012	2013	2014	2015
	CIVILIAN EMPLOYMENT										
	By activity, thousands										
A-X	**All activities**	**..**	**..**	**..**	**..**	**7 131**	**7 487**	**7 626**	**7 786**	**7 903**	**..**
A	Agriculture, hunting and forestry	..	..	..	..	711	719	708	682	687	..
B	Fishing	..	..	..	..	45	49	53	56	56	..
C	Mining and quarrying	..	..	..	..	203	220	251	249	237	..
D	Manufacturing	..	..	..	..	803	860	881	882	898	..
E	Electricity, gas and water supply	..	..	..	..	59	61	56	53	59	..
F	Construction	..	..	..	..	572	608	629	675	663	..
G	Wholesale, retail trade: vehicle repair, household gds	..	..	..	..	1 508	1 558	1 500	1 581	1 587	..
H	Hotels and restaurants	..	..	..	..	242	260	281	279	275	..
I	Transport, storage and communication	..	..	..	..	523	542	558	573	576	..
J	Financial intermediation	..	..	..	..	128	123	136	168	164	..
K	Real estate, renting and business activities	..	..	..	..	445	493	481	491	502	..
L	Public adm., defence; social sec., excl. armed forces	..	..	..	..	389	399	440	419	440	..
M	Education	..	..	..	..	490	515	565	613	627	..
N	Health and social work	..	..	..	..	301	322	349	347	386	..
O	Other community, social, personal service activities	..	..	..	..	229	247	233	239	247	..
P	Private households with employed persons	..	..	..	..	480	507	502	477	497	..
Q	Extra-territorial organisations and bodies	..	..	..	..	2	2	2	2	2	..
X	Not classifiable by economic activities	..	..	..	..	0	0	..	..	..	..
	By sector, thousands										
A-B	Agriculture	..	..	..	..	756	768	761	738	743	..
C-F	Industry	..	..	..	..	1 637	1 750	1 817	1 859	1 856	..
G-Q	Services	..	..	..	..	4 737	4 969	5 047	5 189	5 304	..
	By sector, percentages										
A-B	Agriculture	..	..	..	..	10.6	10.3	10.0	9.5	9.4	..
C-F	Industry	..	..	..	..	23.0	23.4	23.8	23.9	23.5	..
G-Q	Services	..	..	..	..	66.4	66.4	66.2	66.6	67.1	..
	EMPLOYEES										
	By activity, thousands										
A-X	**All activities**	**..**	**..**	**..**	**..**	**..**	**..**	**..**	**..**	**..**	**..**
A	Agriculture, hunting and forestry	..	..	..	..	..	..	..	..	..	..
B	Fishing	..	..	..	..	..	..	..	..	..	..
C	Mining and quarrying	..	..	..	..	..	..	..	..	..	..
D	Manufacturing	..	..	..	..	..	..	..	..	..	..
E	Electricity, gas and water supply	..	..	..	..	..	..	..	..	..	..
F	Construction	..	..	..	..	..	..	..	..	..	..
G	Wholesale, retail trade: vehicle repair, household gds	..	..	..	..	..	..	..	..	..	..
H	Hotels and restaurants	..	..	..	..	..	..	..	..	..	..
I	Transport, storage and communication	..	..	..	..	..	..	..	..	..	..
J	Financial intermediation	..	..	..	..	..	..	..	..	..	..
K	Real estate, renting and business activities	..	..	..	..	..	..	..	..	..	..
L	Public adm., defence; social sec., excl. armed forces	..	..	..	..	..	..	..	..	..	..
M	Education	..	..	..	..	..	..	..	..	..	..
N	Health and social work	..	..	..	..	..	..	..	..	..	..
O	Other community, social, personal service activities	..	..	..	..	..	..	..	..	..	..
P	Private households with employed persons	..	..	..	..	..	..	..	..	..	..
Q	Extra-territorial organisations and bodies	..	..	..	..	..	..	..	..	..	..
X	Not classifiable by economic activities	..	..	..	..	..	..	..	..	..	..
	By sector, thousands										
A-B	Agriculture	..	..	..	..	..	..	..	..	..	..
C-F	Industry	..	..	..	..	..	..	..	..	..	..
G-Q	Services	..	..	..	..	..	..	..	..	..	..
	By sector, percentages										
A-B	Agriculture	..	..	..	..	..	..	..	..	..	..
C-F	Industry	..	..	..	..	..	..	..	..	..	..
G-Q	Services	..	..	..	..	..	..	..	..	..	..

Note: Detailed metadata:http://metalinks.oecd.org/lfs/20170518/87289
Disclaimer: http://oe.cd/disclaimer

CZECH REPUBLIC

Table 1. Labour force

Annual average estimates

	2006	2007	2008	2009	2010	2011	2012	2013	2014	2015
Civilian labour force, thousands										
All persons	5 183	5 184	5 216	5 272	5 254	5 242	5 239	5 289	5 280	5 296
Males	2 896	2 917	2 951	2 985	2 975	2 953	2 940	2 954	2 952	2 949
Females	2 287	2 267	2 266	2 287	2 279	2 289	2 298	2 335	2 328	2 346
Unemployed, thousands										
All persons	371	276	230	352	384	354	367	369	324	268
Males	169	124	103	175	191	172	178	175	151	125
Females	202	153	127	177	193	181	189	194	172	143
Civilian employment, thousands										
All persons	4 811	4 908	4 986	4 920	4 870	4 888	4 872	4 920	4 957	5 028
Males	2 727	2 793	2 848	2 810	2 784	2 780	2 762	2 779	2 801	2 824
Females	2 085	2 115	2 138	2 110	2 086	2 108	2 109	2 142	2 155	2 203
Civilian employment (%)										
All persons	100.0	100.0	100.0	100.0	100.0	100.0	100.0	100.0	100.0	100.0
Males	56.7	56.9	57.1	57.1	57.2	56.9	56.7	56.5	56.5	56.2
Females	43.3	43.1	42.9	42.9	42.8	43.1	43.3	43.5	43.5	43.8
Unemployment rate (% of civilian labour force)										
All persons	7.2	5.3	4.4	6.7	7.3	6.7	7.0	7.0	6.1	5.1
Males	5.8	4.2	3.5	5.9	6.4	5.8	6.1	5.9	5.1	4.3
Females	8.8	6.7	5.6	7.7	8.5	7.9	8.2	8.3	7.4	6.1
CIVIL. EMPL. - PROFESSIONAL STATUS, thousands										
All activities	**4 811**	**4 908**	**4 986**	**4 920**	**4 870**	**4 888**	**4 872**	**4 920**	**4 957**	**5 028**
Employees	4 031	4 111	4 180	4 092	4 004	4 005	3 971	4 039	4 062	4 153
Employers and persons working on own account	747	766	775	798	836	858	872	835	866	844
Unpaid family workers	32	30	31	29	29	26	28	47	30	30
Employees as % of civilian employment	**83.8**	**83.8**	**83.8**	**83.2**	**82.2**	**81.9**	**81.5**	**82.1**	**81.9**	**82.6**
Part-time employment (%)										
Part-time as % of employment	3.3	3.5	3.5	3.9	4.3	3.9	4.3	4.9	4.8	4.7
Male share of part time employment	27.2	27.7	27.9	31.3	30.8	27.1	30.3	28.8	29.5	30.5
Female share of part time employment	72.8	72.3	72.1	68.7	69.2	72.9	69.7	71.2	70.5	69.5
Male part-time as % of male employment	1.6	1.7	1.7	2.1	2.3	1.9	2.3	2.5	2.5	2.5
Female part-time as % of female employment	5.6	5.9	5.8	6.2	7.0	6.6	7.0	8.0	7.7	7.4
Duration of unemployment (% of total unemployment)										
Less than one month	4.8	6.1	6.7	8.1	6.4	7.2	6.4	6.5	7.5	7.1
More than 1 month and less than 3 months	8.1	9.1	10.4	16.5	12.0	13.2	13.2	12.3	13.2	11.9
More than 3 months and less than 6 months	12.1	13.2	13.6	20.4	15.4	16.4	16.5	15.6	15.3	14.6
More than 6 months and less than 1 year	19.8	18.2	19.2	23.8	22.9	21.6	20.5	20.6	19.5	18.1
More than 1 year	55.2	53.4	50.2	31.2	43.3	41.6	43.4	44.9	44.5	48.3

Note: Detailed metadata: http://metalinks.oecd.org/lfs/20170518/352d6, http://metalinks.oecd.org/lfs/20170518/87289, http://metalinks.oecd.org/lfs/20170518/67a4c and http://metalinks.oecd.org/lfs/20170518/3193e.

Disclaimer: http://oe.cd/disclaimer

CZECH REPUBLIC

Table 2. Participation rates and unemployment rates by age and sex

Annual average estimates, percentage

	2006	2007	2008	2009	2010	2011	2012	2013	2014	2015
Participation rates										
Males										
15-19	10.0	8.7	8.4	9.1	8.4	8.0	8.1	7.0	8.7	7.3
20-24	63.6	62.8	60.8	62.1	60.0	58.2	58.7	59.4	59.9	60.2
25-34	94.8	95.0	94.1	94.4	95.2	94.7	94.3	94.6	94.8	94.2
35-44	97.2	96.6	97.1	97.0	97.2	97.1	97.1	97.3	97.0	97.1
45-54	92.6	93.5	93.1	93.7	93.9	94.0	94.8	95.2	94.8	94.5
55-59	83.2	81.6	84.7	84.0	85.3	85.7	86.4	87.1	88.5	88.1
60-64	36.1	39.3	40.7	40.2	38.2	38.6	41.1	44.8	47.7	49.4
15-24	37.7	36.7	35.9	37.3	36.2	35.6	36.4	36.8	38.1	37.4
25-54	94.8	95.0	94.8	95.1	95.5	95.3	95.5	95.8	95.6	95.4
55-64	62.7	62.4	64.2	63.2	62.5	62.6	64.0	66.1	67.9	68.3
65 and over	6.7	7.1	7.2	7.5	7.1	6.7	6.8	7.1	7.1	7.9
15-64	78.2	78.1	78.1	78.5	78.6	78.7	79.5	80.5	81.2	81.4
Females										
15-19	6.8	5.5	6.3	6.6	5.3	5.2	5.0	4.8	5.8	5.9
20-24	50.1	47.0	44.4	43.5	42.5	39.8	42.3	42.1	41.1	43.6
25-34	68.2	67.3	66.2	66.5	65.8	66.5	65.7	68.4	67.9	67.6
35-44	88.4	86.6	85.3	85.3	85.2	85.7	85.9	85.5	84.8	84.0
45-54	89.8	89.7	89.9	90.2	90.2	90.3	92.0	92.4	92.1	92.5
55-59	51.1	53.1	55.7	58.0	60.2	63.3	66.6	70.3	74.4	77.2
60-64	13.1	14.9	15.1	15.5	15.5	16.0	17.2	19.3	20.4	22.4
15-24	29.1	26.9	26.1	26.1	25.3	24.2	25.9	26.1	26.1	27.4
25-54	81.3	80.3	79.6	79.9	79.8	80.4	80.9	81.9	81.6	81.4
55-64	34.0	35.2	36.1	37.2	38.0	39.4	41.6	44.2	46.3	48.3
65 and over	2.5	2.7	2.8	3.2	3.2	3.3	3.3	3.8	3.5	4.1
15-64	62.3	61.5	61.0	61.5	61.5	62.2	63.5	65.1	65.6	66.5
All persons										
15-24	33.5	31.9	31.1	31.8	30.9	30.1	31.3	31.5	32.2	32.5
25-54	88.1	87.8	87.3	87.7	87.8	88.0	88.3	89.1	88.8	88.6
55-64	47.7	48.2	49.5	49.6	49.7	50.6	52.4	54.8	56.8	58.0
65 and over	4.1	4.5	4.5	4.9	4.8	4.6	4.7	5.2	5.0	5.7
15-64	70.3	69.8	69.7	70.1	70.2	70.5	71.6	72.9	73.5	74.0
Unemployment rates										
Males										
15-19	38.3	25.2	21.7	33.4	38.6	40.0	48.3	40.1	35.8	31.1
20-24	13.4	8.7	8.4	14.5	15.8	15.6	16.7	16.7	12.8	9.5
25-34	5.1	3.4	3.0	5.9	6.0	5.4	6.2	6.3	5.7	5.5
35-44	3.9	3.1	2.3	3.9	4.0	3.7	3.6	3.8	3.3	2.7
45-54	5.1	4.0	3.1	4.5	5.6	5.0	4.7	4.6	4.2	3.2
55-59	5.8	5.2	4.0	6.0	7.5	6.8	6.5	5.8	4.9	4.5
60-64	3.1	2.7	2.2	4.5	4.1	3.7	4.1	4.6	4.1	3.3
15-24	16.6	10.6	9.8	16.6	18.3	18.1	19.9	18.6	15.0	11.3
25-54	4.7	3.5	2.8	4.8	5.2	4.6	4.8	4.9	4.3	3.7
55-64	5.1	4.5	3.5	5.6	6.5	5.9	5.7	5.4	4.6	4.0
65 and over	2.1	1.2	0.9	0.5	0.8	0.9	2.5	1.2	1.1	1.1
15-64	5.9	4.3	3.5	5.9	6.5	5.9	6.1	6.0	5.2	4.3
Total	5.8	4.2	3.5	5.8	6.4	5.8	6.0	5.9	5.1	4.2
Females										
15-19	39.2	29.7	28.1	36.1	40.2	44.6	43.6	47.6	38.5	32.7
20-24	16.0	8.9	7.6	14.1	16.1	15.1	16.7	17.0	14.9	12.6
25-34	9.3	7.8	6.5	9.5	10.1	9.1	9.7	9.6	8.9	7.4
35-44	8.0	6.4	4.8	6.4	7.4	7.2	7.5	8.0	7.0	5.8
45-54	7.8	5.9	5.1	6.3	6.8	6.7	6.5	6.4	5.9	4.5
55-59	6.3	5.5	5.1	6.5	7.2	6.4	6.8	7.1	6.1	5.8
60-64	2.6	1.9	2.7	3.0	3.6	3.0	3.0	3.6	2.9	2.0
15-24	18.6	11.0	9.9	16.7	18.5	17.9	19.0	19.4	17.1	14.4
25-54	8.3	6.7	5.4	7.3	8.0	7.6	7.8	7.9	7.1	5.8
55-64	5.6	4.8	4.6	5.8	6.5	5.7	6.0	6.4	5.4	4.9
65 and over	3.7	1.0	0.8	0.8	2.5	2.2	3.4	2.0	1.4	1.2
15-64	8.9	6.8	5.7	7.8	8.5	8.0	8.3	8.4	7.5	6.2
Total	8.8	6.7	5.6	7.7	8.5	7.9	8.2	8.3	7.4	6.1
All persons										
15-24	17.5	10.7	9.9	16.6	18.3	18.0	19.5	19.0	15.9	12.6
25-54	6.4	4.9	4.0	5.9	6.4	5.9	6.1	6.2	5.6	4.6
55-64	5.3	4.6	3.9	5.7	6.5	5.8	5.8	5.8	4.9	4.4
65 and over	2.7	1.1	0.9	0.6	1.5	1.4	2.9	1.5	1.3	1.1
15-64	7.2	5.4	4.4	6.8	7.4	6.8	7.0	7.0	6.2	5.1

Note: Detailed metadata at:http://metalinks.oecd.org/lfs/20170518/6f97b
Disclaimer: http://oe.cd/disclaimer

Table 3. Civilian employment and employees: breakdown by activity - ISIC Rev. 4

Annual average estimates

		2006	2007	2008	2009	2010	2011	2012	2013	2014	2015
	CIVILIAN EMPLOYMENT										
	By activity, thousands										
A-U	**All activities**	**4 811.3**	**4 907.7**	**4 986.2**	**4 919.4**	**4 870.2**	**4 887.7**	**4 871.8**	**4 920.4**	**4 956.6**	**5 027.5**
A	Agriculture, hunting and forestry	174.2	169.0	158.8	153.8	151.3	145.8	149.2	149.6	136.7	147.5
B-F	**Industry**	**1 929.2**	**1 975.8**	**2 027.2**	**1 903.1**	**1 855.7**	**1 882.8**	**1 864.3**	**1 851.9**	**1 892.1**	**1 917.0**
B	Mining and quarrying	54.5	53.8	55.2	52.2	47.9	46.5	43.3	41.1	35.7	37.8
C	Manufacturing	1 310.6	1 348.3	1 378.5	1 242.7	1 235.9	1 294.0	1 299.1	1 285.3	1 329.8	1 376.8
D	Electricity, gas, steam, air cond. supply	59.3	56.2	60.1	57.7	56.7	58.0	50.9	54.0	57.2	49.2
E	Water supply, sewerage, waste mgt, remediation	50.1	51.6	52.7	53.8	50.2	51.2	46.0	51.3	55.4	57.1
F	Construction	454.7	465.8	480.8	496.7	465.0	433.1	425.0	420.3	413.9	396.0
G-U	**Services**	**2 707.8**	**2 763.0**	**2 800.2**	**2 862.5**	**2 863.3**	**2 859.1**	**2 858.4**	**2 918.9**	**2 927.7**	**2 963.0**
G	Wholesale, retail trade, vehicle, motorcycle repair	599.7	598.9	619.2	630.9	593.8	602.1	601.9	605.3	590.2	615.7
H	Transportation and storage	320.5	323.2	327.5	330.7	328.1	324.0	308.9	301.9	295.9	297.6
I	Accommodation and food service activities	187.1	181.5	176.9	186.0	190.1	187.3	177.5	178.5	195.2	197.2
J	Information and communication	109.3	115.0	117.9	129.2	137.1	147.8	125.3	139.8	148.7	141.5
K	Financial and insurance activities	93.1	102.7	115.9	110.4	115.3	123.7	136.7	137.3	121.5	118.1
L	Real estate activities	31.1	35.6	40.1	40.6	40.0	42.1	45.7	48.8	46.2	44.9
M	Professional, scientific and technical activities	172.0	189.1	195.1	201.7	202.1	200.1	212.4	220.8	222.4	237.5
N	Administrative and support service activities	112.5	119.4	128.0	117.7	112.9	115.3	115.9	129.4	129.8	128.9
O	Public administration, defence, social security	299.6	302.9	300.8	306.7	314.5	301.3	287.2	299.2	301.6	301.9
P	Education	289.6	292.3	283.9	295.6	295.6	296.8	318.9	322.6	326.2	322.8
Q	Human health and social work activities	323.4	331.6	321.3	326.3	339.9	326.7	333.4	339.3	353.5	351.6
R	Arts, entertainment and recreation	78.6	81.4	82.3	83.3	82.9	83.5	80.5	80.3	81.2	81.7
S	Other service activities	86.3	85.8	88.4	91.9	93.7	88.8	91.9	93.0	87.6	90.0
T	Households as employers and own-use activities	3.5	2.7	2.5	10.8	16.0	18.2	20.5	21.9	26.7	31.8
U	Activities of extraterritorial organizations, bodies	1.5	1.0	0.3	0.6	1.1	1.3	1.5	0.6	0.8	1.3
	EMPLOYEES										
	By activity, thousands										
A-U	**All activities**	**4 031.5**	**4 111.0**	**4 179.8**	**4 092.1**	**4 004.3**	**4 004.4**	**3 971.2**	**4 038.5**	**4 061.5**	**4 153.3**
A	Agriculture, hunting and forestry	140.2	134.9	125.2	122.8	111.4	103.5	108.8	113.2	100.6	110.1
B-F	**Industry**	**1 662.4**	**1 695.7**	**1 741.2**	**1 614.6**	**1 566.2**	**1 593.6**	**1 578.6**	**1 570.1**	**1 602.8**	**1 653.1**
B	Mining and quarrying	52.9	52.6	54.1	50.3	46.4	46.4	43.1	40.4	35.2	37.8
C	Manufacturing	1 213.5	1 248.6	1 285.5	1 157.3	1 140.9	1 188.3	1 196.1	1 180.7	1 231.6	1 281.7
D	Electricity, gas, steam, air cond. supply	56.5	52.8	55.9	52.7	52.9	54.6	48.5	51.4	53.8	47.4
E	Water supply, sewerage, waste mgt, remediation	47.3	48.6	50.3	51.3	47.2	48.8	43.8	48.6	52.2	53.5
F	Construction	292.2	293.0	295.5	302.9	278.8	255.4	247.2	248.9	229.9	232.7
G-U	**Services**	**2 228.8**	**2 280.5**	**2 313.3**	**2 354.7**	**2 326.7**	**2 307.3**	**2 283.8**	**2 355.2**	**2 358.2**	**2 390.1**
G	Wholesale, retail trade, vehicle, motorcycle repair	457.0	453.7	471.1	485.9	456.3	457.8	449.4	459.2	450.4	474.9
H	Transportation and storage	272.4	281.9	293.7	294.9	291.2	287.4	276.0	272.2	263.9	267.4
I	Accommodation and food service activities	148.7	147.0	142.5	151.5	151.7	150.3	142.4	146.0	161.2	158.8
J	Information and communication	89.6	96.1	95.0	101.5	102.8	111.1	95.1	110.6	115.9	110.1
K	Financial and insurance activities	71.6	77.3	92.8	85.2	86.4	89.8	96.2	98.5	89.2	87.4
L	Real estate activities	21.1	21.8	24.7	25.4	24.1	25.1	24.4	26.4	22.1	22.1
M	Professional, scientific and technical activities	110.0	121.5	106.7	112.9	105.4	105.9	116.9	124.2	113.9	128.3
N	Administrative and support service activities	78.9	83.3	106.0	98.5	92.5	94.5	96.1	106.1	106.4	107.7
O	Public administration, defence, social security	294.6	298.5	297.2	303.9	310.5	298.4	284.8	297.3	299.3	300.8
P	Education	279.5	281.8	271.6	283.3	283.6	281.4	301.0	302.6	306.2	305.8
Q	Human health and social work activities	292.7	305.8	299.6	298.7	310.3	298.2	299.8	305.6	322.8	324.0
R	Arts, entertainment and recreation	59.2	60.3	62.9	63.7	63.9	62.3	59.4	61.5	63.2	59.2
S	Other service activities	49.9	48.7	48.0	46.2	44.8	41.0	38.0	40.7	39.5	37.9
T	Households as employers and own-use activities	2.7	1.9	1.4	2.8	2.0	2.8	2.5	3.6	3.2	3.9
U	Activities of extraterritorial organizations, bodies	1.0	0.8	0.1	0.5	1.1	1.3	1.5	0.6	0.8	1.3

Note: Detailed metadata:http://metalinks.oecd.org/lfs/20170518/87289
Disclaimer: http://oe.cd/disclaimer

DENMARK

Table 1. Labour force

Annual average estimates

	2006	2007	2008	2009	2010	2011	2012	2013	2014	2015
Civilian labour force, thousands										
All persons	2 919	2 915	2 954	2 948	2 924	2 924	2 907	2 890	2 906	2 933
Males	1 548	1 545	1 567	1 557	1 544	1 539	1 527	1 512	1 530	1 553
Females	1 372	1 369	1 387	1 390	1 381	1 385	1 380	1 378	1 375	1 380
Unemployed, thousands										
All persons	114	111	101	177	218	221	219	202	192	181
Males	52	53	50	103	129	118	115	102	98	92
Females	62	58	52	74	89	103	104	100	94	89
Civilian employment, thousands										
All persons	2 805	2 804	2 853	2 771	2 706	2 703	2 689	2 688	2 714	2 752
Males	1 496	1 492	1 517	1 454	1 415	1 421	1 413	1 410	1 433	1 461
Females	1 309	1 312	1 336	1 316	1 292	1 282	1 276	1 278	1 283	1 291
Civilian employment (%)										
All persons	100.0	100.0	100.0	100.0	100.0	100.0	100.0	100.0	100.0	100.0
Males	53.3	53.2	53.2	52.5	52.3	52.6	52.5	52.5	52.8	53.1
Females	46.7	46.8	46.8	47.5	47.7	47.4	47.5	47.5	47.3	46.9
Unemployment rate (% of civilian labour force)										
All persons	3.9	3.8	3.4	6.0	7.5	7.6	7.5	7.0	6.6	6.2
Males	3.3	3.4	3.2	6.6	8.4	7.7	7.5	6.7	6.4	5.9
Females	4.5	4.2	3.7	5.3	6.5	7.5	7.5	7.3	6.8	6.4
CIVIL. EMPL. - PROFESSIONAL STATUS, thousands										
All activities	**2 805**	**2 804**	**2 853**	**2 771**	**2 706**	**2 703**	**2 689**	**2 688**	**2 714**	**2 752**
Employees	2 551	2 551	2 600	2 512	2 460	2 456	2 443	2 446	2 473	2 514
Employers and persons working on own account	235	236	241	248	239	239	239	237	235	230
Unpaid family workers	19	17	12	11	8	7	7	5	6	8
Employees as % of civilian employment	**90.9**	**91.0**	**91.2**	**90.7**	**90.9**	**90.9**	**90.9**	**91.0**	**91.1**	**91.3**
Part-time employment (%)										
Part-time as % of employment	17.9	17.3	17.8	18.8	19.2	19.2	19.4	19.2	19.7	20.0
Male share of part time employment	35.7	36.7	38.7	38.0	36.8	37.9	39.1	38.9	39.0	39.7
Female share of part time employment	64.3	63.3	61.3	62.0	63.2	62.1	60.9	61.1	61.0	60.3
Male part-time as % of male employment	12.0	11.9	13.0	13.6	13.5	13.8	14.4	14.2	14.6	15.0
Female part-time as % of female employment	24.6	23.4	23.3	24.5	25.4	25.2	24.9	24.7	25.4	25.8
Duration of unemployment (% of total unemployment)										
Less than one month	25.5	29.2	34.7	22.7	17.0	16.5	15.7	17.6	18.0	18.0
More than 1 month and less than 3 months	21.6	25.5	25.8	28.0	23.2	21.9	20.5	21.5	21.9	21.3
More than 3 months and less than 6 months	18.6	16.4	17.6	23.7	21.1	19.4	19.1	19.0	19.2	18.1
More than 6 months and less than 1 year	13.6	12.8	8.5	16.1	18.5	17.8	16.7	16.4	15.6	15.7
More than 1 year	20.8	16.1	13.5	9.5	20.2	24.4	28.0	25.5	25.2	26.9

Note: Detailed metadata: http://metalinks.oecd.org/lfs/20170518/b959b, http://metalinks.oecd.org/lfs/20170518/87289, http://metalinks.oecd.org/lfs/20170518/dcbcc and http://metalinks.oecd.org/lfs/20170518/5d4a9.

Disclaimer: http://oe.cd/disclaimer

Table 2. Participation rates and unemployment rates by age and sex

Annual average estimates, percentage

	2006	2007	2008	2009	2010	2011	2012	2013	2014	2015
Participation rates										
Males										
15-19	61.9	62.2	64.2	63.3	58.0	57.7	53.5	50.0	49.7	49.3
20-24	80.4	82.8	82.1	80.7	77.7	76.8	74.7	71.9	71.9	73.1
25-34	92.0	92.3	92.5	90.8	90.0	89.3	88.5	88.4	87.2	87.3
35-44	93.8	94.0	94.8	93.6	94.3	93.9	92.5	92.5	93.4	93.5
45-54	90.9	90.4	92.2	91.8	91.3	91.0	90.6	89.4	90.1	91.3
55-59	87.2	86.8	87.9	88.9	86.1	84.5	86.6	85.7	86.0	86.2
60-64	50.6	47.4	47.2	48.8	50.2	52.2	52.4	53.8	58.2	58.3
15-24	70.5	72.0	72.8	71.7	67.6	67.1	64.1	61.1	61.0	61.7
25-54	92.3	92.3	93.3	92.2	92.0	91.5	90.6	90.2	90.3	90.8
55-64	69.6	66.9	66.9	68.1	67.8	68.3	69.9	70.2	72.6	72.7
65 and over	8.5	8.8	8.7	8.4	9.0	9.5	10.2	9.7	10.2	11.0
15-64	84.1	83.7	84.3	83.6	82.6	82.3	81.4	80.6	81.1	81.6
Females										
15-19	64.6	62.8	66.3	63.0	61.0	60.1	57.5	54.7	53.2	53.7
20-24	74.5	76.1	77.0	77.4	74.1	74.1	70.4	69.8	70.2	70.4
25-34	83.3	83.1	84.5	85.2	82.8	81.6	81.5	80.8	79.4	79.5
35-44	87.3	87.7	87.6	87.7	86.4	87.2	86.9	87.0	86.0	85.8
45-54	85.4	84.8	86.9	86.4	86.2	84.9	85.5	86.0	85.3	84.3
55-59	79.2	79.5	79.1	78.7	78.8	79.3	79.5	79.3	78.8	80.9
60-64	31.6	31.5	28.5	29.7	33.9	37.3	38.3	39.9	41.2	43.3
15-24	69.3	69.1	71.5	70.0	67.4	67.1	64.0	62.4	62.0	62.5
25-54	85.4	85.3	86.4	86.5	85.3	84.7	84.9	84.8	83.8	83.4
55-64	56.7	55.1	53.0	53.5	55.9	58.0	58.9	59.9	60.3	62.6
65 and over	2.5	2.8	2.7	2.6	3.0	3.7	4.1	3.7	4.5	3.6
15-64	77.0	76.4	77.0	76.8	76.0	76.1	75.8	75.6	75.0	75.3
All persons										
15-24	69.9	70.6	72.2	70.9	67.5	67.1	64.1	61.7	61.5	62.1
25-54	88.9	88.9	89.9	89.4	88.7	88.2	87.8	87.5	87.1	87.1
55-64	63.2	61.0	59.9	60.8	61.8	63.2	64.4	65.0	66.4	67.6
65 and over	5.1	5.4	5.3	5.2	5.7	6.3	6.8	6.4	7.1	6.9
15-64	80.6	80.1	80.7	80.2	79.4	79.3	78.6	78.1	78.1	78.5
Unemployment rates										
Males										
15-19	10.8	9.8	7.9	15.0	18.8	19.0	17.8	17.9	16.7	13.5
20-24	5.4	5.9	7.0	11.8	13.9	13.1	12.6	11.8	11.8	10.4
25-34	3.0	3.6	3.3	7.4	9.6	9.0	9.3	7.3	7.6	7.3
35-44	2.1	2.6	2.5	4.8	6.4	5.0	5.9	4.9	4.4	4.5
45-54	2.2	2.0	1.7	5.3	6.2	5.6	5.2	5.3	4.6	4.7
55-59	4.3	3.5	3.1	6.1	8.6	7.6	6.3	5.6	5.5	4.2
60-64	2.2	2.1	1.3	2.4	3.6	5.0	4.6	4.5	4.3	3.7
15-24	7.9	7.6	7.4	13.3	16.1	15.7	14.8	14.3	13.7	11.6
25-54	2.4	2.7	2.5	5.7	7.3	6.3	6.6	5.7	5.4	5.4
55-64	3.5	3.0	2.4	4.7	6.7	6.6	5.7	5.2	5.1	4.0
65 and over	0.4	1.8	0.7	0.0	1.2	1.0	0.4	0.6	0.2	0.9
15-64	3.4	3.5	3.2	6.8	8.5	7.9	7.7	6.9	6.6	6.1
Total	3.3	3.4	3.2	6.6	8.4	7.7	7.5	6.7	6.4	5.9
Females										
15-19	8.1	8.5	10.9	12.5	13.9	15.4	15.4	13.9	12.3	10.7
20-24	6.9	6.4	6.6	8.4	9.9	10.5	11.9	10.3	10.9	9.6
25-34	5.2	4.9	3.9	6.7	7.8	10.5	9.8	10.0	9.3	8.6
35-44	4.0	3.1	2.6	4.3	5.5	6.1	6.1	6.2	5.8	5.1
45-54	2.9	2.9	2.1	3.1	4.6	5.0	5.1	5.2	4.8	5.1
55-59	5.2	4.7	3.4	4.0	4.8	5.6	6.4	5.7	4.7	5.0
60-64	1.7	2.1	1.3	1.8	2.0	2.8	2.9	3.8	4.1	4.5
15-24	7.5	7.4	8.7	10.3	11.8	12.7	13.5	11.8	11.5	10.1
25-54	4.0	3.6	2.8	4.6	5.9	6.9	6.8	6.9	6.4	6.1
55-64	4.3	4.0	2.8	3.4	4.0	4.7	5.3	5.1	4.5	4.8
65 and over	0.0	2.2	0.7	0.3	0.2	0.9	1.1	0.0	0.6	0.2
15-64	4.6	4.2	3.8	5.4	6.5	7.6	7.7	7.4	6.9	6.5
Total	4.5	4.2	3.7	5.3	6.5	7.5	7.5	7.3	6.8	6.4
All persons										
15-24	7.7	7.5	8.0	11.8	14.0	14.2	14.1	13.1	12.6	10.8
25-54	3.2	3.1	2.6	5.2	6.6	6.6	6.7	6.3	5.9	5.7
55-64	3.9	3.4	2.6	4.1	5.5	5.7	5.5	5.1	4.8	4.4
65 and over	0.3	1.9	0.7	0.1	0.9	0.9	0.6	0.4	0.3	0.7
15-64	4.0	3.8	3.5	6.1	7.6	7.7	7.7	7.2	6.8	6.3

Note: Detailed metadata at:http://metalinks.oecd.org/lfs/20170518/6f97b
Disclaimer: http://oe.cd/disclaimer

DENMARK

Table 3. Civilian employment and employees: breakdown by activity - ISIC Rev. 4

Annual average estimates

		2006	2007	2008	2009	2010	2011	2012	2013	2014	2015
	CIVILIAN EMPLOYMENT										
	By activity, thousands										
A-U	**All activities**	**2 759.0**	**2 752.0**	**2 852.8**	**2 770.5**	**2 706.1**	**2 702.7**	**2 688.6**	**2 687.6**	**2 714.1**	**2 752.0**
A	Agriculture, hunting and forestry	75.0	74.0	72.6	71.5	65.5	64.8	69.6	68.1	67.2	68.5
B-F	**Industry**	**648.0**	**644.0**	**658.8**	**..**	**..**	**..**	**529.2**	**522.2**	**521.3**	**529.2**
B	Mining and quarrying	6.0	4.0	3.6	..	..	..	5.5	5.9	5.6	5.6
C	Manufacturing	405.0	411.0	421.1	353.8	340.9	342.3	333.8	325.0	321.8	328.6
D	Electricity, gas, steam, air cond. supply	14.0	15.0	15.3	15.8	15.8	16.5	16.9	16.0	14.5	13.8
E	Water supply, sewerage, waste mgt, remediation	22.0	21.0	22.0	14.4	12.5	15.0	15.9	15.9	16.3	15.8
F	Construction	201.0	193.0	196.8	173.9	158.1	159.5	157.1	159.4	163.1	165.4
G-U	**Services**	**2 036.0**	**2 034.0**	**2 121.4**	**..**	**..**	**..**	**2 089.8**	**2 097.3**	**2 125.6**	**2 154.3**
G	Wholesale, retail trade, vehicle, motorcycle repair	407.0	410.0	436.4	416.8	396.7	392.0	380.8	380.3	377.5	397.5
H	Transportation and storage	148.0	146.0	143.2	138.8	125.7	129.5	130.1	125.8	132.1	126.3
I	Accommodation and food service activities	77.0	81.0	85.7	89.8	87.9	94.5	99.0	99.9	104.9	119.4
J	Information and communication	109.0	103.0	111.8	106.5	111.8	110.1	107.9	111.0	109.6	114.2
K	Financial and insurance activities	95.0	86.0	86.4	92.7	87.0	84.7	82.1	78.1	78.0	74.1
L	Real estate activities	28.0	30.0	32.4	26.2	26.7	27.5	26.8	24.4	27.4	32.0
M	Professional, scientific and technical activities	144.0	133.0	139.3	139.8	139.6	138.1	136.0	133.9	141.8	147.5
N	Administrative and support service activities	69.0	74.0	77.1	87.1	88.8	84.8	86.3	93.2	96.5	105.4
O	Public administration, defence, social security	140.0	137.0	170.2	176.1	157.7	151.1	154.5	159.7	150.1	144.7
P	Education	211.0	215.0	206.5	219.3	230.6	241.9	245.1	249.2	256.7	261.5
Q	Human health and social work activities	484.0	497.0	502.5	506.5	518.4	509.3	497.3	496.1	504.5	478.9
R	Arts, entertainment and recreation	54.0	55.0	57.2	64.1	60.9	62.5	64.3	62.4	65.7	69.4
S	Other service activities	65.0	63.0	64.7	64.5	69.5	66.2	68.6	70.0	68.6	70.9
T	Households as employers and own-use activities	1.0	4.0	3.1	5.8	5.7	..	5.8	5.8	..	..
U	Activities of extraterritorial organizations, bodies	4.0	4.0	4.7	1.0	2.0	..	..	..	..	..
	EMPLOYEES										
	By activity, thousands										
A-U	**All activities**	**2 514.0**	**2 507.0**	**2 600.4**	**2 511.5**	**2 459.8**	**2 456.4**	**2 443.3**	**2 445.6**	**2 473.2**	**2 513.9**
A	Agriculture, hunting and forestry	39.0	37.0	36.4	37.3	34.5	32.0	34.9	34.0	36.6	42.5
B-F	**Industry**	**596.0**	**592.0**	**605.0**	**..**	**..**	**..**	**484.7**	**478.2**	**477.9**	**485.8**
B	Mining and quarrying	6.0	4.0	3.3	..	..	..	5.3	5.9	5.6	5.6
C	Manufacturing	389.0	396.0	406.7	340.3	326.2	329.4	320.2	312.7	310.3	315.6
D	Electricity, gas, steam, air cond. supply	14.0	15.0	15.3	15.5	15.8	16.5	16.8	15.9	14.4	13.7
E	Water supply, sewerage, waste mgt, remediation	22.0	20.0	22.0	14.0	12.2	14.5	15.7	15.2	15.9	15.7
F	Construction	165.0	157.0	157.7	138.5	125.9	127.8	126.7	128.5	131.7	135.2
G-U	**Services**	**1 879.0**	**1 878.0**	**1 959.0**	**..**	**..**	**..**	**1 923.7**	**1 933.4**	**1 958.7**	**1 985.6**
G	Wholesale, retail trade, vehicle, motorcycle repair	362.0	370.0	396.1	373.1	357.3	354.2	346.3	344.9	344.6	364.3
H	Transportation and storage	138.0	134.0	131.0	126.5	115.6	120.1	120.9	117.4	123.5	117.3
I	Accommodation and food service activities	67.0	71.0	75.9	76.5	78.1	82.1	86.3	88.8	94.1	107.3
J	Information and communication	99.0	93.0	100.1	93.2	101.0	98.7	94.2	96.3	95.5	100.5
K	Financial and insurance activities	93.0	85.0	84.9	91.1	84.9	82.5	79.9	76.1	76.0	71.7
L	Real estate activities	24.0	27.0	28.0	22.4	23.8	24.1	23.0	21.4	24.8	29.3
M	Professional, scientific and technical activities	116.0	106.0	109.8	109.3	106.8	105.4	103.7	102.4	106.1	111.3
N	Administrative and support service activities	58.0	63.0	65.0	74.4	76.2	74.5	74.8	80.1	83.0	91.7
O	Public administration, defence, social security	140.0	137.0	170.1	175.6	157.4	150.8	154.4	159.5	150.0	144.3
P	Education	209.0	210.0	203.2	215.1	226.9	236.7	239.8	244.6	251.4	255.3
Q	Human health and social work activities	465.0	476.0	483.9	486.2	497.1	487.6	476.4	475.4	484.7	460.6
R	Arts, entertainment and recreation	47.0	48.0	50.9	56.4	52.7	54.5	57.2	56.4	58.1	61.9
S	Other service activities	56.0	53.0	52.9	53.5	55.9	53.9	56.1	57.1	55.8	58.3
T	Households as employers and own-use activities	1.0	4.0	3.0	5.8	5.3	..	5.5	5.6	..	..
U	Activities of extraterritorial organizations, bodies	4.0	3.0	4.2	1.0	2.0	..	..	..	..	..

Note: Detailed metadata:http://metalinks.oecd.org/lfs/20170518/87289
Disclaimer: http://oe.cd/disclaimer

ESTONIA

Table 1. Labour force

Annual average estimates

	2006	2007	2008	2009	2010	2011	2012	2013	2014	2015
Civilian labour force, thousands										
All persons	688	686	691	684	679	686	681	678	672	680
Males	348	351	352	347	341	347	345	344	345	347
Females	341	335	339	337	338	340	336	334	327	333
Unemployed, thousands										
All persons	41	32	38	93	114	85	69	59	50	42
Males	22	19	20	58	66	46	38	32	27	22
Females	19	13	17	35	48	39	31	27	22	21
Civilian employment, thousands										
All persons	647	654	653	591	565	601	613	619	622	638
Males	326	332	332	289	275	301	307	313	318	325
Females	321	322	321	302	290	300	305	306	304	313
Civilian employment (%)										
All persons	100.0	100.0	100.0	100.0	100.0	100.0	100.0	100.0	100.0	100.0
Males	50.4	50.7	50.8	48.9	48.6	50.1	50.2	50.5	51.1	51.0
Females	49.6	49.3	49.2	51.1	51.4	49.9	49.8	49.5	48.9	49.0
Unemployment rate (% of civilian labour force)										
All persons	6.0	4.6	5.5	13.6	16.8	12.4	10.1	8.7	7.4	6.2
Males	6.3	5.4	5.8	16.8	19.5	13.1	11.0	9.2	7.9	6.3
Females	5.6	3.8	5.1	10.3	14.1	11.6	9.1	8.2	6.8	6.2
CIVIL. EMPL. - PROFESSIONAL STATUS, thousands										
All activities	**647**	**654**	**653**	**591**	**565**	**601**	**613**	**619**	**622**	**638**
Employees	594	594	601	542	517	549	558	562	566	578
Employers and persons working on own account	52	59	51	49	47	51	53	55	56	59
Unpaid family workers	1	1	1	1	1	2	2	2	1	1
Employees as % of civilian employment	**91.8**	**90.8**	**92.1**	**91.6**	**91.5**	**91.2**	**91.1**	**90.8**	**90.9**	**90.6**
Part-time employment (%)										
Part-time as % of employment	6.8	6.8	6.3	8.5	8.8	8.9	8.2	8.0	7.6	8.6
Male share of part time employment	24.9	26.8	29.6	32.4	32.1	28.3	28.3	30.7	33.9	30.2
Female share of part time employment	75.1	73.2	70.4	67.6	67.9	71.7	71.7	69.3	66.1	69.8
Male part-time as % of male employment	3.3	3.6	3.6	5.6	5.8	5.0	4.6	4.9	5.0	5.1
Female part-time as % of female employment	10.3	10.1	9.0	11.3	11.7	12.9	11.9	11.3	10.3	12.2
Duration of unemployment (% of total unemployment)										
Less than one month	10.2	14.9	18.5	11.2	7.1	9.3	9.0	7.4	10.0	10.5
More than 1 month and less than 3 months	13.7	13.5	18.6	18.3	10.2	10.4	11.0	16.7	15.5	18.0
More than 3 months and less than 6 months	14.4	13.0	15.6	22.1	15.8	10.6	12.3	17.1	14.1	18.3
More than 6 months and less than 1 year	13.1	8.9	16.1	21.0	21.7	12.4	13.0	14.3	15.0	15.0
More than 1 year	48.6	49.8	31.2	27.3	45.3	57.3	54.7	44.5	45.3	38.3

Note: Detailed metadata: http://metalinks.oecd.org/lfs/20170518/e0892, http://metalinks.oecd.org/lfs/20170518/87289, http://metalinks.oecd.org/lfs/20170518/c3247 and http://metalinks.oecd.org/lfs/20170518/0a226.

Disclaimer: http://oe.cd/disclaimer

ESTONIA

Table 2. Participation rates and unemployment rates by age and sex

Annual average estimates, percentage

	2006	2007	2008	2009	2010	2011	2012	2013	2014	2015
Participation rates										
Males										
15-19	14.9	16.7	14.5	13.7	9.4	13.0	14.3	10.2	10.1	13.1
20-24	68.9	72.1	74.8	72.2	68.2	68.0	69.3	65.9	66.4	73.7
25-34	94.9	95.5	95.8	92.9	93.1	93.4	92.8	93.6	93.2	94.9
35-44	95.3	94.2	94.0	94.0	93.6	94.2	94.4	94.3	95.0	93.5
45-54	86.7	89.8	87.2	87.4	87.5	88.3	88.9	88.7	87.5	88.5
55-59	76.2	77.8	78.6	75.5	75.4	77.7	76.7	78.4	77.5	77.5
60-64	41.0	40.7	53.2	56.5	50.8	53.9	51.5	53.3	59.5	56.5
15-24	41.4	44.3	45.4	44.9	42.3	44.8	46.6	43.1	43.1	47.5
25-54	92.4	93.2	92.4	91.5	91.5	92.1	92.1	92.3	92.0	92.4
55-64	61.1	62.4	67.9	67.3	64.3	66.7	65.0	66.7	69.1	67.7
65 and over	25.1	21.9	21.9	19.6	17.5	17.1	21.0	22.1	24.2	23.3
15-64	76.0	77.5	78.1	77.5	76.7	78.2	78.5	78.6	79.3	80.4
Females										
15-19	9.0	11.8	12.2	9.8	9.2	10.6	9.4	10.1	9.8	13.5
20-24	52.1	52.2	60.4	55.0	53.9	55.3	57.0	57.7	56.7	56.3
25-34	77.9	75.8	74.3	73.8	75.5	76.8	74.0	73.2	74.8	75.5
35-44	88.1	85.4	87.1	87.6	88.1	86.8	86.4	86.1	83.2	82.8
45-54	89.4	88.6	89.1	89.6	90.4	90.1	89.6	89.1	87.6	90.4
55-59	74.9	75.8	78.4	80.6	80.4	80.6	79.8	80.3	80.8	81.3
60-64	42.6	41.8	41.6	48.3	46.4	45.4	49.6	52.3	51.6	57.0
15-24	30.4	32.1	37.1	34.0	34.1	36.3	37.1	38.1	37.0	37.7
25-54	85.2	83.4	83.7	83.8	84.8	84.7	83.4	82.8	81.8	82.8
55-64	60.4	61.0	62.2	65.9	64.3	63.5	65.0	66.5	66.5	69.4
65 and over	16.1	16.9	15.9	14.2	14.8	18.3	19.1	19.2	18.6	22.5
15-64	69.4	68.8	70.3	70.5	71.0	71.4	71.3	71.7	71.2	72.9
All persons										
15-24	36.0	38.4	41.4	39.6	38.3	40.7	42.0	40.7	40.1	42.8
25-54	88.8	88.3	88.0	87.6	88.1	88.4	87.7	87.6	87.0	87.7
55-64	60.7	61.6	64.7	66.5	64.3	64.9	65.0	66.6	67.6	68.6
65 and over	19.5	18.8	18.2	16.2	15.8	17.9	19.8	20.3	20.8	22.8
15-64	72.6	73.0	74.1	74.0	73.8	74.7	74.8	75.1	75.2	76.6
Unemployment rates										
Males										
15-19	22.8	22.9	21.8	55.2	69.9	43.8	35.7	27.6	34.8	22.3
20-24	6.7	9.2	10.2	25.9	29.9	19.5	18.6	15.3	15.9	11.6
25-34	5.0	4.3	3.9	14.6	17.4	12.7	10.0	8.8	7.4	5.0
35-44	6.4	4.2	4.0	14.7	15.8	9.3	8.1	7.7	6.1	6.0
45-54	5.8	4.0	7.1	18.1	19.2	12.4	11.4	8.5	8.0	4.9
55-59	8.2	5.7	5.5	14.7	21.9	16.1	12.9	9.1	7.1	6.6
60-64	3.2	10.1	4.8	7.0	14.7	12.5	3.6	6.6	3.8	7.4
15-24	9.7	11.8	12.0	30.0	33.8	22.5	20.8	16.5	17.8	12.9
25-54	5.7	4.2	4.9	15.8	17.4	11.4	9.8	8.3	7.1	5.3
55-64	6.8	6.9	5.3	11.9	19.3	14.8	9.4	8.2	5.8	6.9
65 and over	2.7	1.5	0.9	0.0	3.1	3.2	3.5	5.6	3.5	3.0
15-64	6.3	5.5	5.9	17.0	19.6	13.2	11.0	9.1	7.9	6.3
Total	6.2	5.4	5.7	16.6	19.2	13.0	10.8	9.0	7.8	6.2
Females										
15-19	33.0	15.3	29.8	44.5	46.3	40.4	30.0	31.7	17.2	20.9
20-24	12.0	5.3	7.8	18.3	27.2	17.8	17.1	18.2	9.1	10.6
25-34	5.1	3.7	5.7	11.3	13.4	12.8	11.8	9.5	9.9	5.7
35-44	5.4	5.2	4.8	9.4	12.9	10.7	6.8	8.1	6.2	6.2
45-54	5.7	3.6	4.1	8.7	12.1	11.2	9.4	7.3	5.8	5.5
55-59	2.1	1.3	3.3	8.4	17.1	10.2	6.2	5.8	6.1	7.6
60-64	2.0	0.0	2.6	5.1	8.1	6.7	4.1	2.1	3.6	2.1
15-24	15.1	7.2	11.3	21.8	29.5	20.6	18.5	19.7	10.0	12.2
25-54	5.4	4.2	4.8	9.7	12.7	11.5	9.2	8.2	7.2	5.8
55-64	2.1	0.9	3.1	7.3	14.0	9.0	5.4	4.4	5.1	5.4
65 and over	1.6	0.0	3.0	7.3	3.2	4.5	4.3	1.0	2.5	4.4
15-64	5.8	3.9	5.2	10.4	14.5	11.9	9.3	8.5	7.0	6.2
Total	5.6	3.8	5.1	10.3	14.1	11.6	9.1	8.2	6.8	6.1
All persons										
15-24	11.9	9.9	11.7	26.6	32.0	21.7	19.8	17.9	14.3	12.6
25-54	5.6	4.2	4.9	12.8	15.1	11.5	9.5	8.3	7.2	5.5
55-64	4.1	3.6	4.1	9.3	16.3	11.6	7.2	6.0	5.4	6.0
65 and over	2.1	0.7	2.0	4.0	3.2	4.0	4.0	2.9	2.9	3.8
15-64	6.1	4.7	5.6	13.8	17.1	12.6	10.2	8.8	7.5	6.3

Note: Detailed metadata at:http://metalinks.oecd.org/lfs/20170518/6f97b
Disclaimer: http://oe.cd/disclaimer

ESTONIA

Table 3. Civilian employment and employees: breakdown by activity - ISIC Rev. 4

Annual average estimates

		2006	2007	2008	2009	2010	2011	2012	2013	2014	2015
	CIVILIAN EMPLOYMENT										
	By activity, thousands										
A-U	**All activities**	**647.4**	**654.1**	**652.9**	**591.1**	**564.7**	**601.1**	**612.6**	**619.2**	**622.4**	**637.8**
A	Agriculture, hunting and forestry	31.9	30.8	25.5	24.0	23.9	26.6	27.6	26.5	24.1	25.0
B-F	**Industry**	**217.0**	**230.0**	**230.9**	**186.4**	**171.9**	**195.6**	**191.1**	**187.9**	**188.1**	**196.1**
B	Mining and quarrying	5.3	5.5	5.9	6.3	6.7	5.8	4.9	4.8	4.2	3.1
C	Manufacturing	133.4	130.8	133.9	112.2	106.6	119.1	115.5	116.4	114.0	120.6
D	Electricity, gas, steam, air cond. supply	11.5	8.8	8.1	7.5	8.6	8.1	9.2	7.1	8.1	7.6
E	Water supply, sewerage, waste mgt, remediation	2.0	2.3	2.4	2.3	2.3	3.7	3.3	3.0	3.1	3.0
F	Construction	64.8	82.6	80.6	58.1	47.7	58.9	58.2	56.6	58.7	61.8
G-U	**Services**	**398.5**	**393.3**	**396.5**	**380.7**	**368.9**	**378.9**	**393.9**	**404.8**	**410.2**	**416.7**
G	Wholesale, retail trade, vehicle, motorcycle repair	88.1	87.0	92.4	83.0	80.0	81.1	79.1	81.1	81.2	83.9
H	Transportation and storage	57.7	54.3	51.0	50.6	44.4	48.3	51.0	46.9	50.7	46.7
I	Accommodation and food service activities	22.0	22.0	23.0	19.3	18.9	18.4	18.8	23.4	25.8	26.1
J	Information and communication	15.1	13.7	15.6	14.7	12.7	16.7	18.5	19.7	22.1	26.3
K	Financial and insurance activities	7.5	9.5	10.5	11.4	9.4	10.3	10.9	10.2	8.2	9.5
L	Real estate activities	10.1	9.8	10.3	9.1	10.1	10.7	10.7	11.7	11.5	10.3
M	Professional, scientific and technical activities	17.5	17.9	21.0	21.0	21.0	23.1	23.2	26.2	26.7	25.5
N	Administrative and support service activities	16.1	18.2	17.2	17.1	19.1	17.4	21.3	22.7	18.8	18.6
O	Public administration, defence, social security	36.0	35.4	35.2	34.2	37.1	37.3	37.7	40.9	42.8	39.4
P	Education	58.9	54.7	59.7	61.9	55.7	56.5	61.8	56.1	55.0	60.6
Q	Human health and social work activities	36.6	36.1	30.8	32.9	34.2	34.6	34.5	36.4	38.6	39.1
R	Arts, entertainment and recreation	18.6	17.8	15.1	14.1	14.6	14.2	14.9	17.1	16.6	14.2
S	Other service activities	14.4	16.8	14.7	11.3	11.7	10.5	11.4	12.4	12.3	16.7
T	Households as employers and own-use activities	..	..	..	..	..	..	..	..	..	..
U	Activities of extraterritorial organizations, bodies	..	..	..	..	..	..	..	..	..	..
	EMPLOYEES										
	By activity, thousands										
A-U	**All activities**	**594.4**	**593.9**	**601.4**	**541.5**	**516.6**	**548.5**	**558.1**	**562.4**	**565.5**	**577.9**
A	Agriculture, hunting and forestry	22.9	19.7	16.9	17.8	17.5	18.2	20.7	20.4	18.3	18.6
B-F	**Industry**	**201.5**	**211.1**	**218.7**	**175.1**	**161.4**	**183.0**	**178.5**	**174.7**	**174.7**	**181.4**
B	Mining and quarrying	5.3	5.5	5.9	6.3	6.7	5.8	4.9	4.7	4.0	3.1
C	Manufacturing	128.1	124.8	130.1	108.0	101.9	114.9	111.3	111.5	108.6	114.9
D	Electricity, gas, steam, air cond. supply	11.4	8.7	7.7	7.1	8.6	8.1	9.1	7.1	8.0	7.5
E	Water supply, sewerage, waste mgt, remediation	2.0	2.3	2.3	2.3	2.3	3.7	3.2	3.0	3.1	2.9
F	Construction	54.7	69.8	72.7	51.4	41.9	50.5	50.0	48.4	51.0	53.0
G-U	**Services**	**370.0**	**363.1**	**365.8**	**348.6**	**337.7**	**347.3**	**358.9**	**367.3**	**372.5**	**377.9**
G	Wholesale, retail trade, vehicle, motorcycle repair	78.0	76.9	83.4	74.8	71.4	73.2	70.5	72.3	71.4	72.2
H	Transportation and storage	53.9	49.9	46.0	46.1	40.5	43.2	45.8	43.1	46.4	42.5
I	Accommodation and food service activities	21.0	21.0	21.7	17.3	18.0	17.2	17.0	21.7	24.1	24.8
J	Information and communication	13.8	13.1	14.9	13.3	11.2	15.1	15.7	16.7	19.7	23.7
K	Financial and insurance activities	6.9	8.9	10.0	11.3	9.4	10.0	10.3	9.6	7.9	9.3
L	Real estate activities	9.8	8.8	9.0	7.7	8.4	9.0	10.0	10.6	10.2	8.3
M	Professional, scientific and technical activities	14.0	14.1	16.1	15.0	15.1	16.7	16.9	18.6	19.1	20.0
N	Administrative and support service activities	15.1	17.2	16.3	16.2	18.1	16.9	19.8	21.0	16.9	17.0
O	Public administration, defence, social security	35.9	35.4	35.2	34.2	37.1	37.3	37.7	40.9	42.8	39.4
P	Education	58.3	54.1	58.4	61.0	54.6	55.5	60.2	54.8	54.3	59.7
Q	Human health and social work activities	35.4	35.2	30.4	31.7	32.9	33.3	33.5	34.9	37.3	37.3
R	Arts, entertainment and recreation	17.2	16.4	13.8	12.6	13.1	12.4	13.0	14.8	15.0	12.3
S	Other service activities	10.7	12.0	10.4	7.3	8.2	7.8	8.5	8.4	7.4	11.6
T	Households as employers and own-use activities	0.0	0.0	0.0	0.0	0.0	0.0	..	..	..	..
U	Activities of extraterritorial organizations, bodies	0.0	0.0	0.0	0.0	0.0	0.0	..	..	..	..

Note: Detailed metadata:http://metalinks.oecd.org/lfs/20170518/87289
Disclaimer: http://oe.cd/disclaimer

FINLAND

Table 1. Labour force

Annual average estimates

	2006	2007	2008	2009	2010	2011	2012	2013	2014	2015
Civilian labour force, thousands										
All persons	2 638	2 666	2 694	2 670	2 662	2 673	2 681	2 668	2 671	2 680
Males	1 357	1 371	1 391	1 369	1 375	1 385	1 383	1 375	1 375	1 377
Females	1 281	1 295	1 303	1 300	1 286	1 287	1 297	1 292	1 296	1 303
Unemployed, thousands										
All persons	204	183	172	221	224	209	207	219	232	252
Males	101	90	85	122	126	117	115	122	129	137
Females	104	93	87	99	98	91	92	97	103	115
Civilian employment, thousands										
All persons	2 434	2 483	2 522	2 449	2 438	2 464	2 474	2 448	2 439	2 428
Males	1 257	1 281	1 306	1 247	1 250	1 268	1 268	1 253	1 246	1 240
Females	1 177	1 202	1 216	1 202	1 188	1 196	1 206	1 195	1 193	1 188
Civilian employment (%)										
All persons	100.0	100.0	100.0	100.0	100.0	100.0	100.0	100.0	100.0	100.0
Males	51.6	51.6	51.8	50.9	51.3	51.5	51.3	51.2	51.1	51.1
Females	48.4	48.4	48.2	49.1	48.7	48.5	48.7	48.8	48.9	48.9
Unemployment rate (% of civilian labour force)										
All persons	7.7	6.9	6.4	8.3	8.4	7.8	7.7	8.2	8.7	9.4
Males	7.4	6.6	6.1	8.9	9.2	8.4	8.3	8.9	9.4	9.9
Females	8.1	7.2	6.7	7.6	7.6	7.1	7.1	7.5	7.9	8.8
CIVIL. EMPL. - PROFESSIONAL STATUS, thousands										
All activities	**2 434**	**2 483**	**2 522**	**2 449**	**2 438**	**2 465**	**2 474**	**2 448**	**2 439**	**2 428**
Employees	2 120	2 169	2 198	2 114	2 110	2 134	2 137	2 118	2 096	2 081
Employers and persons working on own account	301	300	311	321	314	319	325	319	331	335
Unpaid family workers	13	14	13	13	14	12	12	11	12	11
Employees as % of civilian employment	**87.1**	**87.4**	**87.2**	**86.3**	**86.5**	**86.6**	**86.4**	**86.5**	**85.9**	**85.7**
Part-time employment (%)										
Part-time as % of employment	11.4	11.7	11.5	12.2	12.5	12.7	13.0	13.0	13.3	13.4
Male share of part time employment	37.1	36.3	37.0	36.4	37.8	39.0	38.3	37.8	38.6	40.5
Female share of part time employment	62.9	63.7	63.0	63.6	62.2	61.0	61.7	62.2	61.4	59.5
Male part-time as % of male employment	8.1	8.2	8.2	8.7	9.2	9.6	9.7	9.6	10.0	10.6
Female part-time as % of female employment	14.9	15.5	15.1	15.9	16.0	16.0	16.5	16.7	16.8	16.4
Duration of unemployment (% of total unemployment)										
Less than one month	10.3	14.0	15.0	12.7	12.3	13.6	13.0	12.3	11.7	11.8
More than 1 month and less than 3 months	29.2	28.1	33.9	33.1	28.9	31.0	31.8	31.9	30.0	29.3
More than 3 months and less than 6 months	20.8	20.0	19.6	22.6	19.4	19.7	19.1	19.8	20.6	19.3
More than 6 months and less than 1 year	14.9	14.9	13.3	15.0	15.9	13.1	14.4	14.8	14.6	14.5
More than 1 year	24.8	23.0	18.2	16.6	23.6	22.6	21.7	21.2	23.1	25.1

Note: Detailed metadata: http://metalinks.oecd.org/lfs/20170518/ab603, http://metalinks.oecd.org/lfs/20170518/87289, http://metalinks.oecd.org/lfs/20170518/27dc8 and http://metalinks.oecd.org/lfs/20170518/50705.

Disclaimer: http://oe.cd/disclaimer

FINLAND

Table 2. Participation rates and unemployment rates by age and sex

Annual average estimates, percentage

	2006	2007	2008	2009	2010	2011	2012	2013	2014	2015
Participation rates										
Males										
15-19	35.1	35.5	34.7	26.0	29.9	32.3	31.7	25.8	32.9	33.1
20-24	77.4	78.0	79.3	68.5	73.7	74.7	74.1	67.4	72.5	72.6
25-34	90.9	91.0	92.1	90.8	90.6	90.3	89.2	89.3	88.2	88.8
35-44	92.9	92.5	93.2	93.3	92.6	92.9	92.9	92.2	92.0	90.9
45-54	87.3	87.5	88.5	88.7	88.9	89.4	89.6	88.8	88.7	89.1
55-59	71.2	71.4	74.1	75.0	76.0	77.5	76.9	76.4	77.2	78.6
60-64	41.2	43.4	44.9	42.0	44.4	45.6	47.2	47.7	46.8	47.8
15-24	56.3	56.3	56.4	47.2	52.1	53.7	53.6	47.8	54.1	54.1
25-54	90.3	90.3	91.2	90.8	90.6	90.8	90.5	90.0	89.6	89.6
55-64	58.7	59.2	60.5	58.9	60.0	61.4	61.7	61.6	61.9	63.1
65 and over	7.7	10.3	10.7	10.0	11.0	11.9	12.4	12.5	13.7	14.5
15-64	77.5	77.4	78.1	75.8	76.7	77.5	77.3	76.0	77.1	77.4
Females										
15-19	33.5	37.2	36.9	34.5	32.9	32.5	35.6	36.7	35.5	35.6
20-24	66.9	69.3	70.4	68.8	67.1	69.2	67.9	68.5	68.7	69.3
25-34	79.2	79.6	79.9	79.7	77.2	76.9	76.6	76.1	75.7	76.1
35-44	86.7	87.3	87.6	87.3	86.6	86.7	86.3	84.7	84.7	84.8
45-54	89.0	89.2	89.4	89.1	88.8	89.0	89.2	88.9	89.4	89.3
55-59	74.8	75.1	76.3	79.0	79.9	79.3	81.5	82.0	83.0	84.6
60-64	36.3	38.6	40.6	40.9	42.0	42.6	44.2	46.1	49.0	50.3
15-24	50.8	53.7	53.7	51.2	49.4	50.6	51.9	52.8	52.5	53.3
25-54	85.3	85.6	85.9	85.6	84.4	84.4	84.2	83.4	83.4	83.5
55-64	58.1	58.3	59.0	59.8	60.3	60.5	62.8	64.1	65.8	67.4
65 and over	4.4	4.4	4.0	4.7	5.0	5.8	6.5	6.5	6.9	7.9
15-64	73.2	73.9	74.0	73.5	72.5	72.7	73.4	73.5	73.8	74.4
All persons										
15-24	53.6	55.0	55.1	49.2	50.8	52.2	52.7	50.2	53.3	53.7
25-54	87.8	88.0	88.6	88.2	87.6	87.6	87.4	86.8	86.6	86.6
55-64	58.4	58.8	59.7	59.3	60.2	60.9	62.2	62.9	63.9	65.3
65 and over	5.9	7.1	7.1	7.1	7.8	8.7	9.3	9.3	10.1	11.0
15-64	75.4	75.7	76.1	74.6	74.6	75.1	75.4	74.8	75.5	75.9
Unemployment rates										
Males										
15-19	23.7	23.0	23.3	36.4	28.0	24.1	25.0	34.1	25.5	27.5
20-24	13.8	10.9	11.5	20.0	19.0	17.3	14.7	19.2	18.6	20.5
25-34	6.0	5.6	5.1	8.5	7.9	7.9	7.6	7.9	8.6	9.1
35-44	4.7	3.9	3.7	5.9	6.7	6.1	5.8	6.1	6.8	6.8
45-54	6.2	5.1	4.1	6.8	7.7	6.2	6.5	6.6	7.3	7.6
55-59	7.4	8.2	6.7	7.5	8.2	8.8	8.4	7.9	9.2	9.8
60-64	4.9	4.3	3.8	6.3	5.7	5.6	7.6	7.6	6.9	8.0
15-24	16.9	14.8	15.3	24.5	21.6	19.3	17.7	23.0	20.6	22.5
25-54	5.6	4.8	4.3	7.1	7.4	6.7	6.6	6.9	7.6	7.9
55-64	6.7	6.9	5.7	7.1	7.3	7.6	8.1	7.8	8.3	9.1
65 and over	0.0	0.0	0.0	0.0	0.0	0.0	0.0	0.0	0.0	0.0
15-64	7.3	6.5	6.0	9.1	9.2	8.5	8.3	9.0	9.4	10.0
Total	7.3	6.4	5.9	9.0	9.0	8.3	8.2	8.7	9.1	9.7
Females										
15-19	26.9	24.1	25.4	28.1	29.1	28.3	28.1	27.6	27.3	28.3
20-24	14.4	13.0	11.4	13.9	13.5	13.6	12.7	11.7	13.4	15.7
25-34	8.1	6.7	6.6	8.0	7.4	7.0	7.5	8.2	8.2	9.7
35-44	6.2	5.9	5.4	5.2	6.3	5.0	5.0	6.3	5.9	6.6
45-54	5.9	5.0	4.4	5.4	5.4	4.8	4.8	5.2	5.8	6.5
55-59	7.8	6.6	6.0	6.5	5.8	5.2	5.0	6.3	5.8	6.9
60-64	3.5	4.5	3.9	3.7	5.7	5.7	4.6	4.5	7.4	7.4
15-24	18.4	16.8	16.2	18.8	18.9	18.4	18.0	17.2	18.0	19.6
25-54	6.6	5.8	5.4	6.1	6.3	5.5	5.7	6.4	6.5	7.5
55-64	6.6	6.0	5.3	5.5	5.8	5.4	4.9	5.6	6.4	7.1
65 and over	0.0	..	0.0	0.0	0.0	0.0	0.0	0.0	0.0	0.0
15-64	8.1	7.3	6.8	7.6	7.8	7.2	7.1	7.7	8.0	9.0
Total	8.0	7.3	6.7	7.5	7.7	7.1	7.0	7.6	7.9	8.8
All persons										
15-24	17.6	15.7	15.7	21.6	20.3	18.9	17.8	20.0	19.3	21.1
25-54	6.1	5.3	4.8	6.6	6.9	6.2	6.2	6.7	7.1	7.7
55-64	6.7	6.5	5.5	6.3	6.5	6.5	6.4	6.7	7.3	8.0
65 and over	0.0	0.0	0.0	0.0	0.0	0.0	0.0	0.0	0.0	0.0
15-64	7.7	6.9	6.4	8.4	8.5	7.9	7.8	8.3	8.7	9.5

Note: Detailed metadata at:http://metalinks.oecd.org/lfs/20170518/6f97b
Disclaimer: http://oe.cd/disclaimer

Table 3. Civilian employment and employees: breakdown by activity - ISIC Rev. 4

Annual average estimates

		2006	2007	2008	2009	2010	2011	2012	2013	2014	2015
	CIVILIAN EMPLOYMENT										
	By activity, thousands										
A-U	**All activities**	**2 434.0**	**2 482.0**	**2 522.0**	**2 449.0**	**2 438.0**	**2 464.0**	**2 474.0**	**2 448.0**	**2 439.0**	**2 428.0**
A	Agriculture, hunting and forestry	113.0	113.0	114.0	113.0	108.0	104.0	103.0	101.0	104.0	103.0
B-F	**Industry**	**613.0**	**625.0**	**634.0**	**586.0**	**567.0**	**565.0**	**563.0**	**559.0**	**533.0**	**526.0**
B	Mining and quarrying	5.0	5.0	5.0	5.0	7.0	6.0	6.0	6.0	6.0	6.0
C	Manufacturing	419.0	423.0	417.0	379.0	362.0	359.0	357.0	350.0	331.0	328.0
D	Electricity, gas, steam, air cond. supply	14.0	13.0	15.0	16.0	15.0	14.0	14.0	14.0	14.0	13.0
E	Water supply, sewerage, waste mgt, remediation	11.0	10.0	11.0	11.0	11.0	10.0	11.0	13.0	13.0	11.0
F	Construction	164.0	174.0	186.0	175.0	172.0	176.0	175.0	176.0	169.0	168.0
G-U	**Services**	**1 708.0**	**1 744.0**	**1 774.0**	**1 750.0**	**1 763.0**	**1 795.0**	**1 808.0**	**1 788.0**	**1 802.0**	**1 799.0**
G	Wholesale, retail trade, vehicle, motorcycle repair	298.0	305.0	311.0	296.0	298.0	303.0	300.0	296.0	290.0	284.0
H	Transportation and storage	154.0	151.0	153.0	153.0	156.0	147.0	144.0	142.0	140.0	137.0
I	Accommodation and food service activities	78.0	84.0	88.0	85.0	83.0	83.0	86.0	86.0	86.0	87.0
J	Information and communication	98.0	95.0	95.0	94.0	95.0	99.0	101.0	100.0	100.0	106.0
K	Financial and insurance activities	48.0	51.0	52.0	51.0	49.0	54.0	51.0	49.0	50.0	49.0
L	Real estate activities	19.0	19.0	20.0	19.0	21.0	22.0	23.0	23.0	23.0	24.0
M	Professional, scientific and technical activities	132.0	140.0	151.0	146.0	150.0	155.0	161.0	164.0	169.0	171.0
N	Administrative and support service activities	102.0	109.0	102.0	98.0	100.0	98.0	100.0	96.0	101.0	107.0
O	Public administration, defence, social security	114.0	110.0	108.0	108.0	107.0	107.0	104.0	103.0	97.0	97.0
P	Education	171.0	168.0	165.0	164.0	174.0	179.0	175.0	175.0	180.0	179.0
Q	Human health and social work activities	364.0	370.0	382.0	388.0	379.0	396.0	409.0	399.0	402.0	404.0
R	Arts, entertainment and recreation	50.0	51.0	52.0	53.0	55.0	59.0	59.0	62.0	64.0	61.0
S	Other service activities	69.0	75.0	75.0	75.0	75.0	73.0	74.0	73.0	76.0	73.0
T	Households as employers and own-use activities	7.0	8.0	9.0	9.0	8.0	8.0	8.0	8.0	10.0	9.0
U	Activities of extraterritorial organizations, bodies	1.0	1.0	1.0	1.0	1.0	0.0	1.0	1.0	1.0	1.0
	EMPLOYEES										
	By activity, thousands										
A-U	**All activities**	**2 120.0**	**2 169.0**	**2 198.0**	**2 114.0**	**2 110.0**	**2 134.0**	**2 137.0**	**2 118.0**	**2 096.0**	**2 081.0**
A	Agriculture, hunting and forestry	33.0	32.0	35.0	34.0	33.0	33.0	31.0	33.0	32.0	32.0
B-F	**Industry**	**548.0**	**564.0**	**566.0**	**517.0**	**505.0**	**502.0**	**496.0**	**493.0**	**466.0**	**460.0**
B	Mining and quarrying	5.0	4.0	4.0	4.0	6.0	6.0	6.0	6.0	5.0	6.0
C	Manufacturing	395.0	400.0	392.0	355.0	341.0	337.0	333.0	327.0	308.0	305.0
D	Electricity, gas, steam, air cond. supply	14.0	13.0	14.0	16.0	15.0	14.0	14.0	14.0	14.0	13.0
E	Water supply, sewerage, waste mgt, remediation	10.0	10.0	11.0	10.0	11.0	10.0	10.0	12.0	12.0	10.0
F	Construction	124.0	137.0	145.0	132.0	132.0	135.0	133.0	134.0	127.0	126.0
G-U	**Services**	**1 539.0**	**1 573.0**	**1 597.0**	**1 563.0**	**1 572.0**	**1 599.0**	**1 610.0**	**1 592.0**	**1 598.0**	**1 589.0**
G	Wholesale, retail trade, vehicle, motorcycle repair	254.0	264.0	271.0	257.0	258.0	262.0	261.0	259.0	251.0	245.0
H	Transportation and storage	134.0	131.0	132.0	129.0	131.0	124.0	120.0	121.0	120.0	116.0
I	Accommodation and food service activities	68.0	73.0	78.0	74.0	71.0	73.0	76.0	76.0	74.0	75.0
J	Information and communication	91.0	89.0	89.0	86.0	86.0	91.0	92.0	91.0	90.0	95.0
K	Financial and insurance activities	45.0	49.0	49.0	49.0	47.0	51.0	49.0	47.0	48.0	46.0
L	Real estate activities	16.0	16.0	17.0	16.0	17.0	18.0	19.0	18.0	20.0	20.0
M	Professional, scientific and technical activities	106.0	110.0	119.0	116.0	120.0	121.0	123.0	126.0	130.0	130.0
N	Administrative and support service activities	93.0	101.0	91.0	84.0	87.0	86.0	89.0	85.0	89.0	94.0
O	Public administration, defence, social security	113.0	110.0	108.0	107.0	107.0	107.0	104.0	103.0	97.0	97.0
P	Education	167.0	165.0	161.0	161.0	170.0	174.0	172.0	172.0	176.0	174.0
Q	Human health and social work activities	349.0	355.0	364.0	369.0	362.0	377.0	389.0	378.0	381.0	382.0
R	Arts, entertainment and recreation	39.0	41.0	40.0	41.0	43.0	45.0	46.0	46.0	48.0	47.0
S	Other service activities	52.0	55.0	56.0	55.0	53.0	52.0	52.0	52.0	54.0	53.0
T	Households as employers and own-use activities	7.0	8.0	8.0	8.0	8.0	8.0	8.0	8.0	10.0	9.0
U	Activities of extraterritorial organizations, bodies	1.0	1.0	1.0	1.0	1.0	0.0	1.0	1.0	1.0	1.0

Note: Detailed metadata:http://metalinks.oecd.org/lfs/20170518/87289
Disclaimer: http://oe.cd/disclaimer

FRANCE

Table 1. Labour force

Annual average estimates

	2006	2007	2008	2009	2010	2011	2012	2013	2014	2015
Civilian labour force, thousands										
All persons	28 079	28 242	28 220	28 421	28 509	28 702	28 978	29 177	29 297	..
Males	14 748	14 788	14 679	14 718	14 724	14 825	15 017	15 121	15 177	..
Females	13 331	13 454	13 541	13 703	13 785	13 877	13 961	14 056	14 120	..
Unemployed, thousands										
All persons	2 321	2 122	1 971	2 458	2 505	2 489	2 674	2 824	2 838	..
Males	1 143	1 062	987	1 281	1 288	1 262	1 406	1 492	1 518	..
Females	1 178	1 060	984	1 177	1 217	1 227	1 268	1 332	1 320	..
Civilian employment, thousands										
All persons	25 758	26 120	26 249	25 963	26 004	26 213	26 304	26 353	26 459	..
Males	13 605	13 726	13 692	13 437	13 436	13 563	13 611	13 629	13 660	..
Females	12 153	12 394	12 557	12 526	12 568	12 650	12 693	12 724	12 800	..
Civilian employment (%)										
All persons	100.0	100.0	100.0	100.0	100.0	100.0	100.0	100.0	100.0	..
Males	52.8	52.6	52.2	51.8	51.7	51.7	51.7	51.7	51.6	..
Females	47.2	47.4	47.8	48.2	48.3	48.3	48.3	48.3	48.4	..
Unemployment rate (% of civilian labour force)										
All persons	8.3	7.5	7.0	8.6	8.8	8.7	9.2	9.7	9.7	..
Males	7.8	7.2	6.7	8.7	8.7	8.5	9.4	9.9	10.0	..
Females	8.8	7.9	7.3	8.6	8.8	8.8	9.1	9.5	9.3	..
CIVIL. EMPL. - PROFESSIONAL STATUS, thousands										
All activities	**25 758**	**26 120**	**26 249**	**25 963**	**26 004**	**26 213**	**26 304**	**26 353**	**26 459**	**..**
Employees	23 433	23 775	23 886	23 585	23 561	23 674	23 677	23 624	23 659	..
Employers and persons working on own account	2 325	2 346	2 363	2 378	2 443	2 540	2 627	2 729	2 800	..
Unpaid family workers	0	0	0	0	0	0	..	..	..	..
Employees as % of civilian employment	**91.0**	**91.0**	**91.0**	**90.8**	**90.6**	**90.3**	**90.0**	**89.6**	**89.4**	**..**
Part-time employment (%)										
Part-time as % of employment	13.2	13.3	13.0	13.5	13.7	13.7	13.9	14.0	14.3	14.4
Male share of part time employment	20.2	19.5	20.1	20.1	21.9	22.6	22.5	23.0	24.4	24.8
Female share of part time employment	79.8	80.5	79.9	79.9	78.1	77.4	77.5	77.0	75.6	75.2
Male part-time as % of male employment	5.0	4.9	4.9	5.1	5.7	5.9	6.0	6.2	6.7	6.9
Female part-time as % of female employment	22.6	22.8	22.1	22.7	22.5	22.3	22.6	22.5	22.5	22.3
Duration of unemployment (% of total unemployment)										
Less than one month	13.1	13.7	14.3	12.8	12.2	11.9	12.3	4.9	4.6	4.4
More than 1 month and less than 3 months	16.6	17.8	19.6	18.9	17.1	17.2	17.4	18.0	16.0	15.8
More than 3 months and less than 6 months	10.3	11.1	11.5	12.9	11.1	11.1	11.1	17.6	16.5	16.3
More than 6 months and less than 1 year	18.5	17.7	17.6	20.6	19.7	18.7	19.2	19.1	18.7	19.2
More than 1 year	41.5	39.7	37.1	34.9	39.9	41.1	40.0	40.5	44.2	44.3

Note: Detailed metadata: http://metalinks.oecd.org/lfs/20170518/eef8a, http://metalinks.oecd.org/lfs/20170518/87289, http://metalinks.oecd.org/lfs/20170518/4a372 and http://metalinks.oecd.org/lfs/20170518/cb271.

Disclaimer: http://oe.cd/disclaimer

Table 2. Participation rates and unemployment rates by age and sex

Annual average estimates, percentage

	2006	2007	2008	2009	2010	2011	2012	2013	2014	2015
Participation rates										
Males										
15-19	19.5	20.6	19.3	19.1	19.6	17.9	17.4	17.2	16.8	16.2
20-24	65.8	64.5	66.1	67.4	65.9	65.0	64.3	64.7	65.4	66.8
25-34	94.4	94.6	94.7	94.6	94.4	93.6	93.1	93.5	93.3	92.5
35-44	95.8	95.7	96.0	95.9	95.3	95.1	95.1	94.7	94.8	94.4
45-54	92.0	92.1	92.5	92.4	92.9	92.4	92.4	91.8	91.3	91.2
55-59	61.3	61.5	61.8	65.2	68.8	72.1	76.6	77.6	77.8	78.7
60-64	15.9	17.3	18.9	20.1	20.0	21.1	24.7	26.5	27.3	30.2
15-24	42.0	41.9	42.2	42.9	42.6	41.3	40.8	40.8	40.5	40.5
25-54	94.1	94.1	94.4	94.3	94.2	93.7	93.6	93.3	93.1	92.7
55-64	42.7	42.5	42.4	44.0	45.0	46.8	50.8	52.3	53.1	55.1
65 and over	1.5	1.9	2.0	2.0	2.3	2.7	3.1	3.1	3.3	3.6
15-64	74.9	74.7	74.7	75.0	74.9	74.6	75.3	75.5	75.4	75.5
Females										
15-19	12.3	12.4	12.3	13.1	12.2	12.2	11.6	11.8	11.6	11.0
20-24	56.0	57.4	57.0	58.6	57.3	56.0	55.4	55.6	56.1	58.2
25-34	79.7	80.8	81.5	81.3	81.6	80.9	80.9	81.7	80.9	80.2
35-44	83.0	83.6	84.5	85.0	84.9	84.7	85.0	85.0	85.3	85.2
45-54	81.1	81.4	82.2	82.8	83.4	83.1	83.1	83.5	83.8	83.5
55-59	54.1	54.7	56.0	58.8	60.7	64.4	67.6	68.6	70.2	71.2
60-64	14.1	15.2	14.8	15.6	17.4	17.9	20.9	23.1	26.6	29.0
15-24	34.1	34.9	34.7	36.2	35.2	34.5	34.0	33.9	33.7	34.2
25-54	81.3	82.0	82.8	83.1	83.4	83.0	83.0	83.5	83.4	83.0
55-64	37.6	37.6	37.3	38.5	39.5	41.2	44.3	46.0	48.6	50.4
65 and over	0.7	0.9	1.0	0.9	1.0	1.4	1.7	1.7	1.7	1.9
15-64	64.5	64.9	65.2	65.7	65.8	65.7	66.3	66.9	67.4	67.6
All persons										
15-24	38.1	38.4	38.5	39.6	38.9	37.9	37.4	37.4	37.1	37.3
25-54	87.6	87.9	88.5	88.6	88.7	88.2	88.2	88.3	88.2	87.8
55-64	40.1	40.0	39.8	41.2	42.2	43.9	47.4	49.0	50.7	52.6
65 and over	1.1	1.3	1.4	1.4	1.5	1.9	2.3	2.3	2.4	2.7
15-64	69.6	69.7	69.9	70.3	70.3	70.1	70.7	71.1	71.4	71.5
Unemployment rates										
Males										
15-19	25.8	22.8	20.7	27.9	25.9	27.8	31.2	29.6	30.8	31.4
20-24	18.7	16.8	17.9	22.9	21.0	19.6	22.2	22.2	22.8	23.4
25-34	8.4	8.1	7.0	9.6	10.0	10.0	11.1	12.3	12.3	12.2
35-44	6.0	5.7	5.0	6.4	6.8	6.7	7.3	7.6	7.9	8.1
45-54	5.1	4.7	4.5	5.2	5.3	5.6	6.2	6.7	6.7	7.6
55-59	5.3	4.7	4.3	5.7	6.4	6.2	6.9	8.0	8.2	7.5
60-64	4.4	4.3	3.8	5.7	4.6	4.2	5.1	6.0	7.0	8.6
15-24	20.4	18.3	18.5	24.0	22.2	21.4	24.1	23.8	24.5	25.1
25-54	6.5	6.1	5.5	7.0	7.3	7.3	8.1	8.8	8.9	9.2
55-64	5.2	4.7	4.2	5.7	6.0	5.8	6.5	7.5	7.9	7.8
65 and over	0.8	1.4	3.1	3.6	2.3	0.9	1.0	2.6	2.5	2.1
15-64	7.9	7.3	6.7	8.7	8.7	8.6	9.5	10.1	10.3	10.6
Total	7.9	7.3	6.7	8.7	8.7	8.5	9.4	10.0	10.2	10.5
Females										
15-19	33.7	30.2	28.1	34.6	34.8	31.3	34.2	35.3	34.9	33.7
20-24	20.1	17.1	15.9	18.8	20.6	20.8	20.9	22.1	19.6	20.5
25-34	10.1	9.6	8.4	10.1	10.4	10.8	11.0	11.3	11.9	11.7
35-44	8.1	6.8	6.7	7.4	7.8	7.9	7.9	8.0	8.0	7.9
45-54	6.0	5.5	5.1	6.0	5.9	6.0	6.7	7.1	6.9	6.6
55-59	5.0	4.4	3.9	5.4	5.8	6.1	6.1	6.9	6.9	7.0
60-64	3.3	2.4	2.8	3.9	4.4	4.0	5.5	5.4	6.3	5.7
15-24	22.5	19.5	18.1	21.6	23.0	22.6	23.1	24.4	22.2	22.7
25-54	8.0	7.2	6.7	7.7	7.9	8.1	8.4	8.7	8.8	8.6
55-64	4.7	4.1	3.7	5.1	5.5	5.6	5.9	6.5	6.7	6.6
65 and over	2.2	1.4	1.8	2.3	2.6	1.6	1.8	2.7	2.9	1.8
15-64	9.1	8.1	7.5	8.8	9.1	9.2	9.4	9.8	9.7	9.6
Total	9.1	8.1	7.4	8.8	9.1	9.1	9.4	9.8	9.6	9.5
All persons										
15-24	21.3	18.8	18.3	22.9	22.6	21.9	23.7	24.1	23.5	24.0
25-54	7.2	6.6	6.0	7.3	7.6	7.7	8.2	8.7	8.8	8.9
55-64	5.0	4.4	4.0	5.4	5.8	5.7	6.2	7.0	7.3	7.2
65 and over	1.4	1.4	2.6	3.1	2.4	1.2	1.3	2.6	2.7	2.0
15-64	8.5	7.7	7.1	8.8	8.9	8.9	9.5	10.0	10.0	10.1

Note: Detailed metadata at:http://metalinks.oecd.org/lfs/20170518/6f97b
Disclaimer: http://oe.cd/disclaimer

FRANCE

Table 3. Civilian employment and employees: breakdown by activity - ISIC Rev. 4

Annual average estimates

		2006	2007	2008	2009	2010	2011	2012	2013	2014	2015
	CIVILIAN EMPLOYMENT										
	By activity, thousands										
A-U	**All activities**	..	..	..	..	..	..	..	..	..	..
A	Agriculture, hunting and forestry	..	..	..	..	..	..	..	..	..	..
B-F	**Industry**	..	..	..	..	..	..	..	..	..	..
B	Mining and quarrying	..	..	..	..	..	..	..	..	..	..
C	Manufacturing	..	..	..	..	..	..	..	..	..	..
D	Electricity, gas, steam, air cond. supply	..	..	..	..	..	..	..	..	..	..
E	Water supply, sewerage, waste mgt, remediation	..	..	..	..	..	..	..	..	..	..
F	Construction	..	..	..	..	..	..	..	..	..	..
G-U	**Services**	..	..	..	..	..	..	..	..	..	..
G	Wholesale, retail trade, vehicle, motorcycle repair	..	..	..	..	..	..	..	..	..	..
H	Transportation and storage	..	..	..	..	..	..	..	..	..	..
I	Accommodation and food service activities	..	..	..	..	..	..	..	..	..	..
J	Information and communication	..	..	..	..	..	..	..	..	..	..
K	Financial and insurance activities	..	..	..	..	..	..	..	..	..	..
L	Real estate activities	..	..	..	..	..	..	..	..	..	..
M	Professional, scientific and technical activities	..	..	..	..	..	..	..	..	..	..
N	Administrative and support service activities	..	..	..	..	..	..	..	..	..	..
O	Public administration, defence, social security	..	..	..	..	..	..	..	..	..	..
P	Education	..	..	..	..	..	..	..	..	..	..
Q	Human health and social work activities	..	..	..	..	..	..	..	..	..	..
R	Arts, entertainment and recreation	..	..	..	..	..	..	..	..	..	..
S	Other service activities	..	..	..	..	..	..	..	..	..	..
T	Households as employers and own-use activities	..	..	..	..	..	..	..	..	..	..
U	Activities of extraterritorial organizations, bodies	..	..	..	..	..	..	..	..	..	..
	EMPLOYEES										
	By activity, thousands										
A-U	**All activities**	**23 433.4**	**23 774.9**	**23 886.2**	**23 585.1**	**23 561.1**	**23 673.7**	**23 677.0**	**23 624.2**	**23 658.6**	..
A	Agriculture, hunting and forestry	251.0	242.4	231.5	225.8	223.1	223.5	227.4	231.4	237.2	..
B-F	**Industry**	**5 080.5**	**5 087.6**	**5 069.5**	**4 917.0**	**4 761.0**	**4 710.0**	**4 680.9**	**4 613.0**	**4 536.3**	..
B	Mining and quarrying	28.2	27.2	27.0	25.7	24.7	24.1	23.6	22.9	22.4	..
C	Manufacturing	3 320.4	3 266.5	3 208.4	3 075.5	2 946.5	2 906.5	2 883.9	2 839.4	2 793.7	..
D	Electricity, gas, steam, air cond. supply	166.3	164.4	161.8	164.6	164.6	163.8	166.1	167.9	170.1	..
E	Water supply, sewerage, waste mgt, remediation	162.8	167.0	169.8	170.4	171.8	173.4	175.0	176.1	174.6	..
F	Construction	1 402.7	1 462.5	1 502.5	1 480.7	1 453.4	1 442.2	1 432.4	1 406.8	1 375.5	..
G-U	**Services**	**18 101.9**	**18 444.8**	**18 585.2**	**18 442.3**	**18 576.9**	**18 740.2**	**18 768.7**	**18 779.8**	**18 885.1**	..
G	Wholesale, retail trade, vehicle, motorcycle repair	3 006.5	3 039.4	3 049.1	3 011.4	3 003.1	3 021.8	3 027.9	3 003.1	3 000.2	..
H	Transportation and storage	1 352.8	1 358.8	1 367.3	1 348.3	1 341.9	1 352.6	1 350.3	1 344.6	1 337.5	..
I	Accommodation and food service activities	898.4	921.2	926.1	920.9	945.0	966.8	977.5	974.1	976.3	..
J	Information and communication	663.5	678.8	694.3	693.4	688.1	696.3	703.6	706.9	707.1	..
K	Financial and insurance activities	802.2	823.0	829.6	826.9	825.2	834.0	840.0	839.3	841.7	..
L	Real estate activities	229.6	240.6	243.1	233.1	234.7	236.9	235.5	232.4	230.3	..
M	Professional, scientific and technical activities	1 172.7	1 205.7	1 232.4	1 231.0	1 238.9	1 273.8	1 292.7	1 301.7	1 320.2	..
N	Administrative and support service activities	1 615.7	1 683.9	1 669.3	1 523.6	1 605.9	1 661.0	1 623.0	1 609.1	1 625.1	..
O	Public administration, defence, social security	2 513.0	2 543.3	2 565.7	2 592.2	2 590.1	2 579.4	2 575.3	2 590.4	2 612.1	..
P	Education	1 642.0	1 633.5	1 598.9	1 570.6	1 560.3	1 545.4	1 535.8	1 557.2	1 582.4	..
Q	Human health and social work activities	2 972.8	3 041.9	3 112.1	3 169.1	3 208.8	3 246.0	3 287.7	3 326.3	3 359.6	..
R	Arts, entertainment and recreation	241.6	252.5	259.8	267.0	269.2	269.5	273.6	272.3	274.0	..
S	Other service activities	514.6	522.5	526.5	539.5	548.0	547.6	547.6	549.7	551.9	..
T	Households as employers and own-use activities	457.4	479.7	489.9	494.9	497.5	488.7	477.8	452.3	446.5	..
U	Activities of extraterritorial organizations, bodies	19.0	19.9	21.0	20.3	20.3	20.3	20.3	20.3	20.3	..

Note: Detailed metadata:http://metalinks.oecd.org/lfs/20170518/87289
Disclaimer: http://oe.cd/disclaimer

GERMANY

Table 1. Labour force

Annual average estimates

	2006	2007	2008	2009	2010	2011	2012	2013	2014	2015
Civilian labour force, thousands										
All persons	41 206	41 364	41 481	41 507	41 495	40 997	41 153	41 522	41 779	41 971
Males	22 471	22 472	22 535	22 472	22 412	21 963	22 081	22 206	22 331	22 414
Females	18 735	18 893	18 947	19 037	19 083	19 034	19 073	19 316	19 448	19 557
Unemployed, thousands										
All persons	4 257	3 601	3 136	3 228	2 946	2 399	2 222	2 179	2 088	1 947
Males	2 344	1 938	1 686	1 836	1 696	1 336	1 235	1 230	1 188	1 123
Females	1 913	1 663	1 450	1 393	1 249	1 063	987	949	900	824
Civilian employment, thousands										
All persons	36 949	37 763	38 345	38 279	38 549	38 598	38 931	39 343	39 691	40 024
Males	20 127	20 534	20 849	20 636	20 716	20 627	20 846	20 976	21 143	21 291
Females	16 822	17 230	17 497	17 644	17 834	17 971	18 086	18 367	18 548	18 733
Civilian employment (%)										
All persons	100.0	100.0	100.0	100.0	100.0	100.0	100.0	100.0	100.0	100.0
Males	54.5	54.4	54.4	53.9	53.7	53.4	53.5	53.3	53.3	53.2
Females	45.5	45.6	45.6	46.1	46.3	46.6	46.5	46.7	46.7	46.8
Unemployment rate (% of civilian labour force)										
All persons	10.3	8.7	7.6	7.8	7.1	5.9	5.4	5.2	5.0	4.6
Males	10.4	8.6	7.5	8.2	7.6	6.1	5.6	5.5	5.3	5.0
Females	10.2	8.8	7.7	7.3	6.5	5.6	5.2	4.9	4.6	4.2
CIVIL. EMPL. - PROFESSIONAL STATUS, thousands										
All activities	**36 949**	**37 763**	**38 346**	**38 279**	**38 549**	**38 598**	**38 932**	**39 343**	**39 691**	**40 025**
Employees	32 437	33 207	33 854	33 820	34 070	34 074	34 407	34 920	35 325	35 705
Employers and persons working on own account	4 131	4 160	4 143	4 215	4 258	4 295	4 314	4 235	4 190	4 160
Unpaid family workers	382	396	349	244	220	230	211	188	176	160
Employees as % of civilian employment	**87.8**	**87.9**	**88.3**	**88.4**	**88.4**	**88.3**	**88.4**	**88.8**	**89.0**	**89.2**
Part-time employment (%)										
Part-time as % of employment	21.8	22.0	21.8	21.9	21.8	22.3	22.2	22.6	22.3	22.4
Male share of part time employment	19.1	19.3	19.7	19.6	19.1	20.3	20.8	21.4	21.9	22.1
Female share of part time employment	80.9	80.7	80.3	80.4	80.9	79.7	79.2	78.6	78.1	77.9
Male part-time as % of male employment	7.6	7.8	7.9	7.9	7.8	8.4	8.6	9.0	9.1	9.3
Female part-time as % of female employment	39.0	39.1	38.5	38.3	38.2	38.3	38.0	38.1	37.5	37.4
Duration of unemployment (% of total unemployment)										
Less than one month	5.8	6.3	6.8	7.7	7.6	9.2	9.9	9.4	9.9	10.4
More than 1 month and less than 3 months	11.7	12.6	13.8	15.6	14.7	15.1	15.9	16.0	16.3	15.8
More than 3 months and less than 6 months	11.3	11.4	12.9	14.9	14.3	13.1	14.2	14.4	14.2	14.4
More than 6 months and less than 1 year	14.9	13.2	14.0	16.3	16.1	14.7	14.5	15.6	15.3	15.4
More than 1 year	56.4	56.6	52.5	45.5	47.3	47.9	45.4	44.7	44.3	44.0

Note: Detailed metadata: http://metalinks.oecd.org/lfs/20170518/c3c9c, http://metalinks.oecd.org/lfs/20170518/87289, http://metalinks.oecd.org/lfs/20170518/10f96 and http://metalinks.oecd.org/lfs/20170518/4642d.

Disclaimer: http://oe.cd/disclaimer

GERMANY

Table 2. Participation rates and unemployment rates by age and sex

Annual average estimates, percentage

	2006	2007	2008	2009	2010	2011	2012	2013	2014	2015
Participation rates										
Males										
15-19	33.9	35.0	35.7	34.7	33.6	33.1	31.0	31.2	30.9	29.4
20-24	74.2	74.7	74.9	74.3	73.2	73.9	72.1	71.8	70.9	70.3
25-34	91.0	91.0	90.7	90.6	90.7	90.8	90.8	90.6	90.2	90.0
35-44	96.3	96.2	96.0	95.6	95.6	95.5	95.4	95.2	95.0	94.5
45-54	93.1	93.2	92.9	92.8	92.6	93.0	92.9	92.8	92.5	92.8
55-59	82.2	82.9	83.6	84.1	84.8	85.6	85.7	85.9	86.3	86.1
60-64	42.5	45.3	46.8	50.8	53.7	56.2	58.9	61.8	63.3	62.7
15-24	54.0	54.9	55.6	55.2	54.7	55.2	53.2	52.9	52.1	50.5
25-54	93.8	93.8	93.5	93.2	93.1	93.2	93.1	92.9	92.6	92.5
55-64	63.7	65.8	67.2	69.3	70.7	71.8	73.1	74.5	75.5	75.3
65 and over	5.0	5.3	5.7	5.9	5.7	6.6	7.1	7.7	8.2	8.6
15-64	81.4	81.8	82.1	82.2	82.4	82.7	82.5	82.6	82.5	82.1
Females										
15-19	27.9	29.8	29.3	28.3	27.3	28.1	25.9	26.9	25.8	25.8
20-24	67.1	67.7	68.6	67.9	67.3	68.2	66.8	67.5	67.2	66.5
25-34	76.4	76.7	76.3	77.7	77.9	79.4	79.2	79.6	79.6	79.7
35-44	82.3	82.3	82.1	82.3	82.4	83.0	83.2	82.9	82.8	82.8
45-54	81.3	81.8	82.0	82.3	82.9	83.4	83.8	84.1	84.3	84.5
55-59	65.7	66.9	67.7	68.9	70.3	72.6	73.5	75.0	75.8	76.2
60-64	24.4	27.4	29.4	32.9	35.5	38.9	41.2	45.5	48.8	50.2
15-24	47.6	49.0	49.5	49.2	48.9	50.0	48.0	48.7	47.7	47.1
25-54	80.3	80.6	80.5	81.0	81.3	82.1	82.2	82.4	82.4	82.5
55-64	46.3	48.9	50.6	52.9	54.5	56.8	58.2	60.8	62.9	63.8
65 and over	2.3	2.5	2.6	2.7	2.8	3.1	3.3	3.6	3.9	4.1
15-64	68.5	69.4	69.7	70.4	70.8	71.9	71.9	72.6	72.9	73.1
All persons										
15-24	50.9	52.0	52.7	52.3	51.8	52.6	50.7	50.8	50.0	48.8
25-54	87.1	87.2	87.0	87.2	87.3	87.7	87.7	87.7	87.6	87.6
55-64	54.9	57.2	58.7	61.0	62.5	64.1	65.4	67.5	69.1	69.4
65 and over	3.5	3.7	4.0	4.1	4.0	4.6	5.0	5.4	5.8	6.1
15-64	75.0	75.6	75.9	76.4	76.6	77.3	77.2	77.6	77.7	77.6
Unemployment rates										
Males										
15-19	14.0	12.6	10.6	10.7	10.4	9.7	9.0	8.8	9.0	7.8
20-24	14.5	12.0	10.7	12.5	10.5	8.8	8.5	8.4	8.1	7.9
25-34	11.2	9.3	8.2	9.7	8.7	7.0	6.4	6.6	6.3	6.1
35-44	8.4	7.0	6.1	6.7	6.5	5.0	4.7	4.5	4.5	4.3
45-54	9.7	7.7	6.6	7.1	6.4	5.1	4.5	4.4	4.3	3.9
55-59	12.4	10.0	8.3	8.1	7.9	6.3	5.7	5.8	5.1	4.9
60-64	11.1	9.0	7.7	7.5	8.3	6.8	6.8	6.5	6.2	5.7
15-24	14.3	12.2	10.7	12.0	10.4	9.1	8.6	8.5	8.4	7.9
25-54	9.6	7.8	6.9	7.6	7.1	5.6	5.1	5.1	5.0	4.7
55-64	12.0	9.7	8.1	8.0	8.1	6.5	6.1	6.1	5.5	5.2
65 and over	0.6	1.1	1.0	1.2	0.7	0.9	0.8	0.9	0.8	0.8
15-64	10.5	8.6	7.5	8.2	7.6	6.1	5.7	5.6	5.4	5.1
Total	10.3	8.5	7.4	8.1	7.5	6.0	5.5	5.5	5.3	5.0
Females										
15-19	14.3	13.0	11.4	11.9	10.9	10.1	9.0	7.9	8.4	8.0
20-24	11.9	10.3	9.5	9.1	8.1	7.0	6.7	6.8	6.6	5.9
25-34	9.9	8.9	7.8	7.6	7.0	5.9	5.5	5.6	5.2	4.7
35-44	9.1	7.6	6.8	6.6	5.8	4.9	4.7	4.3	4.2	3.9
45-54	9.7	8.2	7.1	6.7	5.9	4.8	4.5	4.2	3.9	3.6
55-59	13.8	11.9	9.5	8.3	7.4	6.4	5.4	4.8	4.2	3.9
60-64	10.4	9.3	7.4	7.4	7.0	6.2	5.8	6.0	5.4	4.5
15-24	12.6	11.1	10.0	9.8	8.8	7.8	7.3	7.1	7.1	6.5
25-54	9.5	8.1	7.2	6.9	6.2	5.2	4.9	4.6	4.4	4.0
55-64	13.0	11.2	8.9	8.0	7.3	6.3	5.5	5.2	4.6	4.1
65 and over	1.4	0.9	0.8	0.8	0.8	0.7	1.3	0.9	0.6	0.8
15-64	10.3	8.9	7.7	7.4	6.6	5.7	5.2	5.0	4.7	4.3
Total	10.2	8.8	7.7	7.3	6.6	5.6	5.2	4.9	4.6	4.2
All persons										
15-24	13.6	11.7	10.4	11.0	9.7	8.5	8.0	7.8	7.8	7.2
25-54	9.6	8.0	7.0	7.3	6.6	5.4	5.0	4.9	4.7	4.4
55-64	12.4	10.3	8.5	8.0	7.7	6.4	5.9	5.7	5.1	4.7
65 and over	0.9	1.0	0.9	1.0	0.7	0.8	1.0	0.9	0.7	0.8
15-64	10.4	8.7	7.6	7.8	7.2	5.9	5.5	5.3	5.1	4.7

Note: Detailed metadata at:http://metalinks.oecd.org/lfs/20170518/6f97b

Disclaimer: http://oe.cd/disclaimer

GERMANY

Table 3. Civilian employment and employees: breakdown by activity - ISIC Rev. 4

Annual average estimates

		2006	2007	2008	2009	2010	2011	2012	2013	2014	2015
	CIVILIAN EMPLOYMENT										
	By activity, thousands										
A-U	**All activities**	..	..	..	**38 279.0**	**38 549.0**	**38 598.0**	**38 933.0**	**39 342.0**	**39 692.0**	**40 025.0**
A	Agriculture, hunting and forestry	..	..	..	647.0	633.0	638.0	611.0	572.0	570.0	560.0
B-F	**Industry**	..	..	..	**11 078.0**	**10 990.0**	**10 952.0**	**11 028.0**	**10 976.0**	**11 181.0**	**11 130.0**
B	Mining and quarrying	..	..	..	104.0	96.0	97.0	93.0	83.0	88.0	82.0
C	Manufacturing	..	..	..	7 848.0	7 747.0	7 694.0	7 715.0	7 645.0	7 806.0	7 757.0
D	Electricity, gas, steam, air cond. supply	..	..	..	335.0	350.0	362.0	377.0	354.0	335.0	341.0
E	Water supply, sewerage, waste mgt, remediation	..	..	..	225.0	211.0	222.0	220.0	210.0	221.0	227.0
F	Construction	..	..	..	2 566.0	2 586.0	2 577.0	2 623.0	2 684.0	2 731.0	2 723.0
G-U	**Services**	..	..	..	**26 554.0**	**26 926.0**	**27 008.0**	**27 294.0**	**27 794.0**	**27 941.0**	**28 335.0**
G	Wholesale, retail trade, vehicle, motorcycle repair	..	..	..	5 197.0	5 264.0	5 232.0	5 213.0	5 678.0	5 612.0	5 668.0
H	Transportation and storage	..	..	..	1 820.0	1 819.0	1 834.0	1 869.0	1 912.0	1 924.0	1 957.0
I	Accommodation and food service activities	..	..	..	1 489.0	1 488.0	1 473.0	1 504.0	1 509.0	1 527.0	1 548.0
J	Information and communication	..	..	..	1 225.0	1 233.0	1 238.0	1 279.0	1 152.0	1 164.0	1 198.0
K	Financial and insurance activities	..	..	..	1 323.0	1 321.0	1 289.0	1 290.0	1 277.0	1 274.0	1 247.0
L	Real estate activities	..	..	..	276.0	267.0	269.0	271.0	221.0	195.0	213.0
M	Professional, scientific and technical activities	..	..	..	1 904.0	1 923.0	2 008.0	1 986.0	2 139.0	2 166.0	2 222.0
N	Administrative and support service activities	..	..	..	1 935.0	2 028.0	2 038.0	2 066.0	1 928.0	1 953.0	2 020.0
O	Public administration, defence, social security	..	..	..	2 580.0	2 619.0	2 556.0	2 580.0	2 615.0	2 631.0	2 589.0
P	Education	..	..	..	2 370.0	2 371.0	2 419.0	2 471.0	2 544.0	2 593.0	2 637.0
Q	Human health and social work activities	..	..	..	4 527.0	4 685.0	4 766.0	4 871.0	4 855.0	4 968.0	5 104.0
R	Arts, entertainment and recreation	..	..	..	536.0	552.0	529.0	551.0	533.0	536.0	560.0
S	Other service activities	..	..	..	1 140.0	1 118.0	1 108.0	1 100.0	1 175.0	1 147.0	1 134.0
T	Households as employers and own-use activities	..	..	..	203.0	208.0	222.0	217.0	236.0	230.0	217.0
U	Activities of extraterritorial organizations, bodies	..	..	..	29.0	32.0	27.0	26.0	20.0	21.0	18.0
	EMPLOYEES										
	By activity, thousands										
A-U	**All activities**	..	..	..	**33 820.0**	**34 071.0**	**34 073.0**	**34 409.0**	**34 923.0**	**35 325.0**	**35 705.0**
A	Agriculture, hunting and forestry	..	..	..	291.0	291.0	290.0	282.0	271.0	272.0	281.0
B-F	**Industry**	..	..	..	**10 260.0**	**10 161.0**	**10 129.0**	**10 180.0**	**10 134.0**	**10 351.0**	**10 325.0**
B	Mining and quarrying	..	..	..	100.0	94.0	95.0	92.0	82.0	86.0	81.0
C	Manufacturing	..	..	..	7 526.0	7 422.0	7 380.0	7 394.0	7 324.0	7 496.0	7 455.0
D	Electricity, gas, steam, air cond. supply	..	..	..	329.0	343.0	355.0	365.0	346.0	328.0	333.0
E	Water supply, sewerage, waste mgt, remediation	..	..	..	219.0	203.0	212.0	210.0	202.0	212.0	218.0
F	Construction	..	..	..	2 086.0	2 099.0	2 087.0	2 119.0	2 180.0	2 229.0	2 238.0
G-U	**Services**	..	..	..	**23 269.0**	**23 619.0**	**23 654.0**	**23 947.0**	**24 518.0**	**24 702.0**	**25 099.0**
G	Wholesale, retail trade, vehicle, motorcycle repair	..	..	..	4 542.0	4 621.0	4 611.0	4 603.0	5 070.0	5 027.0	5 105.0
H	Transportation and storage	..	..	..	1 702.0	1 701.0	1 716.0	1 753.0	1 800.0	1 816.0	1 850.0
I	Accommodation and food service activities	..	..	..	1 222.0	1 226.0	1 219.0	1 254.0	1 270.0	1 287.0	1 311.0
J	Information and communication	..	..	..	1 032.0	1 041.0	1 040.0	1 073.0	963.0	980.0	1 015.0
K	Financial and insurance activities	..	..	..	1 164.0	1 168.0	1 142.0	1 148.0	1 141.0	1 132.0	1 105.0
L	Real estate activities	..	..	..	209.0	203.0	197.0	201.0	164.0	141.0	157.0
M	Professional, scientific and technical activities	..	..	..	1 341.0	1 333.0	1 388.0	1 373.0	1 540.0	1 570.0	1 632.0
N	Administrative and support service activities	..	..	..	1 685.0	1 776.0	1 778.0	1 808.0	1 654.0	1 695.0	1 750.0
O	Public administration, defence, social security	..	..	..	2 580.0	2 619.0	2 556.0	2 580.0	2 615.0	2 631.0	2 589.0
P	Education	..	..	..	2 210.0	2 217.0	2 248.0	2 293.0	2 365.0	2 410.0	2 448.0
Q	Human health and social work activities	..	..	..	4 107.0	4 258.0	4 325.0	4 427.0	4 430.0	4 526.0	4 647.0
R	Arts, entertainment and recreation	..	..	..	361.0	366.0	346.0	359.0	358.0	359.0	372.0
S	Other service activities	..	..	..	896.0	869.0	857.0	851.0	912.0	896.0	898.0
T	Households as employers and own-use activities	..	..	..	189.0	192.0	204.0	198.0	216.0	211.0	202.0
U	Activities of extraterritorial organizations, bodies	..	..	..	29.0	32.0	27.0	26.0	20.0	21.0	18.0

Note: Detailed metadata:http://metalinks.oecd.org/lfs/20170518/87289
Disclaimer: http://oe.cd/disclaimer

GREECE

Table 1. Labour force

Annual average estimates

	2006	2007	2008	2009	2010	2011	2012	2013	2014	2015
Civilian labour force, thousands										
All persons	4 972	4 981	5 004	5 040	5 041	4 940	4 893	4 863	4 819	4 806
Males	2 928	2 923	2 942	2 927	2 898	2 827	2 768	2 744	2 697	2 661
Females	2 044	2 058	2 062	2 113	2 144	2 113	2 125	2 119	2 122	2 144
Unemployed, thousands										
All persons	441	409	367	456	605	816	1 163	1 328	1 280	1 180
Males	165	146	139	189	274	391	580	667	634	573
Females	276	263	228	267	330	425	583	660	646	607
Civilian employment, thousands										
All persons	4 532	4 572	4 637	4 585	4 437	4 124	3 730	3 535	3 539	3 626
Males	2 763	2 778	2 803	2 739	2 623	2 436	2 187	2 076	2 062	2 088
Females	1 768	1 795	1 834	1 846	1 813	1 688	1 543	1 459	1 477	1 538
Civilian employment (%)										
All persons	100.0	100.0	100.0	100.0	100.0	100.0	100.0	100.0	100.0	100.0
Males	61.0	60.7	60.4	59.7	59.1	59.1	58.6	58.7	58.3	57.6
Females	39.0	39.3	39.6	40.3	40.9	40.9	41.4	41.3	41.7	42.4
Unemployment rate (% of civilian labour force)										
All persons	8.9	8.2	7.3	9.0	12.0	16.5	23.8	27.3	26.6	24.6
Males	5.6	5.0	4.7	6.4	9.5	13.8	21.0	24.3	23.5	21.5
Females	13.5	12.8	11.0	12.6	15.4	20.1	27.4	31.2	30.4	28.3
CIVIL. EMPL. - PROFESSIONAL STATUS, thousands										
All activities	**4 532**	**4 572**	**4 637**	**4 585**	**4 437**	**4 124**	**3 730**	**3 535**	**3 539**	**3 626**
Employees	2 903	2 947	3 028	2 977	2 877	2 636	2 367	2 231	2 285	2 349
Employers and persons working on own account	1 335	1 331	1 337	1 341	1 316	1 256	1 177	1 130	1 092	1 115
Unpaid family workers	294	294	271	266	244	232	186	174	161	161
Employees as % of civilian employment	**64.1**	**64.5**	**65.3**	**64.9**	**64.9**	**63.9**	**63.4**	**63.1**	**64.6**	**64.8**
Part-time employment (%)										
Part-time as % of employment	7.4	7.7	7.9	8.5	8.9	9.1	9.8	10.3	11.2	11.1
Male share of part time employment	33.0	32.3	32.3	32.0	33.7	36.6	36.3	37.7	39.2	38.1
Female share of part time employment	67.0	67.7	67.7	68.0	66.3	63.4	63.7	62.3	60.8	61.9
Male part-time as % of male employment	4.0	4.1	4.2	4.6	5.1	5.6	6.1	6.6	7.5	7.3
Female part-time as % of female employment	12.8	13.3	13.6	14.4	14.5	14.0	15.1	15.6	16.2	16.3
Duration of unemployment (% of total unemployment)										
Less than one month	3.9	5.6	6.6	7.2	6.4	5.1	4.0	3.1	2.5	2.8
More than 1 month and less than 3 months	9.5	13.7	15.6	17.8	15.3	13.5	9.7	6.9	6.1	5.9
More than 3 months and less than 6 months	14.7	14.9	14.7	16.6	15.8	14.4	11.7	9.2	7.5	7.2
More than 6 months and less than 1 year	17.8	16.0	15.9	18.0	17.9	17.7	15.5	13.7	10.3	10.9
More than 1 year	54.1	49.7	47.1	40.4	44.6	49.3	59.1	67.1	73.5	73.1

Note: Detailed metadata: http://metalinks.oecd.org/lfs/20170518/e04ed, http://metalinks.oecd.org/lfs/20170518/87289, http://metalinks.oecd.org/lfs/20170518/9f4f0 and http://metalinks.oecd.org/lfs/20170518/7b044.

Disclaimer: http://oe.cd/disclaimer

Table 2. Participation rates and unemployment rates by age and sex

Annual average estimates, percentage

	2006	2007	2008	2009	2010	2011	2012	2013	2014	2015
Participation rates										
Males										
15-19	12.4	11.5	10.4	10.7	9.1	8.6	9.4	8.8	7.2	5.5
20-24	56.2	54.9	54.9	55.2	56.3	55.8	53.8	55.2	52.6	49.5
25-34	94.2	94.1	93.9	93.9	93.7	92.9	92.9	93.3	92.9	91.7
35-44	97.1	97.1	97.0	96.8	96.5	96.2	96.3	96.3	96.2	96.5
45-54	92.6	92.1	91.9	92.3	92.1	91.1	91.2	90.7	90.0	90.7
55-59	74.2	76.0	76.5	74.3	74.9	74.3	72.9	71.7	70.9	72.4
60-64	45.0	44.2	45.5	45.5	44.4	40.3	37.5	37.2	36.2	37.6
15-24	35.8	34.4	34.0	33.9	33.0	31.7	31.2	31.6	30.0	27.7
25-54	94.7	94.6	94.4	94.4	94.2	93.5	93.6	93.6	93.1	93.1
55-64	61.1	60.9	61.0	60.2	60.2	57.3	55.2	55.0	53.4	54.9
65 and over	7.3	7.1	7.2	6.8	6.4	5.6	4.6	4.3	4.5	4.4
15-64	78.5	78.4	78.4	78.5	78.3	77.2	76.9	76.9	76.0	75.9
Females										
15-19	7.5	7.5	7.1	6.9	6.1	6.1	7.0	6.5	6.5	4.9
20-24	47.9	46.8	44.8	47.4	46.6	46.5	47.3	45.5	45.2	45.1
25-34	76.2	74.9	75.0	76.8	77.3	77.9	81.0	81.5	81.9	83.0
35-44	72.2	72.7	72.9	74.0	76.0	76.5	76.8	77.4	78.4	81.4
45-54	58.2	58.9	59.9	62.0	63.3	63.7	64.3	64.5	67.2	69.5
55-59	33.7	35.7	37.8	39.2	41.2	39.2	40.8	40.5	38.5	38.2
60-64	21.7	20.6	19.9	20.3	21.4	20.6	19.0	20.8	21.0	21.1
15-24	28.6	27.5	26.1	27.4	27.1	26.6	27.0	25.3	26.1	24.3
25-54	69.2	69.2	69.5	71.1	72.4	72.8	74.0	74.3	75.6	77.7
55-64	28.0	28.2	28.7	29.5	31.1	29.9	30.0	31.0	29.9	29.5
65 and over	2.0	2.1	2.0	2.2	2.1	2.0	1.4	1.4	1.5	2.1
15-64	55.0	54.8	55.0	56.5	57.5	57.5	58.3	58.3	59.0	59.9
All persons										
15-24	32.2	31.0	30.1	30.7	30.0	29.1	29.1	28.4	28.0	26.0
25-54	82.0	81.8	81.9	82.8	83.2	83.1	83.7	83.9	84.3	85.4
55-64	44.2	44.2	44.4	44.4	45.2	43.1	42.1	42.4	41.1	41.6
65 and over	4.3	4.3	4.3	4.2	4.0	3.6	2.8	2.7	2.8	3.1
15-64	66.7	66.5	66.7	67.4	67.8	67.3	67.5	67.5	67.4	67.8
Unemployment rates										
Males										
15-19	25.9	19.7	19.2	23.3	34.9	48.6	56.0	65.5	55.8	49.9
20-24	16.0	14.7	16.5	18.8	25.6	37.3	47.1	51.8	46.2	44.7
25-34	7.8	8.0	7.5	9.4	13.3	21.1	29.8	32.8	32.7	29.0
35-44	4.0	3.4	3.2	5.1	7.8	11.5	17.3	20.3	19.3	17.8
45-54	2.9	2.4	2.6	4.8	7.2	11.1	16.1	18.4	17.7	17.0
55-59	3.4	3.3	2.8	4.3	6.7	9.6	14.5	16.7	18.9	18.7
60-64	2.4	2.2	3.0	3.7	5.1	6.7	11.9	15.7	15.3	16.9
15-24	17.6	15.5	16.9	19.5	26.8	38.8	48.5	53.8	47.4	45.2
25-54	5.0	4.7	4.5	6.5	9.5	14.6	21.0	23.7	23.0	20.9
55-64	3.1	2.9	2.9	4.1	6.1	8.6	13.6	16.4	17.7	18.1
65 and over	0.9	1.1	1.1	0.9	1.4	1.7	4.3	10.4	12.4	12.3
15-64	5.8	5.3	5.2	7.1	10.2	15.4	21.8	24.7	23.8	21.9
Total	5.7	5.2	5.1	7.0	10.0	15.1	21.5	24.5	23.6	21.7
Females										
15-19	41.2	36.9	36.0	43.4	45.2	68.1	78.9	80.8	68.5	68.4
20-24	33.2	30.9	27.2	31.8	39.7	49.4	60.7	61.2	56.7	53.4
25-34	17.0	16.4	15.0	16.4	21.0	28.4	34.4	39.8	37.3	35.2
35-44	11.1	10.6	9.7	11.5	14.1	18.4	25.4	28.5	27.8	27.6
45-54	8.0	7.9	7.0	8.4	10.6	14.1	20.7	23.5	24.0	23.6
55-59	6.3	5.6	5.3	7.0	7.7	9.4	14.4	17.7	17.6	18.8
60-64	2.9	2.0	1.4	2.8	4.2	5.5	10.4	12.3	14.1	12.5
15-24	34.2	31.7	28.3	33.3	40.3	51.6	63.1	63.8	58.1	55.0
25-54	12.5	12.0	10.9	12.4	15.5	20.6	27.1	30.9	29.8	28.7
55-64	5.0	4.3	3.9	5.5	6.5	8.1	13.1	15.9	16.4	16.5
65 and over	2.0	1.1	0.2	0.7	1.3	4.6	4.8	5.7	6.7	6.3
15-64	13.9	13.0	11.6	13.4	16.5	21.7	28.4	31.6	30.4	29.1
Total	13.8	12.9	11.5	13.3	16.3	21.5	28.2	31.3	30.2	28.9
All persons										
15-24	25.0	22.7	21.9	25.7	33.0	44.7	55.3	58.3	52.4	49.8
25-54	8.2	7.8	7.2	9.0	12.1	17.2	23.7	26.9	26.0	24.4
55-64	3.7	3.4	3.2	4.6	6.2	8.4	13.5	16.2	17.2	17.5
65 and over	1.2	1.1	0.8	0.8	1.3	2.6	4.4	9.1	10.8	10.0
15-64	9.1	8.5	7.9	9.8	12.9	18.1	24.7	27.7	26.7	25.1

Note: Detailed metadata at:http://metalinks.oecd.org/lfs/20170518/6f97b
Disclaimer: http://oe.cd/disclaimer

GREECE

Table 3. Civilian employment and employees: breakdown by activity - ISIC Rev. 4

Annual average estimates

		2006	2007	2008	2009	2010	2011	2012	2013	2014	2015
	CIVILIAN EMPLOYMENT										
	By activity, thousands										
A-U	**All activities**	**..**	**..**	**4 637.3**	**4 584.6**	**4 436.5**	**4 124.2**	**3 729.9**	**3 535.0**	**3 539.1**	**3 625.5**
A	Agriculture, hunting and forestry	..	..	516.0	526.0	546.6	503.6	484.3	481.1	475.9	472.4
B-F	**Industry**	**..**	**..**	**1 031.2**	**965.7**	**883.2**	**729.3**	**615.0**	**552.3**	**531.8**	**538.8**
B	Mining and quarrying	..	..	17.7	13.8	13.0	10.1	9.9	10.7	11.5	9.5
C	Manufacturing	..	..	545.2	522.3	482.5	410.7	351.0	326.8	318.5	332.0
D	Electricity, gas, steam, air cond. supply	..	..	36.0	30.4	27.3	22.3	25.6	26.5	28.1	25.2
E	Water supply, sewerage, waste mgt, remediation	..	..	30.2	30.1	32.2	27.6	19.7	22.9	25.6	22.7
F	Construction	..	..	402.1	369.1	328.2	258.7	208.8	165.4	148.2	149.4
G-U	**Services**	**..**	**..**	**3 090.1**	**3 093.0**	**3 006.8**	**2 891.3**	**2 630.6**	**2 501.6**	**2 531.3**	**2 614.4**
G	Wholesale, retail trade, vehicle, motorcycle repair	..	..	845.1	841.2	806.0	770.3	671.0	639.0	624.5	657.3
H	Transportation and storage	..	..	217.2	221.2	203.7	202.7	177.1	172.4	173.1	169.6
I	Accommodation and food service activities	..	..	333.3	322.1	306.5	304.6	274.7	263.7	302.2	333.7
J	Information and communication	..	..	76.6	85.3	89.4	79.6	71.3	76.5	75.6	74.3
K	Financial and insurance activities	..	..	124.4	116.3	116.3	111.2	121.0	110.5	95.2	87.1
L	Real estate activities	..	..	9.3	8.8	6.5	4.5	6.3	2.3	2.3	6.1
M	Professional, scientific and technical activities	..	..	226.1	237.7	217.2	211.6	217.3	193.5	185.8	216.1
N	Administrative and support service activities	..	..	79.5	80.0	75.3	82.7	72.2	59.8	86.3	85.5
O	Public administration, defence, social security	..	..	384.1	380.7	373.3	360.6	315.9	323.0	314.3	304.9
P	Education	..	..	326.6	335.6	332.3	310.7	301.2	277.4	293.3	297.9
Q	Human health and social work activities	..	..	234.6	229.1	249.4	237.1	226.8	217.1	209.7	213.0
R	Arts, entertainment and recreation	..	..	60.0	56.8	49.3	48.1	40.9	40.6	48.3	42.1
S	Other service activities	..	..	96.9	88.5	88.1	87.2	75.1	70.9	71.8	77.2
T	Households as employers and own-use activities	..	..	74.7	88.5	91.9	78.5	57.6	53.4	47.7	47.5
U	Activities of extraterritorial organizations, bodies	..	..	1.8	1.1	1.5	2.0	2.2	1.4	1.3	2.1
	EMPLOYEES										
	By activity, thousands										
A-U	**All activities**	**..**	**..**	**3 028.4**	**2 977.2**	**2 877.1**	**2 635.9**	**2 366.6**	**2 231.0**	**2 285.3**	**2 349.4**
A	Agriculture, hunting and forestry	..	..	40.1	46.4	53.3	49.3	49.6	43.6	42.8	49.2
B-F	**Industry**	**..**	**..**	**772.4**	**713.6**	**642.0**	**526.7**	**429.2**	**379.9**	**388.0**	**388.2**
B	Mining and quarrying	..	..	16.1	12.4	11.9	8.3	8.8	9.7	10.6	8.6
C	Manufacturing	..	..	406.6	386.7	356.8	302.5	254.5	232.4	236.7	246.6
D	Electricity, gas, steam, air cond. supply	..	..	35.2	29.8	26.7	21.8	25.1	25.4	27.5	24.0
E	Water supply, sewerage, waste mgt, remediation	..	..	29.1	29.4	31.5	26.5	19.6	21.8	25.0	22.0
F	Construction	..	..	285.4	255.3	215.2	167.7	121.2	90.6	88.3	86.9
G-U	**Services**	**..**	**..**	**2 215.9**	**2 217.2**	**2 181.8**	**2 059.9**	**1 887.8**	**1 807.5**	**1 854.4**	**1 912.0**
G	Wholesale, retail trade, vehicle, motorcycle repair	..	..	451.1	452.8	456.2	432.8	379.4	366.7	364.5	392.4
H	Transportation and storage	..	..	156.1	154.6	143.8	138.2	119.0	116.4	118.8	119.2
I	Accommodation and food service activities	..	..	197.5	196.7	184.3	176.0	162.5	156.4	200.4	221.0
J	Information and communication	..	..	69.5	75.9	81.2	70.5	62.8	68.8	65.8	67.3
K	Financial and insurance activities	..	..	111.9	104.5	105.0	99.3	107.0	97.9	82.2	73.5
L	Real estate activities	..	..	1.6	1.4	1.2	0.7	1.9	0.0	0.2	2.5
M	Professional, scientific and technical activities	..	..	106.7	111.3	93.1	80.5	83.6	83.8	78.9	94.6
N	Administrative and support service activities	..	..	65.7	64.6	60.0	65.9	61.2	47.6	74.0	70.2
O	Public administration, defence, social security	..	..	384.1	380.7	373.3	360.6	315.9	323.0	314.3	304.9
P	Education	..	..	301.2	308.1	304.2	285.0	280.1	255.1	269.0	274.4
Q	Human health and social work activities	..	..	199.9	195.4	211.8	195.7	191.3	175.3	166.4	168.1
R	Arts, entertainment and recreation	..	..	44.2	40.7	33.1	31.2	27.1	30.1	33.5	32.2
S	Other service activities	..	..	55.4	47.5	46.2	46.7	39.8	37.6	42.3	44.9
T	Households as employers and own-use activities	..	..	69.4	82.0	87.0	74.6	53.7	47.3	43.2	45.1
U	Activities of extraterritorial organizations, bodies	..	..	1.8	1.1	1.5	2.0	2.2	1.4	1.1	1.7

Note: Detailed metadata:http://metalinks.oecd.org/lfs/20170518/87289
Disclaimer: http://oe.cd/disclaimer

HUNGARY

Table 1. Labour force

Annual average estimates

	2006	2007	2008	2009	2010	2011	2012	2013	2014	2015
Civilian labour force, thousands										
All persons	4 203	4 177	4 139	4 137	4 175	4 206	4 282	4 315	4 425	4 502
Males	2 267	2 261	2 238	2 234	2 234	2 257	2 296	2 327	2 386	2 432
Females	1 935	1 916	1 902	1 903	1 941	1 949	1 986	1 988	2 039	2 070
Unemployed, thousands										
All persons	318	312	326	418	469	466	473	441	343	308
Males	165	164	174	232	262	252	262	239	182	162
Females	154	149	153	186	208	215	211	202	162	146
Civilian employment, thousands										
All persons	3 885	3 866	3 814	3 720	3 706	3 741	3 810	3 874	4 083	4 194
Males	2 103	2 099	2 065	2 002	1 972	2 005	2 035	2 088	2 205	2 270
Females	1 782	1 767	1 749	1 717	1 734	1 735	1 775	1 786	1 878	1 924
Civilian employment (%)										
All persons	100.0	100.0	100.0	100.0	100.0	100.0	100.0	100.0	100.0	100.0
Males	54.1	54.3	54.1	53.8	53.2	53.6	53.4	53.9	54.0	54.1
Females	45.9	45.7	45.9	46.2	46.8	46.4	46.6	46.1	46.0	45.9
Unemployment rate (% of civilian labour force)										
All persons	7.6	7.5	7.9	10.1	11.2	11.1	11.0	10.2	7.8	6.8
Males	7.3	7.2	7.8	10.4	11.7	11.1	11.4	10.3	7.6	6.7
Females	7.9	7.8	8.0	9.8	10.7	11.0	10.6	10.2	7.9	7.0
CIVIL. EMPL. - PROFESSIONAL STATUS, thousands										
All activities	**3 885**	**3 866**	**3 814**	**3 720**	**3 706**	**3 741**	**3 810**	**3 874**	**4 083**	**4 194**
Employees	3 386	3 379	3 344	3 247	3 247	3 284	3 361	3 435	3 634	3 737
Employers and persons working on own account	480	469	457	458	447	441	434	426	436	445
Unpaid family workers	20	18	13	15	12	16	15	13	13	11
Employees as % of civilian employment	**87.1**	**87.4**	**87.7**	**87.3**	**87.6**	**87.8**	**88.2**	**88.7**	**89.0**	**89.1**
Part-time employment (%)										
Part-time as % of employment	2.9	3.1	3.4	3.8	4.0	5.2	5.2	4.9	4.5	4.4
Male share of part time employment	29.4	31.4	35.3	35.5	34.3	38.8	35.1	37.5	37.2	36.4
Female share of part time employment	70.6	68.6	64.7	64.5	65.7	61.2	64.9	62.5	62.8	63.6
Male part-time as % of male employment	1.6	1.8	2.3	2.6	2.6	3.9	3.5	3.5	3.2	3.0
Female part-time as % of female employment	4.4	4.5	4.6	5.2	5.4	6.7	7.0	6.5	6.0	6.0
Duration of unemployment (% of total unemployment)										
Less than one month	4.6	4.8	4.7	4.8	3.8	6.4	8.6	11.6	11.3	11.1
More than 1 month and less than 3 months	10.8	11.5	11.5	11.7	9.5	10.8	9.1	7.7	8.7	9.9
More than 3 months and less than 6 months	16.2	14.6	14.7	16.9	13.7	14.1	13.3	11.4	11.7	12.4
More than 6 months and less than 1 year	22.1	21.6	21.8	24.2	22.8	19.8	22.5	19.6	19.4	19.9
More than 1 year	46.3	47.5	47.3	42.4	50.3	48.8	46.6	49.8	48.9	46.7

Note: Detailed metadata: http://metalinks.oecd.org/lfs/20170518/90a8c, http://metalinks.oecd.org/lfs/20170518/87289, http://metalinks.oecd.org/lfs/20170518/e23e2 and http://metalinks.oecd.org/lfs/20170518/e98e5.

Disclaimer: http://oe.cd/disclaimer

HUNGARY

Table 2. Participation rates and unemployment rates by age and sex

Annual average estimates, percentage

	2006	2007	2008	2009	2010	2011	2012	2013	2014	2015
Participation rates										
Males										
15-19	6.6	5.7	5.6	4.8	4.3	4.1	4.7	5.8	6.5	8.2
20-24	52.6	52.1	50.6	49.5	49.5	48.5	49.1	53.0	55.6	56.2
25-34	91.4	91.0	90.9	90.2	89.9	90.3	91.2	90.4	92.4	92.0
35-44	89.5	90.2	90.3	90.3	90.5	91.0	92.0	92.5	94.2	94.8
45-54	79.0	79.6	80.0	79.8	80.6	82.4	84.1	84.7	86.0	88.3
55-59	61.3	60.6	57.9	60.6	62.2	64.0	67.4	71.4	75.0	77.9
60-64	19.2	18.4	16.8	17.3	17.2	18.4	18.4	22.6	29.6	38.2
15-24	30.2	29.5	28.7	27.7	27.5	27.0	27.9	31.0	33.0	34.4
25-54	86.9	87.2	87.3	87.1	87.3	88.2	89.4	89.5	91.2	92.0
55-64	43.0	42.1	39.8	41.5	42.2	43.7	45.4	49.0	53.2	57.8
65 and over	4.3	4.7	4.8	5.0	4.7	5.4	5.3	4.9	4.5	4.7
15-64	68.9	68.6	68.0	67.7	67.8	68.4	69.6	71.0	73.4	75.3
Females										
15-19	3.9	3.1	3.0	3.0	3.1	2.6	2.8	3.7	4.6	4.9
20-24	41.2	39.3	38.8	38.8	39.6	39.2	42.2	41.1	43.9	46.2
25-34	67.4	67.0	65.9	65.3	66.1	66.0	67.9	69.2	70.4	70.7
35-44	77.1	77.4	77.9	78.4	78.5	77.7	79.1	79.0	80.9	81.2
45-54	75.6	75.8	76.5	77.2	79.1	79.5	82.2	82.7	84.5	86.1
55-59	44.0	41.9	40.9	43.7	50.5	54.7	54.3	55.7	60.5	63.2
60-64	8.9	9.6	10.1	10.1	10.0	11.7	11.8	11.8	14.1	18.6
15-24	23.2	21.8	21.5	21.5	22.0	21.5	23.4	23.6	25.9	27.5
25-54	73.2	73.2	73.3	73.6	74.6	74.4	76.4	77.1	78.8	79.6
55-64	27.7	26.9	26.6	28.1	31.7	34.8	34.5	34.7	37.4	39.9
65 and over	1.7	2.3	2.3	2.2	2.4	2.7	2.7	2.5	2.3	2.7
15-64	55.5	54.9	54.7	55.0	56.3	56.6	58.0	58.6	60.7	62.2
All persons										
15-24	26.7	25.7	25.1	24.7	24.8	24.3	25.7	27.4	29.5	31.0
25-54	79.9	80.1	80.3	80.3	80.9	81.3	82.9	83.3	85.0	85.8
55-64	34.5	33.7	32.6	34.1	36.5	38.8	39.5	41.2	44.6	48.1
65 and over	2.7	3.2	3.3	3.3	3.4	3.8	3.8	3.5	3.2	3.5
15-64	62.0	61.6	61.2	61.2	61.9	62.4	63.7	64.7	67.0	68.6
Unemployment rates										
Males										
15-19	38.2	35.6	37.6	49.0	49.6	43.0	53.4	51.2	40.9	28.2
20-24	16.3	15.5	16.9	25.9	26.0	25.7	27.0	23.1	17.9	17.1
25-34	7.2	7.2	7.6	10.3	12.3	10.1	12.1	10.8	7.6	6.8
35-44	6.2	5.8	6.6	8.7	9.7	9.8	9.3	8.1	5.9	4.6
45-54	5.4	6.2	6.5	8.5	9.9	9.8	9.4	8.4	6.2	5.7
55-59	4.6	5.4	5.9	7.4	9.4	11.1	9.1	9.0	5.9	5.1
60-64	2.0	2.0	2.1	3.3	4.4	5.3	7.3	6.9	9.0	7.6
15-24	18.7	17.4	18.9	27.8	27.8	27.0	29.1	25.6	20.0	18.3
25-54	6.4	6.5	7.0	9.2	10.7	9.9	10.3	9.1	6.5	5.6
55-64	4.1	4.8	5.2	6.6	8.5	10.0	8.8	8.6	6.7	6.0
65 and over	1.3	0.6	0.6	0.0	0.6	0.5	1.0	1.0	2.2	3.3
15-64	7.2	7.2	7.7	10.4	11.7	11.2	11.4	10.3	7.6	6.6
Total	7.1	7.1	7.7	10.3	11.6	11.1	11.3	10.2	7.6	6.6
Females										
15-19	36.2	35.9	37.9	50.6	39.3	43.8	48.7	54.1	34.8	40.6
20-24	18.4	17.6	19.1	22.7	23.5	23.5	25.8	25.8	19.7	13.8
25-34	8.3	8.6	8.5	10.7	11.9	11.4	11.3	10.4	9.5	8.4
35-44	7.8	7.7	7.2	8.5	9.7	10.0	9.0	9.0	7.0	6.5
45-54	6.1	5.7	6.5	8.1	9.0	10.2	9.2	8.3	5.5	5.2
55-59	3.7	4.4	5.4	6.8	7.7	8.8	8.6	7.7	6.2	5.1
60-64	5.0	1.6	3.6	3.8	4.3	5.6	5.2	6.2	5.1	7.0
15-24	19.8	18.9	20.4	24.6	24.6	24.7	27.1	27.9	20.9	16.0
25-54	7.4	7.3	7.4	9.0	10.1	10.4	9.7	9.2	7.2	6.6
55-64	3.9	3.9	5.1	6.3	7.2	8.3	8.0	7.5	6.0	5.5
65 and over	1.1	0.8	2.3	2.4	0.0	1.4	5.3	3.6	2.2	1.4
15-64	7.9	7.8	8.0	9.8	10.7	11.1	10.7	10.2	8.0	7.1
Total	7.9	7.7	8.0	9.7	10.7	11.0	10.6	10.1	7.9	7.0
All persons										
15-24	19.2	18.0	19.5	26.4	26.4	26.0	28.2	26.6	20.4	17.3
25-54	6.8	6.9	7.2	9.1	10.4	10.2	10.0	9.1	6.8	6.0
55-64	4.0	4.4	5.1	6.5	7.9	9.2	8.4	8.1	6.4	5.8
65 and over	1.2	0.7	1.3	1.0	0.3	0.9	2.8	2.1	2.2	2.5
15-64	7.5	7.5	7.9	10.1	11.3	11.1	11.1	10.2	7.8	6.8

Note: Detailed metadata at:http://metalinks.oecd.org/lfs/20170518/6f97b
Disclaimer: http://oe.cd/disclaimer

Table 3. Civilian employment and employees: breakdown by activity - ISIC Rev. 4

Annual average estimates

		2006	2007	2008	2009	2010	2011	2012	2013	2014	2015
	CIVILIAN EMPLOYMENT										
	By activity, thousands										
A-U	**All activities**	..	..	**3 813.7**	**3 719.5**	**3 706.4**	**3 740.8**	**3 810.1**	**3 874.2**	**4 066.7**	**4 187.3**
A	Agriculture, hunting and forestry	..	..	168.1	174.9	172.8	184.6	192.7	184.6	189.6	203.2
B-F	**Industry**	..	..	**1 239.8**	**1 167.4**	**1 147.2**	**1 161.3**	**1 140.8**	**1 165.1**	**1 249.3**	**1 273.2**
B	Mining and quarrying	..	..	8.5	8.7	11.3	11.1	9.1	7.5	9.3	9.1
C	Manufacturing	..	..	841.6	786.0	777.7	800.0	789.2	819.3	888.7	901.7
D	Electricity, gas, steam, air cond. supply	..	..	33.9	38.5	37.4	38.0	35.9	31.4	37.0	34.1
E	Water supply, sewerage, waste mgt, remediation	..	..	47.5	46.3	47.3	51.5	63.4	61.4	55.9	56.5
F	Construction	..	..	308.3	287.9	273.5	260.7	243.2	245.5	258.4	271.9
G-U	**Services**	..	..	**2 405.8**	**2 377.2**	**2 386.4**	**2 394.9**	**2 476.6**	**2 524.5**	**2 627.8**	**2 710.9**
G	Wholesale, retail trade, vehicle, motorcycle repair	..	..	571.8	540.3	530.6	534.7	539.3	528.6	548.2	539.4
H	Transportation and storage	..	..	258.0	251.9	254.2	255.0	258.5	259.5	258.7	268.6
I	Accommodation and food service activities	..	..	157.7	151.3	149.1	157.5	161.8	158.0	168.1	183.3
J	Information and communication	..	..	95.5	89.7	94.4	89.8	102.0	111.0	102.8	102.6
K	Financial and insurance activities	..	..	93.5	95.8	90.6	90.7	91.6	96.1	95.2	87.4
L	Real estate activities	..	..	20.3	20.2	20.8	21.8	23.1	20.6	20.2	18.8
M	Professional, scientific and technical activities	..	..	145.1	136.9	135.3	134.1	131.0	148.8	151.6	156.9
N	Administrative and support service activities	..	..	104.1	113.8	107.6	110.3	131.0	136.6	146.1	153.3
O	Public administration, defence, social security	..	..	252.4	278.1	293.8	290.4	305.7	348.1	384.7	430.7
P	Education	..	..	309.3	315.6	318.2	317.4	315.5	309.2	323.1	318.3
Q	Human health and social work activities	..	..	243.2	238.6	247.7	251.1	263.8	261.5	267.0	269.3
R	Arts, entertainment and recreation	..	..	64.1	57.7	58.1	59.9	63.1	56.1	63.0	79.7
S	Other service activities	..	..	87.8	84.4	81.9	78.3	85.2	83.3	94.0	96.5
T	Households as employers and own-use activities	..	..	2.2	3.0	3.2	2.3	2.7	3.7	3.8	4.5
U	Activities of extraterritorial organizations, bodies	..	..	0.6	0.0	0.9	1.6	2.3	3.4	1.3	1.5
	EMPLOYEES										
	By activity, thousands										
A-U	**All activities**	..	..	**3 343.8**	**3 246.6**	**3 246.8**	**3 283.9**	**3 360.6**	**3 435.4**	**3 618.2**	**3 730.6**
A	Agriculture, hunting and forestry	..	..	114.0	114.2	115.1	128.5	130.0	122.6	125.8	137.6
B-F	**Industry**	..	..	**1 133.8**	**1 063.6**	**1 045.1**	**1 063.5**	**1 050.9**	**1 074.7**	**1 156.5**	**1 176.2**
B	Mining and quarrying	..	..	8.0	8.1	11.0	10.6	8.2	7.3	9.2	9.0
C	Manufacturing	..	..	800.5	744.2	735.2	761.1	753.6	779.3	848.3	860.2
D	Electricity, gas, steam, air cond. supply	..	..	33.7	38.1	36.9	37.7	35.5	30.8	36.7	34.1
E	Water supply, sewerage, waste mgt, remediation	..	..	46.7	45.2	46.3	50.4	62.3	60.2	54.1	55.0
F	Construction	..	..	244.9	228.0	215.7	203.7	191.3	197.1	208.2	217.9
G-U	**Services**	..	..	**2 096.0**	**2 068.8**	**2 086.6**	**2 091.9**	**2 179.7**	**2 238.1**	**2 335.9**	**2 416.9**
G	Wholesale, retail trade, vehicle, motorcycle repair	..	..	469.2	441.2	437.6	445.9	446.3	442.4	461.3	459.9
H	Transportation and storage	..	..	234.6	228.0	231.2	228.8	234.5	237.9	238.5	245.2
I	Accommodation and food service activities	..	..	134.8	126.5	125.1	133.5	138.8	138.0	147.8	163.4
J	Information and communication	..	..	80.7	74.1	78.1	74.3	85.5	89.9	87.3	88.8
K	Financial and insurance activities	..	..	80.0	81.9	79.3	77.9	80.8	85.4	83.5	77.2
L	Real estate activities	..	..	16.0	16.0	15.5	16.6	18.0	16.7	15.2	16.3
M	Professional, scientific and technical activities	..	..	96.8	89.5	90.1	84.5	88.5	100.4	99.8	100.6
N	Administrative and support service activities	..	..	91.5	99.6	94.1	96.0	114.7	122.8	129.7	135.8
O	Public administration, defence, social security	..	..	251.3	277.8	292.3	287.9	304.2	347.2	383.6	429.6
P	Education	..	..	302.7	307.7	308.0	310.1	310.6	303.0	315.9	311.6
Q	Human health and social work activities	..	..	228.5	225.7	234.6	235.0	247.8	247.4	253.9	254.6
R	Arts, entertainment and recreation	..	..	53.5	48.9	47.2	49.7	52.0	46.1	54.5	68.9
S	Other service activities	..	..	53.8	49.0	49.5	48.0	53.2	53.8	60.0	59.3
T	Households as employers and own-use activities	..	..	2.0	3.0	3.1	2.2	2.6	3.7	3.6	4.4
U	Activities of extraterritorial organizations, bodies	..	..	0.6	0.0	0.9	1.5	2.2	3.4	1.3	1.3

Note: Detailed metadata:http://metalinks.oecd.org/lfs/20170518/87289
Disclaimer: http://oe.cd/disclaimer

ICELAND

Table 1. Labour force

Annual average estimates

	2006	2007	2008	2009	2010	2011	2012	2013	2014	2015
Civilian labour force, thousands										
All persons	175	181	184	181	181	180	180	185	187	191
Males	95	99	100	97	95	94	94	97	98	100
Females	80	83	84	84	86	86	86	88	89	91
Unemployed, thousands										
All persons	5	4	6	13	14	13	11	10	9	8
Males	3	2	3	8	8	7	6	5	5	4
Females	2	2	2	5	6	5	5	4	4	4
Civilian employment, thousands										
All persons	170	177	179	168	167	167	169	175	178	184
Males	92	97	97	88	87	87	88	91	93	96
Females	78	81	81	80	80	80	81	84	85	88
Civilian employment (%)										
All persons	100.0	100.0	100.0	100.0	100.0	100.0	100.0	100.0	100.0	100.0
Males	54.3	54.5	54.4	52.6	52.1	52.0	52.0	52.1	52.2	52.3
Females	45.7	45.5	45.6	47.4	47.9	48.0	48.0	47.9	47.8	47.7
Unemployment rate (% of civilian labour force)										
All persons	2.9	2.3	3.0	7.2	7.6	7.1	6.0	5.4	5.0	4.0
Males	2.7	2.3	3.3	8.6	8.3	7.8	6.4	5.7	5.1	3.9
Females	3.1	2.3	2.6	5.7	6.7	6.2	5.7	5.1	4.9	4.1
CIVIL. EMPL. - PROFESSIONAL STATUS, thousands										
All activities	**170**	**177**	**179**	**168**	**167**	**167**	**169**	**175**	**178**	**184**
Employees	145	153	156	148	146	146	148	153	155	161
Employers and persons working on own account	25	24	22	20	21	21	20	22	22	22
Unpaid family workers	0	0	0	0	0	0	1	1	1	1
Employees as % of civilian employment	**85.2**	**86.2**	**87.3**	**87.8**	**87.1**	**87.2**	**87.4**	**87.3**	**87.4**	**87.5**
Part-time employment (%)										
Part-time as % of employment	16.0	15.9	15.1	17.5	18.4	17.0	17.3	17.4	16.7	17.2
Male share of part time employment	25.8	27.3	28.8	30.0	32.4	32.0	34.2	32.5	33.8	34.4
Female share of part time employment	74.2	72.7	71.2	70.0	67.6	68.0	65.8	67.5	66.2	65.6
Male part-time as % of male employment	7.6	8.0	8.0	10.0	11.4	10.4	11.4	10.9	10.8	11.3
Female part-time as % of female employment	26.0	25.4	23.6	25.8	25.9	24.1	23.7	24.6	23.2	23.7
Duration of unemployment (% of total unemployment)										
Less than one month	58.2	56.9	43.3	19.5	16.1	18.6	20.9	21.6	26.7	31.3
More than 1 month and less than 3 months	19.0	24.7	38.1	30.1	23.0	21.2	20.1	26.6	22.3	24.7
More than 3 months and less than 6 months	9.1	7.3	11.2	25.8	18.4	19.0	18.2	17.6	19.7	15.9
More than 6 months and less than 1 year	6.3	3.1	3.4	17.6	21.2	13.4	12.8	12.2	17.7	11.9
More than 1 year	7.3	8.0	4.1	6.9	21.3	27.8	27.9	21.9	13.6	16.1

Note: Detailed metadata: http://metalinks.oecd.org/lfs/20170518/e100c, http://metalinks.oecd.org/lfs/20170518/87289, http://metalinks.oecd.org/lfs/20170518/ea991 and http://metalinks.oecd.org/lfs/20170518/7374a.

Disclaimer: http://oe.cd/disclaimer

Table 2. Participation rates and unemployment rates by age and sex

Annual average estimates, percentage

	2006	2007	2008	2009	2010	2011	2012	2013	2014	2015
Participation rates										
Males										
15-19	74.4	74.4	70.9	61.1	64.1	65.2	65.7	67.8	69.3	70.9
20-24	80.2	84.9	82.9	79.1	78.1	78.1	80.6	81.5	82.1	82.9
25-34	94.5	93.8	93.9	90.6	91.0	90.6	89.7	91.6	88.5	91.9
35-44	96.3	95.9	96.1	95.4	95.3	94.8	94.4	93.2	95.5	96.5
45-54	96.7	96.2	95.0	95.2	94.0	92.9	93.0	93.6	94.9	93.4
55-59	92.9	92.7	95.1	92.4	91.5	92.3	90.4	93.0	92.8	95.0
60-64	87.5	87.6	85.6	85.5	84.7	84.5	82.9	86.6	87.4	87.5
15-24	77.6	80.0	77.4	70.7	71.7	72.3	74.0	75.5	76.6	77.7
25-54	95.8	95.3	95.0	93.7	93.4	92.7	92.3	92.8	92.9	93.9
55-64	90.6	90.4	90.9	89.3	88.4	88.7	86.9	90.0	90.3	91.5
65 and over	46.0	39.8	41.9	42.8	45.0	42.7	40.8	42.5	46.5	48.3
15-64	91.4	91.6	90.9	88.4	88.2	87.8	87.6	88.8	89.1	90.3
Females										
15-19	81.2	81.3	79.3	74.8	74.8	74.1	75.1	82.5	74.0	78.6
20-24	82.1	79.1	80.4	77.4	77.9	77.3	82.0	82.4	81.6	83.6
25-34	83.1	81.4	80.2	79.0	78.7	81.0	82.1	83.4	83.4	84.0
35-44	85.0	88.4	85.3	87.0	90.0	86.6	87.5	87.9	87.8	87.8
45-54	88.8	86.5	87.7	88.4	87.6	88.2	88.5	88.4	87.8	90.6
55-59	88.6	87.1	85.4	87.5	85.4	84.1	80.9	80.2	85.2	83.1
60-64	73.0	72.7	69.2	66.7	73.0	74.1	75.9	76.6	80.9	82.9
15-24	81.7	80.1	79.9	76.2	76.5	75.9	78.8	82.5	78.4	81.5
25-54	85.6	85.4	84.4	84.7	85.3	85.2	86.1	86.6	86.3	87.5
55-64	81.7	80.7	78.1	78.1	79.8	79.5	78.6	78.5	83.3	83.0
65 and over	21.5	27.7	29.2	27.7	27.8	25.9	27.2	28.2	27.5	29.6
15-64	84.2	83.6	82.5	82.0	82.7	82.4	83.3	84.3	84.2	85.5
All persons										
15-24	79.5	80.1	78.6	73.4	74.0	74.1	76.3	78.9	77.5	79.5
25-54	90.9	90.6	89.9	89.3	89.4	89.0	89.2	89.7	89.6	90.7
55-64	86.3	85.7	84.7	83.8	84.2	84.1	82.8	84.3	86.8	87.3
65 and over	33.3	33.5	35.4	35.0	36.2	34.1	34.0	35.3	36.9	38.9
15-64	88.0	87.8	86.9	85.3	85.5	85.2	85.5	86.6	86.7	87.9
Unemployment rates										
Males										
15-19	14.9	12.6	13.2	21.5	21.2	22.7	20.2	19.5	17.4	15.0
20-24	4.7	4.4	5.9	18.9	16.4	15.5	11.1	9.9	10.4	7.9
25-34	2.0	1.6	3.1	11.0	11.4	7.9	7.2	5.7	5.1	3.1
35-44	1.4	0.9	1.3	5.3	5.1	3.8	3.2	4.3	4.0	2.5
45-54	2.0	1.0	2.2	5.3	4.5	5.2	3.9	3.0	2.2	2.1
55-59	1.3	0.7	2.3	2.9	5.0	8.3	4.0	2.9	3.2	3.3
60-64	1.8	1.1	2.8	7.4	5.4	5.6	5.3	3.3	2.7	3.0
15-24	9.2	8.0	9.0	19.9	18.3	18.4	14.7	13.6	13.1	10.7
25-54	1.8	1.2	2.2	7.2	7.0	5.6	4.8	4.4	3.8	2.6
55-64	1.5	0.9	2.5	4.9	5.1	7.1	4.6	3.1	2.9	3.2
65 and over	0.0	2.4	1.9	2.7	3.6	3.4	4.0	4.4	2.0	0.8
15-64	3.0	2.3	3.4	8.9	8.6	8.1	6.5	5.8	5.2	4.1
Total	2.8	2.3	3.3	8.6	8.3	7.8	6.4	5.7	5.1	3.9
Females										
15-19	10.1	8.3	10.3	14.9	17.1	12.4	12.5	10.0	10.2	9.8
20-24	5.1	4.6	5.1	9.7	11.6	9.4	12.3	6.1	4.7	4.6
25-34	4.2	1.6	2.3	8.2	8.1	9.3	6.0	7.9	7.5	5.6
35-44	1.1	1.7	1.3	3.8	4.3	4.1	4.0	4.7	4.5	3.6
45-54	1.1	1.4	1.6	3.0	4.5	3.7	3.3	2.4	3.0	2.4
55-59	1.4	0.5	1.0	2.1	2.5	3.1	4.2	4.3	4.5	3.4
60-64	2.2	1.4	..	2.3	5.0	4.2	3.7	2.3	1.5	3.1
15-24	7.5	6.3	7.5	12.0	14.1	10.7	12.4	7.8	6.9	6.7
25-54	2.1	1.6	1.7	4.9	5.6	5.7	4.4	4.9	5.0	3.8
55-64	1.7	0.9	0.6	2.2	3.5	3.6	4.0	3.4	3.2	3.3
65 and over	5.0	1.1	1.2	2.2	3.5	5.3	2.3	1.1	1.5	0.5
15-64	3.1	2.4	2.6	5.8	6.8	6.2	5.8	5.2	5.0	4.3
Total	3.1	2.3	2.6	5.7	6.7	6.2	5.7	5.1	4.9	4.1
All persons										
15-24	8.4	7.2	8.2	16.0	16.2	14.6	13.6	10.7	10.0	8.7
25-54	1.9	1.3	2.0	6.2	6.3	5.6	4.6	4.6	4.3	3.2
55-64	1.6	0.9	1.6	3.6	4.4	5.4	4.3	3.2	3.1	3.2
65 and over	1.7	1.9	1.6	2.5	3.6	4.1	3.3	3.1	1.8	0.7
15-64	3.0	2.3	3.0	7.4	7.7	7.2	6.2	5.5	5.1	4.2

Note: Detailed metadata at:http://metalinks.oecd.org/lfs/20170518/6f97b
Disclaimer: http://oe.cd/disclaimer

Table 3. Civilian employment and employees: breakdown by activity - ISIC Rev. 4

Annual average estimates

		2006	2007	2008	2009	2010	2011	2012	2013	2014	2015
	CIVILIAN EMPLOYMENT										
	By activity, thousands										
A-U	**All activities**	..	..	**179.1**	**168.0**	**167.4**	**167.4**	**169.3**	**174.9**	**177.7**	**183.7**
A	Agriculture, hunting and forestry	..	..	8.3	8.7	9.9	10.1	9.6	8.0	8.0	7.8
B-F	**Industry**	..	..	**39.1**	**32.1**	**30.3**	**30.3**	**30.6**	**32.5**	**32.7**	**32.7**
B	Mining and quarrying	..	..	0.1	0.1	0.2	0.0	0.0	0.1	0.2	0.2
C	Manufacturing	..	..	18.7	17.9	17.3	18.2	19.5	20.0	19.7	18.8
D	Electricity, gas, steam, air cond. supply	..	..	1.7	1.5	1.5	1.5	1.1	1.3	1.4	1.5
E	Water supply, sewerage, waste mgt, remediation	..	..	0.9	0.9	0.7	0.6	0.8	0.7	0.9	0.9
F	Construction	..	..	17.7	11.7	10.5	10.0	9.3	10.5	10.5	11.4
G-U	**Services**	..	..	**131.7**	**127.2**	**127.3**	**127.0**	**129.0**	**134.4**	**137.0**	**143.2**
G	Wholesale, retail trade, vehicle, motorcycle repair	..	..	23.2	21.1	20.5	21.6	22.3	23.5	23.2	23.8
H	Transportation and storage	..	..	9.3	9.8	9.0	9.0	8.8	9.2	10.1	11.3
I	Accommodation and food service activities	..	..	6.4	7.7	7.9	8.7	8.1	10.1	10.6	11.1
J	Information and communication	..	..	7.6	8.0	7.1	7.2	7.1	7.4	8.1	9.3
K	Financial and insurance activities	..	..	9.0	7.9	8.0	8.3	7.5	7.1	6.8	6.3
L	Real estate activities	..	..	1.3	0.7	0.8	0.8	0.8	0.8	0.7	0.9
M	Professional, scientific and technical activities	..	..	9.5	9.5	9.8	10.1	9.8	10.0	10.6	11.3
N	Administrative and support service activities	..	..	4.3	4.0	4.2	4.5	5.1	5.2	6.3	5.7
O	Public administration, defence, social security	..	..	9.7	9.1	8.5	7.1	9.0	9.0	7.6	7.5
P	Education	..	..	21.6	20.4	20.6	18.4	19.5	20.5	22.0	23.5
Q	Human health and social work activities	..	..	20.0	19.5	21.2	20.5	19.2	20.6	20.3	20.9
R	Arts, entertainment and recreation	..	..	5.9	5.1	5.0	5.6	6.1	6.1	5.9	6.3
S	Other service activities	..	..	3.9	4.1	4.5	5.1	5.4	4.7	4.7	5.1
T	Households as employers and own-use activities	..	..	0.0	0.1	0.0	0.0	0.0	0.0	0.0	0.0
U	Activities of extraterritorial organizations, bodies	..	..	0.1	0.2	0.1	0.1	0.2	0.2	0.2	0.1
	EMPLOYEES										
	By activity, thousands										
A-U	**All activities**	..	..	**156.3**	**147.5**	**145.8**	**146.0**	**147.8**	**152.8**	**155.5**	**160.8**
A	Agriculture, hunting and forestry	..	..	4.6	5.0	5.8	5.9	5.9	4.6	5.1	5.1
B-F	**Industry**	..	..	**32.1**	**26.9**	**25.2**	**25.9**	**26.0**	**27.3**	**27.3**	**27.3**
B	Mining and quarrying	..	..	0.1	0.1	0.2	0.0	0.0	0.1	0.2	0.2
C	Manufacturing	..	..	17.0	16.3	15.7	16.6	17.8	18.2	18.0	17.0
D	Electricity, gas, steam, air cond. supply	..	..	1.7	1.5	1.5	1.5	1.0	1.3	1.4	1.5
E	Water supply, sewerage, waste mgt, remediation	..	..	0.9	0.7	0.6	0.6	0.7	0.6	0.8	0.9
F	Construction	..	..	12.5	8.2	7.2	7.2	6.4	7.2	6.9	7.9
G-U	**Services**	..	..	**119.7**	**115.6**	**114.7**	**114.2**	**115.9**	**120.8**	**123.1**	**128.4**
G	Wholesale, retail trade, vehicle, motorcycle repair	..	..	21.2	19.0	18.2	19.3	20.2	21.2	21.1	21.7
H	Transportation and storage	..	..	7.8	8.4	7.8	7.8	7.9	8.4	9.2	10.1
I	Accommodation and food service activities	..	..	5.9	7.0	7.1	8.0	7.4	9.0	9.5	9.9
J	Information and communication	..	..	6.7	7.0	6.2	6.6	6.3	6.3	6.9	7.8
K	Financial and insurance activities	..	..	8.8	7.8	7.7	8.0	7.1	6.9	6.6	6.2
L	Real estate activities	..	..	0.8	0.6	0.6	0.6	0.5	0.6	0.3	0.4
M	Professional, scientific and technical activities	..	..	7.4	7.6	7.8	8.3	7.6	7.7	8.2	8.8
N	Administrative and support service activities	..	..	3.8	3.5	3.8	3.7	4.2	4.6	5.5	5.1
O	Public administration, defence, social security	..	..	9.6	9.0	8.4	7.1	8.9	9.0	7.5	7.5
P	Education	..	..	21.3	19.9	19.9	17.9	18.9	19.9	21.3	22.9
Q	Human health and social work activities	..	..	18.7	18.2	19.7	18.7	17.5	18.7	18.4	19.3
R	Arts, entertainment and recreation	..	..	4.6	4.1	4.0	4.5	5.1	4.9	4.8	5.0
S	Other service activities	..	..	3.1	3.4	3.4	3.7	4.0	3.5	3.5	3.7
T	Households as employers and own-use activities	..	..	0.0	0.1	0.0	0.0	0.0	0.0	0.0	0.0
U	Activities of extraterritorial organizations, bodies	..	..	0.1	0.1	0.1	0.1	0.2	0.2	0.2	0.1

Note: Detailed metadata:http://metalinks.oecd.org/lfs/20170518/87289
Disclaimer: http://oe.cd/disclaimer

IRELAND

Table 1. Labour force

Annual average estimates

	2006	2007	2008	2009	2010	2011	2012	2013	2014	2015
Civilian labour force, thousands										
All persons	2 128	2 237	2 271	2 243	2 191	2 171	2 152	2 164	2 150	2 165
Males	1 226	1 277	1 289	1 260	1 216	1 200	1 187	1 189	1 186	1 192
Females	901	960	983	983	975	971	965	975	963	973
Unemployed, thousands										
All persons	99	108	131	275	305	317	323	301	255	211
Males	58	63	87	194	208	214	216	190	161	132
Females	41	44	44	81	97	103	107	111	93	80
Civilian employment, thousands										
All persons	2 028	2 129	2 140	1 968	1 886	1 853	1 829	1 863	1 895	1 954
Males	1 168	1 213	1 202	1 066	1 008	986	971	1 000	1 025	1 061
Females	860	916	938	902	878	868	859	864	870	894
Civilian employment (%)										
All persons	100.0	100.0	100.0	100.0	100.0	100.0	100.0	100.0	100.0	100.0
Males	57.6	57.0	56.2	54.2	53.5	53.2	53.1	53.6	54.1	54.3
Females	42.4	43.0	43.8	45.8	46.5	46.8	46.9	46.4	45.9	45.7
Unemployment rate (% of civilian labour force)										
All persons	4.7	4.8	5.8	12.3	13.9	14.6	15.0	13.9	11.8	9.8
Males	4.7	4.9	6.7	15.4	17.1	17.8	18.2	15.9	13.6	11.0
Females	4.5	4.6	4.5	8.2	10.0	10.6	11.0	11.4	9.7	8.2
CIVIL. EMPL. - PROFESSIONAL STATUS, thousands										
All activities	**2 028**	**2 129**	**2 140**	**1 968**	**1 886**	**1 853**	**1 829**	**1 863**	**1 895**	**1 954**
Employees	1 700	1 773	1 773	1 623	1 563	1 546	1 524	1 544	1 566	1 611
Employers and persons working on own account	317	342	352	331	307	296	292	304	316	328
Unpaid family workers	12	14	16	15	16	11	13	15	14	15
Employees as % of civilian employment	**83.8**	**83.3**	**82.8**	**82.5**	**82.9**	**83.4**	**83.3**	**82.9**	**82.6**	**82.5**
Part-time employment (%)										
Part-time as % of employment	19.3	19.9	20.9	23.8	24.9	25.7	25.0	24.2	23.4	23.3
Male share of part time employment	20.6	20.2	21.3	23.8	24.9	25.5	26.7	28.1	27.8	27.9
Female share of part time employment	79.4	79.8	78.7	76.2	75.1	74.5	73.3	71.9	72.2	72.1
Male part-time as % of male employment	7.2	7.4	8.3	11.0	12.1	12.8	13.1	13.1	12.5	12.3
Female part-time as % of female employment	34.3	35.0	35.5	37.4	38.2	39.1	37.5	36.2	35.4	35.4
Duration of unemployment (% of total unemployment)										
Less than one month	23.4	9.1	8.6	7.5	4.4	4.3	4.0	4.4	4.5	4.8
More than 1 month and less than 3 months	9.8	24.1	25.7	19.6	11.8	9.7	9.7	10.1	10.7	10.9
More than 3 months and less than 6 months	16.7	18.9	20.3	19.6	13.7	10.9	10.6	10.6	11.1	12.3
More than 6 months and less than 1 year	18.5	17.9	18.8	24.3	21.0	15.8	14.0	14.3	14.5	14.4
More than 1 year	31.6	30.0	26.5	29.1	49.1	59.3	61.7	60.6	59.2	57.6

Note: Detailed metadata: http://metalinks.oecd.org/lfs/20170518/50b89, http://metalinks.oecd.org/lfs/20170518/87289, http://metalinks.oecd.org/lfs/20170518/00c6a and http://metalinks.oecd.org/lfs/20170518/c5099.

Disclaimer: http://oe.cd/disclaimer

IRELAND

Table 2. Participation rates and unemployment rates by age and sex

Annual average estimates, percentage

	2006	2007	2008	2009	2010	2011	2012	2013	2014	2015
Participation rates										
Males										
15-19	32.3	31.1	27.6	23.2	18.4	16.1	18.0	16.9	15.0	16.4
20-24	82.1	82.0	80.5	76.4	71.2	68.3	67.1	67.9	66.5	65.1
25-34	93.4	92.3	92.5	91.6	90.6	89.0	90.0	88.1	88.7	88.3
35-44	93.6	93.1	92.8	92.4	91.6	91.7	91.2	91.9	92.1	92.2
45-54	88.9	89.1	89.1	87.5	86.8	86.6	86.1	88.4	88.0	88.5
55-59	76.4	77.5	76.3	76.6	74.2	74.1	73.4	76.3	77.9	79.7
60-64	58.1	60.6	60.5	57.1	55.1	55.7	54.6	56.4	57.3	62.4
15-24	59.3	59.6	56.8	51.7	45.9	42.6	42.3	41.5	38.9	38.3
25-54	92.2	91.7	91.7	90.7	89.9	89.2	89.3	89.5	89.7	89.8
55-64	68.2	69.8	69.0	67.5	65.2	65.4	64.6	66.9	68.3	71.5
65 and over	14.4	16.1	16.5	14.9	13.9	13.8	14.0	14.5	15.6	16.6
15-64	81.6	81.6	81.0	79.3	77.4	76.7	76.7	77.2	77.1	77.6
Females										
15-19	25.4	27.4	25.1	21.0	15.8	15.9	17.6	17.3	14.2	13.5
20-24	70.4	72.5	71.8	71.0	66.5	64.6	63.5	64.5	59.6	58.3
25-34	78.5	78.7	77.7	77.8	77.4	78.0	76.9	78.3	76.8	76.9
35-44	66.7	68.8	68.8	69.0	68.7	68.3	70.4	71.5	72.9	72.6
45-54	63.9	66.9	67.1	66.8	68.2	67.9	66.4	67.6	67.4	70.4
55-59	48.3	49.0	50.4	52.0	56.2	56.6	55.8	58.2	57.6	59.1
60-64	31.1	31.1	33.3	32.3	33.4	34.5	34.3	34.5	37.4	37.3
15-24	50.1	52.7	51.3	48.8	43.2	41.3	40.9	40.3	35.5	33.8
25-54	70.5	72.2	71.8	71.8	71.9	71.8	71.7	72.8	72.6	73.4
55-64	40.6	40.8	42.5	42.8	45.4	46.2	45.7	47.0	48.1	48.8
65 and over	4.1	4.0	4.5	4.2	4.6	4.6	4.5	5.0	5.2	6.1
15-64	61.9	63.5	63.3	62.8	62.3	62.3	62.2	63.2	62.5	62.8
All persons										
15-24	54.7	56.2	54.1	50.3	44.5	42.0	41.6	40.9	37.3	36.1
25-54	81.5	82.1	81.8	81.3	80.9	80.5	80.3	81.0	81.0	81.4
55-64	54.6	55.5	55.9	55.2	55.4	55.8	55.1	56.9	58.1	60.1
65 and over	8.7	9.4	9.9	9.1	8.8	8.8	8.8	9.4	10.0	10.9
15-64	71.9	72.7	72.2	71.1	69.8	69.5	69.4	70.1	69.7	70.1
Unemployment rates										
Males										
15-19	14.2	18.3	21.8	39.8	41.9	46.3	51.2	43.5	38.9	31.8
20-24	8.1	8.5	13.0	29.8	32.5	33.4	35.6	29.6	25.2	21.8
25-34	5.0	4.9	7.2	18.0	18.8	21.4	20.4	18.1	15.9	12.8
35-44	3.4	3.6	5.1	12.4	14.7	14.9	15.5	13.7	11.5	9.1
45-54	3.7	3.8	4.5	10.4	13.5	13.5	13.9	12.8	10.8	9.5
55-59	3.3	2.9	4.1	7.7	10.6	11.8	14.9	12.9	11.9	9.0
60-64	1.5	1.7	2.8	8.0	10.3	11.2	11.3	11.5	11.2	9.0
15-24	9.6	10.7	14.9	31.9	34.3	35.8	38.9	32.5	28.0	24.2
25-54	4.1	4.2	5.8	14.0	15.9	16.9	16.8	14.9	12.7	10.4
55-64	2.7	2.4	3.6	7.8	10.5	11.6	13.5	12.3	11.6	9.0
65 and over	0.3	0.6	0.3	0.9	0.9	1.2	1.7	2.4	1.4	1.1
15-64	4.8	5.0	6.9	15.7	17.4	18.2	18.6	16.3	14.0	11.4
Total	4.7	4.9	6.7	15.3	17.0	17.7	18.1	15.8	13.5	11.0
Females										
15-19	17.7	16.2	17.2	32.5	38.8	33.8	45.3	42.4	39.1	29.2
20-24	7.9	7.9	7.7	15.6	18.4	21.4	21.7	22.0	22.0	17.8
25-34	3.9	3.9	4.2	8.1	9.8	11.1	10.9	10.9	9.7	7.9
35-44	3.5	3.8	3.3	6.6	8.7	9.2	9.6	9.5	7.4	6.6
45-54	3.1	3.1	2.9	4.5	6.6	7.2	7.9	9.1	7.7	7.3
55-59	2.8	2.5	2.9	3.9	5.7	5.7	5.2	8.3	7.3	6.1
60-64	1.1	1.0	1.8	1.8	4.2	5.4	5.8	8.2	5.6	6.2
15-24	10.2	9.8	9.7	18.8	21.8	23.7	26.7	26.5	25.6	20.3
25-54	3.5	3.7	3.6	6.7	8.6	9.4	9.7	9.9	8.3	7.3
55-64	2.2	2.0	2.5	3.2	5.2	5.6	5.4	8.3	6.7	6.1
65 and over	0.0	1.9	0.0	1.7	3.1	0.7	0.8	2.6	1.8	3.0
15-64	4.6	4.7	4.6	8.3	10.1	10.8	11.2	11.5	9.8	8.3
Total	4.5	4.6	4.5	8.3	10.0	10.6	11.0	11.4	9.6	8.2
All persons										
15-24	9.9	10.3	12.4	25.5	28.3	29.9	33.0	29.6	26.9	22.4
25-54	3.9	4.0	4.8	10.8	12.6	13.5	13.6	12.6	10.7	9.0
55-64	2.5	2.3	3.2	6.0	8.3	9.1	10.1	10.7	9.6	7.8
65 and over	0.2	0.9	0.2	1.1	1.5	1.1	1.4	2.4	1.5	1.7
15-64	4.7	4.9	5.9	12.5	14.1	14.9	15.3	14.1	12.1	10.0

Note: Detailed metadata at:http://metalinks.oecd.org/lfs/20170518/6f97b
Disclaimer: http://oe.cd/disclaimer

IRELAND

Table 3. Civilian employment and employees: breakdown by activity - ISIC Rev. 3

Annual average estimates

		2006	2007	2008	2009	2010	2011	2012	2013	2014	2015
CIVILIAN EMPLOYMENT											
	By activity, thousands										
A-X	**All activities**	**2 028**	**2 129**	**2 140**	**1 968**	**1 885**	**1 853**	**1 829**	**1 863**	**1 895**	**..**
A	Agriculture, hunting and forestry	111	112	121	102	87	90	92	108	112	..
B	Fishing	3	2	2	2	3	2	2	3	3	..
C	Mining and quarrying	11	11	11	8	8	6	7	7	6	..
D	Manufacturing	270	276	266	239	221	220	212	217	217	..
E	Electricity, gas and water supply	11	13	14	15	14	12	13	12	13	..
F	Construction	266	289	262	173	138	116	107	107	112	..
G	Wholesale, retail trade: vehicle repair, household gds	284	303	316	287	279	276	270	272	270	..
H	Hotels and restaurants	126	134	130	127	128	115	120	131	137	..
I	Transport, storage and communication	122	125	120	125	118	124	115	110	115	..
J	Financial intermediation	85	91	96	100	95	95	88	90	88	..
K	Real estate, renting and business activities	182	198	207	191	191	198	200	207	214	..
L	Public adm., defence; social sec., excl. armed forces	97	96	97	103	99	92	93	88	92	..
M	Education	134	139	145	146	144	146	144	147	150	..
N	Health and social work	205	215	226	234	241	247	252	248	251	..
O	Other community, social, personal service activities	101	107	105	101	99	99	102	106	103	..
P	Private households with employed persons	9	9	10	8	8	8	7	7	7	..
Q	Extra-territorial organisations and bodies	1	1	1	1	1	2	3	4	5	..
X	Not classifiable by economic activities	11	7	10	8	11	6	2	2	2	..
	By sector, thousands										
A-B	Agriculture	114	115	123	104	90	93	94	111	115	..
C-F	Industry	558	589	553	435	381	355	339	344	348	..
G-Q	Services	1 345	1 418	1 454	1 422	1 404	1 401	1 395	1 407	1 431	..
	By sector, percentages										
A-B	Agriculture	5.6	5.4	5.8	5.3	4.8	5.0	5.1	6.0	6.1	..
C-F	Industry	27.5	27.7	25.9	22.1	20.2	19.1	18.5	18.4	18.4	..
G-Q	Services	66.3	66.6	67.9	72.3	74.5	75.6	76.2	75.5	75.5	..
EMPLOYEES											
	By activity, thousands										
A-X	**All activities**	**1 700**	**1 773**	**1 773**	**1 623**	**1 562**	**1 546**	**1 524**	**1 544**	**1 566**	**..**
A	Agriculture, hunting and forestry	24	24	26	19	18	22	21	25	26	..
B	Fishing	2	1	1	1	2	2	1	2	3	..
C	Mining and quarrying	10	10	10	7	7	5	5	7	6	..
D	Manufacturing	248	252	240	214	199	202	194	197	196	..
E	Electricity, gas and water supply	11	12	14	14	13	11	12	11	13	..
F	Construction	202	215	187	112	85	75	67	68	69	..
G	Wholesale, retail trade: vehicle repair, household gds	247	262	276	248	241	238	235	236	232	..
H	Hotels and restaurants	110	118	115	113	110	100	104	117	122	..
I	Transport, storage and communication	97	99	94	96	92	96	91	86	90	..
J	Financial intermediation	82	87	92	95	91	91	84	85	83	..
K	Real estate, renting and business activities	149	159	166	149	149	152	156	160	169	..
L	Public adm., defence; social sec., excl. armed forces	96	96	97	102	98	92	92	87	91	..
M	Education	129	134	139	140	138	138	138	141	144	..
N	Health and social work	194	203	216	220	227	233	236	232	236	..
O	Other community, social, personal service activities	83	86	83	79	77	77	79	80	76	..
P	Private households with employed persons	7	8	9	7	6	6	6	6	5	..
Q	Extra-territorial organisations and bodies	1	1	1	1	1	2	3	4	5	..
X	Not classifiable by economic activities	10	7	9	7	10	5	2	2	2	..
	By sector, thousands										
A-B	Agriculture	25	25	27	20	19	23	22	27	28	..
C-F	Industry	470	489	450	347	304	293	278	282	283	..
G-Q	Services	1 194	1 252	1 287	1 249	1 229	1 225	1 223	1 233	1 252	..
	By sector, percentages										
A-B	Agriculture	1.5	1.4	1.5	1.2	1.2	1.5	1.4	1.7	1.8	..
C-F	Industry	27.7	27.6	25.4	21.4	19.5	19.0	18.2	18.3	18.1	..
G-Q	Services	70.3	70.6	72.6	77.0	78.7	79.2	80.2	79.9	80.0	..

Note: Detailed metadata:http://metalinks.oecd.org/lfs/20170518/87289

Disclaimer: http://oe.cd/disclaimer

ISRAEL

Table 1. Labour force

Annual average estimates

	2006	2007	2008	2009	2010	2011	2012	2013	2014	2015
Civilian labour force, thousands										
All persons	2 817	2 904	2 964	3 073	3 147	3 204	3 606	3 678	3 778	3 846
Males	1 504	1 549	1 582	1 625	1 664	1 699	1 918	1 956	1 998	2 032
Females	1 313	1 355	1 382	1 448	1 483	1 505	1 688	1 722	1 781	1 813
Unemployed, thousands										
All persons	236	212	180	232	209	180	247	228	223	202
Males	119	105	91	123	113	95	130	121	117	104
Females	118	107	90	109	96	85	118	108	105	98
Civilian employment, thousands										
All persons	2 581	2 692	2 784	2 841	2 938	3 025	3 359	3 450	3 556	3 644
Males	1 385	1 444	1 491	1 502	1 552	1 604	1 788	1 835	1 880	1 928
Females	1 196	1 248	1 293	1 339	1 387	1 421	1 571	1 614	1 675	1 715
Civilian employment (%)										
All persons	100.0	100.0	100.0	100.0	100.0	100.0	100.0	100.0	100.0	100.0
Males	53.7	53.7	53.6	52.9	52.8	53.0	53.2	53.2	52.9	52.9
Females	46.3	46.3	46.4	47.1	47.2	47.0	46.8	46.8	47.1	47.1
Unemployment rate (% of civilian labour force)										
All persons	8.4	7.3	6.1	7.5	6.6	5.6	6.9	6.2	5.9	5.3
Males	7.9	6.8	5.7	7.6	6.8	5.6	6.8	6.2	5.9	5.1
Females	9.0	7.9	6.5	7.5	6.5	5.6	7.0	6.2	5.9	5.4
CIVIL. EMPL. - PROFESSIONAL STATUS, thousands										
All activities	**2 581**	**2 692**	**2 784**	**2 841**	**2 938**	**3 025**	**3 359**	**3 450**	**3 556**	**3 644**
Employees	2 242	2 351	2 431	2 475	2 564	2 642	2 933	3 015	3 111	3 183
Employers and persons working on own account	332	335	347	360	369	378	422	430	442	457
Unpaid family workers	7	6	6	6	6	5	5	4	4	4
Employees as % of civilian employment	**86.9**	**87.3**	**87.3**	**87.1**	**87.2**	**87.3**	**87.3**	**87.4**	**87.5**	**87.4**
Part-time employment (%)										
Part-time as % of employment	16.6	16.1	16.0	16.1	15.2	14.9	16.1	15.9	16.0	15.9
Male share of part time employment	26.1	26.7	27.7	27.4	27.1	28.3	32.1	31.5	31.4	31.7
Female share of part time employment	73.9	73.3	72.3	72.6	72.9	71.7	67.9	68.5	68.6	68.3
Male part-time as % of male employment	8.2	8.1	8.4	8.4	7.9	8.0	9.6	9.4	9.4	9.4
Female part-time as % of female employment	26.2	25.3	24.5	24.5	23.3	22.5	23.6	23.4	23.5	23.3
Duration of unemployment (% of total unemployment)										
Less than one month	19.5	23.3	22.5	20.6	22.6	22.9	29.2	28.7	30.7	30.1
More than 1 month and less than 3 months	22.8	22.4	24.6	25.5	24.2	26.5	26.4	27.2	27.9	27.4
More than 3 months and less than 6 months	16.1	15.6	16.8	18.8	16.3	17.6	16.9	17.2	17.4	17.2
More than 6 months and less than 1 year	14.3	13.9	13.3	14.8	14.6	12.8	14.2	14.2	13.4	13.8
More than 1 year	27.3	24.9	22.7	20.3	22.4	20.2	13.3	12.7	10.6	11.5

Note: Detailed metadata: http://metalinks.oecd.org/lfs/20170518/70b5c, http://metalinks.oecd.org/lfs/20170518/87289, http://metalinks.oecd.org/lfs/20170518/ce73f and http://metalinks.oecd.org/lfs/20170518/61ef2.

Disclaimer: http://oe.cd/disclaimer

Table 2. Participation rates and unemployment rates by age and sex

Annual average estimates, percentage

	2006	2007	2008	2009	2010	2011	2012	2013	2014	2015
Participation rates										
Males										
15-19	42.4	40.1	38.8	33.4	35.4	33.5	29.2	30.3	29.4	29.7
20-24	75.4	78.2	77.5	76.9	75.0	73.1	73.3	73.7	74.3	72.7
25-34	85.3	86.1	86.9	84.7	84.9	85.0	84.8	84.2	84.5	85.2
35-44	88.0	88.7	88.7	89.6	90.0	89.3	90.0	89.8	90.2	90.1
45-54	86.5	86.2	85.7	86.6	86.5	85.8	85.9	85.5	85.7	86.4
55-59	74.8	75.0	75.5	74.9	74.6	76.8	79.3	81.7	80.7	79.8
60-64	60.2	63.0	63.2	65.3	67.0	67.4	71.1	71.1	71.4	73.1
15-24	58.3	58.3	57.1	54.4	54.4	52.6	50.4	51.0	50.9	49.9
25-54	86.5	87.0	87.1	86.8	87.0	86.7	86.9	86.5	86.8	87.3
55-64	69.4	70.3	70.4	70.8	71.3	72.6	75.5	76.7	76.2	76.6
65 and over	18.4	18.5	19.4	19.8	21.1	22.9	24.8	26.6	27.0	26.9
15-64	76.7	77.0	76.8	76.1	76.3	75.9	75.9	76.0	76.1	76.1
Females										
15-19	36.3	34.5	31.5	29.8	29.4	27.0	29.9	29.3	30.2	29.8
20-24	71.7	70.9	70.7	73.6	72.8	70.3	68.3	68.4	68.4	68.2
25-34	73.9	75.2	75.7	76.6	77.2	77.7	77.6	77.6	79.7	78.0
35-44	74.9	75.8	75.7	77.2	76.2	76.7	77.5	77.6	78.9	79.3
45-54	69.4	70.1	69.8	71.0	71.4	71.3	75.2	75.3	76.0	76.6
55-59	59.9	60.6	61.2	63.9	64.5	65.1	66.4	67.1	69.1	69.9
60-64	35.6	41.2	44.4	45.3	47.6	48.6	48.2	50.7	51.2	53.4
15-24	53.7	52.5	50.8	51.0	50.7	48.1	48.6	48.2	48.5	48.0
25-54	72.9	73.9	74.0	75.2	75.2	75.6	76.9	77.0	78.4	78.1
55-64	50.2	52.4	53.7	55.3	56.4	56.9	57.6	59.1	60.3	61.8
65 and over	5.3	5.1	5.6	6.6	7.2	7.5	10.4	11.2	11.9	13.0
15-64	65.0	65.5	65.3	66.3	66.4	66.1	67.1	67.3	68.4	68.3
All persons										
15-24	56.0	55.5	54.0	52.7	52.6	50.4	49.5	49.6	49.7	49.0
25-54	79.6	80.3	80.4	80.9	81.0	81.0	81.8	81.7	82.6	82.6
55-64	59.7	61.2	61.9	63.0	63.7	64.6	66.3	67.6	67.9	68.9
65 and over	10.9	10.8	11.6	12.3	13.3	14.2	16.7	17.9	18.6	19.1
15-64	70.8	71.2	71.0	71.2	71.3	71.0	71.5	71.6	72.2	72.2
Unemployment rates										
Males										
15-19	19.9	19.5	14.1	16.6	19.1	14.2	16.3	14.1	13.6	12.3
20-24	15.8	13.0	10.7	15.1	12.7	10.8	9.6	8.8	8.6	7.4
25-34	7.9	6.8	5.8	8.8	8.2	7.5	7.3	6.9	7.0	5.3
35-44	7.1	7.1	6.4	8.0	6.9	5.3	5.4	4.5	4.0	3.9
45-54	11.6	8.6	8.4	10.3	8.9	6.7	5.2	5.1	4.8	4.2
55-59	6.8	6.3	4.8	6.2	5.4	5.2	5.2	5.2	4.3	4.7
60-64	12.6	9.6	7.7	8.5	8.8	6.8	5.0	4.8	4.3	4.0
15-24	17.3	15.3	11.9	15.6	14.8	11.9	11.6	10.4	10.1	8.9
25-54	8.7	7.4	6.7	8.9	7.9	6.5	6.1	5.5	5.3	4.5
55-64	8.7	7.4	5.9	7.1	6.8	5.9	5.1	5.0	4.3	4.4
65 and over	7.9	8.6	6.1	6.4	5.7	5.7	4.7	4.2	4.0	3.5
15-64	10.4	9.0	7.6	9.9	9.0	7.4	6.8	6.3	6.0	5.2
Total	10.4	9.0	7.6	9.8	8.9	7.3	6.8	6.2	5.9	5.1
Females										
15-19	22.9	19.0	10.8	14.7	17.6	14.0	13.1	10.8	12.7	10.9
20-24	18.0	16.5	14.1	13.4	11.9	10.8	12.5	10.6	10.4	9.1
25-34	9.0	9.0	7.2	8.7	7.6	6.7	7.9	7.4	6.2	6.2
35-44	10.7	9.1	8.1	9.9	7.3	7.1	5.7	5.3	4.9	4.4
45-54	7.5	6.6	5.1	6.8	5.9	4.7	4.4	4.3	4.1	3.7
55-59	6.8	4.9	5.1	6.0	5.0	4.3	4.3	4.1	4.3	3.4
60-64	8.9	8.1	6.4	7.6	7.0	6.1	4.5	3.1	3.2	3.4
15-24	19.7	17.3	13.1	13.8	13.6	11.7	12.7	10.7	11.1	9.7
25-54	9.1	8.4	6.9	8.6	7.1	6.3	6.2	5.8	5.2	4.9
55-64	7.4	6.0	5.6	6.6	5.8	5.0	4.4	3.7	3.9	3.4
65 and over	0.0	0.0	0.0	0.0	0.0	0.0	3.5	2.8	3.1	3.1
15-64	11.2	9.9	8.0	9.3	8.1	7.1	7.1	6.3	6.0	5.5
Total	11.0	9.8	7.8	9.1	7.9	6.9	7.0	6.2	5.9	5.4
All persons										
15-24	18.4	16.3	12.5	14.7	14.3	11.8	12.1	10.5	10.6	9.3
25-54	8.9	7.8	6.8	8.8	7.5	6.4	6.1	5.7	5.3	4.7
55-64	8.1	6.8	5.8	6.9	6.4	5.5	4.8	4.4	4.1	3.9
65 and over	5.7	6.3	4.4	4.5	3.9	4.0	4.3	3.7	3.7	3.3
15-64	10.8	9.4	7.8	9.6	8.6	7.2	7.0	6.3	6.0	5.3

Note: Detailed metadata at:http://metalinks.oecd.org/lfs/20170518/6f97b
Disclaimer: http://oe.cd/disclaimer

Table 3. Civilian employment and employees: breakdown by activity - ISIC Rev. 4

Annual average estimates

		2006	2007	2008	2009	2010	2011	2012	2013	2014	2015
	CIVILIAN EMPLOYMENT										
	By activity, thousands										
A-U	**All activities**	..	..	..	..	..	..	..	**3 449.5**	**3 555.8**	**3 643.8**
A	Agriculture, hunting and forestry	..	..	..	..	..	..	..	43.1	40.0	37.3
B-F	**Industry**	..	..	..	..	..	..	..	**609.0**	**622.0**	**633.9**
B	Mining and quarrying	..	..	..	..	..	..	..	3.3	3.0	3.2
C	Manufacturing	..	..	..	..	..	..	..	408.4	417.0	418.8
D	Electricity, gas, steam, air cond. supply	..	..	..	..	..	..	..	15.4	16.0	15.9
E	Water supply, sewerage, waste mgt, remediation	..	..	..	..	..	..	..	16.1	14.0	15.1
F	Construction	..	..	..	..	..	..	..	165.8	172.0	180.9
G-U	**Services**	..	..	..	..	..	..	..	**2 797.5**	**2 893.8**	**2 972.6**
G	Wholesale, retail trade, vehicle, motorcycle repair	..	..	..	..	..	..	..	402.7	406.0	420.1
H	Transportation and storage	..	..	..	..	..	..	..	146.6	147.0	151.1
I	Accommodation and food service activities	..	..	..	..	..	..	..	150.3	153.0	154.2
J	Information and communication	..	..	..	..	..	..	..	165.9	174.0	180.1
K	Financial and insurance activities	..	..	..	..	..	..	..	118.5	125.0	123.9
L	Real estate activities	..	..	..	..	..	..	..	28.2	29.0	28.0
M	Professional, scientific and technical activities	..	..	..	..	..	..	..	237.0	253.0	257.7
N	Administrative and support service activities	..	..	..	..	..	..	..	147.7	147.0	152.9
O	Public administration, defence, social security	..	..	..	..	..	..	..	362.7	367.0	371.0
P	Education	..	..	..	..	..	..	..	413.2	434.0	455.3
Q	Human health and social work activities	..	..	..	..	..	..	..	353.9	377.0	392.5
R	Arts, entertainment and recreation	..	..	..	..	..	..	..	61.4	67.0	66.8
S	Other service activities	..	..	..	..	..	..	..	89.4	87.0	84.7
T	Households as employers and own-use activities	..	..	..	..	..	..	..	64.1	67.0	66.1
U	Activities of extraterritorial organizations, bodies	..	..	..	..	..	..	..	2.2	3.0	3.0
	EMPLOYEES										
	By activity, thousands										
A-U	**All activities**	..	..	..	..	..	..	..	..	..	..
A	Agriculture, hunting and forestry	..	..	..	..	..	..	..	..	..	..
B-F	**Industry**	..	..	..	..	..	..	..	..	..	..
B	Mining and quarrying	..	..	..	..	..	..	..	..	..	..
C	Manufacturing	..	..	..	..	..	..	..	..	..	..
D	Electricity, gas, steam, air cond. supply	..	..	..	..	..	..	..	..	..	..
E	Water supply, sewerage, waste mgt, remediation	..	..	..	..	..	..	..	..	..	..
F	Construction	..	..	..	..	..	..	..	..	..	..
G-U	**Services**	..	..	..	..	..	..	..	..	..	..
G	Wholesale, retail trade, vehicle, motorcycle repair	..	..	..	..	..	..	..	..	..	..
H	Transportation and storage	..	..	..	..	..	..	..	..	..	..
I	Accommodation and food service activities	..	..	..	..	..	..	..	..	..	..
J	Information and communication	..	..	..	..	..	..	..	..	..	..
K	Financial and insurance activities	..	..	..	..	..	..	..	..	..	..
L	Real estate activities	..	..	..	..	..	..	..	..	..	..
M	Professional, scientific and technical activities	..	..	..	..	..	..	..	..	..	..
N	Administrative and support service activities	..	..	..	..	..	..	..	..	..	..
O	Public administration, defence, social security	..	..	..	..	..	..	..	..	..	..
P	Education	..	..	..	..	..	..	..	..	..	..
Q	Human health and social work activities	..	..	..	..	..	..	..	..	..	..
R	Arts, entertainment and recreation	..	..	..	..	..	..	..	..	..	..
S	Other service activities	..	..	..	..	..	..	..	..	..	..
T	Households as employers and own-use activities	..	..	..	..	..	..	..	..	..	..
U	Activities of extraterritorial organizations, bodies	..	..	..	..	..	..	..	..	..	..

Note: Detailed metadata:http://metalinks.oecd.org/lfs/20170518/87289
Disclaimer: http://oe.cd/disclaimer

Table 1. Labour force

Annual average estimates

	2006	2007	2008	2009	2010	2011	2012	2013	2014	2015
Civilian labour force, thousands										
All persons	24 164	24 126	24 512	24 357	24 325	24 420	24 991	25 017	25 278	25 249
Males	14 300	14 277	14 388	14 275	14 208	14 190	14 368	14 355	14 456	14 509
Females	9 864	9 850	10 124	10 082	10 117	10 230	10 623	10 663	10 822	10 740
Unemployed, thousands										
All persons	1 654	1 481	1 664	1 907	2 056	2 061	2 691	3 069	3 236	3 033
Males	788	708	804	976	1 084	1 084	1 434	1 674	1 742	1 669
Females	866	773	861	930	972	977	1 257	1 394	1 494	1 364
Civilian employment, thousands										
All persons	22 509	22 646	22 848	22 450	22 269	22 359	22 300	21 949	22 042	22 216
Males	13 511	13 569	13 584	13 299	13 124	13 105	12 934	12 680	12 714	12 840
Females	8 998	9 077	9 264	9 151	9 146	9 254	9 366	9 268	9 328	9 376
Civilian employment (%)										
All persons	100.0	100.0	100.0	100.0	100.0	100.0	100.0	100.0	100.0	100.0
Males	60.0	59.9	59.5	59.2	58.9	58.6	58.0	57.8	57.7	57.8
Females	40.0	40.1	40.5	40.8	41.1	41.4	42.0	42.2	42.3	42.2
Unemployment rate (% of civilian labour force)										
All persons	6.8	6.1	6.8	7.8	8.5	8.4	10.8	12.3	12.8	12.0
Males	5.5	5.0	5.6	6.8	7.6	7.6	10.0	11.7	12.1	11.5
Females	8.8	7.8	8.5	9.2	9.6	9.5	11.8	13.1	13.8	12.7
CIVIL. EMPL. - PROFESSIONAL STATUS, thousands										
All activities	**22 509**	**22 646**	**22 848**	**22 450**	**22 269**	**22 359**	**22 300**	**21 949**	**22 042**	**22 216**
Employees	16 500	16 664	16 971	16 782	16 575	16 700	16 679	16 441	16 543	16 738
Employers and persons working on own account	5 592	5 563	5 481	5 312	5 329	5 301	5 294	5 192	5 189	5 170
Unpaid family workers	418	418	396	356	366	357	327	316	309	307
Employees as % of civilian employment	**73.3**	**73.6**	**74.3**	**74.8**	**74.4**	**74.7**	**74.8**	**74.9**	**75.1**	**75.3**
Part-time employment (%)										
Part-time as % of employment	15.0	15.3	16.0	15.9	16.4	16.7	17.8	18.5	18.8	18.7
Male share of part time employment	22.2	21.8	22.9	22.3	22.9	23.1	24.7	25.9	26.6	26.5
Female share of part time employment	77.8	78.2	77.1	77.7	77.1	76.9	75.3	74.1	73.4	73.5
Male part-time as % of male employment	5.5	5.5	6.1	6.0	6.3	6.5	7.5	8.3	8.6	8.5
Female part-time as % of female employment	29.3	29.8	30.5	30.5	31.0	31.2	32.2	32.8	32.9	32.8
Duration of unemployment (% of total unemployment)										
Less than one month	7.2	8.3	8.5	7.4	6.9	6.4	5.3	4.8	4.4	5.6
More than 1 month and less than 3 months	14.7	15.6	16.1	14.6	13.2	11.6	11.8	10.8	10.0	10.3
More than 3 months and less than 6 months	14.6	15.1	15.5	16.4	15.3	15.1	14.2	13.0	11.9	11.9
More than 6 months and less than 1 year	14.0	13.5	14.1	17.0	16.1	15.0	15.6	14.5	12.4	13.3
More than 1 year	49.6	47.5	45.7	44.6	48.5	52.0	53.2	56.9	61.4	58.9

Note: Detailed metadata: http://metalinks.oecd.org/lfs/20170518/8ec1c, http://metalinks.oecd.org/lfs/20170518/87289, http://metalinks.oecd.org/lfs/20170518/cf8fa and http://metalinks.oecd.org/lfs/20170518/0a573.

Disclaimer: http://oe.cd/disclaimer

ITALY

Table 2. Participation rates and unemployment rates by age and sex

Annual average estimates, percentage

	2006	2007	2008	2009	2010	2011	2012	2013	2014	2015
Participation rates										
Males										
15-19	15.1	13.7	16.8	14.2	13.6	11.5	12.7	10.7	10.9	10.6
20-24	58.9	57.6	57.7	55.7	54.1	52.3	54.2	51.2	51.7	51.0
25-34	87.4	86.9	86.8	85.0	84.1	83.5	84.0	81.7	80.9	81.1
35-44	94.6	94.1	93.9	93.0	92.5	92.3	92.4	91.5	90.9	91.0
45-54	91.6	91.5	91.8	91.2	90.6	90.7	90.6	90.2	89.6	89.4
55-59	58.0	60.3	62.2	66.0	68.3	70.7	74.2	75.5	77.5	78.6
60-64	28.9	29.7	29.9	30.1	30.7	30.7	32.6	36.6	41.3	46.2
15-24	37.6	36.0	39.7	37.4	36.3	34.5	36.3	33.9	34.3	33.7
25-54	91.3	91.0	91.0	90.0	89.4	89.2	89.4	88.3	87.7	87.7
55-64	45.0	46.2	46.8	48.4	49.5	50.5	53.6	56.6	60.2	63.3
65 and over	6.2	6.1	6.3	5.8	5.7	5.7	6.1	6.2	6.5	6.6
15-64	74.5	74.3	75.5	74.7	74.2	73.9	74.8	74.4	74.7	75.2
Females										
15-19	8.4	8.4	10.5	8.5	7.7	7.7	8.6	7.6	6.9	6.6
20-24	43.8	41.5	42.0	39.7	39.2	38.3	39.7	39.2	39.1	36.9
25-34	67.0	66.0	67.0	65.9	64.5	64.3	66.0	64.5	64.9	63.9
35-44	67.2	66.6	67.9	67.3	67.5	67.7	69.1	69.2	69.7	69.0
45-54	58.3	59.3	60.7	60.2	61.2	61.8	64.2	64.2	64.2	64.4
55-59	32.8	34.5	36.4	39.5	41.7	45.0	48.4	49.9	51.1	51.6
60-64	10.2	10.8	11.8	12.1	12.2	13.0	15.8	18.7	24.4	26.4
15-24	26.9	25.4	28.3	26.1	25.5	25.1	26.5	25.8	25.5	24.0
25-54	64.4	64.1	65.3	64.6	64.5	64.7	66.5	66.1	66.4	65.9
55-64	22.5	23.4	24.6	26.0	26.9	28.8	32.2	34.7	38.3	39.6
65 and over	1.2	1.2	1.3	1.3	1.3	1.4	1.4	1.5	1.6	1.7
15-64	50.8	50.6	52.4	51.8	51.8	52.2	54.2	54.3	55.2	54.9
All persons										
15-24	32.3	30.8	34.1	31.9	31.0	29.9	31.5	30.0	30.0	29.0
25-54	77.8	77.5	78.1	77.2	76.9	76.9	77.8	77.1	77.0	76.8
55-64	33.4	34.5	35.4	36.9	37.9	39.3	42.5	45.3	48.9	51.1
65 and over	3.3	3.3	3.4	3.2	3.2	3.2	3.4	3.5	3.7	3.8
15-64	62.6	62.4	63.9	63.2	62.9	63.0	64.4	64.3	64.9	65.0
Unemployment rates										
Males										
15-19	28.7	27.9	30.4	36.9	41.8	44.2	55.2	60.3	62.2	57.1
20-24	17.0	16.2	16.2	20.4	23.9	24.2	29.9	35.7	38.0	35.9
25-34	7.5	6.6	7.3	9.0	10.4	10.2	13.6	16.5	17.3	16.4
35-44	3.4	3.3	4.0	4.9	5.4	5.6	7.4	8.6	9.3	8.9
45-54	2.8	2.5	3.1	4.2	4.7	4.7	6.2	7.8	8.0	7.8
55-59	2.8	2.5	3.4	4.0	4.0	4.6	5.8	7.0	6.7	6.7
60-64	3.0	2.7	3.0	3.3	3.6	4.4	6.2	6.2	5.2	5.8
15-24	19.2	18.4	18.8	23.2	26.9	27.1	33.7	39.0	41.3	38.8
25-54	4.5	4.0	4.7	5.8	6.5	6.5	8.6	10.3	10.8	10.4
55-64	2.9	2.6	3.3	3.7	3.9	4.6	5.9	6.7	6.2	6.4
65 and over	1.0	0.5	1.2	0.7	1.1	1.0	1.3	1.6	1.3	1.5
15-64	5.5	5.0	5.6	6.8	7.6	7.7	10.0	11.7	12.1	11.6
Total	5.4	4.9	5.5	6.7	7.5	7.5	9.8	11.5	11.9	11.3
Females										
15-19	40.4	37.4	40.9	45.0	51.8	55.5	58.0	68.2	71.7	66.1
20-24	22.8	20.6	21.5	25.8	26.0	28.5	34.3	37.7	41.1	39.5
25-34	11.4	10.4	10.8	12.5	14.0	13.6	16.5	19.3	20.1	19.6
35-44	7.1	6.6	7.4	8.0	8.1	8.1	10.2	11.4	12.3	11.0
45-54	4.6	4.1	4.8	4.9	5.3	5.5	7.3	8.2	9.1	8.2
55-59	2.5	2.1	2.9	3.0	3.0	2.6	4.4	4.5	5.0	4.8
60-64	4.4	1.9	2.5	2.2	2.8	2.8	3.4	3.2	3.2	3.1
15-24	25.4	23.3	24.7	28.5	29.4	32.1	37.6	41.5	44.7	42.6
25-54	7.8	7.1	7.7	8.4	8.9	8.8	10.9	12.3	13.2	12.2
55-64	2.9	2.1	2.9	2.8	3.0	2.7	4.2	4.2	4.4	4.3
65 and over	2.7	1.1	3.1	2.3	1.2	1.3	3.5	2.1	1.4	2.7
15-64	8.8	7.9	8.5	9.3	9.7	9.6	11.9	13.2	13.9	12.8
Total	8.8	7.8	8.5	9.2	9.6	9.5	11.8	13.1	13.8	12.7
All persons										
15-24	21.8	20.4	21.2	25.3	27.9	29.2	35.3	40.0	42.7	40.3
25-54	5.9	5.3	6.0	6.9	7.5	7.5	9.6	11.2	11.8	11.2
55-64	2.9	2.4	3.1	3.4	3.6	3.8	5.3	5.7	5.5	5.5
65 and over	1.3	0.7	1.6	1.0	1.2	1.1	1.8	1.7	1.3	1.8
15-64	6.9	6.2	6.8	7.9	8.5	8.5	10.8	12.3	12.9	12.1

Note: Detailed metadata at:http://metalinks.oecd.org/lfs/20170518/6f97b
Disclaimer: http://oe.cd/disclaimer

Table 3. Civilian employment and employees: breakdown by activity - ISIC Rev. 4

Annual average estimates

		2006	2007	2008	2009	2010	2011	2012	2013	2014	2015
	CIVILIAN EMPLOYMENT										
	By activity, thousands										
A-U	**All activities**	**..**	**..**	**22 847.9**	**22 450.5**	**22 269.1**	**22 358.7**	**22 299.9**	**21 948.8**	**22 041.8**	**22 215.6**
A	Agriculture, hunting and forestry	..	..	854.1	837.7	849.1	831.9	833.4	799.2	811.7	842.8
B-F	**Industry**	**..**	**..**	**6 881.0**	**6 636.7**	**6 444.5**	**6 392.8**	**6 224.3**	**6 001.8**	**5 993.4**	**5 975.6**
B	Mining and quarrying	..	..	35.7	33.0	35.4	38.2	35.3	37.5	38.9	34.1
C	Manufacturing	..	..	4 597.6	4 379.0	4 195.5	4 226.1	4 131.4	4 062.6	4 134.2	4 121.8
D	Electricity, gas, steam, air cond. supply	..	..	117.3	114.4	113.4	129.5	136.5	123.9	107.8	113.9
E	Water supply, sewerage, waste mgt, remediation	..	..	177.9	193.8	211.2	207.8	221.3	224.6	228.4	237.6
F	Construction	..	..	1 952.5	1 916.5	1 889.0	1 791.2	1 699.9	1 553.2	1 484.1	1 468.3
G-U	**Services**	**..**	**..**	**15 112.7**	**14 976.0**	**14 975.5**	**15 134.0**	**15 242.2**	**15 147.8**	**15 236.7**	**15 397.1**
G	Wholesale, retail trade, vehicle, motorcycle repair	..	..	3 452.3	3 363.6	3 305.4	3 252.2	3 331.2	3 287.5	3 226.5	3 194.2
H	Transportation and storage	..	..	1 064.5	1 059.8	1 057.3	1 073.8	1 045.2	1 033.6	1 039.1	1 033.0
I	Accommodation and food service activities	..	..	1 159.7	1 146.8	1 166.4	1 189.1	1 247.2	1 227.6	1 269.4	1 334.0
J	Information and communication	..	..	541.5	536.6	522.6	544.4	554.7	549.0	551.4	561.5
K	Financial and insurance activities	..	..	646.7	641.5	656.4	649.0	640.1	626.8	611.6	643.7
L	Real estate activities	..	..	121.6	130.3	137.8	144.2	140.5	145.9	125.7	132.3
M	Professional, scientific and technical activities	..	..	1 437.5	1 402.4	1 415.9	1 386.6	1 344.8	1 361.8	1 403.5	1 415.8
N	Administrative and support service activities	..	..	839.7	823.3	832.4	850.9	867.0	894.9	907.4	968.4
O	Public administration, defence, social security	..	..	1 190.6	1 165.2	1 147.7	1 197.5	1 106.7	1 064.9	1 043.8	1 045.0
P	Education	..	..	1 596.3	1 573.3	1 537.2	1 537.2	1 494.3	1 489.4	1 512.7	1 508.2
Q	Human health and social work activities	..	..	1 633.0	1 642.1	1 637.8	1 684.1	1 774.2	1 765.2	1 804.2	1 796.2
R	Arts, entertainment and recreation	..	..	246.4	250.9	262.1	264.2	282.6	292.7	297.8	303.2
S	Other service activities	..	..	736.2	759.0	761.6	722.6	713.2	687.5	652.1	658.8
T	Households as employers and own-use activities	..	..	410.6	458.2	522.0	623.9	689.9	707.6	776.1	786.5
U	Activities of extraterritorial organizations, bodies	..	..	36.1	23.1	12.9	14.3	10.5	13.4	15.5	16.3
	EMPLOYEES										
	By activity, thousands										
A-U	**All activities**	**..**	**..**	**16 970.9**	**16 782.2**	**16 574.8**	**16 700.2**	**16 679.1**	**16 440.7**	**16 543.1**	**16 738.5**
A	Agriculture, hunting and forestry	..	..	399.2	389.1	397.2	400.8	415.8	396.5	406.1	428.5
B-F	**Industry**	**..**	**..**	**5 480.4**	**5 290.1**	**5 110.8**	**5 102.8**	**4 986.1**	**4 820.4**	**4 817.5**	**4 836.9**
B	Mining and quarrying	..	..	31.1	29.1	32.0	34.7	31.2	31.6	36.2	33.3
C	Manufacturing	..	..	3 931.4	3 770.9	3 607.3	3 654.7	3 586.3	3 540.9	3 600.8	3 605.0
D	Electricity, gas, steam, air cond. supply	..	..	113.3	110.6	107.9	121.5	128.4	117.8	103.1	108.1
E	Water supply, sewerage, waste mgt, remediation	..	..	166.1	182.6	194.9	194.1	207.5	210.6	216.1	227.0
F	Construction	..	..	1 238.5	1 196.8	1 168.7	1 097.8	1 032.7	919.4	861.4	863.5
G-U	**Services**	**..**	**..**	**11 091.3**	**11 103.1**	**11 066.8**	**11 196.6**	**11 277.3**	**11 223.8**	**11 319.4**	**11 473.1**
G	Wholesale, retail trade, vehicle, motorcycle repair	..	..	2 044.3	2 000.7	1 957.3	1 914.0	2 007.6	1 976.6	1 938.5	1 915.7
H	Transportation and storage	..	..	898.9	897.8	903.8	918.6	894.8	892.8	904.6	903.4
I	Accommodation and food service activities	..	..	773.2	779.3	795.2	803.4	863.1	837.6	861.9	935.8
J	Information and communication	..	..	416.1	420.7	409.2	405.0	416.3	419.5	420.1	427.4
K	Financial and insurance activities	..	..	537.3	538.9	550.8	535.7	520.7	511.7	503.5	526.6
L	Real estate activities	..	..	46.7	59.2	60.9	66.1	69.0	70.5	59.8	58.6
M	Professional, scientific and technical activities	..	..	612.4	601.3	594.4	573.0	525.4	539.0	559.8	550.0
N	Administrative and support service activities	..	..	690.1	697.4	702.0	711.8	713.5	746.8	756.5	815.2
O	Public administration, defence, social security	..	..	1 166.0	1 146.8	1 133.9	1 179.9	1 095.1	1 052.2	1 031.6	1 036.7
P	Education	..	..	1 503.3	1 484.8	1 445.3	1 448.3	1 404.1	1 399.1	1 420.4	1 412.8
Q	Human health and social work activities	..	..	1 404.7	1 415.7	1 398.8	1 438.5	1 508.8	1 490.0	1 518.7	1 518.8
R	Arts, entertainment and recreation	..	..	137.0	140.9	143.4	150.7	159.5	165.6	180.1	190.1
S	Other service activities	..	..	416.3	438.7	437.3	418.8	402.5	409.1	382.7	391.1
T	Households as employers and own-use activities	..	..	410.5	458.2	521.9	619.2	687.2	699.9	766.2	775.0
U	Activities of extraterritorial organizations, bodies	..	..	34.5	22.7	12.6	13.5	9.6	13.3	15.0	16.0

Note: Detailed metadata:http://metalinks.oecd.org/lfs/20170518/87289
Disclaimer: http://oe.cd/disclaimer

JAPAN

Table 1. Labour force

Annual average estimates

	2006	2007	2008	2009	2010	2011	2012	2013	2014	2015
Civilian labour force, thousands										
All persons	66 640	66 840	66 740	66 500 |	66 320	65 910	65 550	65 770	65 870	65 980
Males	39 030	39 170	39 040	38 690 |	38 500	38 220	37 890	37 730	37 630	37 560
Females	27 610	27 680	27 710	27 820 |	27 830	27 680	27 660	28 040	28 240	28 420
Unemployed, thousands										
All persons	2 750	2 570	2 650	3 360 |	3 340	3 020	2 850	2 650	2 360	2 220
Males	1 680	1 540	1 590	2 030 |	2 070	1 870	1 730	1 620	1 410	1 340
Females	1 070	1 040	1 070	1 330 |	1 270	1 150	1 120	1 030	950	880
Civilian employment, thousands										
All persons	63 890	64 270	64 090	63 140 |	62 980	62 890	62 700	63 110	63 510	63 760
Males	37 350	37 630	37 450	36 660 |	36 430	36 360	36 160	36 100	36 210	36 220
Females	26 540	26 650	26 640	26 490 |	26 560	26 530	26 540	27 010	27 290	27 540
Civilian employment (%)										
All persons	100.0	100.0	100.0	100.0 |	100.0	100.0	100.0	100.0	100.0	100.0
Males	58.5	58.5	58.4	58.1 |	57.8	57.8	57.7	57.2	57.0	56.8
Females	41.5	41.5	41.6	42.0 |	42.2	42.2	42.3	42.8	43.0	43.2
Unemployment rate (% of civilian labour force)										
All persons	4.1	3.8	4.0	5.1 |	5.0	4.6	4.3	4.0	3.6	3.4
Males	4.3	3.9	4.1	5.2 |	5.4	4.9	4.6	4.3	3.7	3.6
Females	3.9	3.8	3.9	4.8 |	4.6	4.2	4.0	3.7	3.4	3.1
CIVIL. EMPL. - PROFESSIONAL STATUS, thousands										
All activities	**63 820**	**64 120**	**63 850**	**62 820 |**	**62 570**	**59 770**	**62 700**	**63 110**	**63 510**	**63 760**
Employees	54 720	55 230	55 240	54 600 |	54 630	52 440	55 040	55 530	55 950	56 400
Employers and persons working on own account	6 330	6 220	6 070	5 940 |	5 790	5 350	5 590	5 540	5 560	5 430
Unpaid family workers	2 470	2 360	2 240	2 020 |	1 890	1 740	1 800	1 740	1 680	1 620
Employees as % of civilian employment	**85.7**	**86.1**	**86.5**	**86.9 |**	**87.3**	**87.7**	**87.8**	**88.0**	**88.1**	**88.5**
Part-time employment (%)										
Part-time as % of employment	18.0	18.9	19.6	20.3	20.2	20.6	20.5	21.9	22.7	22.7
Male share of part time employment	27.6	28.5	29.6	30.1	29.7	29.0	29.2	29.7	30.2	30.2
Female share of part time employment	72.4	71.5	70.4	69.9	70.3	71.0	70.8	70.3	69.8	69.8
Male part-time as % of male employment	8.5	9.2	9.9	10.5	10.4	10.3	10.3	11.3	12.0	12.0
Female part-time as % of female employment	31.3	32.6	33.2	33.8	33.9	34.8	34.5	36.2	37.2	36.9
Duration of unemployment (% of total unemployment)										
Less than one month	15.2	15.8	14.7	13.5	9.9	10.9	12.2	11.3	12.2	12.6
More than 1 month and less than 3 months	20.4	21.1	21.7	22.4	18.9	18.6	18.0	18.7	21.4	21.0
More than 3 months and less than 6 months	16.3	15.0	16.7	17.8	15.5	15.0	15.1	14.0	14.4	15.9
More than 6 months and less than 1 year	15.2	16.2	13.6	17.8	18.0	16.1	16.2	14.8	14.4	15.0
More than 1 year	33.0	32.0	33.3	28.5	37.6	39.4	38.5	41.2	37.6	35.5

Note: Detailed metadata: http://metalinks.oecd.org/lfs/20170518/30293, http://metalinks.oecd.org/lfs/20170518/87289, http://metalinks.oecd.org/lfs/20170518/3c071 and http://metalinks.oecd.org/lfs/20170518/6bbf2.

Disclaimer: http://oe.cd/disclaimer

JAPAN

Table 2. Participation rates and unemployment rates by age and sex

Annual average estimates, percentage

	2006	2007	2008	2009	2010	2011	2012	2013	2014	2015
Participation rates										
Males										
15-19	16.4	16.4	16.1	14.7	14.5	13.6	14.8	15.2	15.9	16.0
20-24	69.1	70.0	69.1	67.6	67.1	67.4	67.4	67.7	68.6	68.8
25-34	95.3	95.8	95.5	95.2	95.3	95.1	94.6	94.7	94.7	94.4
35-44	96.9	96.8	96.8	96.8	96.8	96.6	96.3	96.4	96.4	96.2
45-54	96.3	96.3	96.4	96.1	96.4	95.8	95.6	95.8	95.4	95.6
55-59	93.4	93.1	92.7	92.4	92.8	92.6	92.2	92.7	93.2	93.1
60-64	70.9	74.4	76.4	76.3	76.0	75.6	75.6	76.0	77.6	78.9
15-24	44.7	45.1	44.5	43.0	42.3	41.7	41.5	41.8	42.7	43.0
25-54	96.1	96.3	96.3	96.1	96.2	95.9	95.6	95.7	95.6	95.5
55-64	83.8	84.9	85.1	84.4	83.9	83.1	82.9	83.5	84.8	85.6
65 and over	29.2	29.7	29.7	29.4	28.8	28.4	28.7	29.5	30.2	31.1
15-64	84.8	85.2	85.2	84.8	84.8	84.4	84.3	84.6	84.9	85.0
Females										
15-19	16.6	16.2	16.2	16.2	15.6	15.0	14.6	15.9	16.3	16.8
20-24	70.1	69.5	69.5	69.9	69.4	69.1	68.4	70.3	69.8	68.5
25-34	68.6	69.3	70.1	71.6	72.2	72.2	72.9	74.3	74.8	75.4
35-44	67.3	68.0	67.8	68.3	68.7	69.0	69.8	71.4	72.6	73.4
45-54	72.2	73.2	73.4	73.9	74.3	74.2	74.6	75.7	76.3	76.8
55-59	60.3	60.8	61.6	62.5	63.3	63.8	64.4	66.5	68.1	69.0
60-64	40.2	42.2	43.6	44.6	45.7	45.8	46.0	47.4	48.7	50.6
15-24	45.3	44.7	44.7	44.8	44.0	43.3	42.0	43.5	43.4	43.1
25-54	69.3	70.1	70.3	71.1	71.6	71.6	72.3	73.6	74.5	75.2
55-64	51.5	52.5	53.1	53.5	53.9	53.7	54.0	55.8	57.5	59.2
65 and over	12.9	13.0	13.0	13.1	13.3	13.2	13.4	13.8	14.5	15.3
15-64	61.3	61.9	62.2	62.9	63.2	63.0	63.4	65.0	66.0	66.7
All persons										
15-24	45.0	44.9	44.6	43.9	43.1	42.5	41.8	42.6	43.0	43.0
25-54	82.8	83.3	83.4	83.7	84.0	83.9	84.0	84.8	85.1	85.4
55-64	67.3	68.4	68.8	68.7	68.7	68.2	68.2	69.4	71.0	72.2
65 and over	19.8	20.1	20.2	20.1	19.9	19.7	19.9	20.5	21.3	22.1
15-64	73.1	73.6	73.8	73.9	74.0	73.8	73.9	74.9	75.5	75.9
Unemployment rates										
Males										
15-19	9.3	9.4	9.8	10.9	11.1	10.0	8.7	6.4	6.1	6.1
20-24	8.7	8.0	7.5	9.9	10.3	8.8	8.8	7.9	7.3	5.9
25-34	5.3	4.9	5.2	6.6	6.6	6.0	5.7	5.7	4.8	4.8
35-44	3.1	3.0	3.2	4.4	4.2	3.9	3.8	3.7	3.3	3.0
45-54	3.1	2.9	3.1	3.9	4.1	3.5	3.4	3.4	2.9	2.9
55-59	4.0	3.5	3.7	4.7	5.2	4.4	4.1	3.9	3.4	3.1
60-64	5.4	5.0	5.1	6.3	7.1	6.2	5.7	4.9	4.3	4.2
15-24	8.8	8.3	7.9	10.1	10.4	8.9	8.7	7.6	7.1	5.9
25-54	3.9	3.6	3.8	4.9	4.9	4.4	4.3	4.2	3.6	3.5
55-64	4.5	4.1	4.3	5.4	6.1	5.3	4.9	4.4	3.8	3.7
65 and over	2.8	2.6	2.5	3.3	3.0	2.9	2.9	3.0	2.8	2.6
15-64	4.4	4.1	4.3	5.5	5.6	5.0	4.7	4.5	4.0	3.7
Total	4.3	4.0	4.1	5.3	5.4	4.8	4.6	4.3	3.8	3.6
Females										
15-19	9.6	8.0	6.1	8.3	6.5	7.1	7.0	6.4	4.2	4.1
20-24	6.7	6.9	6.6	8.0	8.3	7.1	7.1	6.1	5.7	5.3
25-34	5.1	5.1	5.4	6.1	5.6	5.4	5.0	4.7	4.2	4.3
35-44	3.8	3.9	3.8	4.9	5.0	4.6	4.4	3.9	3.5	3.0
45-54	2.6	2.6	2.8	3.8	3.8	3.3	3.4	3.1	3.1	2.7
55-59	2.8	2.2	2.6	3.1	3.2	2.8	2.7	2.7	2.7	2.3
60-64	3.0	2.8	2.5	3.8	3.5	3.4	3.3	3.0	2.2	2.3
15-24	7.2	7.1	6.6	8.1	8.0	7.1	7.1	6.2	5.4	5.1
25-54	3.9	3.9	4.0	4.9	4.8	4.4	4.3	3.9	3.5	3.3
55-64	2.8	2.4	2.6	3.4	3.3	3.1	3.0	2.8	2.5	2.3
65 and over	0.5	1.0	1.4	1.4	0.9	0.9	1.3	1.2	1.5	1.0
15-64	4.1	3.9	4.0	5.0	4.8	4.4	4.3	3.9	3.5	3.3
Total	3.8	3.7	3.8	4.7	4.5	4.1	4.0	3.7	3.3	3.0
All persons										
15-24	8.0	7.7	7.2	9.1	9.2	8.0	7.9	6.9	6.3	5.5
25-54	3.9	3.7	3.9	4.9	4.9	4.4	4.3	4.1	3.6	3.4
55-64	3.9	3.4	3.6	4.6	5.0	4.4	4.1	3.8	3.3	3.1
65 and over	1.9	2.0	2.1	2.6	2.2	2.2	2.3	2.3	2.3	2.0
15-64	4.3	4.1	4.2	5.3	5.3	4.8	4.6	4.3	3.8	3.5

Note: Detailed metadata at:http://metalinks.oecd.org/lfs/20170518/6f97b
Disclaimer: http://oe.cd/disclaimer

Table 3. Civilian employment and employees: breakdown by activity - ISIC Rev. 4

Annual average estimates

		2006	2007	2008	2009	2010	2011	2012	2013	2014	2015
	CIVILIAN EMPLOYMENT										
	By activity, thousands										
A-U	**All activities**	**63 820.0**	**64 120.0**	**63 850.0**	**62 820.0**	**62 570.0**	**59 770.0**	**62 700.0**	**63 110.0**	**63 510.0**	**63 760.0**
A	Agriculture, hunting and forestry	2 720.0	2 720.0	2 680.0	2 620.0	2 520.0	2 230.0	2 400.0	2 330.0	2 300.0	2 280.0
B-F	**Industry**	**18 200.0**	**18 140.0**	**17 780.0**	**16 910.0**	**16 440.0**	**15 570.0**	**16 260.0**	**16 290.0**	**16 370.0**	**16 260.0**
B	Mining and quarrying	30.0	40.0	30.0	30.0	30.0	30.0	30.0	30.0	30.0	30.0
C	Manufacturing	11 930.0	11 940.0	11 740.0	11 040.0	10 780.0	10 240.0	10 590.0	10 660.0	10 680.0	10 620.0
D	Electricity, gas, steam, air cond. supply	650.0	640.0	640.0	670.0	650.0	570.0	610.0	610.0	610.0	610.0
E	Water supply, sewerage, waste mgt, remediation	0.0	0.0	0.0	0.0	0.0	0.0	0.0	0.0	0.0	0.0
F	Construction	5 590.0	5 520.0	5 370.0	5 170.0	4 980.0	4 730.0	5 030.0	4 990.0	5 050.0	5 000.0
G-U	**Services**	**42 900.0**	**43 260.0**	**43 390.0**	**43 290.0**	**43 610.0**	**41 970.0**	**44 040.0**	**44 490.0**	**44 840.0**	**45 220.0**
G	Wholesale, retail trade, vehicle, motorcycle repair	11 100.0	11 130.0	11 010.0	10 880.0	10 900.0	10 370.0	10 750.0	10 890.0	10 910.0	10 830.0
H	Transportation and storage	3 650.0	3 640.0	3 620.0	3 660.0	3 660.0	3 500.0	3 610.0	3 700.0	3 680.0	3 660.0
I	Accommodation and food service activities	3 740.0	3 800.0	3 730.0	3 800.0	3 870.0	3 650.0	3 760.0	3 840.0	3 850.0	3 830.0
J	Information and communication	1 800.0	1 920.0	1 890.0	1 930.0	1 960.0	1 850.0	1 880.0	1 920.0	2 030.0	2 090.0
K	Financial and insurance activities	1 930.0	1 920.0	2 000.0	1 990.0	1 920.0	1 790.0	1 890.0	1 910.0	1 790.0	1 800.0
L	Real estate activities	790.0	850.0	830.0	830.0	830.0	840.0	850.0	830.0	860.0	920.0
M	Professional, scientific and technical activities	2 040.0	1 980.0	2 000.0	1 950.0	1 980.0	1 990.0	2 050.0	2 070.0	2 120.0	2 140.0
N	Administrative and support service activities	3 470.0	3 590.0	3 670.0	3 420.0	3 360.0	3 230.0	3 450.0	2 820.0	2 780.0	2 940.0
O	Public administration, defence, social security	2 260.0	2 310.0	2 260.0	2 250.0	2 240.0	2 140.0	2 280.0	2 320.0	2 380.0	2 340.0
P	Education	2 820.0	2 790.0	2 830.0	2 870.0	2 880.0	2 800.0	2 950.0	2 990.0	3 010.0	3 030.0
Q	Human health and social work activities	5 710.0	5 790.0	5 980.0	6 210.0	6 530.0	6 480.0	7 060.0	7 350.0	7 570.0	7 840.0
R	Arts, entertainment and recreation	790.0	750.0	770.0	770.0	790.0	760.0	770.0	770.0	730.0	710.0
S	Other service activities	2 080.0	2 010.0	2 040.0	2 100.0	2 050.0	1 980.0	2 080.0	2 140.0	2 110.0	2 060.0
T	Households as employers and own-use activities	0.0	0.0	0.0	0.0	0.0	0.0	0.0	0.0	0.0	0.0
U	Activities of extraterritorial organizations, bodies	30.0	20.0	20.0	20.0	20.0	20.0	30.0	30.0	20.0	30.0
	EMPLOYEES										
	By activity, thousands										
A-U	**All activities**	**54 720.0**	**55 230.0**	**55 240.0**	**54 600.0**	**54 630.0**	**52 440.0**	**55 040.0**	**55 530.0**	**55 950.0**	**56 400.0**
A	Agriculture, hunting and forestry	490.0	520.0	540.0	570.0	590.0	550.0	570.0	580.0	610.0	610.0
B-F	**Industry**	**16 280.0**	**16 310.0**	**16 050.0**	**15 320.0**	**14 920.0**	**14 150.0**	..	..	..	..
B	Mining and quarrying	30.0	40.0	30.0	30.0	30.0	30.0	30.0	20.0	30.0	30.0
C	Manufacturing	11 080.0	11 150.0	11 020.0	10 410.0	10 200.0	9 710.0	10 030.0	10 110.0	10 100.0	10 060.0
D	Electricity, gas, steam, air cond. supply	640.0	630.0	630.0	660.0	640.0	560.0	600.0	600.0	600.0	600.0
E	Water supply, sewerage, waste mgt, remediation	0.0	0.0	0.0	0.0	0.0	0.0	..	..	..	..
F	Construction	4 530.0	4 490.0	4 370.0	4 220.0	4 050.0	3 850.0	4 110.0	4 080.0	4 100.0	4 070.0
G-U	**Services**	**37 950.0**	**38 400.0**	**38 650.0**	**38 710.0**	**39 120.0**	**37 740.0**	..	..	..	..
G	Wholesale, retail trade, vehicle, motorcycle repair	9 680.0	9 730.0	9 660.0	9 600.0	9 670.0	9 260.0	9 630.0	9 810.0	9 860.0	9 850.0
H	Transportation and storage	3 470.0	3 470.0	3 450.0	3 490.0	3 510.0	3 360.0	3 460.0	3 550.0	3 540.0	3 530.0
I	Accommodation and food service activities	2 930.0	3 010.0	3 010.0	3 080.0	3 160.0	3 010.0	3 110.0	3 200.0	3 230.0	3 240.0
J	Information and communication	1 740.0	1 850.0	1 820.0	1 850.0	1 880.0	1 770.0	1 800.0	1 840.0	1 940.0	2 000.0
K	Financial and insurance activities	1 870.0	1 860.0	1 950.0	1 950.0	1 870.0	1 750.0	1 850.0	1 860.0	1 740.0	1 770.0
L	Real estate activities	680.0	730.0	710.0	700.0	710.0	700.0	720.0	710.0	750.0	800.0
M	Professional, scientific and technical activities	1 510.0	1 480.0	1 490.0	1 470.0	1 510.0	1 530.0	1 570.0	1 580.0	1 630.0	1 660.0
N	Administrative and support service activities	3 210.0	3 300.0	3 380.0	3 130.0	3 100.0	2 970.0	3 160.0	2 530.0	2 490.0	2 640.0
O	Public administration, defence, social security	2 260.0	2 310.0	2 260.0	2 250.0	2 240.0	2 140.0	2 280.0	2 320.0	2 380.0	2 340.0
P	Education	2 550.0	2 540.0	2 580.0	2 610.0	2 610.0	2 540.0	2 670.0	2 730.0	2 740.0	2 780.0
Q	Human health and social work activities	5 360.0	5 470.0	5 650.0	5 880.0	6 200.0	6 180.0	6 760.0	7 040.0	7 240.0	7 510.0
R	Arts, entertainment and recreation	750.0	720.0	720.0	730.0	740.0	710.0	720.0	730.0	690.0	670.0
S	Other service activities	1 500.0	1 450.0	1 490.0	1 540.0	1 520.0	1 470.0	1 550.0	1 600.0	1 560.0	1 530.0
T	Households as employers and own-use activities	0.0	0.0	0.0	0.0	0.0	0.0	0.0	..	..	..
U	Activities of extraterritorial organizations, bodies	30.0	20.0	20.0	20.0	20.0	20.0	30.0	30.0	20.0	30.0

Note: Detailed metadata at: http://metalinks.oecd.org/lfs/20170518/60d8f.
Disclaimer: http://oe.cd/disclaimer

KOREA

Table 1. Labour force

Annual average estimates

	2006	2007	2008	2009	2010	2011	2012	2013	2014	2015
Civilian labour force, thousands										
All persons	23 978	24 216	24 347	24 394	24 748	25 099	25 501	25 873	26 536	26 913
Males	13 978	14 124	14 208	14 318	14 492	14 683	14 891	15 071	15 387	15 543
Females	10 001	10 092	10 139	10 076	10 256	10 416	10 609	10 802	11 149	11 370
Unemployed, thousands										
All persons	827	783	769	889	920	855	820	807	937	976
Males	533	517	505	584	577	530	504	498	548	572
Females	294	266	265	304	342	325	316	309	389	405
Civilian employment, thousands										
All persons	23 151	23 433	23 577	23 506	23 829	24 244	24 681	25 066	25 599	25 936
Males	13 444	13 607	13 703	13 734	13 915	14 153	14 387	14 573	14 839	14 971
Females	9 706	9 826	9 874	9 772	9 914	10 091	10 294	10 494	10 761	10 965
Civilian employment (%)										
All persons	100.0	100.0	100.0	100.0	100.0	100.0	100.0	100.0	100.0	100.0
Males	58.1	58.1	58.1	58.4	58.4	58.4	58.3	58.1	58.0	57.7
Females	41.9	41.9	41.9	41.6	41.6	41.6	41.7	41.9	42.0	42.3
Unemployment rate (% of civilian labour force)										
All persons	3.5	3.2	3.2	3.6	3.7	3.4	3.2	3.1	3.5	3.6
Males	3.8	3.7	3.6	4.1	4.0	3.6	3.4	3.3	3.6	3.7
Females	2.9	2.6	2.6	3.0	3.3	3.1	3.0	2.9	3.5	3.6
CIVIL. EMPL. - PROFESSIONAL STATUS, thousands										
All activities	**23 151**	**23 433**	**23 577**	**23 506**	**23 829**	**24 244**	**24 681**	**25 067**	**25 600**	**25 936**
Employees	15 551	15 970	16 206	16 454	16 971	17 397	17 712	18 195	18 743	19 230
Employers and persons working on own account	6 135	6 049	5 970	5 711	5 593	5 594	5 718	5 651	5 652	5 563
Unpaid family workers	1 466	1 413	1 401	1 341	1 266	1 254	1 251	1 221	1 205	1 144
Employees as % of civilian employment	**67.2**	**68.2**	**68.7**	**70.0**	**71.2**	**71.8**	**71.8**	**72.6**	**73.2**	**74.1**
Part-time employment (%)										
Part-time as % of employment	8.8	8.9	9.3	9.9	10.7	13.5	10.2	11.1	10.5	10.6
Male share of part time employment	41.5	41.1	41.0	40.7	39.7	43.4	39.0	39.5	37.8	37.4
Female share of part time employment	58.5	58.9	59.0	59.3	60.3	56.6	61.0	60.5	62.2	62.6
Male part-time as % of male employment	6.3	6.3	6.5	6.9	7.2	10.0	6.8	7.5	6.8	6.9
Female part-time as % of female employment	12.3	12.5	13.2	14.2	15.5	18.5	15.0	16.2	15.6	15.9
Duration of unemployment (% of total unemployment)										
Less than one month	..	..	..	..	..	..	..	..	..	..
More than 1 month and less than 3 months	61.2	60.1	62.3	63.9	67.2	67.5	63.9	63.9	63.3	59.5
More than 3 months and less than 6 months	27.5	28.2	28.0	27.2	25.9	25.7	27.6	28.2	29.2	30.6
More than 6 months and less than 1 year	10.2	11.2	9.3	8.5	6.6	6.4	8.2	7.5	7.3	9.6
More than 1 year	1.1	0.6	0.4	0.5	0.3	0.4	0.3	0.4	0.2	0.4

Note: Detailed metadata: http://metalinks.oecd.org/lfs/20170518/eab55, http://metalinks.oecd.org/lfs/20170518/87289, http://metalinks.oecd.org/lfs/20170518/d3971 and http://metalinks.oecd.org/lfs/20170518/3228a.

Disclaimer: http://oe.cd/disclaimer

Table 2. Participation rates and unemployment rates by age and sex

Annual average estimates, percentage

	2006	2007	2008	2009	2010	2011	2012	2013	2014	2015
Participation rates										
Males										
15-19	6.3	6.5	5.6	5.0	5.5	6.3	6.3	6.6	7.6	7.7
20-24	48.4	47.3	43.8	44.0	42.7	42.3	43.4	42.1	44.4	46.1
25-34	86.1	85.0	84.4	84.2	84.4	84.9	84.8	84.9	85.7	85.6
35-44	94.6	94.7	94.7	93.8	94.1	94.3	94.4	94.2	94.9	94.5
45-54	91.6	91.6	91.9	91.5	91.9	91.7	92.2	92.4	92.8	92.5
55-59	79.9	82.6	82.3	82.7	83.4	83.8	84.7	85.5	87.4	86.7
60-64	68.6	69.4	68.6	68.8	70.2	72.2	72.3	73.0	74.2	74.7
15-24	24.3	23.1	21.0	20.4	20.2	20.6	22.1	22.5	24.6	25.9
25-54	90.8	90.5	90.5	90.0	90.3	90.5	90.7	90.7	91.3	91.1
55-64	74.9	76.8	76.3	76.6	77.7	78.9	79.6	80.4	82.0	81.8
65 and over	41.9	42.9	41.9	41.5	40.6	40.6	41.6	42.6	43.0	42.2
15-64	77.7	77.6	77.3	76.9	77.1	77.4	77.6	77.6	78.6	78.6
Females										
15-19	8.9	8.1	7.5	7.5	8.5	9.0	9.1	8.7	9.4	9.9
20-24	59.1	56.5	54.5	53.0	53.5	52.3	53.5	52.2	54.6	56.3
25-34	60.1	61.0	61.3	60.5	62.1	63.0	63.4	64.5	66.0	66.9
35-44	62.5	62.5	62.1	60.8	60.9	60.7	60.1	59.9	60.5	60.5
45-54	61.8	62.5	63.3	63.3	63.5	64.6	65.1	66.0	67.9	68.9
55-59	49.7	50.6	52.5	51.9	53.4	54.0	54.8	56.0	57.8	58.6
60-64	43.8	43.9	42.3	42.0	41.5	42.2	43.9	45.0	46.3	48.2
15-24	35.5	32.7	31.1	30.0	30.4	30.1	30.9	30.6	32.5	34.1
25-54	61.5	62.0	62.3	61.5	62.2	62.8	62.8	63.4	64.8	65.4
55-64	47.0	47.6	47.9	47.5	48.1	48.9	50.2	51.4	53.0	54.2
65 and over	22.7	23.3	22.9	22.2	21.7	21.8	23.0	23.4	24.0	23.4
15-64	54.8	54.8	54.7	53.9	54.5	54.9	55.2	55.6	57.0	57.9
All persons										
15-24	30.2	28.2	26.3	25.4	25.5	25.5	26.6	26.6	28.6	30.1
25-54	76.3	76.4	76.6	76.0	76.4	76.9	77.0	77.3	78.2	78.5
55-64	60.7	62.0	61.8	61.8	62.7	63.7	64.7	65.7	67.3	67.8
65 and over	30.5	31.3	30.6	30.1	29.4	29.5	30.7	31.4	31.9	31.3
15-64	66.2	66.2	66.0	65.4	65.8	66.2	66.4	66.6	67.8	68.3
Unemployment rates										
Males										
15-19	10.9	9.3	12.6	15.3	15.6	12.2	9.5	11.3	10.2	10.4
20-24	11.8	11.8	11.3	11.3	10.4	12.1	9.8	9.5	11.4	11.5
25-34	5.9	5.9	5.6	6.6	6.5	5.6	5.3	6.1	6.1	6.2
35-44	2.6	2.7	2.8	3.2	2.9	2.6	2.6	2.2	2.3	2.4
45-54	2.6	2.2	2.2	2.9	2.6	2.3	2.0	1.8	2.1	2.0
55-59	3.1	2.6	2.7	2.8	3.1	2.5	2.7	2.5	2.6	3.2
60-64	2.9	2.8	2.3	2.7	3.8	3.7	3.5	3.2	3.4	3.6
15-24	11.7	11.4	11.5	11.9	11.2	12.1	9.7	9.8	11.2	11.3
25-54	3.6	3.6	3.5	4.1	3.8	3.4	3.2	3.2	3.3	3.3
55-64	3.0	2.7	2.6	2.8	3.4	3.0	3.0	2.8	2.9	3.3
65 and over	1.0	0.9	1.2	1.6	2.6	2.5	2.3	1.6	2.2	2.6
15-64	4.0	3.8	3.7	4.3	4.1	3.7	3.5	3.4	3.7	3.8
Total	3.8	3.7	3.6	4.1	4.0	3.6	3.4	3.3	3.6	3.7
Females										
15-19	10.5	8.9	8.5	10.2	9.6	9.7	8.3	9.5	8.4	10.7
20-24	8.8	6.9	7.9	8.3	8.9	7.8	8.5	9.0	9.3	9.8
25-34	3.8	3.7	3.7	4.3	4.3	4.5	4.0	4.1	5.0	4.5
35-44	2.0	2.1	2.0	2.4	2.7	2.5	2.3	2.1	2.7	3.0
45-54	1.6	1.4	1.6	1.8	1.9	1.8	1.7	1.7	2.3	2.3
55-59	1.2	1.3	1.2	1.7	2.0	1.5	1.7	1.4	2.2	2.3
60-64	1.4	1.5	0.9	1.5	2.6	2.0	1.8	0.9	1.3	1.5
15-24	9.0	7.1	8.0	8.5	9.0	8.1	8.5	9.0	9.2	10.0
25-54	2.5	2.4	2.4	2.8	2.9	2.9	2.6	2.6	3.3	3.2
55-64	1.2	1.4	1.1	1.7	2.2	1.7	1.7	1.2	1.9	2.0
65 and over	0.2	0.3	0.3	0.6	2.0	2.0	1.8	1.3	1.8	2.1
15-64	3.1	2.8	2.8	3.2	3.4	3.2	3.1	3.0	3.6	3.7
Total	2.9	2.6	2.6	3.0	3.3	3.1	3.0	2.9	3.5	3.6
All persons										
15-24	10.0	8.8	9.3	9.8	9.8	9.6	9.0	9.3	10.0	10.5
25-54	3.2	3.1	3.0	3.6	3.5	3.2	3.0	2.9	3.3	3.3
55-64	2.3	2.2	2.0	2.3	2.9	2.5	2.5	2.1	2.5	2.8
65 and over	0.6	0.7	0.8	1.1	2.3	2.3	2.1	1.5	2.0	2.4
15-64	3.6	3.4	3.3	3.8	3.8	3.5	3.3	3.2	3.7	3.7

Note: Detailed metadata at:http://metalinks.oecd.org/lfs/20170518/6f97b
Disclaimer: http://oe.cd/disclaimer

Table 3. Civilian employment and employees: breakdown by activity - ISIC Rev. 4

Annual average estimates

		2006	2007	2008	2009	2010	2011	2012	2013	2014	2015
	CIVILIAN EMPLOYMENT										
	By activity, thousands										
A-U	**All activities**	**23 150.8**	**23 432.8**	**23 577.3**	**23 505.7**	**23 828.7**	**24 244.2**	**24 680.7**	**25 066.5**	**25 599.6**	**25 936.3**
A	Agriculture, hunting and forestry	1 781.0	1 722.9	1 686.0	1 648.3	1 566.6	1 541.7	1 527.9	1 520.2	1 452.0	1 345.1
B-F	**Industry**	**6 043.3**	**6 027.0**	**5 953.6**	**5 747.0**	**5 945.0**	**6 005.3**	**6 041.3**	**6 116.7**	**6 309.0**	**6 503.3**
B	Mining and quarrying	16.1	16.4	22.9	22.8	21.1	17.0	14.7	15.8	13.4	13.5
C	Manufacturing	4 056.6	4 014.2	3 962.6	3 836.3	4 027.6	4 091.0	4 105.1	4 184.0	4 329.8	4 485.9
D	Electricity, gas, steam, air cond. supply	75.9	86.0	90.3	95.8	78.6	75.7	75.8	90.3	82.8	92.8
E	Water supply, sewerage, waste mgt, remediation	61.8	61.5	66.2	71.9	64.8	70.8	73.0	72.8	87.3	88.1
F	Construction	1 832.9	1 848.9	1 811.7	1 720.2	1 753.0	1 750.8	1 772.8	1 753.8	1 795.8	1 822.9
G-U	**Services**	**15 326.5**	**15 682.9**	**15 937.8**	**16 110.3**	**16 317.1**	**16 697.3**	**17 111.4**	**17 429.7**	**17 838.6**	**18 088.0**
G	Wholesale, retail trade, vehicle, motorcycle repair	3 710.8	3 672.8	3 631.3	3 599.9	3 580.3	3 638.2	3 688.9	3 659.7	3 791.5	3 783.3
H	Transportation and storage	1 192.7	1 246.9	1 247.8	1 247.0	1 280.0	1 332.1	1 379.6	1 413.3	1 406.9	1 409.3
I	Accommodation and food service activities	2 049.3	2 049.2	2 043.8	1 936.3	1 889.2	1 853.6	1 906.3	1 970.7	2 097.5	2 179.0
J	Information and communication	650.9	633.9	626.8	652.1	667.8	702.9	700.3	692.1	713.8	771.5
K	Financial and insurance activities	785.7	806.1	821.3	766.3	807.8	845.6	841.6	863.8	837.4	789.2
L	Real estate activities	499.4	505.3	488.8	500.3	516.9	486.0	485.8	485.1	507.6	534.6
M	Professional, scientific and technical activities	680.9	701.7	756.5	843.8	883.2	960.8	1 028.0	1 021.9	1 024.3	1 047.8
N	Administrative and support service activities	818.7	953.5	973.8	944.3	1 022.8	1 086.6	1 116.6	1 173.3	1 180.1	1 248.4
O	Public administration, defence, social security	801.4	796.8	840.3	1 031.7	960.1	951.3	951.4	965.7	957.3	936.3
P	Education	1 701.5	1 739.7	1 783.8	1 831.4	1 798.8	1 686.2	1 743.7	1 747.8	1 806.8	1 817.7
Q	Human health and social work activities	680.9	739.8	842.3	997.9	1 152.7	1 311.2	1 399.3	1 554.3	1 693.1	1 769.9
R	Arts, entertainment and recreation	378.8	370.7	418.8	390.4	379.7	416.8	408.8	392.2	393.4	424.3
S	Other service activities	1 218.8	1 291.3	1 297.2	1 211.6	1 216.3	1 261.6	1 286.2	1 312.4	1 299.3	1 277.0
T	Households as employers and own-use activities	138.2	160.6	149.8	146.5	149.7	153.1	166.4	171.4	115.8	82.2
U	Activities of extraterritorial organizations, bodies	19.6	15.4	16.3	12.5	13.4	12.8	9.3	7.5	14.2	18.4
	EMPLOYEES										
	By activity, thousands										
A-U	**All activities**	**15 550.6**	**15 970.2**	**16 206.4**	**16 453.7**	**16 970.6**	**17 397.1**	**17 712.1**	**18 194.7**	**18 742.5**	**19 229.8**
A	Agriculture, hunting and forestry	160.8	170.3	163.6	172.7	174.5	173.4	153.3	147.3	140.3	135.2
B-F	**Industry**	**4 948.8**	**5 000.6**	**4 963.8**	**4 816.7**	**4 956.4**	**5 012.5**	**5 032.5**	**5 174.8**	**5 364.5**	**5 569.3**
B	Mining and quarrying	14.9	16.2	21.9	20.4	18.9	15.6	12.9	14.5	13.2	12.5
C	Manufacturing	3 445.1	3 421.9	3 373.3	3 277.1	3 439.6	3 508.8	3 548.8	3 668.0	3 826.3	3 996.3
D	Electricity, gas, steam, air cond. supply	73.3	84.7	89.7	95.0	77.4	74.9	75.0	89.4	80.9	91.1
E	Water supply, sewerage, waste mgt, remediation	54.7	56.7	58.3	63.1	58.3	65.5	67.1	66.4	78.6	81.0
F	Construction	1 360.8	1 421.1	1 420.6	1 361.1	1 362.2	1 347.7	1 328.7	1 336.5	1 365.5	1 388.4
G-U	**Services**	**10 441.0**	**10 799.3**	**11 079.0**	**11 464.3**	**11 839.7**	**12 211.2**	**12 526.3**	**12 872.6**	**13 237.7**	**13 525.3**
G	Wholesale, retail trade, vehicle, motorcycle repair	1 909.0	1 964.2	1 942.4	1 945.9	2 014.8	2 102.2	2 130.2	2 141.0	2 277.4	2 264.1
H	Transportation and storage	667.3	667.4	679.5	676.2	697.1	711.2	735.4	748.6	767.4	773.5
I	Accommodation and food service activities	1 123.2	1 132.5	1 143.8	1 105.3	1 136.0	1 096.0	1 112.0	1 193.8	1 282.8	1 379.8
J	Information and communication	596.3	585.6	575.7	608.5	608.0	636.2	643.5	638.6	647.4	703.3
K	Financial and insurance activities	732.4	754.4	778.1	737.2	778.4	812.5	809.6	833.8	806.6	758.8
L	Real estate activities	303.1	301.6	287.0	313.4	337.9	312.2	320.8	333.6	359.0	369.1
M	Professional, scientific and technical activities	565.2	593.0	634.3	717.5	752.1	838.7	888.7	888.9	876.7	896.8
N	Administrative and support service activities	773.8	904.2	918.6	893.1	971.4	1 041.5	1 069.9	1 118.7	1 109.5	1 176.7
O	Public administration, defence, social security	801.2	796.5	840.1	1 031.4	960.1	951.2	951.2	965.5	957.3	936.1
P	Education	1 351.2	1 371.3	1 418.7	1 465.0	1 439.6	1 359.6	1 398.4	1 379.0	1 426.0	1 456.3
Q	Human health and social work activities	623.7	679.3	776.8	926.2	1 077.0	1 232.4	1 322.2	1 461.2	1 596.0	1 670.9
R	Arts, entertainment and recreation	231.9	230.7	261.3	239.8	234.3	245.8	247.1	247.0	236.1	279.4
S	Other service activities	610.3	646.8	659.9	648.5	673.2	709.3	726.0	750.8	781.8	773.6
T	Households as employers and own-use activities	132.7	156.4	146.3	143.7	146.4	149.5	161.8	164.7	99.5	68.5
U	Activities of extraterritorial organizations, bodies	19.6	15.3	16.4	12.5	13.2	12.7	9.2	7.4	14.2	18.4

Note: Detailed metadata:http://metalinks.oecd.org/lfs/20170518/87289
Disclaimer: http://oe.cd/disclaimer

LATVIA

Table 1. Labour force

Annual average estimates

	2006	2007	2008	2009	2010	2011	2012	2013	2014	2015
Civilian labour force, thousands										
All persons	1 109	1 126	1 143	1 101	1 057	1 028	1 031	1 014	992	994
Males	567	578	580	550	521	512	511	504	497	499
Females	542	548	564	552	535	517	520	510	495	495
Unemployed, thousands										
All persons	78	68	89	193	206	167	155	120	108	98
Males	42	38	49	115	119	95	83	64	59	55
Females	37	31	40	78	87	71	73	57	49	43
Civilian employment, thousands										
All persons	1 031	1 057	1 055	909	851	862	876	894	885	896
Males	526	540	531	435	403	416	428	441	439	444
Females	505	517	524	474	448	445	447	453	446	452
Civilian employment (%)										
All persons	100.0	100.0	100.0	100.0	100.0	100.0	100.0	100.0	100.0	100.0
Males	51.0	51.1	50.4	47.9	47.3	48.3	48.9	49.3	49.6	49.5
Females	49.0	48.9	49.6	52.1	52.7	51.7	51.1	50.7	50.4	50.5
Unemployment rate (% of civilian labour force)										
All persons	..	..	..	..	..	..	..	..	..	..
Males	..	..	..	..	..	..	..	..	..	..
Females	..	..	..	..	..	..	..	..	..	..
CIVIL. EMPL. - PROFESSIONAL STATUS, thousands										
All activities	**1 031**	**1 057**	**1 055**	**909**	**851**	**862**	**876**	**894**	**885**	**896**
Employees	911	941	947	804	753	764	776	790	782	783
Employers and persons working on own account	104	98	94	91	86	88	92	96	95	106
Unpaid family workers	16	18	14	14	12	10	8	8	7	7
Employees as % of civilian employment	**88.3**	**89.0**	**89.8**	**88.5**	**88.5**	**88.7**	**88.6**	**88.4**	**88.4**	**87.4**
Part-time employment (%)										
Part-time as % of employment	5.3	5.4	6.0	7.4	8.2	8.0	8.3	7.6	6.6	6.8
Male share of part time employment	32.3	32.5	32.0	35.7	35.1	36.4	34.4	34.5	30.8	30.3
Female share of part time employment	67.7	67.5	68.0	64.3	64.9	63.6	65.6	65.5	69.2	69.7
Male part-time as % of male employment	3.4	3.4	3.8	5.5	6.1	6.1	5.9	5.4	4.1	4.2
Female part-time as % of female employment	7.3	7.4	8.2	9.0	10.0	9.8	10.7	9.9	9.0	9.4
Duration of unemployment (% of total unemployment)										
Less than one month	11.2	17.7	12.5	6.7	4.0	5.1	5.6	7.9	6.6	6.6
More than 1 month and less than 3 months	16.3	18.1	21.8	17.1	9.0	10.0	12.5	11.8	12.8	12.1
More than 3 months and less than 6 months	21.8	21.1	24.0	23.3	17.4	13.4	14.1	14.8	18.0	17.7
More than 6 months and less than 1 year	16.8	16.0	17.7	27.1	24.6	17.0	15.7	17.0	19.6	18.1
More than 1 year	33.9	27.1	24.0	25.8	45.0	54.5	52.1	48.5	43.1	45.5

Note: Detailed metadata: http://metalinks.oecd.org/lfs/20170518/354e9, http://metalinks.oecd.org/lfs/20170518/87289, http://metalinks.oecd.org/lfs/20170518/1b9ee and http://metalinks.oecd.org/lfs/20170518/8b433.

Disclaimer: http://oe.cd/disclaimer

LATVIA

Table 2. Participation rates and unemployment rates by age and sex

Annual average estimates, percentage

	2006	2007	2008	2009	2010	2011	2012	2013	2014	2015
Participation rates										
Males										
15-19	18.9	19.3	16.0	14.4	10.7	7.8	10.6	9.6	10.4	11.5
20-24	77.6	79.0	79.7	74.6	68.7	67.7	69.1	65.8	70.0	70.2
25-34	91.0	93.3	93.2	92.0	93.8	92.7	92.0	93.3	93.3	93.1
35-44	92.4	92.2	94.0	93.1	91.1	92.1	92.7	91.5	91.7	92.2
45-54	87.0	89.4	88.8	88.3	88.1	87.7	89.0	86.9	86.3	86.5
55-59	75.0	79.6	83.3	78.9	76.8	80.0	79.6	78.9	79.2	78.9
60-64	52.0	52.3	48.7	42.5	36.4	41.9	44.2	42.7	44.3	54.4
15-24	47.5	49.2	49.0	46.4	42.2	41.1	44.0	42.6	45.3	45.2
25-54	90.2	91.6	92.0	91.1	91.0	90.8	91.2	90.6	90.5	90.6
55-64	64.3	67.6	68.2	62.8	58.5	62.5	63.2	62.2	63.7	68.0
65 and over	16.8	17.7	19.3	12.5	8.2	7.7	9.4	10.7	9.5	10.5
15-64	76.1	77.9	78.3	76.6	75.3	75.8	77.1	76.6	77.8	78.9
Females										
15-19	11.1	13.3	9.4	9.1	8.7	8.1	9.1	8.7	5.1	6.5
20-24	58.1	58.2	61.9	59.5	61.2	53.7	56.1	55.2	56.3	59.7
25-34	76.9	76.6	80.3	80.4	82.7	82.2	82.4	81.6	79.9	82.2
35-44	86.6	85.7	89.8	89.5	88.9	86.2	87.6	86.4	85.3	86.3
45-54	82.9	85.5	86.4	87.4	87.2	87.3	87.0	86.1	86.6	85.3
55-59	68.7	73.4	76.9	78.7	78.0	78.9	81.7	80.4	78.6	78.1
60-64	34.7	35.3	38.3	37.3	31.2	33.8	39.2	39.8	43.0	47.2
15-24	34.0	35.8	36.5	35.9	37.2	33.7	36.1	36.0	35.3	37.1
25-54	82.2	82.8	85.6	85.9	86.3	85.3	85.7	84.8	84.0	84.6
55-64	52.1	55.7	59.2	59.5	55.7	57.1	60.8	60.5	61.7	63.5
65 and over	8.0	8.4	8.9	6.8	5.0	4.8	5.2	6.1	5.8	6.2
15-64	66.4	67.8	70.3	70.7	70.8	70.1	72.0	71.6	71.6	72.8
All persons										
15-24	40.9	42.6	42.8	41.2	39.7	37.5	40.1	39.4	40.4	41.3
25-54	86.1	87.1	88.7	88.4	88.6	88.0	88.4	87.6	87.2	87.6
55-64	57.3	60.7	63.0	60.9	56.9	59.4	61.8	61.3	62.6	65.5
65 and over	10.8	11.4	12.3	8.6	6.1	5.7	6.6	7.6	7.0	7.6
15-64	71.0	72.6	74.2	73.5	73.0	72.8	74.4	74.0	74.6	75.7
Unemployment rates										
Males										
15-19	26.3	20.0	30.3	58.2	64.6	63.7	62.3	29.6	30.2	31.1
20-24	8.3	8.8	11.0	32.7	33.8	28.3	23.8	21.0	18.2	16.4
25-34	6.8	5.5	7.9	20.3	20.8	17.9	13.8	11.8	10.6	9.4
35-44	5.7	6.4	7.2	18.0	21.1	16.4	13.9	11.1	11.1	10.2
45-54	7.0	6.4	8.2	19.0	21.9	17.8	16.9	12.6	12.0	11.9
55-59	9.7	6.4	9.6	19.4	21.5	20.3	18.2	12.3	12.9	12.5
60-64	4.7	1.9	4.2	13.2	15.6	10.8	10.8	9.3	8.6	10.1
15-24	11.9	11.0	14.0	36.4	37.3	31.3	27.8	21.8	19.4	18.0
25-54	6.5	6.1	7.8	19.1	21.2	17.4	14.9	11.8	11.2	10.4
55-64	7.9	4.9	7.9	17.5	19.8	17.4	15.8	11.4	11.6	11.6
65 and over	2.8	2.0	0.3	4.9	7.4	1.8	2.8	4.6	2.2	1.2
15-64	7.5	6.7	8.7	21.4	23.0	18.9	16.5	12.8	12.1	11.4
Total	7.3	6.5	8.4	20.9	22.7	18.6	16.2	12.6	11.8	11.1
Females										
15-19	28.1	18.5	30.3	57.7	61.1	53.1	55.7	42.8	40.1	22.0
20-24	13.6	8.0	10.6	25.3	31.6	27.9	26.3	22.9	18.7	13.5
25-34	6.1	6.5	7.6	14.0	16.2	13.8	12.7	10.3	10.6	8.9
35-44	4.9	4.6	7.0	12.7	14.1	11.4	12.5	9.3	9.6	9.0
45-54	6.6	5.1	6.3	13.2	14.5	11.9	12.5	11.1	8.4	7.9
55-59	6.3	4.8	5.8	12.4	14.4	15.9	17.2	11.3	10.0	8.8
60-64	4.2	2.5	2.8	7.0	9.4	5.7	6.4	6.9	5.5	4.6
15-24	16.0	10.0	13.1	29.2	34.8	30.6	29.5	24.9	20.0	14.2
25-54	5.8	5.3	6.9	13.3	14.9	12.3	12.5	10.3	9.5	8.6
55-64	5.6	4.1	4.9	10.9	13.0	13.0	13.8	9.9	8.5	7.3
65 and over	1.9	3.2	1.4	1.1	2.6	2.6	3.0	2.6	1.4	4.6
15-64	6.9	5.7	7.3	14.6	16.6	14.1	14.2	11.4	10.1	8.8
Total	6.7	5.6	7.1	14.1	16.3	13.8	14.0	11.1	9.8	8.6
All persons										
15-24	13.6	10.6	13.6	33.3	36.2	31.0	28.5	23.2	19.6	16.3
25-54	6.2	5.7	7.4	16.2	18.0	14.8	13.7	11.0	10.4	9.5
55-64	6.7	4.5	6.3	13.8	16.0	14.9	14.7	10.5	9.9	9.3
65 and over	2.3	2.6	0.8	2.9	4.7	2.3	2.9	3.5	1.8	3.1
15-64	7.2	6.2	8.0	18.0	19.8	16.5	15.3	12.1	11.1	10.1

Note: Detailed metadata at:http://metalinks.oecd.org/lfs/20170518/6f97b
Disclaimer: http://oe.cd/disclaimer

LATVIA

Table 3. Civilian employment and employees: breakdown by activity - ISIC Rev. 4

Annual average estimates

		2006	2007	2008	2009	2010	2011	2012	2013	2014	2015
	CIVILIAN EMPLOYMENT										
	By activity, thousands										
A-U	**All activities**	**..**	**..**	**1 054.9**	**908.5**	**850.7**	**861.6**	**875.6**	**893.9**	**884.6**	**896.1**
A	Agriculture, hunting and forestry	..	..	83.9	79.5	73.3	76.6	73.3	71.9	66.3	71.1
B-F	**Industry**	**..**	**..**	**310.0**	**221.2**	**196.2**	**..**	**205.4**	**213.6**	**210.9**	**211.8**
B	Mining and quarrying	..	..	2.6	3.0	3.8	..	2.8	2.8	3.7	3.9
C	Manufacturing	..	..	156.4	120.0	112.2	114.4	122.5	125.7	118.8	116.3
D	Electricity, gas, steam, air cond. supply	..	..	15.3	13.4	12.7	11.6	11.0	11.6	10.0	12.6
E	Water supply, sewerage, waste mgt, remediation	..	..	11.6	12.5	9.9	7.7	6.8	6.2	5.2	7.1
F	Construction	..	..	124.1	72.3	57.6	60.9	62.3	67.3	73.2	71.9
G-U	**Services**	**..**	**..**	**661.0**	**607.8**	**581.2**	**..**	**596.9**	**608.4**	**607.4**	**613.2**
G	Wholesale, retail trade, vehicle, motorcycle repair	..	..	168.6	149.7	135.9	136.2	127.4	133.4	132.3	128.9
H	Transportation and storage	..	..	88.1	79.0	71.4	73.2	75.1	77.3	84.8	85.3
I	Accommodation and food service activities	..	..	28.6	23.0	26.1	25.2	28.3	26.5	29.3	30.4
J	Information and communication	..	..	24.3	21.5	26.7	25.3	21.5	24.3	26.3	26.0
K	Financial and insurance activities	..	..	17.7	19.7	16.4	17.3	24.2	21.0	17.9	20.6
L	Real estate activities	..	..	9.1	13.0	17.9	17.5	23.0	22.7	20.7	20.7
M	Professional, scientific and technical activities	..	..	26.3	22.4	23.0	23.7	27.7	34.4	36.1	36.2
N	Administrative and support service activities	..	..	29.7	27.5	30.5	32.7	25.5	24.6	24.3	24.8
O	Public administration, defence, social security	..	..	83.9	70.5	59.7	59.4	58.9	61.3	58.6	59.1
P	Education	..	..	86.8	83.4	84.5	88.8	92.1	94.6	85.1	83.4
Q	Human health and social work activities	..	..	48.2	50.3	49.5	51.6	51.2	47.7	52.0	55.8
R	Arts, entertainment and recreation	..	..	26.5	23.6	18.7	16.6	23.0	21.5	22.4	22.4
S	Other service activities	..	..	18.9	20.3	18.0	18.1	17.3	16.8	14.7	18.0
T	Households as employers and own-use activities	..	..	3.8	3.5	..	..	..	..	2.3	..
U	Activities of extraterritorial organizations, bodies	..	..	..	..	..	..	..	..	..	..
	EMPLOYEES										
	By activity, thousands										
A-U	**All activities**	**..**	**..**	**946.8**	**803.8**	**752.9**	**763.9**	**776.1**	**790.4**	**782.4**	**783.0**
A	Agriculture, hunting and forestry	..	..	..	..	..	..	..	..	..	..
B-F	**Industry**	**..**	**..**	**..**	**..**	**..**	**..**	**..**	**..**	**..**	**..**
B	Mining and quarrying	..	..	2.4	2.9	..	..	2.7	..	3.6	3.8
C	Manufacturing	..	..	147.5	113.4	105.3	106.9	114.2	118.6	111.2	107.6
D	Electricity, gas, steam, air cond. supply	..	..	14.7	12.2	12.4	11.6	11.0	11.6	10.0	12.2
E	Water supply, sewerage, waste mgt, remediation	..	..	11.5	12.3	9.8	7.6	6.8	5.6	5.1	6.9
F	Construction	..	..	111.1	62.4	51.0	52.7	53.6	58.2	63.5	61.6
G-U	**Services**	**..**	**..**	**..**	**..**	**..**	**..**	**..**	**..**	**..**	**..**
G	Wholesale, retail trade, vehicle, motorcycle repair	..	..	153.0	134.5	120.7	123.8	114.5	120.5	120.0	116.3
H	Transportation and storage	..	..	85.5	75.9	67.1	70.1	72.8	74.4	80.9	80.8
I	Accommodation and food service activities	..	..	27.2	22.0	25.0	24.5	25.5	23.2	27.2	28.3
J	Information and communication	..	..	22.5	20.0	24.0	22.3	19.6	21.2	22.0	21.7
K	Financial and insurance activities	..	..	17.4	18.8	15.6	16.5	23.4	20.6	17.2	20.0
L	Real estate activities	..	..	8.1	11.5	16.3	16.3	21.1	20.0	17.7	18.1
M	Professional, scientific and technical activities	..	..	21.7	15.3	16.6	17.6	21.4	24.9	25.3	25.2
N	Administrative and support service activities	..	..	28.7	26.1	29.3	31.3	23.4	21.9	21.5	21.1
O	Public administration, defence, social security	..	..	83.5	70.2	59.5	59.3	58.8	61.2	58.5	59.0
P	Education	..	..	85.9	82.2	83.9	87.4	90.8	92.9	84.0	81.5
Q	Human health and social work activities	..	..	44.8	46.4	47.1	48.2	46.9	45.1	49.8	52.0
R	Arts, entertainment and recreation	..	..	25.3	22.9	17.2	14.6	20.4	18.0	19.5	19.7
S	Other service activities	..	..	14.5	15.1	11.5	11.1	10.6	10.5	9.2	11.2
T	Households as employers and own-use activities	..	..	1.5	..	..	..	..	..	..	..
U	Activities of extraterritorial organizations, bodies	..	..	..	..	..	..	..	..	..	..

Note: Detailed metadata:http://metalinks.oecd.org/lfs/20170518/87289
Disclaimer: http://oe.cd/disclaimer

LUXEMBOURG

Table 1. Labour force

Annual average estimates

	2006	2007	2008	2009	2010	2011	2012	2013	2014	2015
Civilian labour force, thousands										
All persons	329	343	360	367	375	385	394	404	414	424
Males	..	..	..	..	..	..	..	..	..	..
Females	..	..	..	..	..	..	..	..	..	..
Unemployed, thousands										
All persons	9	9	9	12	14	14	15	17	18	18
Males	5	6	6	8	9	9	8	9	10	..
Females	5	5	5	6	7	7	7	8	9	..
Civilian employment, thousands										
All persons	319	333	349	352	360	370	379	387	396	406
Males	..	..	..	..	..	..	..	..	..	..
Females	..	..	..	..	..	..	..	..	..	..
Civilian employment (%)										
All persons	100.0	100.0	100.0	100.0	100.0	100.0	100.0	100.0	100.0	100.0
Males	..	..	..	..	..	..	..	..	..	..
Females	..	..	..	..	..	..	..	..	..	..
Unemployment rate (% of civilian labour force)										
All persons	4.2	4.2	4.2	5.4	5.8	5.7	6.1	6.9	7.1	6.8
Males	..	..	..	..	..	..	..	..	..	..
Females	..	..	..	..	..	..	..	..	..	..
CIVIL. EMPL. - PROFESSIONAL STATUS, thousands										
All activities	**319**	**333**	**349**	**352**	**359**	**368**	**379**	**387**	**396**	**406**
Employees	299	313	328	332	338	347	356	363	371	381
Employers and persons working on own account	20	20	20	20	21	21	23	24	24	25
Unpaid family workers	0	0	0	0	0	0	0	0	0	0
Employees as % of civilian employment	**93.7**	**94.0**	**94.2**	**94.2**	**94.2**	**94.2**	**94.0**	**93.8**	**93.8**	**93.9**
Part-time employment (%)										
Part-time as % of employment	12.7	13.1	13.4	16.4	15.8	16.0	15.5	15.3	15.5	14.9
Male share of part time employment	6.9	6.1	7.4	18.8	16.3	17.8	19.5	19.7	19.9	19.2
Female share of part time employment	93.1	93.9	92.6	81.2	83.7	82.2	80.5	80.3	80.1	80.8
Male part-time as % of male employment	1.5	1.4	1.7	5.4	4.6	5.0	5.4	5.4	5.6	5.2
Female part-time as % of female employment	27.2	27.6	28.9	31.1	30.4	30.2	28.1	27.7	27.7	26.7
Duration of unemployment (% of total unemployment)										
Less than one month	6.5	6.5	11.3	6.2	13.2	7.8	7.5	5.2	8.9	13.9
More than 1 month and less than 3 months	20.0	21.0	20.9	21.5	18.3	20.6	23.6	22.4	23.2	16.7
More than 3 months and less than 6 months	23.4	23.1	18.7	23.6	23.2	18.8	18.3	23.5	20.5	19.7
More than 6 months and less than 1 year	20.6	20.7	16.7	25.6	16.0	24.0	20.3	18.4	19.9	21.3
More than 1 year	29.5	28.7	32.4	23.1	29.3	28.8	30.3	30.4	27.4	28.4

Note: Detailed metadata: http://metalinks.oecd.org/lfs/20170518/5b5c3, http://metalinks.oecd.org/lfs/20170518/87289, http://metalinks.oecd.org/lfs/20170518/23393 and http://metalinks.oecd.org/lfs/20170518/24585.

Disclaimer: http://oe.cd/disclaimer

Table 2. Participation rates and unemployment rates by age and sex

Annual average estimates, percentage

	2006	2007	2008	2009	2010	2011	2012	2013	2014	2015
Participation rates										
Males										
15-19	10.3	10.7	12.9	15.4	12.1	9.8	11.8	13.2	15.2	18.1
20-24	52.0	50.1	49.9	54.7	42.6	42.9	46.4	47.2	45.9	53.6
25-34	95.0	93.2	91.6	92.9	94.5	92.5	92.4	91.5	93.1	93.3
35-44	97.2	97.9	96.5	97.0	97.0	96.0	97.1	97.0	97.5	96.0
45-54	93.4	93.2	92.6	91.9	92.8	93.0	94.2	94.3	94.0	92.6
55-59	58.3	55.1	56.6	64.7	67.2	66.3	65.4	66.4	69.1	65.3
60-64	15.0	13.1	18.2	26.6	26.2	26.3	27.2	30.7	30.8	20.8
15-24	30.6	30.6	30.9	34.9	26.8	26.3	28.8	29.8	29.6	36.2
25-54	95.3	94.9	93.7	94.1	94.8	93.9	94.6	94.4	94.9	93.9
55-64	38.9	36.4	39.7	47.7	48.8	48.4	48.3	50.5	52.1	45.5
65 and over	0.7	0.6	1.0	6.7	5.4	5.4	5.5	6.5	6.4	4.3
15-64	75.3	75.0	74.7	76.6	76.0	75.0	75.9	76.3	77.2	76.0
Females										
15-19	7.1	7.2	5.4	11.3	6.3	6.0	6.4	9.4	7.7	16.8
20-24	43.5	38.2	49.8	48.0	39.0	40.7	43.1	34.6	39.0	50.4
25-34	82.6	83.9	79.1	83.7	82.2	83.4	84.4	84.0	85.3	86.1
35-44	75.7	75.3	72.7	76.2	77.0	78.0	79.9	82.7	83.6	85.8
45-54	63.9	65.3	67.2	65.9	70.2	70.2	73.3	74.9	73.9	72.1
55-59	41.8	43.9	44.2	44.5	46.3	45.2	48.8	46.9	52.7	51.1
60-64	10.4	10.1	13.2	13.6	14.7	16.6	18.5	18.5	16.4	15.7
15-24	25.0	22.3	27.1	29.5	22.7	23.4	24.7	21.8	23.0	34.1
25-54	73.8	74.7	72.9	75.3	76.4	77.1	79.2	80.5	80.9	81.3
55-64	28.5	29.1	30.3	30.6	32.0	32.1	35.2	34.2	36.5	35.0
65 and over	0.5	0.3	0.9	1.4	1.9	2.2	1.9	1.7	2.2	2.2
15-64	58.2	58.9	58.7	60.7	60.3	60.7	62.8	63.2	64.2	65.6
All persons										
15-24	27.8	26.5	29.0	32.3	24.7	24.9	26.8	25.9	26.3	35.2
25-54	84.5	84.7	83.4	84.8	85.7	85.6	87.0	87.5	88.0	87.7
55-64	33.6	32.7	35.1	39.4	40.6	40.4	41.9	42.5	44.5	40.3
65 and over	0.6	0.5	0.9	3.7	3.4	3.6	3.5	3.9	4.1	3.2
15-64	66.7	66.9	66.8	68.7	68.2	67.9	69.4	69.9	70.8	70.9
Unemployment rates										
Males										
15-19	28.9	19.4	11.6	23.5	23.8	15.6	23.9	23.9	25.3	29.4
20-24	14.5	12.3	12.8	14.7	15.8	12.8	17.5	17.2	26.4	15.5
25-34	4.2	4.8	5.6	5.4	3.6	4.0	5.2	6.9	5.8	5.1
35-44	2.2	2.0	3.1	2.5	2.7	2.7	2.9	4.0	4.6	4.7
45-54	2.0	2.0	2.9	2.8	2.8	3.3	3.4	3.2	3.7	5.1
55-59	0.4	2.8	2.5	1.6	2.8	3.3	2.1	3.7	4.9	4.8
60-64	1.1	0.0	2.2	4.7	0.9	2.3	1.4	6.0	2.9	8.0
15-24	17.0	13.5	12.5	16.7	17.6	13.3	18.9	18.7	26.1	18.9
25-54	2.7	2.8	3.8	3.5	3.0	3.3	3.8	4.6	4.7	5.0
55-64	0.5	2.3	2.5	2.4	2.4	3.0	1.9	4.3	4.4	5.4
65 and over	0.0	0.0	9.5	0.0	0.8	0.0	0.0	0.0	2.3	1.4
15-64	3.6	3.6	4.3	4.4	3.8	3.9	4.6	5.5	6.0	6.2
Total	3.5	3.6	4.3	4.4	3.8	3.8	4.5	5.4	5.9	6.1
Females										
15-19	42.6	36.2	46.1	21.1	12.4	27.3	19.2	20.0	28.1	17.9
20-24	10.6	13.8	21.6	17.0	9.8	19.8	18.5	8.4	16.0	14.9
25-34	6.5	5.6	6.3	6.0	6.4	6.0	6.9	8.0	6.5	9.0
35-44	5.9	2.8	3.6	6.2	4.4	5.6	5.0	6.4	4.8	4.6
45-54	5.1	3.7	4.0	2.7	4.3	4.9	3.8	4.1	3.9	7.1
55-59	2.9	1.7	2.1	4.2	1.6	2.0	2.5	4.0	4.8	3.3
60-64	0.0	2.0	6.8	3.1	4.2	3.6	2.3	9.3	1.6	5.5
15-24	15.2	17.5	24.1	17.8	10.2	20.8	18.6	10.9	18.1	15.7
25-54	5.8	4.0	4.6	5.2	5.0	5.5	5.3	6.2	5.1	6.9
55-64	2.5	1.7	3.0	4.0	2.2	2.4	2.5	5.3	4.2	3.8
65 and over	0.0	0.0	0.0	8.3	0.0	5.0	0.0	0.0	4.1	3.9
15-64	6.3	4.7	6.1	6.1	5.1	6.3	5.9	6.4	5.8	7.4
Total	6.2	4.7	6.0	6.1	5.1	6.3	5.9	6.4	5.8	7.3
All persons										
15-24	16.2	15.2	17.9	17.2	14.2	16.8	18.8	15.5	22.6	17.3
25-54	4.1	3.4	4.2	4.2	3.9	4.3	4.5	5.3	4.9	5.8
55-64	1.4	2.1	2.7	3.0	2.3	2.8	2.1	4.7	4.3	4.7
65 and over	0.0	0.0	4.4	1.8	0.6	1.7	0.0	0.0	2.8	2.4
15-64	4.7	4.1	5.1	5.2	4.4	4.9	5.2	5.9	5.9	6.7

Note: Detailed metadata at:http://metalinks.oecd.org/lfs/20170518/6f97b
Disclaimer: http://oe.cd/disclaimer

LUXEMBOURG

Table 3. Civilian employment and employees: breakdown by activity - ISIC Rev. 4

Annual average estimates

		2006	2007	2008	2009	2010	2011	2012	2013	2014	2015
CIVILIAN EMPLOYMENT											
	By activity, thousands										
A-U	**All activities**	**318.8**	**333.0**	**349.7**	**353.4**	**359.7**	**370.1**	**378.6**	**386.6**	**395.6**	**405.6**
A	Agriculture, hunting and forestry	4.9	5.2	4.3	4.3	4.4	4.5	4.5	4.6	4.6	4.6
B-F	**Industry**	**73.9**	**75.4**	**77.5**	**76.4**	**76.5**	**77.7**	**78.0**	**76.8**	**77.1**	**78.2**
B	Mining and quarrying	0.3	0.3	0.3	0.3	0.3	0.3	0.3	0.3	0.3	0.2
C	Manufacturing	33.9	33.5	33.9	32.8	32.7	33.2	33.0	32.2	32.0	32.3
D	Electricity, gas, steam, air cond. supply	1.3	1.4	1.4	1.4	1.4	1.3	1.3	1.4	1.4	1.5
E	Water supply, sewerage, waste mgt, remediation	2.3	2.3	2.5	2.6	2.6	2.7	2.7	2.6	2.6	2.7
F	Construction	36.1	37.9	39.4	39.3	39.5	40.2	40.7	40.3	40.8	41.5
G-U	**Services**	**240.0**	**252.4**	**267.9**	**272.7**	**278.8**	**287.9**	**296.1**	**305.2**	**313.9**	**322.8**
G	Wholesale, retail trade, vehicle, motorcycle repair	42.7	43.4	44.6	45.2	46.5	48.1	49.4	48.6	49.3	50.2
H	Transportation and storage	21.7	23.1	24.8	24.6	24.4	24.7	24.8	23.9	23.6	23.8
I	Accommodation and food service activities	15.2	15.5	16.3	16.5	17.1	17.8	18.9	18.3	19.0	19.5
J	Information and communication	11.4	12.7	13.6	13.9	14.1	14.9	15.2	16.6	17.4	18.0
K	Financial and insurance activities	35.7	38.2	41.3	41.4	41.1	41.7	42.5	42.6	43.3	44.4
L	Real estate activities	2.3	2.5	2.8	2.9	3.0	3.1	3.3	3.4	3.5	3.7
M	Professional, scientific and technical activities	22.3	24.4	27.4	29.0	29.5	30.8	32.1	33.9	35.9	37.8
N	Administrative and support service activities	19.3	21.0	22.0	20.6	21.9	22.2	22.4	22.5	23.5	24.8
O	Public administration, defence, social security	17.0	17.1	17.9	18.6	18.7	19.1	19.6	21.5	22.6	23.0
P	Education	14.7	15.0	15.6	16.1	16.6	17.4	17.9	18.1	18.3	18.7
Q	Human health and social work activities	23.9	25.0	27.1	28.5	30.4	32.0	33.6	39.0	40.3	41.4
R	Arts, entertainment and recreation	3.2	3.3	3.4	3.7	3.7	3.9	4.0	3.8	3.9	4.0
S	Other service activities	5.9	6.1	6.5	6.8	7.0	7.2	7.3	7.8	7.9	8.0
T	Households as employers and own-use activities	4.7	4.9	4.7	4.8	4.9	5.0	5.2	5.3	5.5	5.6
U	Activities of extraterritorial organizations, bodies	0.0	0.0	0.0	0.0	0.0	0.0	0.0	0.0	0.0	0.0
EMPLOYEES											
	By activity, thousands										
A-U	**All activities**	**298.9**	**313.0**	**328.6**	**331.9**	**337.8**	**347.7**	**356.0**	**362.8**	**371.2**	**380.8**
A	Agriculture, hunting and forestry	1.7	1.8	1.8	2.0	2.1	2.2	2.3	2.1	2.2	2.3
B-F	**Industry**	**72.0**	**73.7**	**75.6**	**74.6**	**74.6**	**75.9**	**76.1**	**75.3**	**75.8**	**77.0**
B	Mining and quarrying	0.3	0.3	0.3	0.3	0.3	0.3	0.3	0.3	0.3	0.2
C	Manufacturing	33.4	33.1	33.4	32.4	32.2	32.7	32.5	31.8	31.6	32.0
D	Electricity, gas, steam, air cond. supply	1.3	1.4	1.4	1.4	1.4	1.3	1.3	1.4	1.4	1.5
E	Water supply, sewerage, waste mgt, remediation	2.3	2.3	2.4	2.6	2.6	2.7	2.7	2.5	2.6	2.7
F	Construction	34.7	36.6	38.1	37.9	38.1	38.9	39.3	39.3	39.9	40.6
G-U	**Services**	**225.2**	**237.5**	**251.2**	**255.3**	**261.1**	**269.6**	**277.6**	**285.4**	**293.2**	**301.5**
G	Wholesale, retail trade, vehicle, motorcycle repair	38.9	39.9	40.8	14.4	42.6	44.2	45.4	45.2	46.2	47.0
H	Transportation and storage	21.3	22.7	24.3	24.1	23.9	24.2	24.2	23.4	23.2	23.4
I	Accommodation and food service activities	12.8	13.2	13.6	14.0	14.6	15.3	16.3	16.6	17.2	17.6
J	Information and communication	10.9	12.2	13.0	13.4	13.5	14.3	14.5	16.1	16.9	17.5
K	Financial and insurance activities	35.7	38.2	41.3	41.4	41.1	41.7	42.5	42.6	43.3	44.4
L	Real estate activities	1.3	1.5	1.7	1.7	1.8	1.9	2.1	2.1	2.2	2.3
M	Professional, scientific and technical activities	19.2	21.2	23.7	25.0	25.3	26.4	27.6	28.5	29.8	31.5
N	Administrative and support service activities	18.8	20.4	21.5	20.1	21.4	21.7	21.8	22.1	23.1	24.4
O	Public administration, defence, social security	17.0	17.1	17.9	18.6	18.7	19.1	19.6	21.5	22.6	23.0
P	Education	14.4	14.7	15.1	15.6	16.0	16.8	17.3	17.6	17.7	18.1
Q	Human health and social work activities	22.6	23.6	25.3	26.6	28.4	30.0	31.6	34.8	36.1	37.1
R	Arts, entertainment and recreation	2.6	2.8	2.8	3.0	3.0	3.2	3.2	3.1	3.2	3.2
S	Other service activities	5.0	5.1	5.3	5.6	5.8	5.9	6.0	6.4	6.3	6.4
T	Households as employers and own-use activities	4.7	4.9	4.7	4.8	4.9	5.0	5.2	5.3	5.5	5.6
U	Activities of extraterritorial organizations, bodies	0.0	0.0	0.0	0.0	0.0	0.0	0.0	0.0	0.0	0.0

Note: Detailed metadata:http://metalinks.oecd.org/lfs/20170518/87289
Disclaimer: http://oe.cd/disclaimer

MEXICO

Table 1. Labour force

Annual average estimates

	2006	2007	2008	2009	2010	2011	2012	2013	2014	2015
Civilian labour force, thousands										
All persons	43 234	44 063	45 121	45 416 |	49 133	49 482	51 477	51 896	51 837	52 624
Males	27 165	27 469	28 091	28 438 |	30 648	30 939	31 742	31 939	32 177	32 684
Females	16 069	16 594	17 031	16 978 |	18 485	18 543	19 735	19 957	19 660	19 940
Unemployed, thousands										
All persons	1 367	1 496	1 584	2 352 |	2 536	2 591	2 474	2 600	2 535	2 288
Males	806	879	921	1 538 |	1 591	1 623	1 518	1 605	1 586	1 374
Females	561	617	663	815 |	945	968	956	995	949	913
Civilian employment, thousands										
All persons	41 867	42 567	43 538	43 063 |	46 598	46 892	49 003	49 296	49 302	50 336
Males	26 359	26 590	27 170	26 900 |	29 057	29 316	30 224	30 334	30 591	31 309
Females	15 508	15 977	16 368	16 163 |	17 540	17 575	18 779	18 962	18 711	19 027
Civilian employment (%)										
All persons	100.0	100.0	100.0	100.0	100.0	100.0	100.0	100.0	100.0	100.0
Males	63.0	62.5	62.4	62.5 |	62.4	62.5	61.7	61.5	62.0	62.2
Females	37.0	37.5	37.6	37.5 |	37.6	37.5	38.3	38.5	38.0	37.8
Unemployment rate (% of civilian labour force)										
All persons	3.2	3.4	3.5	5.2 |	5.2	5.2	4.8	5.0	4.9	4.3
Males	3.0	3.2	3.3	5.4 |	5.2	5.2	4.8	5.0	4.9	4.2
Females	3.5	3.7	3.9	4.8 |	5.1	5.2	4.8	5.0	4.8	4.6
CIVIL. EMPL. - PROFESSIONAL STATUS, thousands										
All activities	**41 867**	**42 567**	**43 538**	**43 063**	**46 598**	**46 892**	**49 003**	**49 296**	**49 302**	**50 336**
Employees	27 440	27 950	28 763	28 513	30 438	31 095	32 492	33 033	33 493	34 169
Employers and persons working on own account	11 658	11 859	12 027	11 895	13 101	12 946	13 487	13 466	13 086	13 427
Unpaid family workers	2 769	2 758	2 748	2 655	3 059	2 851	3 024	2 797	2 722	2 740
Employees as % of civilian employment	**65.5**	**65.7**	**66.1**	**66.2**	**65.3**	**66.3**	**66.3**	**67.0**	**67.9**	**67.9**
Part-time employment (%)										
Part-time as % of employment	17.0	17.7	17.7	18.1	18.9	18.2	19.4	19.0	18.7	18.2
Male share of part time employment	39.4	40.0	41.1	41.9	42.3	42.9	43.2	42.4	43.2	42.7
Female share of part time employment	60.6	60.0	58.9	58.1	57.7	57.1	56.8	57.6	56.8	57.3
Male part-time as % of male employment	10.7	11.3	11.7	12.1	12.8	12.5	13.6	13.1	13.0	12.5
Female part-time as % of female employment	27.8	28.2	27.8	28.0	28.8	27.7	28.7	28.4	27.9	27.5
Duration of unemployment (% of total unemployment)										
Less than one month	50.4	50.5	50.7	44.4	42.2	44.9	42.1	44.5	46.5	45.9
More than 1 month and less than 3 months	31.5	32.1	31.5	33.5	34.7	35.3	37.2	35.4	34.7	37.8
More than 3 months and less than 6 months	13.5	12.9	14.7	17.4	17.3	15.7	16.6	15.6	15.5	12.7
More than 6 months and less than 1 year	2.7	2.2	1.7	2.9	3.8	2.1	2.3	3.0	2.1	2.4
More than 1 year	2.0	2.3	1.4	1.7	2.0	1.9	1.8	1.4	1.2	1.2

Note: Detailed metadata: http://metalinks.oecd.org/lfs/20170518/26047, http://metalinks.oecd.org/lfs/20170518/87289, http://metalinks.oecd.org/lfs/20170518/85758 and http://metalinks.oecd.org/lfs/20170518/66432.

Disclaimer: http://oe.cd/disclaimer

Table 2. Participation rates and unemployment rates by age and sex

Annual average estimates, percentage

	2006	2007	2008	2009	2010	2011	2012	2013	2014	2015
Participation rates										
Males										
15-19	49.0	48.0	48.2	45.4	47.9	45.2	46.2	43.8	41.7	40.9
20-24	79.8	79.8	79.8	78.1	78.6	78.1	78.4	78.1	77.7	76.3
25-34	95.3	95.4	95.1	94.6	94.6	94.2	94.7	94.1	94.0	94.2
35-44	96.7	96.6	96.2	95.6	95.9	95.5	95.7	95.7	95.6	95.2
45-54	94.1	93.2	93.5	93.0	93.2	92.9	93.4	92.9	92.5	93.1
55-59	88.2	86.9	86.8	85.0	85.1	83.6	85.4	85.3	85.9	84.9
60-64	74.1	73.3	71.8	69.2	71.1	68.9	71.5	69.3	69.2	69.3
15-24	62.6	61.8	62.0	59.9	61.7	60.4	61.2	59.9	58.8	57.5
25-54	95.5	95.3	95.0	94.5	94.6	94.3	94.7	94.3	94.1	94.2
55-64	82.1	80.9	80.2	78.0	78.9	77.1	79.3	78.2	78.7	78.0
65 and over	46.0	45.1	47.1	43.6	44.5	42.0	42.6	42.1	42.4	43.6
15-64	84.2	83.7	83.6	82.3	82.9	82.3	83.0	82.5	82.1	81.8
Females										
15-19	25.1	24.0	24.3	22.4	22.5	22.0	23.4	22.2	19.9	19.4
20-24	45.1	45.4	46.0	43.6	45.6	44.8	45.9	46.1	45.0	43.4
25-34	50.9	52.0	51.9	52.3	53.8	53.5	55.9	56.5	55.2	55.0
35-44	54.4	54.6	55.9	55.4	56.7	55.8	57.9	57.5	56.7	56.4
45-54	47.4	50.1	50.4	50.2	51.3	51.5	52.9	53.1	52.0	54.0
55-59	35.3	36.6	39.6	38.6	39.9	39.8	41.5	42.7	41.0	41.0
60-64	28.5	28.2	28.4	26.4	30.8	28.7	32.8	31.9	31.7	30.6
15-24	34.4	34.0	34.3	32.1	33.1	32.8	34.1	33.6	32.2	31.0
25-54	51.2	52.4	52.9	52.8	54.1	53.8	55.7	55.9	54.8	55.2
55-64	32.2	32.8	34.5	33.1	35.9	34.9	37.8	38.0	36.9	36.4
65 and over	14.8	14.2	15.1	14.6	15.2	14.3	15.5	14.3	14.0	14.3
15-64	44.4	45.2	45.7	45.0	46.2	45.9	47.7	47.8	46.8	46.6
All persons										
15-24	47.8	47.4	47.7	45.9	47.3	46.5	47.6	46.6	45.6	44.3
25-54	71.6	72.1	72.5	72.2	73.0	72.8	74.0	73.9	73.2	73.5
55-64	55.9	55.5	55.8	54.2	56.2	55.0	57.1	56.8	56.5	55.7
65 and over	29.1	28.2	29.6	27.9	28.6	27.1	27.7	26.8	26.9	27.7
15-64	63.0	63.2	63.5	62.7	63.7	63.3	64.5	64.3	63.7	63.4
Unemployment rates										
Males										
15-19	5.7	6.9	6.4	9.9	9.8	9.7	9.3	8.9	9.7	8.6
20-24	5.0	5.5	5.9	9.3	8.3	9.4	8.9	8.2	8.9	8.2
25-34	3.3	3.3	3.4	5.3	5.5	5.7	4.9	5.8	5.5	4.5
35-44	1.9	2.1	2.2	3.9	3.9	3.6	3.2	3.5	3.6	3.0
45-54	2.1	1.8	2.0	4.0	3.6	3.7	3.3	3.7	3.3	2.8
55-59	1.8	2.0	2.3	3.8	4.1	3.9	3.4	3.6	3.7	2.9
60-64	1.8	1.9	2.2	3.8	3.3	3.4	3.1	3.5	2.8	3.0
15-24	5.3	6.1	6.1	9.6	9.0	9.5	9.1	8.5	9.2	8.3
25-54	2.5	2.5	2.6	4.5	4.4	4.4	3.8	4.4	4.2	3.5
55-64	1.8	2.0	2.2	3.8	3.8	3.7	3.3	3.6	3.4	2.9
65 and over	1.0	1.1	1.0	2.0	1.9	1.7	2.0	2.3	1.2	1.2
15-64	3.0	3.3	3.3	5.5	5.4	5.4	4.9	5.2	5.1	4.4
Total	2.9	3.1	3.2	5.3	5.2	5.2	4.8	5.0	4.9	4.2
Females										
15-19	8.6	7.5	8.3	10.5	10.7	10.5	10.5	10.5	10.4	10.3
20-24	6.6	7.2	8.2	10.4	9.4	10.3	9.5	10.5	10.3	10.2
25-34	3.8	4.4	4.3	5.5	6.3	6.4	6.0	6.1	5.9	5.8
35-44	1.9	2.3	2.5	3.1	3.7	4.1	3.5	3.5	3.4	3.3
45-54	1.7	1.9	1.4	2.2	2.7	2.4	2.4	2.5	2.6	2.2
55-59	1.3	0.8	1.1	1.2	2.2	1.8	1.8	1.7	1.9	1.9
60-64	1.3	0.5	0.7	2.0	1.0	1.0	1.3	0.8	1.3	1.0
15-24	7.4	7.3	8.2	10.4	9.9	10.4	9.8	10.5	10.3	10.3
25-54	2.6	3.0	2.9	3.7	4.4	4.5	4.1	4.2	4.1	3.9
55-64	1.3	0.6	1.0	1.5	1.7	1.5	1.6	1.4	1.7	1.5
65 and over	0.5	0.3	0.6	0.4	0.3	0.6	0.4	0.8	0.5	0.4
15-64	3.6	3.7	3.9	4.9	5.3	5.4	5.0	5.1	5.0	4.7
Total	3.5	3.6	3.8	4.7	5.1	5.2	4.8	5.0	4.8	4.6
All persons										
15-24	6.1	6.6	6.9	9.9	9.3	9.8	9.3	9.2	9.6	9.0
25-54	2.5	2.7	2.7	4.2	4.4	4.4	4.0	4.3	4.1	3.6
55-64	1.6	1.6	1.8	3.0	3.1	2.9	2.7	2.8	2.8	2.4
65 and over	0.9	0.9	0.9	1.5	1.5	1.4	1.5	1.9	1.0	1.0
15-64	3.2	3.4	3.6	5.3	5.3	5.4	5.0	5.2	5.1	4.5

Note: Detailed metadata at:http://metalinks.oecd.org/lfs/20170518/6f97b
Disclaimer: http://oe.cd/disclaimer

Table 3. Civilian employment and employees: breakdown by activity - ISIC Rev. 4

Annual average estimates

		2006	2007	2008	2009	2010	2011	2012	2013	2014	2015
	CIVILIAN EMPLOYMENT										
	By activity, thousands										
A-U	**All activities**	**41 866.8**	**42 567.3**	**43 537.6**	**43 063.1**	**46 597.6**	**46 891.6**	**49 003.4**	**49 296.2**	**49 301.6**	**50 336.1**
A	Agriculture, hunting and forestry	5 905.5	5 655.1	5 651.5	5 558.1	6 417.0	6 245.7	6 573.5	6 594.2	6 679.5	6 772.6
B-F	**Industry**	**10 812.8**	**11 021.8**	**11 219.3**	**10 445.5**	**11 172.4**	**11 449.2**	**11 558.7**	**11 770.2**	**12 134.0**	**12 543.2**
B	Mining and quarrying	164.1	185.9	183.2	196.7	191.1	165.7	206.0	227.4	243.8	233.5
C	Manufacturing	6 955.5	6 995.8	7 108.5	6 442.6	7 010.9	7 269.2	7 382.7	7 646.6	7 837.9	8 038.3
D	Electricity, gas, steam, air cond. supply	119.1	148.8	140.3	153.2	107.1	101.8	118.1	106.5	93.9	110.2
E	Water supply, sewerage, waste mgt, remediation	136.1	126.1	160.0	151.2	191.1	195.7	202.7	211.9	243.8	214.3
F	Construction	3 438.1	3 565.2	3 627.3	3 501.8	3 672.3	3 716.8	3 649.3	3 577.8	3 714.6	3 947.0
G-U	**Services**	**25 148.5**	**25 890.4**	**26 666.8**	**27 059.5**	**29 008.2**	**29 196.6**	**30 871.2**	**30 931.9**	**30 488.1**	**31 020.3**
G	Wholesale, retail trade, vehicle, motorcycle repair	8 130.6	8 418.0	8 522.2	8 538.3	9 313.0	9 210.8	9 715.0	9 665.1	9 496.8	9 571.2
H	Transportation and storage	1 832.2	1 790.2	1 828.2	1 881.2	1 903.5	1 925.1	1 964.7	2 026.0	2 046.7	2 078.5
I	Accommodation and food service activities	2 489.7	2 645.0	2 800.6	2 765.4	3 095.3	3 211.3	3 388.4	3 482.0	3 484.6	3 618.5
J	Information and communication	387.6	342.0	354.2	379.2	374.1	375.4	382.4	427.0	365.5	354.3
K	Financial and insurance activities	362.6	403.6	405.8	385.7	431.5	413.2	531.5	508.5	521.3	494.8
L	Real estate activities	257.3	241.7	249.9	250.4	242.7	271.3	300.3	253.3	256.7	294.3
M	Professional, scientific and technical activities	906.7	954.2	952.6	1 011.8	1 060.4	1 132.7	1 104.0	1 217.2	1 189.3	1 197.2
N	Administrative and support service activities	767.6	869.4	1 010.0	1 032.4	1 104.5	1 137.0	1 222.6	1 239.9	1 305.9	1 336.6
O	Public administration, defence, social security	2 031.5	2 041.2	2 171.1	2 269.8	2 330.7	2 368.8	2 444.3	2 379.4	2 375.0	2 258.7
P	Education	2 252.3	2 318.9	2 326.0	2 392.5	2 510.7	2 544.5	2 612.5	2 609.4	2 512.0	2 598.9
Q	Human health and social work activities	1 159.8	1 212.3	1 252.8	1 354.6	1 386.6	1 353.4	1 494.9	1 532.2	1 503.0	1 548.7
R	Arts, entertainment and recreation	363.7	383.3	393.3	384.6	452.3	420.7	449.3	436.3	429.0	463.3
S	Other service activities	2 153.4	2 109.6	2 226.9	2 231.3	2 406.2	2 440.6	2 719.5	2 657.5	2 455.3	2 546.9
T	Households as employers and own-use activities	1 745.3	1 848.9	1 843.6	1 872.7	2 099.9	2 104.0	2 185.3	2 196.1	2 267.7	2 376.8
U	Activities of extraterritorial organizations, bodies	2.8	7.2	3.8	7.3	5.0	2.5	5.6	4.5	3.6	1.4
	EMPLOYEES										
	By activity, thousands										
A-U	**All activities**	**27 440.2**	**27 950.3**	**28 762.6**	**28 513.1**	**30 437.7**	**31 095.3**	**32 492.1**	**33 033.2**	**33 493.4**	**34 169.1**
A	Agriculture, hunting and forestry	2 204.6	2 011.4	2 101.5	2 118.3	2 430.3	2 547.1	2 663.9	2 664.6	2 776.4	2 881.0
B-F	**Industry**	**8 005.8**	**8 320.8**	**8 404.7**	**7 773.6**	**8 323.8**	**8 585.8**	**8 724.0**	**8 951.6**	**9 322.1**	**9 686.0**
B	Mining and quarrying	154.8	177.3	174.9	186.7	179.8	159.1	196.6	213.3	228.8	227.4
C	Manufacturing	5 236.7	5 342.1	5 411.3	4 826.5	5 293.9	5 558.5	5 652.3	5 922.4	6 174.5	6 354.7
D	Electricity, gas, steam, air cond. supply	118.3	148.2	139.6	152.2	106.2	101.3	116.2	105.7	93.4	109.2
E	Water supply, sewerage, waste mgt, remediation	91.1	92.7	94.3	106.3	121.8	112.1	126.9	138.4	158.9	135.6
F	Construction	2 404.9	2 560.5	2 584.6	2 502.0	2 622.2	2 654.8	2 632.0	2 571.7	2 666.4	2 859.1
G-U	**Services**	**17 229.8**	**17 618.2**	**18 256.4**	**18 621.3**	**19 683.6**	**19 962.3**	**21 104.2**	**21 417.1**	**21 394.9**	**21 602.1**
G	Wholesale, retail trade, vehicle, motorcycle repair	3 874.4	3 900.3	3 996.4	4 027.8	4 407.4	4 328.3	4 657.3	4 805.6	4 801.6	4 797.6
H	Transportation and storage	1 342.1	1 357.8	1 394.1	1 386.4	1 428.4	1 489.0	1 472.7	1 575.2	1 620.0	1 618.3
I	Accommodation and food service activities	1 416.7	1 467.8	1 591.0	1 545.8	1 667.0	1 795.5	1 805.1	1 909.3	1 987.9	1 942.5
J	Information and communication	339.6	322.8	334.9	359.4	353.2	354.5	371.8	400.9	353.0	336.0
K	Financial and insurance activities	350.4	389.9	391.0	369.4	415.2	402.9	511.9	491.5	500.7	480.2
L	Real estate activities	181.6	168.8	181.4	180.2	165.6	184.9	194.3	172.3	177.8	214.9
M	Professional, scientific and technical activities	534.4	533.9	559.2	597.3	599.8	673.4	666.7	735.2	717.9	735.4
N	Administrative and support service activities	654.9	723.0	848.4	875.2	913.9	949.2	1 018.6	1 038.5	1 106.8	1 153.7
O	Public administration, defence, social security	2 017.4	2 029.0	2 156.7	2 255.4	2 305.8	2 351.9	2 419.4	2 362.7	2 359.5	2 241.1
P	Education	2 169.1	2 247.9	2 245.3	2 307.7	2 423.3	2 452.7	2 518.5	2 516.9	2 418.9	2 477.2
Q	Human health and social work activities	973.0	1 016.3	1 030.7	1 145.7	1 142.9	1 149.2	1 255.5	1 280.7	1 311.3	1 311.9
R	Arts, entertainment and recreation	224.9	263.9	248.7	267.1	304.6	258.8	291.4	305.8	290.4	323.8
S	Other service activities	1 124.3	1 065.6	1 146.4	1 158.4	1 206.8	1 211.9	1 417.4	1 355.6	1 241.3	1 339.7
T	Households as employers and own-use activities	1 744.8	1 848.9	1 843.6	1 872.7	2 099.9	2 104.0	2 185.3	2 196.1	2 267.7	2 376.8
U	Activities of extraterritorial organizations, bodies	2.8	6.3	3.8	7.1	5.0	2.5	5.4	4.5	3.6	1.4

Note: Detailed metadata:http://metalinks.oecd.org/lfs/20170518/87289
Disclaimer: http://oe.cd/disclaimer

NETHERLANDS

Table 1. Labour force

Annual average estimates

	2006	2007	2008	2009	2010	2011	2012	2013	2014	2015
Civilian labour force, thousands										
All persons	8 597	8 741	8 836	8 900	8 760	8 726	8 861	8 932	8 896	8 933
Males	4 719	4 765	4 798	4 810	4 734	4 691	4 761	4 804	4 802	4 795
Females	3 878	3 977	4 038	4 089	4 026	4 034	4 100	4 128	4 094	4 137
Unemployed, thousands										
All persons	336	278	243	304	390	434	516	647	660	614
Males	167	133	122	162	208	216	260	346	343	313
Females	169	145	121	142	182	218	255	301	317	301
Civilian employment, thousands										
All persons	8 261	8 464	8 593	8 596	8 370	8 291	8 345	8 285	8 236	8 319
Males	4 552	4 631	4 676	4 648	4 526	4 475	4 501	4 459	4 460	4 482
Females	3 709	3 832	3 917	3 948	3 844	3 816	3 845	3 827	3 776	3 836
Civilian employment (%)										
All persons	100.0	100.0	100.0	100.0	100.0	100.0	100.0	100.0	100.0	100.0
Males	55.1	54.7	54.4	54.1	54.1	54.0	53.9	53.8	54.1	53.9
Females	44.9	45.3	45.6	45.9	45.9	46.0	46.1	46.2	45.9	46.1
Unemployment rate (% of civilian labour force)										
All persons	3.9	3.2	2.8	3.4	4.5	5.0	5.8	7.2	7.4	6.9
Males	3.5	2.8	2.5	3.4	4.4	4.6	5.5	7.2	7.1	6.5
Females	4.4	3.6	3.0	3.5	4.5	5.4	6.2	7.3	7.7	7.3
CIVIL. EMPL. - PROFESSIONAL STATUS, thousands										
All activities	**8 261**	**8 464**	**8 593**	**8 596**	**8 370**	**8 291**	**8 345**	**8 285**	**8 236**	**8 319**
Employees	7 207	7 349	7 461	7 434	7 113	7 035	7 063	6 955	6 868	6 918
Employers and persons working on own account	1 009	1 067	1 092	1 123	1 204	1 205	1 236	1 288	1 328	1 354
Unpaid family workers	45	46	39	39	53	52	46	42	41	47
Employees as % of civilian employment	**87.2**	**86.8**	**86.8**	**86.5**	**85.0**	**84.8**	**84.6**	**83.9**	**83.4**	**83.2**
Part-time employment (%)										
Part-time as % of employment	35.4	35.9	36.1	36.7	37.1	37.0	37.6	38.5	38.3	38.5
Male share of part time employment	24.1	24.5	24.4	25.0	25.0	24.6	25.5	26.7	27.4	27.3
Female share of part time employment	75.9	75.5	75.6	75.0	75.0	75.4	74.5	73.3	72.6	72.7
Male part-time as % of male employment	15.5	16.1	16.2	17.0	17.2	16.9	17.8	19.2	19.4	19.5
Female part-time as % of female employment	59.8	59.9	59.8	59.9	60.6	60.6	60.9	61.1	60.6	60.7
Duration of unemployment (% of total unemployment)										
Less than one month	3.5	5.0	6.7	7.5	6.8	6.7	7.9	6.8	6.2	5.9
More than 1 month and less than 3 months	20.3	22.5	25.7	27.1	25.4	24.5	23.0	19.6	17.5	18.0
More than 3 months and less than 6 months	16.1	16.7	17.9	22.0	19.4	18.7	18.1	18.8	17.0	16.1
More than 6 months and less than 1 year	17.1	16.4	15.3	18.6	20.9	17.0	17.4	19.2	19.4	16.3
More than 1 year	43.0	39.4	34.4	24.8	27.6	33.2	33.5	35.6	39.9	43.6

Note: Detailed metadata: http://metalinks.oecd.org/lfs/20170518/9a730, http://metalinks.oecd.org/lfs/20170518/87289, http://metalinks.oecd.org/lfs/20170518/0f437 and http://metalinks.oecd.org/lfs/20170518/1ae74.

Disclaimer: http://oe.cd/disclaimer

Table 2. Participation rates and unemployment rates by age and sex

Annual average estimates, percentage

	2006	2007	2008	2009	2010	2011	2012	2013	2014	2015
Participation rates										
Males										
15-19	57.7	60.4	63.1	61.3	58.8	57.9	59.2	59.9	58.7	59.0
20-24	80.2	83.0	81.8	81.2	78.3	77.6	77.4	78.3	76.8	75.7
25-34	93.8	94.5	94.8	94.2	93.5	93.0	92.9	92.1	92.0	91.8
35-44	94.4	94.3	95.2	95.2	94.2	93.8	93.8	92.8	93.1	93.2
45-54	92.0	91.9	92.4	92.6	92.3	92.2	92.3	91.9	91.6	91.4
55-59	77.6	81.9	83.9	85.2	85.2	85.7	86.6	86.5	86.4	86.4
60-64	34.6	40.4	46.2	48.0	50.0	51.4	56.0	63.3	65.7	67.9
15-24	68.7	71.4	72.3	71.2	68.5	67.8	68.5	69.3	68.0	67.5
25-54	93.4	93.5	94.1	94.0	93.3	93.0	92.9	92.3	92.2	92.1
55-64	58.8	62.6	65.7	66.8	67.6	68.6	71.6	75.3	76.5	77.6
65 and over	7.1	7.9	8.0	9.0	9.2	8.9	10.8	11.3	12.6	11.4
15-64	82.7	83.8	84.8	84.6	83.8	83.6	84.2	84.7	84.6	84.6
Females										
15-19	56.9	60.9	62.0	61.3	60.8	61.4	63.0	62.0	60.5	61.8
20-24	77.5	78.0	78.6	79.3	78.0	78.1	79.3	78.9	75.6	76.6
25-34	82.9	84.1	85.2	85.9	85.9	85.2	85.5	85.2	84.6	84.8
35-44	79.5	81.0	82.4	83.1	83.0	81.9	82.4	83.5	82.6	82.2
45-54	73.1	75.1	76.8	77.2	78.6	79.3	79.8	79.8	79.4	79.9
55-59	50.4	54.1	56.4	59.6	61.1	64.5	65.8	66.9	67.2	68.1
60-64	19.2	21.7	25.2	26.8	28.8	32.2	36.2	37.9	40.3	44.0
15-24	67.1	69.4	70.2	70.3	69.5	69.9	71.4	70.8	68.4	69.4
25-54	78.4	79.9	81.2	81.8	82.3	81.9	82.4	82.6	82.0	82.1
55-64	36.7	38.9	41.3	43.3	44.9	48.4	51.3	52.9	54.3	56.7
65 and over	2.0	2.5	2.4	3.1	3.2	3.0	3.4	3.3	3.6	3.8
15-64	68.8	70.4	71.7	72.3	72.6	73.1	74.3	74.6	74.0	74.7
All persons										
15-24	67.9	70.4	71.3	70.8	69.0	68.9	69.9	70.0	68.2	68.5
25-54	86.0	86.8	87.7	87.9	87.8	87.5	87.7	87.5	87.1	87.1
55-64	47.8	50.8	53.5	55.1	56.3	58.5	61.5	64.1	65.4	67.1
65 and over	4.2	4.9	4.9	5.7	5.9	5.6	6.8	6.9	7.7	7.3
15-64	75.8	77.1	78.3	78.5	78.2	78.4	79.3	79.7	79.3	79.6
Unemployment rates										
Males										
15-19	9.0	8.8	8.4	9.6	10.7	9.9	11.6	13.5	13.0	14.2
20-24	4.9	4.5	4.7	7.1	7.3	5.8	6.9	8.8	7.3	9.2
25-34	3.3	2.3	2.1	3.5	4.6	4.9	5.5	7.6	7.3	5.7
35-44	3.0	2.0	1.5	2.6	3.1	3.4	4.3	6.1	6.1	4.4
45-54	3.3	2.6	2.0	2.4	3.3	3.5	4.2	5.5	5.5	4.9
55-59	4.3	3.8	3.3	3.3	4.3	4.1	5.1	6.7	7.2	7.1
60-64	4.6	5.2	3.8	3.6	3.7	4.3	4.8	7.2	8.1	10.3
15-24	6.6	6.3	6.3	8.2	8.8	7.5	8.9	10.8	9.7	11.3
25-54	3.2	2.3	1.8	2.8	3.6	3.9	4.6	6.3	6.2	5.0
55-64	4.4	4.2	3.5	3.4	4.1	4.2	5.0	6.9	7.6	8.4
65 and over	0.0	0.0	2.4	0.0	2.0	5.0	5.0	5.8	6.6	5.3
15-64	3.9	3.2	2.8	3.7	4.5	4.5	5.3	7.1	7.0	6.6
Total	3.8	3.1	2.8	3.6	4.4	4.5	5.3	7.1	7.0	6.5
Females										
15-19	12.0	11.1	8.9	9.6	11.7	11.1	13.7	14.5	14.0	14.8
20-24	5.7	5.1	4.5	5.4	6.2	5.6	7.3	8.8	9.3	8.4
25-34	3.7	3.1	2.4	3.2	3.5	3.4	4.4	5.4	5.2	6.1
35-44	4.4	3.5	2.8	2.9	3.7	3.4	4.3	5.2	5.7	6.3
45-54	4.6	3.4	2.7	3.0	3.6	4.0	3.9	5.1	5.9	6.4
55-59	4.3	3.8	3.0	2.8	3.7	4.0	4.3	5.7	6.3	7.0
60-64	3.6	3.9	3.9	3.6	3.9	4.0	4.4	5.0	6.7	8.7
15-24	8.4	7.8	6.4	7.2	8.6	7.9	10.0	11.2	11.3	11.2
25-54	4.2	3.3	2.6	3.0	3.6	3.6	4.2	5.2	5.6	6.3
55-64	4.1	3.8	3.3	3.1	3.7	4.0	4.4	5.5	6.4	7.6
65 and over	8.0	0.0	0.0	0.0	4.7	0.0	4.2	3.3	2.9	3.5
15-64	4.9	4.1	3.4	3.8	4.5	4.4	5.2	6.3	6.7	7.3
Total	5.0	4.1	3.3	3.7	4.5	4.4	5.2	6.3	6.6	7.3
All persons										
15-24	7.5	7.0	6.4	7.7	8.7	7.7	9.5	11.0	10.5	11.3
25-54	3.7	2.8	2.2	2.9	3.6	3.8	4.4	5.8	5.9	5.6
55-64	4.3	4.0	3.4	3.3	4.0	4.1	4.7	6.3	7.1	8.1
65 and over	2.1	0.0	1.8	0.0	2.8	3.5	4.8	5.2	5.7	4.8
15-64	4.3	3.6	3.0	3.7	4.5	4.4	5.3	6.7	6.9	6.9

Note: Detailed metadata at:http://metalinks.oecd.org/lfs/20170518/6f97b
Disclaimer: http://oe.cd/disclaimer

Table 3. Civilian employment and employees: breakdown by activity - ISIC Rev. 4

Annual average estimates

		2006	2007	2008	2009	2010	2011	2012	2013	2014	2015
	CIVILIAN EMPLOYMENT										
	By activity, thousands										
A-U	**All activities**	..	..	**8 592.7**	**8 596.1**	**8 370.2**	**8 291.4**	**8 345.1**	**8 285.2**	**8 236.1**	**8 318.7**
A	Agriculture, hunting and forestry	..	..	223.6	218.1	232.6	206.0	205.1	159.1	174.0	178.0
B-F	**Industry**	..	..	**1 513.7**	**1 425.7**	**1 334.8**	**1 270.3**	**1 291.7**	**1 254.3**	**1 232.0**	**1 260.6**
B	Mining and quarrying	..	..	11.1	11.0	9.0	7.2	9.6	11.0	10.0	13.4
C	Manufacturing	..	..	917.7	847.5	800.5	761.4	767.5	764.5	764.6	786.1
D	Electricity, gas, steam, air cond. supply	..	..	35.1	37.3	34.3	33.2	38.2	31.4	27.4	27.7
E	Water supply, sewerage, waste mgt, remediation	..	..	34.5	36.8	35.0	33.0	35.0	34.6	32.5	30.8
F	Construction	..	..	515.3	493.1	456.0	435.5	441.4	412.8	397.5	402.6
G-U	**Services**	..	..	**6 855.4**	**6 952.3**	**6 802.8**	**6 815.1**	**6 848.3**	**6 871.8**	**6 830.1**	**6 880.1**
G	Wholesale, retail trade, vehicle, motorcycle repair	..	..	1 175.1	1 145.7	1 095.3	1 084.6	1 125.9	1 215.6	1 234.7	1 233.0
H	Transportation and storage	..	..	440.0	419.5	391.5	389.5	389.9	366.8	357.7	356.1
I	Accommodation and food service activities	..	..	339.7	335.2	337.5	335.7	340.4	313.4	325.3	351.8
J	Information and communication	..	..	325.7	309.6	294.2	284.7	283.5	253.9	244.7	255.9
K	Financial and insurance activities	..	..	254.7	241.1	217.1	218.5	219.7	273.9	280.4	268.2
L	Real estate activities	..	..	75.8	71.5	62.9	60.4	64.4	62.7	63.8	67.0
M	Professional, scientific and technical activities	..	..	571.7	522.0	477.2	471.3	490.8	575.8	580.8	585.2
N	Administrative and support service activities	..	..	322.2	319.4	300.1	296.1	309.0	385.6	410.1	429.1
O	Public administration, defence, social security	..	..	563.8	567.3	541.9	538.0	517.7	501.5	490.3	484.8
P	Education	..	..	590.7	592.4	570.9	557.4	557.7	547.5	543.8	557.4
Q	Human health and social work activities	..	..	1 358.3	1 378.2	1 359.8	1 356.2	1 362.1	1 330.2	1 299.1	1 291.0
R	Arts, entertainment and recreation	..	..	172.6	166.0	171.9	165.2	168.6	159.2	159.5	168.6
S	Other service activities	..	..	170.6	183.8	175.6	160.0	176.0	186.5	185.8	180.6
T	Households as employers and own-use activities	..	..	6.1	5.9	4.4	3.5	2.9	6.7	9.5	3.5
U	Activities of extraterritorial organizations, bodies	..	..	1.9	..	2.6	1.5	..	..	..	..
	EMPLOYEES										
	By activity, thousands										
A-U	**All activities**	..	..	**7 461.3**	**7 433.6**	**7 112.7**	**7 034.8**	**7 063.0**	**6 955.2**	**6 867.6**	**6 917.7**
A	Agriculture, hunting and forestry	..	..	108.5	104.3	100.6	100.2	98.1	72.8	75.0	70.2
B-F	**Industry**	..	..	**1 348.0**	**1 263.9**	**1 158.2**	**1 104.6**	**1 117.9**	**1 065.5**	**1 044.8**	**1 077.2**
B	Mining and quarrying	..	..	10.8	11.0	9.0	7.1	9.5	10.6	9.8	13.2
C	Manufacturing	..	..	868.7	798.1	749.6	713.1	716.6	706.3	707.4	729.4
D	Electricity, gas, steam, air cond. supply	..	..	34.7	37.3	34.2	32.8	37.7	30.9	26.4	26.6
E	Water supply, sewerage, waste mgt, remediation	..	..	33.8	35.3	33.6	32.0	33.1	33.6	32.0	30.1
F	Construction	..	..	400.0	382.2	331.8	319.6	321.0	284.1	269.2	277.9
G-U	**Services**	..	..	**6 004.8**	**6 065.4**	**5 853.9**	**5 830.0**	**5 847.0**	**5 816.9**	**5 747.8**	**5 770.3**
G	Wholesale, retail trade, vehicle, motorcycle repair	..	..	1 033.2	1 011.6	956.2	954.4	990.7	1 048.5	1 055.6	1 056.2
H	Transportation and storage	..	..	407.4	390.7	358.0	356.7	359.6	333.3	324.6	322.6
I	Accommodation and food service activities	..	..	291.6	289.2	288.3	286.2	293.5	265.7	271.9	294.0
J	Information and communication	..	..	272.2	260.7	238.0	228.4	225.4	196.1	183.4	191.8
K	Financial and insurance activities	..	..	242.7	228.9	207.3	208.1	208.4	236.1	229.2	217.0
L	Real estate activities	..	..	61.7	57.4	51.6	49.7	53.8	48.1	49.1	52.1
M	Professional, scientific and technical activities	..	..	409.8	373.7	332.4	323.2	322.8	363.7	362.8	358.5
N	Administrative and support service activities	..	..	300.0	292.9	271.9	265.7	277.5	328.0	347.1	363.2
O	Public administration, defence, social security	..	..	560.1	562.7	537.5	533.8	513.8	494.6	481.1	477.0
P	Education	..	..	556.6	558.2	534.7	517.4	514.3	492.8	489.8	496.8
Q	Human health and social work activities	..	..	1 256.6	1 274.2	1 256.0	1 243.7	1 246.2	1 206.1	1 168.1	1 155.2
R	Arts, entertainment and recreation	..	..	116.1	110.4	111.0	106.1	104.7	95.6	91.6	99.1
S	Other service activities	..	..	111.6	122.1	113.1	99.3	111.9	119.6	117.9	108.5
T	Households as employers and own-use activities	..	..	4.4	3.2	2.5	..	..	3.8	4.0	..
U	Activities of extraterritorial organizations, bodies	..	..	1.9	..	2.6	..	..	..	..	..

Note: Detailed metadata:http://metalinks.oecd.org/lfs/20170518/87289
Disclaimer: http://oe.cd/disclaimer

NEW ZEALAND

Table 1. Labour force

Annual average estimates

	2006	2007	2008	2009	2010	2011	2012	2013	2014	2015
Civilian labour force, thousands										
All persons	2 217	2 251	2 271	2 287	2 308	2 340	2 346	2 375	2 446	2 501
Males	1 188	1 202	1 205	1 209	1 220	1 233	1 229	1 242	1 280	1 313
Females	1 029	1 049	1 065	1 078	1 088	1 107	1 117	1 133	1 166	1 188
Unemployed, thousands										
All persons	85	82	95	140	151	152	163	148	141	144
Males	42	41	49	74	76	77	80	70	64	69
Females	43	42	45	67	75	75	83	79	76	75
Civilian employment, thousands										
All persons	2 132	2 168	2 176	2 147	2 157	2 188	2 183	2 227	2 305	2 357
Males	1 146	1 161	1 156	1 136	1 144	1 156	1 149	1 172	1 216	1 244
Females	986	1 008	1 020	1 011	1 013	1 032	1 034	1 055	1 090	1 113
Civilian employment (%)										
All persons	100.0	100.0	100.0	100.0	100.0	100.0	100.0	100.0	100.0	100.0
Males	53.8	53.6	53.1	52.9	53.0	52.8	52.6	52.6	52.8	52.8
Females	46.2	46.5	46.9	47.1	47.0	47.2	47.4	47.4	47.3	47.2
Unemployment rate (% of civilian labour force)										
All persons	3.8	3.6	4.2	6.1	6.5	6.5	6.9	6.2	5.8	5.8
Males	3.5	3.4	4.1	6.1	6.2	6.2	6.5	5.6	5.0	5.3
Females	4.2	4.0	4.2	6.2	6.9	6.8	7.4	7.0	6.5	6.3
CIVIL. EMPL. - PROFESSIONAL STATUS, thousands										
All activities	**2 130**	**2 166**	**2 174**	**2 145**	**2 154**	**2 186**	**2 180**	**2 224**	**2 303**	**2 354**
Employees	1 753	1 793	1 798	1 792	1 804	1 819	1 817	1 881	1 952	2 005
Employers and persons working on own account	357	349	355	330	327	344	340	317	328	327
Unpaid family workers	20	24	21	23	23	22	23	26	24	21
Employees as % of civilian employment	**82.3**	**82.8**	**82.7**	**83.5**	**83.8**	**83.2**	**83.3**	**84.6**	**84.8**	**85.2**
Part-time employment (%)										
Part-time as % of employment	21.2	21.9	22.1	22.4	21.8	22.1	22.3	21.6	21.5	21.3
Male share of part time employment	25.3	26.8	27.1	27.8	27.5	26.6	26.0	26.8	28.0	27.7
Female share of part time employment	74.7	73.2	72.9	72.2	72.5	73.4	74.0	73.2	72.0	72.3
Male part-time as % of male employment	9.9	11.0	11.2	11.8	11.3	11.1	11.0	11.0	11.4	11.2
Female part-time as % of female employment	34.3	34.5	34.4	34.3	33.7	34.4	35.0	33.5	32.7	32.7
Duration of unemployment (% of total unemployment)										
Less than one month	34.5	40.0	38.4	29.0	23.4	25.6	25.4	24.3	25.2	26.8
More than 1 month and less than 3 months	29.5	28.8	33.0	29.6	28.9	27.1	25.6	26.0	25.9	25.4
More than 3 months and less than 6 months	15.2	14.1	13.6	18.1	19.5	18.3	16.7	17.6	16.5	15.4
More than 6 months and less than 1 year	13.2	11.1	10.6	16.9	19.3	20.1	19.1	20.0	18.8	19.3
More than 1 year	7.6	6.0	4.3	6.4	8.9	8.9	13.3	12.2	13.6	13.2

Note: Detailed metadata: http://metalinks.oecd.org/lfs/20170518/5a11d, http://metalinks.oecd.org/lfs/20170518/87289, http://metalinks.oecd.org/lfs/20170518/06efd and http://metalinks.oecd.org/lfs/20170518/629fb.

Disclaimer: http://oe.cd/disclaimer

NEW ZEALAND

Table 2. Participation rates and unemployment rates by age and sex

Annual average estimates, percentage

	2006	2007	2008	2009	2010	2011	2012	2013	2014	2015
Participation rates										
Males										
15-19	53.7	55.1	54.9	51.0	46.7	45.8	42.4	43.5	46.0	46.9
20-24	82.3	80.4	78.2	77.9	77.7	79.4	80.4	77.8	79.6	80.8
25-34	91.3	91.8	92.0	91.1	91.7	91.0	90.7	91.9	91.7	92.2
35-44	93.1	92.8	92.0	92.2	92.6	92.7	91.9	92.5	93.8	93.4
45-54	92.4	91.7	91.4	91.1	91.1	91.9	91.1	91.1	91.8	90.9
55-59	87.2	86.7	87.6	86.9	86.3	87.0	88.1	87.8	87.8	86.6
60-64	73.2	76.0	74.8	77.7	78.8	78.2	77.7	76.6	78.8	79.9
15-24	67.3	67.1	65.9	63.8	61.6	62.2	61.1	60.5	63.0	64.4
25-54	92.3	92.1	91.8	91.5	91.8	91.9	91.3	91.8	92.4	92.2
55-64	81.1	81.9	81.7	82.6	82.7	82.8	83.1	82.5	83.6	83.5
65 and over	17.7	19.6	20.6	21.1	22.6	24.8	25.6	27.0	27.4	27.8
15-64	85.0	84.9	84.4	83.9	83.6	83.7	83.1	83.1	84.1	84.2
Females										
15-19	54.4	56.6	52.5	50.0	48.3	44.9	45.7	43.4	45.1	46.9
20-24	69.0	67.7	68.5	68.4	68.1	69.2	69.0	70.2	71.4	72.1
25-34	71.8	72.6	73.4	72.5	70.0	73.4	73.0	74.0	74.7	74.8
35-44	75.9	76.0	76.8	77.4	77.2	76.5	77.1	77.6	79.7	80.5
45-54	80.9	80.7	81.4	82.0	82.4	82.9	82.4	83.4	83.0	82.0
55-59	71.5	72.7	73.8	74.3	76.8	77.9	77.3	79.1	80.5	78.8
60-64	50.1	53.4	54.3	57.6	60.8	61.0	64.1	65.3	66.9	66.4
15-24	61.5	61.9	60.2	58.9	58.0	57.0	57.4	56.9	58.5	59.9
25-54	76.2	76.5	77.3	77.5	76.8	77.8	77.7	78.5	79.3	79.1
55-64	62.1	64.1	64.8	66.4	69.2	69.8	71.1	72.6	74.2	73.0
65 and over	8.9	9.8	11.1	11.5	12.4	14.0	15.0	15.3	16.0	16.9
15-64	71.0	71.5	71.7	71.8	71.6	72.1	72.4	73.0	74.1	74.1
All persons										
15-24	64.4	64.5	63.0	61.4	59.8	59.6	59.3	58.8	60.8	62.2
25-54	84.0	84.0	84.3	84.2	84.0	84.5	84.2	84.9	85.6	85.4
55-64	71.5	72.9	73.1	74.4	75.8	76.2	77.0	77.4	78.7	78.1
65 and over	13.0	14.3	15.5	16.0	17.1	19.0	20.0	20.8	21.4	22.1
15-64	77.8	78.1	77.9	77.7	77.4	77.7	77.6	77.9	79.0	79.0
Unemployment rates										
Males										
15-19	13.9	15.3	17.3	22.5	23.9	28.1	26.3	24.1	20.8	21.7
20-24	6.3	6.0	7.5	11.6	12.7	12.7	12.9	11.2	10.7	10.8
25-34	3.3	3.1	3.7	5.7	6.2	5.4	6.1	4.7	4.3	4.4
35-44	2.0	1.8	2.4	3.8	3.6	3.9	4.0	3.4	3.0	2.9
45-54	2.3	1.9	2.1	4.0	3.8	3.8	4.3	3.6	3.1	3.3
55-59	2.1	1.7	2.1	3.8	4.0	3.4	4.0	3.4	3.4	3.7
60-64	1.6	1.2	2.5	3.8	3.7	3.1	4.6	4.7	3.2	3.4
15-24	9.5	10.0	11.8	16.2	17.1	18.5	17.6	15.9	14.3	14.6
25-54	2.5	2.2	2.7	4.4	4.5	4.3	4.8	3.9	3.4	3.6
55-64	1.9	1.5	2.2	3.8	3.9	3.2	4.3	3.9	3.3	3.6
65 and over	1.5	0.9	1.5	1.6	2.1	1.6	1.9	2.1	1.8	1.7
15-64	3.6	3.5	4.2	6.3	6.4	6.5	6.8	5.9	5.3	5.5
Total	3.6	3.4	4.1	6.1	6.2	6.3	6.5	5.6	5.0	5.3
Females										
15-19	14.5	13.6	15.0	24.4	26.3	23.3	25.8	24.7	21.3	21.3
20-24	7.1	7.1	7.6	11.8	11.5	11.8	13.5	11.8	12.3	10.7
25-34	3.9	3.7	4.4	5.7	7.6	6.7	7.7	8.0	7.7	7.4
35-44	3.1	3.1	3.0	4.3	5.2	5.8	5.8	5.6	5.3	4.5
45-54	2.0	2.2	2.5	3.4	4.0	4.4	4.8	4.2	4.1	4.0
55-59	2.1	1.5	1.8	2.8	3.2	3.5	3.9	4.4	3.0	4.2
60-64	2.3	1.1	1.7	2.0	2.5	3.1	3.7	3.6	3.2	3.3
15-24	10.5	10.2	11.0	17.4	17.8	16.4	18.4	16.7	15.7	14.7
25-54	3.0	3.0	3.2	4.4	5.4	5.5	6.0	5.8	5.6	5.2
55-64	2.1	1.3	1.7	2.5	2.9	3.4	3.8	4.1	3.1	3.8
65 and over	2.6	0.8	1.0	0.9	1.7	1.9	1.3	1.0	1.3	1.6
15-64	4.2	4.0	4.4	6.3	7.1	6.9	7.6	7.2	6.8	6.6
Total	4.2	4.0	4.3	6.1	6.9	6.8	7.4	7.0	6.5	6.3
All persons										
15-24	9.9	10.1	11.4	16.8	17.4	17.5	18.0	16.3	15.0	14.7
25-54	2.7	2.6	2.9	4.4	4.9	4.9	5.3	4.8	4.4	4.4
55-64	2.0	1.4	2.0	3.2	3.5	3.3	4.1	4.0	3.2	3.7
65 and over	1.9	0.8	1.3	1.3	2.0	1.7	1.7	1.7	1.6	1.6
15-64	3.9	3.8	4.3	6.3	6.7	6.7	7.2	6.5	6.0	6.0

Note: Detailed metadata at:http://metalinks.oecd.org/lfs/20170518/6f97b
Disclaimer: http://oe.cd/disclaimer

NEW ZEALAND

Table 3. Civilian employment and employees: breakdown by activity - ISIC Rev. 4

Annual average estimates

		2006	2007	2008	2009	2010	2011	2012	2013	2014	2015
	CIVILIAN EMPLOYMENT										
	By activity, thousands										
A-U	**All activities**	**..**	**..**	**..**	**..**	**2 149.0**	**2 183.0**	**2 177.0**	**2 218.0**	**2 294.0**	**2 344.0**
A	Agriculture, hunting and forestry	..	..	..	..	145.0	151.0	147.0	143.0	143.0	143.0
B-F	**Industry**	**..**	**..**	**..**	**..**	**450.0**	**444.0**	**439.0**	**449.0**	**478.0**	**517.0**
B	Mining and quarrying	..	..	..	..	7.0	7.0	7.0	7.0	7.0	7.0
C	Manufacturing	..	..	..	..	250.0	251.0	248.0	251.0	251.0	264.0
D	Electricity, gas, steam, air cond. supply	..	..	..	..	10.0	10.0	11.0	11.0	14.0	14.0
E	Water supply, sewerage, waste mgt, remediation	..	..	..	..	7.0	7.0	6.0	7.0	7.0	9.0
F	Construction	..	..	..	..	176.0	169.0	167.0	173.0	199.0	223.0
G-U	**Services**	**..**	**..**	**..**	**..**	**1 554.0**	**1 588.0**	**1 591.0**	**1 626.0**	**1 673.0**	**1 684.0**
G	Wholesale, retail trade, vehicle, motorcycle repair	..	..	..	..	342.0	343.0	330.0	334.0	353.0	347.0
H	Transportation and storage	..	..	..	..	92.0	95.0	105.0	106.0	104.0	101.0
I	Accommodation and food service activities	..	..	..	..	118.0	122.0	121.0	127.0	122.0	130.0
J	Information and communication	..	..	..	..	73.0	77.0	81.0	83.0	85.0	92.0
K	Financial and insurance activities	..	..	..	..	62.0	66.0	69.0	70.0	70.0	69.0
L	Real estate activities	..	..	..	..	28.0	27.0	26.0	27.0	28.0	29.0
M	Professional, scientific and technical activities	..	..	..	..	138.0	135.0	134.0	141.0	141.0	137.0
N	Administrative and support service activities	..	..	..	..	82.0	90.0	92.0	95.0	98.0	97.0
O	Public administration, defence, social security	..	..	..	..	112.0	111.0	108.0	108.0	116.0	116.0
P	Education	..	..	..	..	188.0	199.0	193.0	193.0	197.0	201.0
Q	Human health and social work activities	..	..	..	..	223.0	228.0	229.0	241.0	249.0	254.0
R	Arts, entertainment and recreation	..	..	..	..	41.0	39.0	44.0	42.0	46.0	49.0
S	Other service activities	..	..	..	..	51.0	52.0	56.0	57.0	61.0	62.0
T	Households as employers and own-use activities	..	..	..	..	3.0	3.0	2.0	2.0	2.0	2.0
U	Activities of extraterritorial organizations, bodies	..	..	..	..	1.0	1.0	1.0	0.0	1.0	1.0
	EMPLOYEES										
	By activity, thousands										
A-U	**All activities**	**..**	**..**	**..**	**..**	**1 803.0**	**1 817.0**	**1 814.0**	**1 876.0**	**1 943.0**	**1 997.0**
A	Agriculture, hunting and forestry	..	..	..	..	84.0	83.0	81.0	82.0	83.0	89.0
B-F	**Industry**	**..**	**..**	**..**	**..**	**371.0**	**367.0**	**365.0**	**371.0**	**398.0**	**431.0**
B	Mining and quarrying	..	..	..	..	7.0	7.0	6.0	6.0	7.0	6.0
C	Manufacturing	..	..	..	..	228.0	229.0	225.0	225.0	227.0	240.0
D	Electricity, gas, steam, air cond. supply	..	..	..	..	10.0	9.0	11.0	11.0	14.0	13.0
E	Water supply, sewerage, waste mgt, remediation	..	..	..	..	6.0	5.0	5.0	6.0	7.0	8.0
F	Construction	..	..	..	..	120.0	117.0	118.0	123.0	143.0	164.0
G-U	**Services**	**..**	**..**	**..**	**..**	**1 348.0**	**1 367.0**	**1 368.0**	**1 423.0**	**1 462.0**	**1 477.0**
G	Wholesale, retail trade, vehicle, motorcycle repair	..	..	..	..	301.0	299.0	288.0	297.0	314.0	310.0
H	Transportation and storage	..	..	..	..	79.0	82.0	92.0	93.0	91.0	89.0
I	Accommodation and food service activities	..	..	..	..	102.0	103.0	104.0	108.0	107.0	112.0
J	Information and communication	..	..	..	..	58.0	61.0	64.0	69.0	73.0	76.0
K	Financial and insurance activities	..	..	..	..	58.0	60.0	63.0	64.0	63.0	63.0
L	Real estate activities	..	..	..	..	14.0	12.0	14.0	16.0	15.0	15.0
M	Professional, scientific and technical activities	..	..	..	..	100.0	96.0	95.0	105.0	103.0	105.0
N	Administrative and support service activities	..	..	..	..	63.0	70.0	70.0	76.0	80.0	80.0
O	Public administration, defence, social security	..	..	..	..	110.0	110.0	105.0	106.0	114.0	113.0
P	Education	..	..	..	..	180.0	191.0	184.0	184.0	187.0	189.0
Q	Human health and social work activities	..	..	..	..	206.0	209.0	211.0	224.0	229.0	235.0
R	Arts, entertainment and recreation	..	..	..	..	33.0	31.0	34.0	35.0	38.0	40.0
S	Other service activities	..	..	..	..	40.0	40.0	42.0	44.0	47.0	48.0
T	Households as employers and own-use activities	..	..	..	..	3.0	2.0	2.0	2.0	1.0	1.0
U	Activities of extraterritorial organizations, bodies	..	..	..	..	1.0	1.0	0.0	0.0	0.0	1.0

Note: Detailed metadata:http://metalinks.oecd.org/lfs/20170518/87289
Disclaimer: http://oe.cd/disclaimer

NORWAY

Table 1. Labour force

Annual average estimates

	2006	2007	2008	2009	2010	2011	2012	2013	2014	2015
Civilian labour force, thousands										
All persons	2 429	2 491	2 574	2 573	2 588	2 617	2 668	2 692	2 717	2 756
Males	1 280	1 309	1 354	1 351	1 366	1 376	1 410	1 420	1 432	1 458
Females	1 149	1 182	1 221	1 223	1 222	1 241	1 258	1 272	1 284	1 299
Unemployed, thousands										
All persons	84	63	67	82	94	86	86	95	96	121
Males	45	34	38	49	57	48	51	53	54	68
Females	39	29	30	32	37	38	35	42	42	53
Civilian employment, thousands										
All persons	2 345	2 428	2 506	2 492	2 494	2 532	2 582	2 597	2 620	2 635
Males	1 235	1 275	1 316	1 302	1 309	1 329	1 359	1 367	1 378	1 390
Females	1 110	1 153	1 191	1 190	1 185	1 203	1 223	1 230	1 242	1 246
Civilian employment (%)										
All persons	100.0	100.0	100.0	100.0	100.0	100.0	100.0	100.0	100.0	100.0
Males	52.7	52.5	52.5	52.2	52.5	52.5	52.6	52.6	52.6	52.8
Females	47.3	47.5	47.5	47.8	47.5	47.5	47.4	47.4	47.4	47.3
Unemployment rate (% of civilian labour force)										
All persons	3.5	2.5	2.6	3.2	3.6	3.3	3.2	3.5	3.5	4.4
Males	3.5	2.6	2.8	3.6	4.2	3.5	3.6	3.7	3.8	4.7
Females	3.4	2.5	2.5	2.6	3.0	3.1	2.8	3.3	3.3	4.1
CIVIL. EMPL. - PROFESSIONAL STATUS, thousands										
All activities	**2 345**	**2 426**	**2 506**	**2 492**	**2 494**	**2 532**	**2 582**	**2 597**	**2 620**	**2 635**
Employees	2 144	2 231	2 310	2 289	2 300	2 351	2 399	2 408	2 424	2 445
Employers and persons working on own account	191	188	189	196	188	174	174	176	185	180
Unpaid family workers	8	6	7	6	5	4	5	5	4	5
Employees as % of civilian employment	**91.4**	**92.0**	**92.2**	**91.9**	**92.2**	**92.9**	**92.9**	**92.7**	**92.5**	**92.8**
Part-time employment (%)										
Part-time as % of employment	21.1	20.4	20.3	20.4	20.1	20.0	19.8	19.5	18.8	19.4
Male share of part time employment	26.5	27.1	28.3	29.2	29.7	28.9	30.6	30.6	30.2	32.9
Female share of part time employment	73.5	72.9	71.7	70.8	70.3	71.1	69.4	69.4	69.8	67.1
Male part-time as % of male employment	10.6	10.5	10.9	11.3	11.4	11.0	11.5	11.3	10.8	12.1
Female part-time as % of female employment	32.9	31.6	30.8	30.4	29.8	30.0	29.1	28.8	27.7	27.6
Duration of unemployment (% of total unemployment)										
Less than one month	27.0	33.0	39.1	29.0	26.5	26.0	26.6	26.6	25.8	22.8
More than 1 month and less than 3 months	25.9	26.1	28.3	28.1	25.1	24.6	27.1	26.9	24.7	25.2
More than 3 months and less than 6 months	14.2	15.1	14.2	17.8	17.1	16.9	17.6	17.8	17.7	20.1
More than 6 months and less than 1 year	18.5	17.0	12.4	17.4	21.9	21.0	20.1	19.6	20.2	20.3
More than 1 year	14.5	8.8	6.0	7.7	9.5	11.6	8.7	9.2	11.8	11.7

Note: Detailed metadata: http://metalinks.oecd.org/lfs/20170518/4b916, http://metalinks.oecd.org/lfs/20170518/87289, http://metalinks.oecd.org/lfs/20170518/b0da1 and http://metalinks.oecd.org/lfs/20170518/79e8c.

Disclaimer: http://oe.cd/disclaimer

Table 2. Participation rates and unemployment rates by age and sex

Annual average estimates, percentage

	2006	2007	2008	2009	2010	2011	2012	2013	2014	2015
Participation rates										
Males										
15-19	41.0	42.6	48.5	41.3	40.4	37.8	39.7	39.0	35.7	37.5
20-24	77.2	76.4	78.7	75.9	75.3	73.6	74.0	74.2	72.0	74.3
25-34	90.4	90.0	90.2	90.7	89.1	89.0	88.1	88.4	88.4	88.3
35-44	91.9	93.1	93.2	92.4	92.4	91.4	91.8	91.1	90.5	90.7
45-54	89.2	89.4	90.4	89.4	88.9	88.4	88.8	87.9	89.1	88.3
55-59	82.9	83.6	84.1	83.0	82.9	82.9	83.8	82.7	83.9	83.2
60-64	63.5	65.0	65.7	64.5	63.9	64.7	67.5	68.6	69.3	70.0
15-24	58.2	58.6	62.9	57.9	57.6	55.6	57.1	56.9	54.3	56.3
25-54	90.6	90.9	91.4	90.9	90.2	89.7	89.6	89.2	89.3	89.1
55-64	74.1	74.7	75.0	73.9	73.5	73.9	76.0	76.0	77.0	76.9
65 and over	17.7	19.0	20.0	21.5	23.2	23.2	23.1	23.0	24.4	25.7
15-64	81.4	81.8	82.9	81.4	80.8	80.1	80.7	80.4	80.2	80.5
Females										
15-19	45.6	47.0	51.5	47.6	44.3	43.2	45.3	44.6	41.8	42.6
20-24	71.8	74.9	74.5	71.5	70.3	70.2	70.7	71.5	69.7	70.9
25-34	82.3	82.7	85.6	84.7	82.6	82.5	81.8	81.8	82.0	81.5
35-44	85.0	86.0	86.7	86.5	86.5	86.5	86.1	86.0	86.8	86.7
45-54	82.7	82.9	84.3	84.4	83.7	83.7	84.0	84.1	83.6	83.7
55-59	71.7	74.6	75.5	75.2	75.8	77.1	76.3	76.3	78.1	77.3
60-64	51.1	53.8	53.9	54.7	55.2	56.2	58.1	59.0	59.7	61.8
15-24	58.1	60.3	62.5	59.2	57.1	56.9	58.2	58.5	56.2	57.2
25-54	83.4	84.0	85.6	85.2	84.4	84.3	84.0	84.0	84.1	83.9
55-64	62.2	64.6	64.9	65.0	65.6	66.9	67.5	68.0	69.2	69.8
65 and over	10.6	12.1	13.2	13.6	13.7	14.5	14.6	14.0	14.5	14.8
15-64	74.8	75.9	77.4	76.5	75.6	75.8	75.9	76.1	75.9	76.2
All persons										
15-24	58.1	59.4	62.7	58.5	57.4	56.2	57.6	57.7	55.2	56.7
25-54	87.0	87.5	88.5	88.1	87.4	87.1	86.9	86.7	86.8	86.6
55-64	68.2	69.7	70.0	69.5	69.6	70.5	71.8	72.0	73.1	73.4
65 and over	14.0	15.4	16.4	17.4	18.3	18.7	18.7	18.4	19.4	20.2
15-64	78.2	78.9	80.2	79.0	78.2	78.0	78.4	78.3	78.1	78.4
Unemployment rates										
Males										
15-19	12.1	11.2	13.2	12.8	14.0	12.5	12.7	13.3	11.7	13.7
20-24	6.6	5.9	4.9	8.8	9.1	7.6	8.5	9.2	7.6	9.8
25-34	4.2	2.3	3.0	3.8	5.3	4.3	4.0	4.3	5.3	6.2
35-44	3.2	2.0	1.7	2.6	3.1	2.5	2.7	2.5	2.5	3.8
45-54	1.8	1.4	1.6	2.2	2.2	2.1	2.4	2.1	2.7	2.9
55-59	1.3	1.0	1.2	1.6	1.9	1.4	2.2	1.8	1.9	2.1
60-64	1.2	1.4	1.1	1.4	1.6	1.3	0.8	0.8	1.0	1.4
15-24	8.6	7.9	8.2	10.3	10.9	9.3	10.0	10.6	8.9	11.1
25-54	3.1	1.9	2.0	2.9	3.5	2.9	3.0	2.9	3.5	4.3
55-64	1.3	1.1	1.1	1.5	1.8	1.4	1.6	1.4	1.5	1.8
65 and over	1.1	1.6	0.6	1.6	0.5	0.4	0.6	1.0	0.9	1.1
15-64	3.5	2.6	2.8	3.7	4.2	3.5	3.7	3.8	3.9	4.8
Total	3.5	2.6	2.8	3.6	4.1	3.4	3.6	3.7	3.7	4.6
Females										
15-19	11.1	9.8	10.5	10.7	10.4	10.0	9.4	11.3	8.4	13.3
20-24	7.0	4.5	4.1	6.1	5.9	6.6	5.9	5.6	5.6	6.2
25-34	3.9	2.8	2.7	2.8	3.9	3.7	3.2	4.0	4.6	5.4
35-44	2.8	1.8	1.6	1.9	2.4	2.1	2.1	2.9	2.8	3.7
45-54	1.8	1.3	1.2	1.4	1.6	2.0	1.7	1.9	2.2	2.5
55-59	0.9	0.8	1.0	0.7	1.1	1.2	0.9	1.4	1.2	1.8
60-64	1.1	0.8	0.8	0.4	0.7	1.1	0.9	1.1	0.7	1.2
15-24	8.7	6.6	6.8	8.0	7.7	7.9	7.2	7.7	6.6	8.8
25-54	2.8	2.0	1.8	2.0	2.6	2.6	2.3	2.9	3.2	3.9
55-64	1.0	0.8	0.9	0.6	0.9	1.2	0.9	1.2	1.0	1.6
65 and over	2.2	0.0	0.0	0.4	1.1	1.3	0.3	0.3	0.6	0.6
15-64	3.4	2.5	2.5	2.7	3.1	3.1	2.8	3.4	3.3	4.2
Total	3.4	2.5	2.4	2.6	3.0	3.1	2.8	3.3	3.3	4.1
All persons										
15-24	8.6	7.3	7.5	9.2	9.3	8.6	8.6	9.2	7.8	10.0
25-54	2.9	1.9	2.0	2.5	3.1	2.7	2.7	2.9	3.3	4.1
55-64	1.1	1.0	1.0	1.1	1.4	1.3	1.3	1.3	1.3	1.7
65 and over	1.5	1.0	0.4	1.1	0.7	0.8	0.5	0.7	0.8	0.9
15-64	3.5	2.6	2.6	3.2	3.7	3.3	3.3	3.6	3.6	4.5

Note: Detailed metadata at:http://metalinks.oecd.org/lfs/20170518/6f97b
Disclaimer: http://oe.cd/disclaimer

Table 3. Civilian employment and employees: breakdown by activity - ISIC Rev. 4

Annual average estimates

		2006	2007	2008	2009	2010	2011	2012	2013	2014	2015
	CIVILIAN EMPLOYMENT										
	By activity, thousands										
A-U	**All activities**	..	..	..	**2 492.0**	**2 494.0**	**2 532.0**	**2 582.0**	**2 597.0**	**2 620.0**	**2 635.0**
A	Agriculture, hunting and forestry	..	..	..	67.0	63.0	60.0	57.0	57.0	59.0	53.0
B-F	**Industry**	..	..	..	**504.0**	**492.0**	**512.0**	**520.0**	**524.0**	**535.0**	**528.0**
B	Mining and quarrying	..	..	..	45.0	46.0	53.0	59.0	72.0	77.0	68.0
C	Manufacturing	..	..	..	248.0	236.0	237.0	238.0	228.0	228.0	226.0
D	Electricity, gas, steam, air cond. supply	..	..	..	18.0	18.0	18.0	16.0	15.0	16.0	15.0
E	Water supply, sewerage, waste mgt, remediation	..	..	..	13.0	13.0	14.0	13.0	12.0	13.0	13.0
F	Construction	..	..	..	180.0	179.0	190.0	194.0	197.0	201.0	206.0
G-U	**Services**	..	..	..	**1 921.0**	**1 939.0**	**1 960.0**	**2 005.0**	**2 016.0**	**2 026.0**	**2 054.0**
G	Wholesale, retail trade, vehicle, motorcycle repair	..	..	..	345.0	345.0	349.0	358.0	355.0	348.0	358.0
H	Transportation and storage	..	..	..	134.0	140.0	144.0	143.0	139.0	138.0	144.0
I	Accommodation and food service activities	..	..	..	68.0	69.0	67.0	68.0	69.0	75.0	77.0
J	Information and communication	..	..	..	93.0	91.0	95.0	103.0	105.0	103.0	99.0
K	Financial and insurance activities	..	..	..	53.0	52.0	51.0	52.0	54.0	57.0	53.0
L	Real estate activities	..	..	..	26.0	24.0	20.0	19.0	24.0	26.0	26.0
M	Professional, scientific and technical activities	..	..	..	139.0	137.0	134.0	144.0	149.0	154.0	157.0
N	Administrative and support service activities	..	..	..	99.0	98.0	97.0	100.0	104.0	110.0	118.0
O	Public administration, defence, social security	..	..	..	141.0	143.0	141.0	154.0	155.0	156.0	158.0
P	Education	..	..	..	205.0	208.0	211.0	214.0	220.0	226.0	227.0
Q	Human health and social work activities	..	..	..	518.0	529.0	547.0	545.0	534.0	520.0	521.0
R	Arts, entertainment and recreation	..	..	..	45.0	52.0	51.0	49.0	52.0	56.0	57.0
S	Other service activities	..	..	..	50.0	47.0	48.0	48.0	49.0	48.0	52.0
T	Households as employers and own-use activities	..	..	..	3.0	3.0	3.0	2.0	1.0	2.0	2.0
U	Activities of extraterritorial organizations, bodies	..	..	..	1.0	0.0	0.0	1.0	0.0	1.0	1.0
	EMPLOYEES										
	By activity, thousands										
A-U	**All activities**	..	..	..	**2 287.0**	**2 299.0**	**2 352.0**	**2 397.0**	**2 409.0**	**2 422.0**	**2 445.0**
A	Agriculture, hunting and forestry	..	..	..	24.0	22.0	25.0	24.0	25.0	25.0	23.0
B-F	**Industry**	..	..	..	**464.0**	**456.0**	**478.0**	**483.0**	**489.0**	**495.0**	**494.0**
B	Mining and quarrying	..	..	..	45.0	45.0	52.0	58.0	71.0	76.0	68.0
C	Manufacturing	..	..	..	238.0	228.0	229.0	228.0	219.0	220.0	220.0
D	Electricity, gas, steam, air cond. supply	..	..	..	18.0	18.0	18.0	16.0	15.0	15.0	15.0
E	Water supply, sewerage, waste mgt, remediation	..	..	..	13.0	13.0	14.0	13.0	12.0	13.0	13.0
F	Construction	..	..	..	150.0	152.0	165.0	168.0	172.0	171.0	178.0
G-U	**Services**	..	..	..	**1 799.0**	**1 821.0**	**1 849.0**	**1 890.0**	**1 895.0**	**1 902.0**	**1 928.0**
G	Wholesale, retail trade, vehicle, motorcycle repair	..	..	..	327.0	327.0	331.0	341.0	338.0	331.0	339.0
H	Transportation and storage	..	..	..	122.0	125.0	131.0	130.0	127.0	127.0	133.0
I	Accommodation and food service activities	..	..	..	65.0	65.0	64.0	65.0	64.0	71.0	72.0
J	Information and communication	..	..	..	88.0	87.0	91.0	98.0	100.0	96.0	93.0
K	Financial and insurance activities	..	..	..	52.0	50.0	50.0	51.0	54.0	56.0	52.0
L	Real estate activities	..	..	..	22.0	20.0	17.0	16.0	21.0	23.0	22.0
M	Professional, scientific and technical activities	..	..	..	117.0	116.0	114.0	123.0	127.0	133.0	135.0
N	Administrative and support service activities	..	..	..	92.0	92.0	93.0	95.0	96.0	101.0	110.0
O	Public administration, defence, social security	..	..	..	140.0	143.0	141.0	153.0	155.0	156.0	158.0
P	Education	..	..	..	201.0	204.0	207.0	209.0	215.0	222.0	222.0
Q	Human health and social work activities	..	..	..	496.0	510.0	529.0	528.0	517.0	503.0	503.0
R	Arts, entertainment and recreation	..	..	..	32.0	41.0	38.0	37.0	39.0	40.0	42.0
S	Other service activities	..	..	..	42.0	39.0	40.0	41.0	41.0	40.0	44.0
T	Households as employers and own-use activities	..	..	..	2.0	2.0	3.0	2.0	1.0	2.0	1.0
U	Activities of extraterritorial organizations, bodies	..	..	..	1.0	0.0	0.0	1.0	0.0	1.0	1.0

Note: Detailed metadata:http://metalinks.oecd.org/lfs/20170518/87289
Disclaimer: http://oe.cd/disclaimer

POLAND

Table 1. Labour force

Annual average estimates

	2006	2007	2008	2009	2010	2011	2012	2013	2014	2015
Civilian labour force, thousands										
All persons	16 938	16 859	17 011	17 279	17 123	17 221	17 340	17 361	17 428	17 388
Males	9 283	9 234	9 317	9 455	9 446	9 504	9 551	9 568	9 593	9 569
Females	7 655	7 626	7 694	7 824	7 677	7 717	7 789	7 793	7 835	7 820
Unemployed, thousands										
All persons	2 344	1 619	1 211	1 411	1 650	1 659	1 749	1 793	1 567	1 304
Males	1 202	831	599	734	881	856	900	927	815	701
Females	1 142	788	612	678	769	802	850	866	752	603
Civilian employment, thousands										
All persons	14 594	15 241	15 800	15 868	15 473	15 562	15 591	15 568	15 862	16 084
Males	8 081	8 403	8 718	8 722	8 566	8 648	8 651	8 641	8 778	8 867
Females	6 513	6 838	7 082	7 147	6 908	6 914	6 940	6 927	7 084	7 217
Civilian employment (%)										
All persons	100.0	100.0	100.0	100.0	100.0	100.0	100.0	100.0	100.0	100.0
Males	55.4	55.1	55.2	55.0	55.4	55.6	55.5	55.5	55.3	55.1
Females	44.6	44.9	44.8	45.0	44.6	44.4	44.5	44.5	44.7	44.9
Unemployment rate (% of civilian labour force)										
All persons	13.8	9.6	7.1	8.2	9.6	9.6	10.1	10.3	9.0	7.5
Males	12.9	9.0	6.4	7.8	9.3	9.0	9.4	9.7	8.5	7.3
Females	14.9	10.3	8.0	8.7	10.0	10.4	10.9	11.1	9.6	7.7
CIVIL. EMPL. - PROFESSIONAL STATUS, thousands										
All activities	**14 594**	**15 241**	**15 800**	**15 868**	**15 473**	**15 562**	**15 591**	**15 568**	**15 862**	**16 084**
Employees	11 028	11 666	12 179	12 260	11 918	12 004	12 099	12 170	12 475	12 669
Employers and persons working on own account	2 903	2 932	2 970	2 979	2 955	2 979	2 942	2 885	2 896	2 940
Unpaid family workers	662	643	651	629	601	580	549	514	491	475
Employees as % of civilian employment	**75.6**	**76.5**	**77.1**	**77.3**	**77.0**	**77.1**	**77.6**	**78.2**	**78.6**	**78.8**
Part-time employment (%)										
Part-time as % of employment	10.8	10.1	9.3	8.7	8.7	8.3	8.0	7.7	7.1	6.4
Male share of part time employment	33.0	33.0	31.9	31.6	33.1	33.1	32.4	32.1	32.9	33.0
Female share of part time employment	67.0	67.0	68.1	68.4	66.9	66.9	67.6	67.9	67.1	67.0
Male part-time as % of male employment	6.5	6.0	5.3	5.0	5.2	5.0	4.7	4.5	4.2	3.8
Female part-time as % of female employment	16.3	15.0	14.1	13.1	13.1	12.5	12.2	11.8	10.7	9.6
Duration of unemployment (% of total unemployment)										
Less than one month	7.0	8.2	15.3	14.1	13.2	11.8	11.0	10.9	11.7	11.5
More than 1 month and less than 3 months	10.1	12.3	18.6	20.6	19.2	17.2	16.2	15.3	15.8	11.5
More than 3 months and less than 6 months	13.7	15.2	19.4	20.6	21.1	18.9	18.0	17.5	16.7	19.3
More than 6 months and less than 1 year	18.7	18.4	17.6	19.5	21.0	20.5	20.1	19.8	19.5	18.5
More than 1 year	50.4	45.9	29.0	25.2	25.5	31.6	34.8	36.5	36.2	39.3

Note: Detailed metadata: http://metalinks.oecd.org/lfs/20170518/e873b, http://metalinks.oecd.org/lfs/20170518/87289, http://metalinks.oecd.org/lfs/20170518/889eb and http://metalinks.oecd.org/lfs/20170518/176b0.

Disclaimer: http://oe.cd/disclaimer

POLAND

Table 2. Participation rates and unemployment rates by age and sex

Annual average estimates, percentage

	2006	2007	2008	2009	2010	2011	2012	2013	2014	2015
Participation rates										
Males										
15-19	10.0	9.4	8.7	9.0	9.7	8.8	8.3	7.9	7.9	7.7
20-24	62.5	61.4	62.6	65.3	65.3	64.5	64.1	63.9	64.4	63.9
25-34	92.8	91.9	92.5	93.0	93.0	93.1	92.9	93.0	93.0	92.6
35-44	92.1	92.2	92.8	93.0	93.0	92.5	92.9	92.8	93.0	93.1
45-54	80.2	80.2	81.2	82.0	82.7	83.0	83.6	83.3	84.4	84.9
55-59	51.6	54.7	58.5	61.7	64.6	66.9	68.5	70.2	71.0	71.4
60-64	26.8	28.3	28.8	27.4	28.4	32.7	35.7	39.3	41.5	42.2
15-24	37.5	36.5	36.5	38.1	39.3	38.7	38.5	38.4	38.8	38.4
25-54	88.2	87.9	88.8	89.4	89.6	89.7	90.0	90.0	90.5	90.6
55-64	42.6	44.8	46.8	47.5	48.9	51.6	53.5	55.9	57.2	57.5
65 and over	8.1	7.6	7.6	7.5	7.7	7.8	7.7	7.5	7.9	7.9
15-64	70.1	70.0	70.9	71.8	72.1	72.6	73.3	73.9	74.6	74.8
Females										
15-19	7.1	6.4	6.6	6.3	6.5	5.7	6.0	5.4	5.3	4.0
20-24	51.4	49.4	49.8	49.9	50.1	47.6	47.5	47.0	48.3	46.2
25-34	77.0	76.8	76.4	76.5	77.2	76.8	77.2	77.1	78.0	78.2
35-44	81.9	81.7	82.2	82.9	83.0	82.8	83.0	82.8	82.7	82.0
45-54	68.7	69.6	71.3	73.8	76.1	76.7	77.4	77.5	78.1	78.5
55-59	25.3	26.2	28.5	31.4	36.3	42.2	46.6	50.7	53.2	55.4
60-64	12.3	11.9	11.8	12.1	13.1	13.8	14.2	14.4	16.0	18.6
15-24	30.7	29.3	29.6	29.4	29.6	28.1	28.4	27.9	28.7	27.0
25-54	75.4	75.6	76.3	77.5	78.6	78.6	79.1	79.1	79.6	79.6
55-64	20.3	20.6	21.6	23.2	25.9	29.0	31.3	33.3	35.2	37.3
65 and over	3.3	3.2	3.1	3.0	3.0	3.1	3.0	3.0	2.9	2.7
15-64	56.8	56.5	57.0	57.8	58.5	58.9	59.7	60.1	61.1	61.4
All persons										
15-24	34.2	33.0	33.1	33.8	34.6	33.5	33.6	33.3	33.9	32.9
25-54	81.7	81.7	82.5	83.4	84.1	84.2	84.6	84.6	85.1	85.1
55-64	30.7	31.8	33.3	34.5	36.7	39.6	41.8	44.0	45.6	46.9
65 and over	5.1	4.9	4.8	4.7	4.8	4.9	4.8	4.7	4.8	4.7
15-64	63.4	63.2	63.8	64.7	65.3	65.7	66.5	67.0	67.9	68.1
Unemployment rates										
Males										
15-19	27.8	18.4	15.6	28.1	28.0	28.9	34.1	34.5	35.2	32.7
20-24	28.4	20.2	15.2	19.2	21.7	23.0	23.0	24.4	21.4	19.4
25-34	12.4	8.8	6.3	7.4	9.4	8.8	9.4	9.9	8.9	7.8
35-44	9.7	6.1	4.5	5.3	6.5	6.0	6.5	6.9	5.8	5.1
45-54	11.3	8.1	5.2	6.0	7.6	7.4	7.7	7.4	6.8	5.6
55-59	10.9	7.8	6.4	7.0	8.0	7.4	8.0	8.3	7.4	6.0
60-64	5.9	6.0	3.7	5.8	6.2	7.3	7.9	8.3	6.6	5.8
15-24	28.3	20.0	15.2	20.2	22.4	23.6	24.1	25.4	22.7	20.7
25-54	11.2	7.8	5.4	6.3	7.9	7.5	8.0	8.2	7.2	6.2
55-64	9.8	7.4	5.8	6.7	7.5	7.4	8.0	8.3	7.1	5.9
65 and over	1.4	1.8	1.6	0.6	1.5	1.4	2.0	2.0	2.0	1.4
15-64	13.1	9.1	6.5	7.9	9.5	9.1	9.5	9.8	8.6	7.4
Total	13.0	9.0	6.4	7.8	9.3	9.0	9.4	9.7	8.5	7.3
Females										
15-19	35.3	28.1	26.2	26.2	34.4	41.1	43.1	40.7	37.0	33.4
20-24	31.2	23.3	19.1	20.7	24.4	27.6	28.5	29.0	24.5	20.0
25-34	14.9	10.1	7.9	9.0	10.8	11.6	12.5	12.6	11.0	8.6
35-44	13.1	8.3	5.9	6.6	7.4	7.5	8.4	9.0	7.8	6.3
45-54	12.1	8.6	6.6	6.9	7.8	8.0	8.0	8.4	7.2	6.4
55-59	6.7	6.5	4.8	6.3	7.5	7.2	7.5	7.5	7.3	5.4
60-64	4.6	3.1	3.0	2.8	3.1	2.6	3.3	4.6	3.1	2.9
15-24	31.6	23.8	19.9	21.2	25.4	28.8	30.0	30.1	25.5	20.9
25-54	13.4	9.1	6.8	7.6	8.7	9.1	9.7	10.0	8.7	7.1
55-64	6.2	5.7	4.4	5.5	6.5	6.2	6.6	6.9	6.3	4.8
65 and over	1.5	2.4	1.2	1.1	2.6	1.0	0.9	1.5	1.5	1.6
15-64	15.1	10.4	8.0	8.8	10.1	10.5	11.0	11.2	9.7	7.8
Total	14.9	10.3	7.9	8.7	10.0	10.4	10.9	11.1	9.6	7.7
All persons										
15-24	29.8	21.7	17.3	20.7	23.7	25.8	26.5	27.3	23.9	20.8
25-54	12.2	8.4	6.1	6.9	8.3	8.2	8.8	9.0	7.9	6.6
55-64	8.5	6.8	5.3	6.3	7.1	6.9	7.4	7.7	6.8	5.4
65 and over	1.5	2.0	1.5	0.8	1.9	1.2	1.6	1.8	1.8	1.5
15-64	14.0	9.7	7.2	8.3	9.7	9.8	10.2	10.5	9.1	7.6

Note: Detailed metadata at:http://metalinks.oecd.org/lfs/20170518/6f97b
Disclaimer: http://oe.cd/disclaimer

Table 3. Civilian employment and employees: breakdown by activity - ISIC Rev. 4

Annual average estimates

		2006	2007	2008	2009	2010	2011	2012	2013	2014	2015
	CIVILIAN EMPLOYMENT										
	By activity, thousands										
A-U	**All activities**	..	..	**15 800.0**	**15 868.0**	**15 961.0**	**16 130.7**	**15 591.0**	**15 568.0**	**15 862.0**	**16 084.0**
A	Agriculture, hunting and forestry	..	..	2 206.0	2 107.0	2 050.0	2 044.9	1 960.0	1 867.0	1 820.0	1 849.0
B-F	**Industry**	..	..	**5 036.0**	**4 934.0**	**4 812.0**	**4 933.0**	**4 740.0**	**4 752.0**	**4 836.0**	**4 897.0**
B	Mining and quarrying	..	..	234.0	221.0	230.0	254.8	252.0	268.0	267.0	230.0
C	Manufacturing	..	..	3 228.0	3 059.0	2 961.0	3 025.3	2 906.0	2 969.0	3 036.0	3 107.0
D	Electricity, gas, steam, air cond. supply	..	..	174.0	190.0	182.0	178.2	164.0	167.0	176.0	175.0
E	Water supply, sewerage, waste mgt, remediation	..	..	166.0	156.0	154.0	156.8	165.0	164.0	170.0	178.0
F	Construction	..	..	1 234.0	1 308.0	1 285.0	1 317.9	1 253.0	1 184.0	1 187.0	1 207.0
G-U	**Services**	..	..	**8 558.0**	**8 827.0**	**9 099.0**	**9 152.8**	**8 891.0**	**8 949.0**	**9 206.0**	**9 338.0**
G	Wholesale, retail trade, vehicle, motorcycle repair	..	..	2 326.0	2 332.0	2 376.0	2 376.8	2 270.0	2 226.0	2 296.0	2 329.0
H	Transportation and storage	..	..	897.0	889.0	886.0	900.3	898.0	923.0	927.0	944.0
I	Accommodation and food service activities	..	..	307.0	329.0	350.0	354.9	346.0	330.0	334.0	340.0
J	Information and communication	..	..	295.0	318.0	316.0	315.4	316.0	331.0	356.0	369.0
K	Financial and insurance activities	..	..	340.0	372.0	371.0	389.4	394.0	379.0	376.0	395.0
L	Real estate activities	..	..	143.0	156.0	174.0	170.2	147.0	139.0	158.0	172.0
M	Professional, scientific and technical activities	..	..	411.0	459.0	496.0	512.9	515.0	522.0	555.0	561.0
N	Administrative and support service activities	..	..	363.0	386.0	407.0	444.7	424.0	420.0	456.0	440.0
O	Public administration, defence, social security	..	..	984.0	1 021.0	1 049.0	1 064.3	1 039.0	1 054.0	1 063.0	1 075.0
P	Education	..	..	1 184.0	1 227.0	1 254.0	1 228.4	1 175.0	1 212.0	1 249.0	1 233.0
Q	Human health and social work activities	..	..	857.0	881.0	935.0	924.1	907.0	942.0	935.0	947.0
R	Arts, entertainment and recreation	..	..	197.0	199.0	200.0	196.4	189.0	196.0	208.0	213.0
S	Other service activities	..	..	225.0	229.0	248.0	243.3	233.0	237.0	239.0	245.0
T	Households as employers and own-use activities	..	..	19.0	20.0	24.0	25.4	29.0	29.0	26.0	25.0
U	Activities of extraterritorial organizations, bodies	..	..	..	1.0	1.0	0.9	1.0	1.0	..	1.0
	EMPLOYEES										
	By activity, thousands										
A-U	**All activities**	..	..	**12 179.0**	**12 260.0**	**12 306.0**	**12 481.8**	**12 099.0**	**12 004.0**	**12 475.0**	**12 669.0**
A	Agriculture, hunting and forestry	..	..	215.0	208.0	216.0	223.3	217.0	219.0	219.0	217.0
B-F	**Industry**	..	..	**4 588.0**	**4 454.0**	**4 313.0**	**4 451.0**	**4 265.0**	**4 302.0**	**4 351.0**	**4 418.0**
B	Mining and quarrying	..	..	234.0	220.0	229.0	253.4	249.0	246.0	267.0	230.0
C	Manufacturing	..	..	3 036.0	2 866.0	2 772.0	2 841.0	2 724.0	2 740.0	2 833.0	2 904.0
D	Electricity, gas, steam, air cond. supply	..	..	174.0	190.0	181.0	176.8	163.0	172.0	173.0	171.0
E	Water supply, sewerage, waste mgt, remediation	..	..	156.0	150.0	141.0	151.4	157.0	147.0	166.0	171.0
F	Construction	..	..	988.0	1 028.0	990.0	1 028.4	972.0	997.0	912.0	942.0
G-U	**Services**	..	..	**7 376.0**	**7 598.0**	**7 777.0**	**7 807.5**	**7 617.0**	**7 483.0**	**7 905.0**	**8 034.0**
G	Wholesale, retail trade, vehicle, motorcycle repair	..	..	1 783.0	1 806.0	1 834.0	1 829.1	1 754.0	1 744.0	1 795.0	1 862.0
H	Transportation and storage	..	..	750.0	738.0	741.0	751.5	756.0	729.0	798.0	805.0
I	Accommodation and food service activities	..	..	265.0	278.0	291.0	295.8	293.0	284.0	286.0	287.0
J	Information and communication	..	..	245.0	264.0	264.0	259.6	260.0	247.0	291.0	299.0
K	Financial and insurance activities	..	..	300.0	319.0	320.0	332.2	342.0	314.0	321.0	341.0
L	Real estate activities	..	..	129.0	136.0	151.0	148.4	130.0	143.0	134.0	147.0
M	Professional, scientific and technical activities	..	..	274.0	306.0	325.0	332.0	332.0	316.0	355.0	362.0
N	Administrative and support service activities	..	..	332.0	351.0	372.0	399.1	387.0	387.0	409.0	393.0
O	Public administration, defence, social security	..	..	984.0	1 021.0	1 049.0	1 064.3	1 039.0	1 018.0	1 063.0	1 075.0
P	Education	..	..	1 157.0	1 196.0	1 216.0	1 190.8	1 140.0	1 144.0	1 215.0	1 194.0
Q	Human health and social work activities	..	..	804.0	820.0	857.0	848.2	828.0	815.0	851.0	851.0
R	Arts, entertainment and recreation	..	..	175.0	179.0	177.0	173.2	171.0	167.0	182.0	189.0
S	Other service activities	..	..	153.0	157.0	158.0	153.5	150.0	147.0	156.0	162.0
T	Households as employers and own-use activities	..	..	18.0	19.0	21.0	23.6	26.0	23.0	24.0	23.0
U	Activities of extraterritorial organizations, bodies	..	..	..	1.0	1.0	0.9	1.0	1.0	..	1.0

Note: Detailed metadata:http://metalinks.oecd.org/lfs/20170518/87289
Disclaimer: http://oe.cd/disclaimer

PORTUGAL

Table 1. Labour force

Annual average estimates

<table>
<tr><th></th><th>2006</th><th>2007</th><th>2008</th><th>2009</th><th>2010</th><th>2011</th><th>2012</th><th>2013</th><th>2014</th><th>2015</th></tr>
<tr><td>Civilian labour force, thousands</td><td></td><td></td><td></td><td></td><td></td><td></td><td></td><td></td><td></td><td></td></tr>
<tr><td>All persons</td><td>5 471</td><td>5 499</td><td>5 505</td><td>5 458</td><td>5 465 |</td><td>5 397</td><td>5 352</td><td>5 259</td><td>5 201</td><td>5 167</td></tr>
<tr><td>Males</td><td>2 890</td><td>2 889</td><td>2 887</td><td>2 839</td><td>2 825 |</td><td>2 810</td><td>2 764</td><td>2 701</td><td>2 659</td><td>2 632</td></tr>
<tr><td>Females</td><td>2 582</td><td>2 610</td><td>2 618</td><td>2 618</td><td>2 639 |</td><td>2 588</td><td>2 588</td><td>2 558</td><td>2 542</td><td>2 535</td></tr>
<tr><td>Unemployed, thousands</td><td></td><td></td><td></td><td></td><td></td><td></td><td></td><td></td><td></td><td></td></tr>
<tr><td>All persons</td><td>421</td><td>441</td><td>418</td><td>517</td><td>591 |</td><td>688</td><td>836</td><td>855</td><td>726</td><td>647</td></tr>
<tr><td>Males</td><td>191</td><td>192</td><td>189</td><td>253</td><td>278 |</td><td>350</td><td>434</td><td>436</td><td>362</td><td>323</td></tr>
<tr><td>Females</td><td>230</td><td>248</td><td>229</td><td>265</td><td>314 |</td><td>338</td><td>402</td><td>419</td><td>365</td><td>324</td></tr>
<tr><td>Civilian employment, thousands</td><td></td><td></td><td></td><td></td><td></td><td></td><td></td><td></td><td></td><td></td></tr>
<tr><td>All persons</td><td>5 051</td><td>5 059</td><td>5 087</td><td>4 940</td><td>4 874 |</td><td>4 709</td><td>4 517</td><td>4 404</td><td>4 475</td><td>4 520</td></tr>
<tr><td>Males</td><td>2 699</td><td>2 697</td><td>2 698</td><td>2 587</td><td>2 548 |</td><td>2 459</td><td>2 330</td><td>2 265</td><td>2 297</td><td>2 309</td></tr>
<tr><td>Females</td><td>2 352</td><td>2 362</td><td>2 389</td><td>2 354</td><td>2 326 |</td><td>2 250</td><td>2 187</td><td>2 139</td><td>2 178</td><td>2 212</td></tr>
<tr><td>Civilian employment (%)</td><td></td><td></td><td></td><td></td><td></td><td></td><td></td><td></td><td></td><td></td></tr>
<tr><td>All persons</td><td>100.0</td><td>100.0</td><td>100.0</td><td>100.0</td><td>100.0 |</td><td>100.0</td><td>100.0</td><td>100.0</td><td>100.0</td><td>100.0</td></tr>
<tr><td>Males</td><td>53.4</td><td>53.3</td><td>53.0</td><td>52.4</td><td>52.3 |</td><td>52.2</td><td>51.6</td><td>51.4</td><td>51.3</td><td>51.1</td></tr>
<tr><td>Females</td><td>46.6</td><td>46.7</td><td>47.0</td><td>47.6</td><td>47.7 |</td><td>47.8</td><td>48.4</td><td>48.6</td><td>48.7</td><td>48.9</td></tr>
<tr><td>Unemployment rate (% of civilian labour force)</td><td></td><td></td><td></td><td></td><td></td><td></td><td></td><td></td><td></td><td></td></tr>
<tr><td>All persons</td><td>7.7</td><td>8.0</td><td>7.6</td><td>9.5</td><td>10.8 |</td><td>12.8</td><td>15.6</td><td>16.3</td><td>14.0</td><td>12.5</td></tr>
<tr><td>Males</td><td>6.6</td><td>6.7</td><td>6.5</td><td>8.9</td><td>9.8 |</td><td>12.5</td><td>15.7</td><td>16.1</td><td>13.6</td><td>12.3</td></tr>
<tr><td>Females</td><td>8.9</td><td>9.5</td><td>8.8</td><td>10.1</td><td>11.9 |</td><td>13.1</td><td>15.5</td><td>16.4</td><td>14.3</td><td>12.8</td></tr>
<tr><td>CIVIL. EMPL. - PROFESSIONAL STATUS, thousands</td><td></td><td></td><td></td><td></td><td></td><td></td><td></td><td></td><td></td><td></td></tr>
<tr><td>All activities</td><td>5 051</td><td>5 059</td><td>5 087</td><td>4 940</td><td>4 874 |</td><td>4 709</td><td>4 516</td><td>4 404</td><td>4 475</td><td>4 520</td></tr>
<tr><td>Employees</td><td>3 796</td><td>3 796</td><td>3 842</td><td>3 746</td><td>3 741 |</td><td>3 688</td><td>3 512</td><td>3 432</td><td>3 587</td><td>3 682</td></tr>
<tr><td>Employers and persons working on own account</td><td>1 166</td><td>1 183</td><td>1 196</td><td>1 151</td><td>1 086 |</td><td>992</td><td>974</td><td>942</td><td>865</td><td>815</td></tr>
<tr><td>Unpaid family workers</td><td>62</td><td>54</td><td>46</td><td>43</td><td>46 |</td><td>29</td><td>30</td><td>30</td><td>24</td><td>23</td></tr>
<tr><td>Employees as % of civilian employment</td><td>75.2</td><td>75.0</td><td>75.5</td><td>75.8</td><td>76.8 |</td><td>78.3</td><td>77.8</td><td>77.9</td><td>80.1</td><td>81.5</td></tr>
<tr><td>Part-time employment (%)</td><td></td><td></td><td></td><td></td><td></td><td></td><td></td><td></td><td></td><td></td></tr>
<tr><td>Part-time as % of employment</td><td>9.4</td><td>10.0</td><td>9.9</td><td>9.8</td><td>9.6</td><td>11.7</td><td>12.5</td><td>12.0</td><td>11.0</td><td>10.5</td></tr>
<tr><td>Male share of part time employment</td><td>33.7</td><td>33.3</td><td>31.6</td><td>32.1</td><td>34.2</td><td>40.2</td><td>41.4</td><td>42.0</td><td>42.1</td><td>40.7</td></tr>
<tr><td>Female share of part time employment</td><td>66.3</td><td>66.7</td><td>68.4</td><td>67.9</td><td>65.8</td><td>59.8</td><td>58.6</td><td>58.0</td><td>57.9</td><td>59.3</td></tr>
<tr><td>Male part-time as % of male employment</td><td>5.9</td><td>6.3</td><td>5.9</td><td>6.0</td><td>6.3</td><td>9.1</td><td>10.1</td><td>9.9</td><td>9.1</td><td>8.5</td></tr>
<tr><td>Female part-time as % of female employment</td><td>13.5</td><td>14.4</td><td>14.5</td><td>14.0</td><td>13.2</td><td>14.5</td><td>14.9</td><td>14.1</td><td>12.9</td><td>12.6</td></tr>
<tr><td>Duration of unemployment (% of total unemployment)</td><td></td><td></td><td></td><td></td><td></td><td></td><td></td><td></td><td></td><td></td></tr>
<tr><td>Less than one month</td><td>5.9</td><td>6.3</td><td>7.1</td><td>6.4</td><td>5.2</td><td>5.0</td><td>4.0</td><td>3.2</td><td>3.8</td><td>4.1</td></tr>
<tr><td>More than 1 month and less than 3 months</td><td>12.7</td><td>14.0</td><td>15.3</td><td>14.8</td><td>11.3</td><td>15.2</td><td>13.8</td><td>11.4</td><td>11.7</td><td>13.8</td></tr>
<tr><td>More than 3 months and less than 6 months</td><td>13.4</td><td>14.6</td><td>13.9</td><td>15.1</td><td>13.0</td><td>15.0</td><td>14.6</td><td>12.3</td><td>10.6</td><td>11.7</td></tr>
<tr><td>More than 6 months and less than 1 year</td><td>17.6</td><td>17.9</td><td>16.3</td><td>19.5</td><td>18.2</td><td>16.5</td><td>18.9</td><td>16.9</td><td>14.2</td><td>13.0</td></tr>
<tr><td>More than 1 year</td><td>50.4</td><td>47.2</td><td>47.4</td><td>44.2</td><td>52.2</td><td>48.4</td><td>48.8</td><td>56.4</td><td>59.6</td><td>57.4</td></tr>
</table>

Note: Detailed metadata: http://metalinks.oecd.org/lfs/20170518/78818, http://metalinks.oecd.org/lfs/20170518/87289, http://metalinks.oecd.org/lfs/20170518/f5d98 and http://metalinks.oecd.org/lfs/20170518/e5136.

Disclaimer: http://oe.cd/disclaimer

Table 2. Participation rates and unemployment rates by age and sex

Annual average estimates, percentage

	2006	2007	2008	2009	2010	2011	2012	2013	2014	2015
Participation rates										
Males										
15-19	20.7	20.2	18.4	15.9	14.2	14.8	14.0	13.1	12.5	11.1
20-24	67.3	67.0	67.4	63.5	61.4	65.4	63.8	58.9	57.1	58.0
25-34	92.8	92.4	93.0	92.3	92.1	92.5	91.9	90.6	90.6	89.5
35-44	94.7	94.8	94.9	93.7	94.4	94.6	93.6	92.2	94.2	95.0
45-54	91.0	91.4	91.5	91.4	91.3	90.0	90.8	90.5	89.7	90.2
55-59	71.7	71.7	72.6	73.7	73.4	74.2	72.6	75.6	77.2	77.9
60-64	52.3	53.1	51.7	50.1	49.3	47.8	47.3	48.9	49.6	51.0
15-24	45.5	44.7	43.6	40.1	38.0	40.4	39.2	36.2	34.8	34.2
25-54	92.9	92.9	93.2	92.5	92.7	92.4	92.1	91.1	91.6	91.7
55-64	62.7	63.2	62.9	62.6	62.0	61.6	60.4	62.7	64.0	65.0
65 and over	24.6	24.2	23.4	22.3	22.3	22.2	21.9	20.5	18.3	17.7
15-64	79.2	79.2	79.2	78.2	77.8	78.0	77.3	76.5	76.7	76.7
Females										
15-19	14.2	13.7	12.5	11.8	10.6	12.1	11.3	11.5	10.1	9.9
20-24	58.0	59.5	61.8	61.5	56.9	58.5	57.3	55.0	56.9	55.9
25-34	86.6	86.9	86.9	87.2	88.2	88.8	89.1	89.3	89.0	89.5
35-44	84.7	85.6	85.1	86.0	87.3	87.3	87.7	88.3	88.8	89.0
45-54	76.0	75.2	76.4	76.5	79.0	77.6	78.6	79.5	80.1	80.4
55-59	51.3	56.3	55.2	55.8	56.6	58.2	59.1	59.1	58.9	63.6
60-64	38.4	36.7	37.3	35.5	37.6	33.9	34.3	34.0	35.4	35.3
15-24	37.7	37.8	38.1	37.2	34.2	35.9	34.9	33.8	33.8	32.8
25-54	82.6	82.7	82.9	83.3	84.9	84.5	85.0	85.5	85.8	86.0
55-64	45.2	47.0	46.7	46.0	47.4	46.4	47.0	46.9	47.5	49.9
65 and over	13.2	13.9	13.4	13.3	12.5	9.2	9.6	8.3	7.4	7.2
15-64	68.3	68.7	68.9	68.9	69.7	69.5	69.7	69.8	70.0	70.3
All persons										
15-24	41.7	41.3	40.9	38.7	36.1	38.1	37.1	35.0	34.3	33.5
25-54	87.7	87.7	87.9	87.8	88.7	88.4	88.5	88.3	88.6	88.8
55-64	53.4	54.6	54.3	53.8	54.3	53.6	53.3	54.4	55.3	57.0
65 and over	17.9	18.1	17.6	17.0	16.6	14.5	14.7	13.4	11.9	11.6
15-64	73.6	73.9	73.9	73.4	73.7	73.6	73.4	73.0	73.2	73.4
Unemployment rates										
Males										
15-19	24.9	21.6	21.3	26.1	33.3	47.6	53.3	50.0	48.9	39.9
20-24	12.2	11.7	11.6	17.4	19.0	24.9	33.2	33.9	31.0	27.6
25-34	6.9	7.3	6.7	9.5	10.5	13.4	17.7	18.0	14.5	12.8
35-44	5.0	5.2	5.9	7.8	8.0	10.4	13.1	13.8	10.6	9.7
45-54	5.5	5.8	5.2	8.1	9.4	11.0	13.6	14.9	11.5	10.5
55-59	8.1	8.1	8.2	9.0	11.1	13.1	15.2	14.9	15.5	14.1
60-64	5.9	5.5	5.7	6.9	8.0	10.0	13.3	14.2	14.5	13.8
15-24	14.9	13.8	13.6	19.1	21.6	29.0	36.7	36.7	34.2	29.6
25-54	5.8	6.1	6.0	8.5	9.3	11.6	14.7	15.4	12.0	10.8
55-64	7.3	7.1	7.3	8.2	9.9	11.9	14.5	14.6	15.2	14.0
65 and over	0.1	0.3	0.3	0.3	0.3	0.6	1.3	1.4	1.7	2.2
15-64	7.0	7.0	6.9	9.4	10.4	13.1	16.5	17.0	14.2	12.8
Total	6.5	6.6	6.5	8.8	9.8	12.3	15.6	16.0	13.5	12.2
Females										
15-19	27.2	27.7	28.9	29.4	36.1	51.5	60.6	57.0	49.4	52.6
20-24	16.7	18.8	18.7	20.3	21.9	27.8	35.3	36.1	33.0	31.3
25-34	11.4	12.3	10.8	12.6	15.1	14.8	18.5	19.9	16.5	13.3
35-44	7.8	8.3	7.5	9.1	11.7	11.5	13.5	14.9	12.7	10.8
45-54	7.3	7.5	7.1	8.3	9.4	10.7	12.4	12.3	11.4	11.0
55-59	6.2	6.5	7.0	8.4	9.3	10.1	11.6	13.4	13.2	11.7
60-64	3.7	4.5	3.8	4.4	5.0	8.5	8.9	11.0	8.4	8.8
15-24	18.5	20.3	20.3	21.7	24.0	31.7	39.3	39.6	35.4	34.5
25-54	9.0	9.5	8.6	10.1	12.1	12.3	14.7	15.6	13.4	11.6
55-64	5.2	5.8	5.8	6.9	7.7	9.5	10.7	12.5	11.5	10.7
65 and over	0.1	0.1	0.0	0.3	0.8	1.7	2.0	1.1	1.9	2.9
15-64	9.4	10.1	9.3	10.7	12.5	13.5	16.1	17.0	14.8	13.1
Total	8.9	9.5	8.7	10.1	11.9	13.0	15.5	16.4	14.3	12.7
All persons										
15-24	16.5	16.7	16.7	20.3	22.8	30.3	37.9	38.1	34.8	32.0
25-54	7.3	7.7	7.2	9.2	10.7	11.9	14.7	15.5	12.7	11.2
55-64	6.3	6.5	6.6	7.6	8.9	10.8	12.7	13.7	13.5	12.5
65 and over	0.1	0.2	0.2	0.3	0.5	1.0	1.6	1.3	1.8	2.5
15-64	8.1	8.5	8.0	10.0	11.4	13.3	16.3	17.0	14.5	12.9

Note: Detailed metadata at:http://metalinks.oecd.org/lfs/20170518/6f97b
Disclaimer: http://oe.cd/disclaimer

PORTUGAL

Table 3. Civilian employment and employees: breakdown by activity - ISIC Rev. 4

Annual average estimates

		2006	2007	2008	2009	2010	2011	2012	2013	2014	2015
	CIVILIAN EMPLOYMENT										
	By activity, thousands										
A-U	**All activities**	..	..	**5 086.6**	**4 940.2**	**4 873.5**	**4 709.2**	**4 516.5**	**4 403.5**	**4 475.2**	**4 520.4**
A	Agriculture, hunting and forestry	..	..	585.4	568.8	548.5	483.9	491.4	453.1	389.1	342.5
B-F	**Industry**	..	..	**1 483.4**	**1 381.4**	**1 335.0**	**1 272.9**	**1 143.4**	**1 049.7**	**1 073.5**	**1 107.4**
B	Mining and quarrying	..	..	17.3	17.4	19.2	18.4	13.7	13.2	12.3	12.3
C	Manufacturing	..	..	869.7	825.0	801.7	783.2	740.7	705.0	739.0	769.2
D	Electricity, gas, steam, air cond. supply	..	..	22.6	21.0	15.8	18.4	17.8	15.9	15.1	19.0
E	Water supply, sewerage, waste mgt, remediation	..	..	34.2	28.3	31.5	29.8	28.2	27.3	31.3	29.4
F	Construction	..	..	539.6	489.7	466.8	423.1	343.0	288.3	275.8	277.5
G-U	**Services**	..	..	**3 017.8**	**2 990.0**	**2 990.0**	**2 952.4**	**2 881.7**	**2 900.7**	**3 012.6**	**3 070.5**
G	Wholesale, retail trade, vehicle, motorcycle repair	..	..	750.0	744.7	719.0	692.8	659.9	644.0	669.7	702.3
H	Transportation and storage	..	..	175.0	175.5	174.0	169.0	165.7	179.6	175.3	172.1
I	Accommodation and food service activities	..	..	317.5	291.7	287.0	286.5	276.8	289.0	276.4	258.7
J	Information and communication	..	..	90.9	90.6	103.5	80.3	84.1	89.5	106.2	103.6
K	Financial and insurance activities	..	..	95.0	86.9	86.6	103.7	96.9	86.6	100.2	108.0
L	Real estate activities	..	..	26.7	33.3	27.6	25.0	23.6	27.6	29.7	28.0
M	Professional, scientific and technical activities	..	..	170.9	164.0	154.6	171.6	152.9	167.3	180.7	192.4
N	Administrative and support service activities	..	..	132.5	135.5	152.8	139.3	144.8	141.8	161.1	153.7
O	Public administration, defence, social security	..	..	305.0	298.7	282.3	275.8	258.8	266.4	292.1	279.2
P	Education	..	..	341.8	355.7	366.1	362.8	368.0	354.9	357.0	379.5
Q	Human health and social work activities	..	..	300.7	320.0	347.4	361.4	370.0	368.2	380.4	404.1
R	Arts, entertainment and recreation	..	..	45.5	45.8	36.3	50.7	50.8	50.5	57.3	67.0
S	Other service activities	..	..	89.1	94.8	102.4	94.0	93.1	103.0	107.0	103.3
T	Households as employers and own-use activities	..	..	175.1	150.3	146.4	137.6	134.1	130.5	116.9	116.9
U	Activities of extraterritorial organizations, bodies	..	..	2.0	2.5	4.0	1.8	2.0	1.9	2.6	1.7
	EMPLOYEES										
	By activity, thousands										
A-U	**All activities**	..	..	**3 841.8**	**3 746.1**	**3 740.8**	**3 688.2**	**3 512.3**	**3 431.7**	**3 586.7**	**3 682.4**
A	Agriculture, hunting and forestry	..	..	87.4	81.3	82.3	82.5	82.9	84.7	84.6	79.5
B-F	**Industry**	..	..	**1 266.3**	**1 179.2**	**1 153.4**	**1 097.6**	**984.9**	**906.8**	**935.8**	**968.2**
B	Mining and quarrying	..	..	16.4	16.1	17.7	17.4	13.1	12.4	11.6	12.3
C	Manufacturing	..	..	782.3	742.3	721.9	704.6	663.1	630.7	666.7	697.9
D	Electricity, gas, steam, air cond. supply	..	..	22.0	20.5	15.3	17.5	17.7	15.8	14.6	18.7
E	Water supply, sewerage, waste mgt, remediation	..	..	33.0	27.0	30.1	27.9	25.7	25.4	29.6	28.2
F	Construction	..	..	412.6	373.3	368.4	330.2	265.3	222.5	213.3	211.1
G-U	**Services**	..	..	**2 488.1**	**2 485.6**	**2 505.1**	**2 508.1**	**2 444.5**	**2 440.2**	**2 566.3**	**2 634.7**
G	Wholesale, retail trade, vehicle, motorcycle repair	..	..	541.8	535.5	516.7	514.6	489.2	471.3	503.1	533.5
H	Transportation and storage	..	..	149.5	159.6	156.9	153.6	150.8	161.4	158.1	155.4
I	Accommodation and food service activities	..	..	221.9	213.1	217.0	216.6	206.8	216.1	205.5	197.1
J	Information and communication	..	..	80.9	82.6	93.0	73.4	74.9	77.3	92.9	95.3
K	Financial and insurance activities	..	..	88.9	82.5	78.2	97.3	89.6	78.9	91.4	98.9
L	Real estate activities	..	..	18.5	23.3	21.8	18.1	16.8	20.7	20.8	20.1
M	Professional, scientific and technical activities	..	..	116.3	111.1	106.2	112.1	96.4	104.4	123.4	132.2
N	Administrative and support service activities	..	..	119.5	120.4	140.5	128.2	134.1	131.5	148.3	140.5
O	Public administration, defence, social security	..	..	303.3	297.0	281.8	274.5	257.5	264.9	290.8	278.2
P	Education	..	..	334.5	347.1	353.6	353.3	355.8	343.2	347.3	367.5
Q	Human health and social work activities	..	..	284.3	301.9	325.1	343.5	350.8	348.4	359.0	383.1
R	Arts, entertainment and recreation	..	..	36.4	33.8	30.2	39.1	39.0	40.4	47.7	55.2
S	Other service activities	..	..	54.4	58.2	61.8	55.5	52.7	54.0	62.4	61.5
T	Households as employers and own-use activities	..	..	135.9	116.9	118.4	126.6	128.1	125.9	113.2	114.6
U	Activities of extraterritorial organizations, bodies	..	..	2.0	2.5	4.0	1.8	2.0	1.9	2.6	1.7

Note: Detailed metadata:http://metalinks.oecd.org/lfs/20170518/87289
Disclaimer: http://oe.cd/disclaimer

SLOVAK REPUBLIC

Table 1. Labour force

Annual average estimates

	2006	2007	2008	2009	2010	2011	2012	2013	2014	2015
Civilian labour force, thousands										
All persons	2 655	2 649	2 691	2 690	2 707	2 680	2 707	2 715	2 722	2 738
Males	1 471	1 465	1 488	1 497	1 497	1 496	1 507	1 506	1 510	1 505
Females	1 184	1 184	1 203	1 193	1 209	1 184	1 199	1 210	1 212	1 234
Unemployed, thousands										
All persons	353	292	258	324	389	365	378	386	359	314
Males	180	144	125	171	213	204	204	210	194	155
Females	174	148	133	154	176	161	174	176	165	159
Civilian employment, thousands										
All persons	2 301	2 357	2 434	2 366	2 318	2 315	2 329	2 329	2 363	2 424
Males	1 291	1 322	1 364	1 326	1 285	1 292	1 304	1 295	1 316	1 349
Females	1 010	1 036	1 070	1 039	1 033	1 023	1 026	1 034	1 047	1 075
Civilian employment (%)										
All persons	100.0	100.0	100.0	100.0	100.0	100.0	100.0	100.0	100.0	100.0
Males	56.1	56.1	56.0	56.1	55.4	55.8	56.0	55.6	55.7	55.7
Females	43.9	43.9	44.0	43.9	44.6	44.2	44.0	44.4	44.3	44.3
Unemployment rate (% of civilian labour force)										
All persons	13.3	11.0	9.6	12.1	14.4	13.6	13.9	14.2	13.2	11.5
Males	12.2	9.8	8.4	11.4	14.2	13.6	13.5	14.0	12.8	10.3
Females	14.7	12.5	11.0	12.9	14.6	13.6	14.5	14.5	13.6	12.9
CIVIL. EMPL. - PROFESSIONAL STATUS, thousands										
All activities	**2 301**	**2 357**	**2 434**	**2 366**	**2 318**	**2 315**	**2 329**	**2 329**	**2 363**	**2 424**
Employees	2 003	2 044	2 094	1 995	1 947	1 946	1 969	1 967	1 999	2 057
Employers and persons working on own account	288	301	332	368	367	368	359	361	362	364
Unpaid family workers	1	2	3	3	3	2	2	2	2	4
Employees as % of civilian employment	**87.0**	**86.7**	**86.1**	**84.3**	**84.0**	**84.1**	**84.5**	**84.5**	**84.6**	**84.8**
Part-time employment (%)										
Part-time as % of employment	2.4	2.4	2.6	2.9	3.7	4.0	3.8	4.3	4.9	5.7
Male share of part time employment	30.0	26.0	32.9	41.0	41.4	38.4	40.6	42.0	41.8	40.1
Female share of part time employment	70.0	74.0	67.1	59.0	58.6	61.6	59.4	58.0	58.2	59.9
Male part-time as % of male employment	1.3	1.1	1.5	2.1	2.7	2.7	2.7	3.3	3.7	4.1
Female part-time as % of female employment	3.8	4.0	4.0	4.0	4.8	5.6	5.1	5.6	6.4	7.8
Duration of unemployment (% of total unemployment)										
Less than one month	4.2	5.6	7.5	11.3	6.6	5.9	6.6	6.2	6.4	9.9
More than 1 month and less than 3 months	5.2	5.4	6.0	10.2	6.4	6.4	6.6	5.9	6.2	7.5
More than 3 months and less than 6 months	6.3	6.7	7.9	11.7	9.5	8.6	8.4	7.9	7.4	8.4
More than 6 months and less than 1 year	11.2	11.5	12.6	15.9	18.2	15.1	14.6	13.5	13.2	11.9
More than 1 year	73.1	70.8	66.0	50.9	59.3	64.0	63.7	66.6	66.8	62.3

Note: Detailed metadata: http://metalinks.oecd.org/lfs/20170518/354e9, http://metalinks.oecd.org/lfs/20170518/87289, http://metalinks.oecd.org/lfs/20170518/4892f and http://metalinks.oecd.org/lfs/20170518/e67c8.

Disclaimer: http://oe.cd/disclaimer

SLOVAK REPUBLIC

Table 2. Participation rates and unemployment rates by age and sex

Annual average estimates, percentage

	2006	2007	2008	2009	2010	2011	2012	2013	2014	2015
Participation rates										
Males										
15-19	10.6	9.2	9.1	8.3	6.9	7.8	7.9	7.4	8.0	7.3
20-24	65.5	65.5	63.4	62.7	62.1	62.7	61.7	62.4	62.0	63.0
25-34	95.7	94.6	94.9	94.9	94.2	94.0	94.7	94.9	94.8	94.7
35-44	95.1	94.8	95.1	95.0	94.7	95.3	95.3	95.0	96.0	95.1
45-54	90.5	89.3	90.1	90.5	89.6	90.9	91.0	90.5	90.7	90.5
55-59	76.9	77.1	79.1	78.3	81.0	80.9	82.0	81.9	82.1	81.5
60-64	24.2	27.1	31.4	30.6	29.9	29.4	33.1	32.8	32.0	32.8
15-24	39.3	38.7	37.7	37.0	36.2	37.2	37.1	37.6	38.1	38.3
25-54	93.8	93.0	93.4	93.6	92.9	93.5	93.8	93.6	94.0	93.6
55-64	55.3	56.9	60.0	58.8	59.9	58.7	60.3	59.5	58.9	58.4
65 and over	1.9	1.5	2.8	2.5	2.8	2.9	2.8	2.8	3.3	4.2
15-64	76.3	75.8	76.4	76.3	76.0	76.6	77.1	77.2	77.6	77.5
Females										
15-19	7.2	7.0	5.3	4.8	5.7	5.2	5.5	4.8	4.6	5.3
20-24	51.9	51.0	46.0	43.6	42.8	37.8	38.8	39.1	38.6	40.4
25-34	72.2	71.2	72.8	71.3	70.5	69.7	70.8	69.9	68.6	70.2
35-44	87.8	87.7	89.1	87.2	87.9	85.2	84.1	85.4	85.8	85.0
45-54	85.0	84.2	86.5	85.6	85.8	87.8	87.3	87.5	88.0	87.9
55-59	31.8	35.1	40.9	46.4	51.3	54.7	62.1	65.7	68.2	73.6
60-64	7.1	7.9	7.3	6.5	8.0	9.9	10.0	12.3	14.1	17.2
15-24	30.6	30.1	26.8	25.4	25.5	22.7	23.6	23.7	23.6	24.9
25-54	81.2	80.5	82.2	80.8	80.8	80.4	80.3	80.5	80.4	80.8
55-64	21.0	23.3	26.5	29.1	32.4	34.5	38.0	40.4	42.1	45.8
65 and over	0.7	1.0	0.9	0.9	1.2	1.2	1.1	1.1	1.2	1.5
15-64	60.9	60.7	61.4	60.6	61.3	60.8	61.7	62.4	62.8	64.3
All persons										
15-24	35.1	34.5	32.3	31.3	31.0	30.1	30.5	30.8	31.0	31.7
25-54	87.5	86.8	87.8	87.2	86.9	87.0	87.1	87.2	87.3	87.3
55-64	36.8	38.8	42.0	42.9	45.2	45.9	48.5	49.5	50.1	51.8
65 and over	1.1	1.2	1.6	1.5	1.8	1.8	1.8	1.7	2.0	2.6
15-64	68.5	68.2	68.9	68.4	68.7	68.7	69.4	69.8	70.3	70.9
Unemployment rates										
Males										
15-19	55.7	42.7	37.4	49.1	60.2	67.6	65.0	62.1	51.2	49.6
20-24	22.0	17.4	15.6	25.4	32.2	29.5	31.7	32.3	27.2	23.6
25-34	10.4	9.0	8.3	11.4	14.9	14.5	13.5	15.1	15.3	10.2
35-44	10.7	8.7	6.6	9.2	10.8	9.6	10.3	9.7	8.2	8.0
45-54	10.2	7.9	7.3	9.1	10.8	10.5	10.2	11.5	10.7	9.0
55-59	10.6	8.3	6.2	7.0	11.1	12.0	13.0	12.4	11.1	8.9
60-64	6.3	4.9	2.5	4.2	3.9	6.0	4.8	4.9	5.6	6.5
15-24	26.3	20.3	18.1	27.9	34.7	33.2	35.0	34.9	29.5	25.8
25-54	10.4	8.6	7.5	10.0	12.4	11.8	11.5	12.2	11.5	9.1
55-64	9.8	7.7	5.5	6.4	9.6	10.7	11.0	10.6	9.7	8.2
65 and over	0.0	2.1	2.1	1.5	4.0	0.0	2.0	4.7	7.8	2.7
15-64	12.2	9.8	8.4	11.4	14.3	13.7	13.6	14.0	12.9	10.4
Total	12.2	9.8	8.4	11.4	14.2	13.6	13.5	14.0	12.8	10.3
Females										
15-19	56.9	50.4	48.4	61.1	63.7	66.6	59.3	62.8	65.7	58.3
20-24	23.2	16.1	16.9	23.2	28.3	29.9	29.4	28.5	26.7	24.4
25-34	14.2	13.1	11.7	13.2	14.2	15.3	18.3	17.4	16.2	14.4
35-44	12.8	10.8	9.9	11.4	13.5	11.8	11.1	12.0	11.1	11.6
45-54	13.4	11.8	9.5	10.8	12.2	10.6	11.0	11.7	11.2	10.7
55-59	9.4	9.0	8.7	10.4	12.0	9.6	12.2	12.9	12.6	11.2
60-64	9.6	9.4	7.2	6.4	2.8	5.5	6.7	4.4	6.8	7.9
15-24	27.0	19.9	19.9	26.5	32.0	33.8	32.5	31.6	30.1	27.5
25-54	13.5	11.9	10.3	11.8	13.3	12.5	13.4	13.6	12.7	12.2
55-64	9.4	9.1	8.5	10.0	11.0	9.1	11.6	11.6	11.7	10.6
65 and over	0.0	3.4	0.9	1.0	4.2	6.0	5.6	3.0	4.1	1.6
15-64	14.7	12.6	11.1	12.9	14.6	13.6	14.5	14.6	13.7	12.9
Total	14.7	12.5	11.0	12.9	14.6	13.6	14.5	14.5	13.6	12.9
All persons										
15-24	26.6	20.1	18.8	27.3	33.6	33.4	34.0	33.6	29.7	26.4
25-54	11.8	10.1	8.8	10.8	12.8	12.1	12.4	12.8	12.0	10.5
55-64	9.7	8.1	6.5	7.7	10.1	10.1	11.2	11.0	10.6	9.3
65 and over	0.0	2.8	1.6	1.3	4.1	2.4	3.4	4.1	6.4	2.3
15-64	13.3	11.0	9.6	12.1	14.4	13.7	14.0	14.3	13.2	11.5

Note: Detailed metadata at:http://metalinks.oecd.org/lfs/20170518/6f97b
Disclaimer: http://oe.cd/disclaimer

Table 3. Civilian employment and employees: breakdown by activity - ISIC Rev. 4

Annual average estimates

		2006	2007	2008	2009	2010	2011	2012	2013	2014	2015
	CIVILIAN EMPLOYMENT										
	By activity, thousands										
A-U	**All activities**	..	..	..	**2 365.5**	**2 317.2**	**2 314.8**	**2 328.8**	**2 328.9**	**2 362.7**	**2 423.4**
A	Agriculture, hunting and forestry	..	..	..	84.9	75.0	71.3	75.4	77.1	82.7	77.1
B-F	**Industry**	..	..	..	**897.2**	**860.3**	**867.9**	**874.1**	**834.5**	**837.5**	**875.1**
B	Mining and quarrying	..	..	..	10.8	13.9	11.6	12.7	11.5	9.6	12.0
C	Manufacturing	..	..	..	565.2	530.0	560.7	570.3	539.5	550.4	598.3
D	Electricity, gas, steam, air cond. supply	..	..	..	30.7	27.0	26.4	24.3	23.5	26.6	25.0
E	Water supply, sewerage, waste mgt, remediation	..	..	..	33.4	31.1	28.2	26.1	27.1	27.6	26.2
F	Construction	..	..	..	257.1	258.3	241.0	240.7	232.9	223.3	213.6
G-U	**Services**	..	..	..	**1 383.4**	**1 381.9**	**1 375.6**	**1 379.3**	**1 417.3**	**1 442.5**	**1 471.2**
G	Wholesale, retail trade, vehicle, motorcycle repair	..	..	..	312.7	306.3	298.2	289.9	299.2	284.2	296.9
H	Transportation and storage	..	..	..	151.3	145.4	150.3	157.0	148.5	152.0	161.4
I	Accommodation and food service activities	..	..	..	107.1	103.6	99.1	97.2	112.6	119.2	114.8
J	Information and communication	..	..	..	48.7	55.9	56.5	61.1	51.7	56.6	65.5
K	Financial and insurance activities	..	..	..	50.0	47.8	51.9	51.9	52.4	50.9	39.4
L	Real estate activities	..	..	..	13.0	13.8	10.6	16.0	18.4	14.8	13.3
M	Professional, scientific and technical activities	..	..	..	82.0	75.4	76.3	72.1	70.7	76.5	73.0
N	Administrative and support service activities	..	..	..	58.6	59.5	60.5	61.5	64.2	60.9	64.6
O	Public administration, defence, social security	..	..	..	178.4	189.0	190.2	184.8	200.4	211.0	217.3
P	Education	..	..	..	162.0	165.0	161.7	157.4	163.6	166.9	175.2
Q	Human health and social work activities	..	..	..	149.8	157.1	157.5	161.3	164.1	175.6	181.0
R	Arts, entertainment and recreation	..	..	..	28.7	26.8	26.3	28.2	30.6	37.7	34.7
S	Other service activities	..	..	..	35.2	31.2	29.4	35.0	35.6	31.8	32.4
T	Households as employers and own-use activities	..	..	..	5.1	4.8	6.4	5.4	5.3	3.9	0.6
U	Activities of extraterritorial organizations, bodies	..	..	..	0.9	0.9	0.9	0.8	0.4	1.0	1.3
	EMPLOYEES										
	By activity, thousands										
A-U	**All activities**	..	..	..	**1 994.6**	**1 947.0**	**1 945.9**	**1 968.7**	**1 966.9**	**1 999.1**	**2 056.2**
A	Agriculture, hunting and forestry	..	..	..	69.0	60.1	54.1	62.6	63.8	64.5	59.4
B-F	**Industry**	..	..	..	**743.9**	**703.2**	**713.1**	**727.7**	**692.5**	**701.4**	**733.5**
B	Mining and quarrying	..	..	..	10.8	13.9	11.6	12.6	11.1	9.1	11.3
C	Manufacturing	..	..	..	528.6	489.2	517.8	530.1	496.9	510.1	552.5
D	Electricity, gas, steam, air cond. supply	..	..	..	29.8	26.3	25.2	23.3	21.5	24.4	22.8
E	Water supply, sewerage, waste mgt, remediation	..	..	..	32.3	29.3	26.9	25.4	26.4	27.0	25.4
F	Construction	..	..	..	142.4	144.5	131.6	136.3	136.6	130.8	121.5
G-U	**Services**	..	..	..	**1 181.7**	**1 183.7**	**1 178.7**	**1 178.4**	**1 210.6**	**1 233.2**	**1 263.3**
G	Wholesale, retail trade, vehicle, motorcycle repair	..	..	..	252.8	245.5	240.0	235.8	244.5	234.7	245.4
H	Transportation and storage	..	..	..	135.1	130.7	136.4	142.0	133.6	135.0	145.8
I	Accommodation and food service activities	..	..	..	89.8	87.1	84.9	87.7	98.4	102.4	96.6
J	Information and communication	..	..	..	44.8	48.6	47.4	48.3	41.7	45.2	55.2
K	Financial and insurance activities	..	..	..	39.8	35.9	40.5	39.7	38.3	38.9	28.5
L	Real estate activities	..	..	..	10.0	10.9	7.9	12.1	13.8	11.0	10.6
M	Professional, scientific and technical activities	..	..	..	45.4	43.5	42.3	39.1	37.3	41.3	42.6
N	Administrative and support service activities	..	..	..	50.8	51.6	54.0	55.7	58.6	54.4	56.9
O	Public administration, defence, social security	..	..	..	178.2	188.9	190.2	184.8	200.4	211.0	217.3
P	Education	..	..	..	157.0	160.5	157.5	153.1	160.3	162.6	170.0
Q	Human health and social work activities	..	..	..	134.3	140.7	137.8	140.5	141.3	149.6	147.4
R	Arts, entertainment and recreation	..	..	..	23.9	22.4	22.2	23.1	24.6	29.1	28.3
S	Other service activities	..	..	..	16.7	16.1	15.6	15.7	17.6	17.1	17.4
T	Households as employers and own-use activities	..	..	..	2.0	0.6	1.1	0.4	0.1	0.2	0.0
U	Activities of extraterritorial organizations, bodies	..	..	..	0.9	0.9	0.9	0.8	0.4	1.0	1.3

Note: Detailed metadata:http://metalinks.oecd.org/lfs/20170518/87289

Disclaimer: http://oe.cd/disclaimer

SLOVENIA

Table 1. Labour force

Annual average estimates

	2006	2007	2008	2009	2010	2011	2012	2013	2014	2015
Civilian labour force, thousands										
All persons	1 022	1 035	1 042	1 042	1 041	1 019	1 013	1 008	1 015	1 008
Males	551	562	566	564	565	551	546	546	548	545
Females	472	473	476	478	476	468	468	462	467	463
Unemployed, thousands										
All persons	61	50	46	61	75	83	90	102	99	91
Males	27	22	23	33	42	45	46	52	49	44
Females	34	28	23	28	33	38	44	50	49	47
Civilian employment, thousands										
All persons	961	985	996	981	966	936	924	906	917	917
Males	524	540	543	531	524	506	500	495	499	501
Females	438	446	453	450	443	430	424	411	417	417
Civilian employment (%)										
All persons	100.0	100.0	100.0	100.0	100.0	100.0	100.0	100.0	100.0	100.0
Males	54.5	54.8	54.5	54.1	54.2	54.1	54.1	54.6	54.5	54.6
Females	45.5	45.2	45.5	45.9	45.8	45.9	45.9	45.4	45.5	45.4
Unemployment rate (% of civilian labour force)										
All persons	5.9	4.8	4.4	5.9	7.2	8.2	8.8	10.1	9.7	9.0
Males	4.9	4.0	4.0	5.9	7.4	8.2	8.4	9.5	9.0	8.1
Females	7.2	5.8	4.8	5.8	7.0	8.2	9.4	10.9	10.6	10.1
CIVIL. EMPL. - PROFESSIONAL STATUS, thousands										
All activities	**961**	**985**	**996**	**981**	**966**	**936**	**924**	**906**	**917**	**917**
Employees	806	829	855	822	799	779	774	753	746	766
Employers and persons working on own account	109	109	99	105	119	118	113	109	116	114
Unpaid family workers	47	47	42	54	47	40	37	43	54	37
Employees as % of civilian employment	**83.8**	**84.1**	**85.9**	**83.8**	**82.7**	**83.2**	**83.8**	**83.1**	**81.4**	**83.5**
Part-time employment (%)										
Part-time as % of employment	7.8	7.8	7.5	8.3	9.4	8.6	7.9	8.6	9.6	9.2
Male share of part time employment	42.9	43.8	41.7	42.7	41.5	42.0	40.5	40.9	40.5	40.2
Female share of part time employment	57.1	56.2	58.3	57.3	58.5	58.0	59.5	59.1	59.5	59.8
Male part-time as % of male employment	6.1	6.3	5.7	6.6	7.2	6.7	5.9	6.4	7.1	6.7
Female part-time as % of female employment	9.8	9.7	9.6	10.4	12.1	10.9	10.3	11.2	12.5	12.1
Duration of unemployment (% of total unemployment)										
Less than one month	3.3	5.1	6.4	5.9	4.0	3.7	3.9	3.0	2.2	3.7
More than 1 month and less than 3 months	13.4	17.5	19.2	22.2	13.6	16.3	15.0	12.3	12.3	13.2
More than 3 months and less than 6 months	15.5	16.0	17.0	21.3	19.0	17.1	15.2	14.7	14.0	13.9
More than 6 months and less than 1 year	18.5	15.7	15.2	20.5	20.1	18.7	18.0	19.0	17.0	16.9
More than 1 year	49.3	45.7	42.2	30.1	43.3	44.2	47.9	51.0	54.5	52.3

Note: Detailed metadata: http://metalinks.oecd.org/lfs/20170518/95f6d, http://metalinks.oecd.org/lfs/20170518/87289, http://metalinks.oecd.org/lfs/20170518/69c10 and http://metalinks.oecd.org/lfs/20170518/82500.

Disclaimer: http://oe.cd/disclaimer

SLOVENIA

Table 2. Participation rates and unemployment rates by age and sex

Annual average estimates, percentage

	2006	2007	2008	2009	2010	2011	2012	2013	2014	2015
Participation rates										
Males										
15-19	20.3	23.1	20.9	19.1	18.3	17.8	12.4	13.7	14.8	16.0
20-24	64.6	68.0	68.0	64.7	63.3	59.8	57.5	55.5	55.1	59.4
25-34	92.5	93.3	93.8	92.9	92.6	92.8	93.2	92.6	92.5	92.9
35-44	95.1	94.4	94.1	93.7	94.4	94.2	95.1	95.6	95.2	95.8
45-54	85.9	86.5	87.1	87.5	88.5	88.6	89.0	89.6	89.3	90.1
55-59	61.8	62.9	62.4	61.9	61.7	59.3	62.0	62.2	64.0	67.0
60-64	22.3	22.6	21.1	26.8	27.4	21.5	21.0	25.0	26.0	23.2
15-24	44.4	47.6	47.7	45.4	44.4	42.0	38.1	37.1	36.6	38.9
25-54	91.0	91.3	91.6	91.3	91.7	91.8	92.4	92.6	92.2	92.9
55-64	45.8	46.7	46.4	48.2	47.5	42.7	43.6	45.1	45.7	46.4
65 and over	11.5	12.0	8.5	10.7	10.4	8.6	6.9	7.2	9.1	5.8
15-64	74.9	75.8	75.8	75.6	75.4	73.9	73.7	74.2	74.3	75.4
Females										
15-19	14.3	14.7	16.7	16.0	15.9	12.3	9.0	10.7	13.1	12.9
20-24	56.7	53.9	55.0	52.1	50.8	48.8	48.5	46.9	45.3	47.4
25-34	87.9	88.8	89.2	87.7	88.5	89.1	87.6	86.5	83.6	86.3
35-44	92.5	92.1	91.9	91.4	92.8	92.2	92.8	92.0	93.3	91.8
45-54	81.1	81.5	84.7	85.1	83.7	84.3	87.1	87.7	87.8	87.5
55-59	30.2	31.0	30.3	36.3	35.5	34.9	39.8	40.8	46.7	52.3
60-64	10.3	12.6	11.7	11.7	13.2	10.7	10.5	10.5	13.5	11.7
15-24	36.4	35.4	37.4	35.8	34.8	32.3	30.0	30.2	30.4	31.7
25-54	87.0	87.3	88.5	87.9	88.1	88.4	89.1	88.7	88.3	88.6
55-64	21.4	23.1	22.2	25.6	25.5	23.7	26.5	27.0	31.1	32.9
65 and over	5.4	6.7	4.9	5.6	5.2	4.8	3.7	3.5	5.1	3.1
15-64	66.7	66.6	67.5	67.9	67.4	66.5	66.9	66.6	67.2	67.9
All persons										
15-24	40.6	41.8	42.9	40.9	39.9	37.4	34.4	33.8	33.6	35.3
25-54	89.0	89.3	90.1	89.6	90.0	90.1	90.8	90.7	90.3	90.8
55-64	33.4	34.6	34.2	36.9	36.5	33.3	35.1	36.0	38.4	39.7
65 and over	7.7	8.8	6.4	7.6	7.3	6.3	5.0	5.0	6.7	4.2
15-64	70.9	71.3	71.8	71.8	71.5	70.3	70.4	70.5	70.9	71.8
Unemployment rates										
Males										
15-19	15.3	8.4	8.4	17.5	16.7	14.4	20.8	13.8	15.6	15.9
20-24	10.7	9.6	10.2	13.0	14.9	15.1	20.2	21.3	20.3	18.1
25-34	5.8	4.3	4.1	7.5	9.7	9.7	10.3	11.5	12.0	10.4
35-44	3.2	2.3	2.8	4.1	6.0	6.5	6.0	6.8	5.8	5.4
45-54	4.1	3.7	2.8	4.3	5.6	6.7	6.5	8.6	7.2	6.2
55-59	3.2	3.5	4.1	4.4	4.4	8.5	7.5	7.8	9.5	7.6
60-64	0.8	0.8	1.5	1.5	3.3	3.7	3.3	6.2	6.0	9.9
15-24	11.6	9.4	9.9	13.8	15.2	15.0	20.3	20.1	19.4	17.7
25-54	4.3	3.4	3.3	5.3	7.1	7.6	7.6	8.9	8.3	7.3
55-64	2.7	3.0	3.6	3.8	4.2	7.5	6.6	7.4	8.6	8.1
65 and over	0.0	0.0	0.0	0.0	0.0	0.0	0.0	0.0	0.0	0.0
15-64	5.0	4.1	4.1	6.1	7.6	8.3	8.5	9.6	9.1	8.2
Total	4.9	4.0	4.0	5.9	7.4	8.2	8.4	9.4	8.9	8.0
Females										
15-19	15.0	12.1	12.0	11.4	13.5	15.8	17.5	16.4	18.6	13.8
20-24	17.3	11.0	11.1	13.9	13.9	17.0	21.6	25.1	21.9	14.8
25-34	9.7	8.4	6.1	8.3	10.1	11.4	13.4	16.3	17.1	14.9
35-44	5.3	3.9	3.2	4.2	4.9	5.8	7.0	7.2	8.0	9.0
45-54	4.9	4.4	3.4	3.8	5.4	6.6	6.9	8.5	7.2	7.4
55-59	2.8	4.7	5.1	3.6	4.2	4.6	5.9	6.9	7.8	7.4
60-64	0.0	1.0	4.0	1.5	1.5	1.7	3.1	3.6	1.9	6.1
15-24	16.8	11.2	11.3	13.4	13.8	16.8	21.0	23.7	21.3	14.6
25-54	6.6	5.6	4.2	5.4	6.8	7.9	9.0	10.6	10.5	10.2
55-64	2.2	3.8	4.8	3.2	3.6	4.0	5.4	6.3	6.6	7.2
65 and over	0.0	0.0	0.0	0.0	0.0	0.0	0.0	0.0	0.0	0.0
15-64	7.4	6.0	4.9	5.9	7.2	8.3	9.5	11.1	10.8	10.2
Total	7.2	5.8	4.8	5.8	7.0	8.2	9.4	10.9	10.5	10.0
All persons										
15-24	13.9	10.1	10.4	13.6	14.7	15.7	20.6	21.6	20.2	16.3
25-54	5.4	4.5	3.7	5.3	7.0	7.8	8.3	9.7	9.3	8.7
55-64	2.5	3.3	4.0	3.6	4.0	6.3	6.2	7.0	7.8	7.8
65 and over	0.0	0.0	0.0	0.0	0.0	0.0	0.0	0.0	0.0	0.0
15-64	6.1	5.0	4.5	6.0	7.4	8.3	9.0	10.3	9.9	9.1

Note: Detailed metadata at:http://metalinks.oecd.org/lfs/20170518/6f97b
Disclaimer: http://oe.cd/disclaimer

SLOVENIA

Table 3. Civilian employment and employees: breakdown by activity - ISIC Rev. 4

Annual average estimates

		2006	2007	2008	2009	2010	2011	2012	2013	2014	2015
	CIVILIAN EMPLOYMENT										
	By activity, thousands										
A-U	**All activities**	..	..	**996.1**	**980.7**	**966.0**	**936.1**	**923.8**	**901.4**	**911.4**	**906.3**
A	Agriculture, hunting and forestry	..	..	85.2	89.0	84.8	80.1	77.1	76.6	87.7	64.1
B-F	**Industry**	..	..	**348.2**	**323.4**	**313.5**	**294.9**	**284.7**	**279.7**	**281.9**	**290.1**
B	Mining and quarrying	..	..	3.8	4.0	4.1	4.8	4.3	4.2	2.9	3.1
C	Manufacturing	..	..	260.2	237.6	234.0	216.6	206.5	203.2	206.4	214.7
D	Electricity, gas, steam, air cond. supply	..	..	9.8	8.2	7.4	9.1	9.0	9.0	11.2	10.2
E	Water supply, sewerage, waste mgt, remediation	..	..	7.9	10.1	9.9	10.2	10.2	9.5	9.4	9.2
F	Construction	..	..	66.5	63.5	58.1	54.2	54.7	53.8	52.0	52.9
G-U	**Services**	..	..	**562.7**	**568.3**	**567.7**	**561.1**	**562.0**	**545.1**	**541.7**	**552.0**
G	Wholesale, retail trade, vehicle, motorcycle repair	..	..	119.3	120.8	116.5	112.8	111.5	115.4	109.9	111.4
H	Transportation and storage	..	..	57.0	57.2	51.7	52.7	51.8	48.9	42.1	45.3
I	Accommodation and food service activities	..	..	43.3	41.1	46.5	42.7	39.8	37.9	40.4	46.5
J	Information and communication	..	..	28.8	31.0	32.3	29.9	26.9	29.0	30.8	33.5
K	Financial and insurance activities	..	..	24.0	27.2	26.1	29.3	31.3	25.4	23.9	23.2
L	Real estate activities	..	..	2.5	2.7	2.5	3.3	2.7	3.7	3.1	2.2
M	Professional, scientific and technical activities	..	..	39.9	40.6	42.2	41.9	45.0	42.5	44.7	42.1
N	Administrative and support service activities	..	..	22.2	22.6	21.1	20.6	22.1	20.9	23.3	19.9
O	Public administration, defence, social security	..	..	57.2	60.8	59.3	58.6	61.5	54.8	57.1	55.4
P	Education	..	..	74.4	72.7	76.9	78.5	80.1	61.3	76.2	80.6
Q	Human health and social work activities	..	..	55.5	54.0	56.0	54.8	53.4	55.5	57.4	59.7
R	Arts, entertainment and recreation	..	..	18.5	17.5	18.2	17.9	16.7	18.6	17.7	18.2
S	Other service activities	..	..	14.6	14.6	14.3	13.1	14.0	14.4	15.1	14.0
T	Households as employers and own-use activities	..	..	0.0	0.0	0.0	0.0	0.0	0.2	0.0	0.1
U	Activities of extraterritorial organizations, bodies	..	..	0.0	0.0	0.0	0.0	0.0	0.0	0.0	0.0
	EMPLOYEES										
	By activity, thousands										
A-U	**All activities**	..	..	**855.4**	**821.9**	**799.3**	**778.7**	**773.8**	**748.8**	**741.6**	**756.6**
A	Agriculture, hunting and forestry	..	..	12.9	10.4	9.4	9.8	10.0	8.7	8.7	8.7
B-F	**Industry**	..	..	**324.9**	**295.7**	**283.2**	**267.1**	**258.1**	**255.0**	**254.9**	**261.7**
B	Mining and quarrying	..	..	3.8	3.9	4.1	4.8	4.2	4.1	2.9	3.0
C	Manufacturing	..	..	248.0	223.5	216.4	201.7	193.4	190.6	192.2	199.7
D	Electricity, gas, steam, air cond. supply	..	..	9.7	8.0	7.3	9.1	8.9	8.8	10.9	10.1
E	Water supply, sewerage, waste mgt, remediation	..	..	7.9	10.0	9.7	9.9	10.0	9.3	9.2	9.1
F	Construction	..	..	55.5	50.3	45.7	41.6	41.6	42.1	39.8	39.8
G-U	**Services**	..	..	**517.6**	**515.8**	**506.7**	**501.8**	**505.7**	**485.1**	**477.9**	**486.2**
G	Wholesale, retail trade, vehicle, motorcycle repair	..	..	109.6	108.4	102.0	98.1	99.5	101.1	95.4	94.5
H	Transportation and storage	..	..	49.8	51.1	45.3	45.9	45.4	43.0	36.7	40.4
I	Accommodation and food service activities	..	..	38.4	34.3	39.4	37.3	33.1	31.8	34.3	39.3
J	Information and communication	..	..	26.5	26.3	27.9	26.9	23.8	25.0	25.2	28.0
K	Financial and insurance activities	..	..	23.4	26.2	24.9	27.8	29.8	24.2	22.8	22.6
L	Real estate activities	..	..	2.1	2.0	1.8	2.6	2.1	3.0	2.7	1.8
M	Professional, scientific and technical activities	..	..	31.2	31.5	29.0	28.8	32.9	30.5	29.9	27.0
N	Administrative and support service activities	..	..	20.7	20.8	19.5	17.7	19.9	18.7	20.0	17.4
O	Public administration, defence, social security	..	..	57.1	60.4	58.9	58.3	61.0	54.2	56.9	55.2
P	Education	..	..	73.9	71.6	75.1	76.6	78.7	76.6	74.5	78.9
Q	Human health and social work activities	..	..	53.8	51.7	53.4	53.1	51.6	53.6	55.9	58.3
R	Arts, entertainment and recreation	..	..	16.1	15.6	15.3	14.9	14.3	14.3	14.2	14.1
S	Other service activities	..	..	9.9	10.7	10.5	9.1	8.8	8.9	9.4	8.6
T	Households as employers and own-use activities	..	..	0.0	0.0	0.0	0.0	0.0	0.2	0.0	0.1
U	Activities of extraterritorial organizations, bodies	..	..	0.0	0.0	0.0	0.0	0.0	0.0	0.0	0.0

Note: Detailed metadata:http://metalinks.oecd.org/lfs/20170518/87289
Disclaimer: http://oe.cd/disclaimer

SPAIN

Table 1. Labour force

Annual average estimates

	2006	2007	2008	2009	2010	2011	2012	2013	2014	2015
Civilian labour force, thousands										
All persons	21 692	22 336	22 966	23 150	23 258	23 331	23 345	23 102	22 858	22 831
Males	12 530	12 813	13 035	12 933	12 863	12 768	12 651	12 440	12 276	12 239
Females	9 161	9 523	9 932	10 217	10 394	10 563	10 694	10 662	10 582	10 592
Unemployed, thousands										
All persons	1 839	1 845	2 594	4 151	4 639	5 011	5 810	6 050	5 610	5 055
Males	799	826	1 318	2 297	2 535	2 704	3 130	3 204	2 916	2 559
Females	1 040	1 020	1 276	1 854	2 104	2 306	2 680	2 845	2 694	2 496
Civilian employment, thousands										
All persons	19 853	20 491	20 373	19 000	18 619	18 321	17 536	17 052	17 249	17 776
Males	11 731	11 988	11 717	10 636	10 329	10 064	9 521	9 236	9 360	9 681
Females	8 122	8 503	8 656	8 363	8 290	8 257	8 014	7 816	7 888	8 096
Civilian employment (%)										
All persons	100.0	100.0	100.0	100.0	100.0	100.0	100.0	100.0	100.0	100.0
Males	59.1	58.5	57.5	56.0	55.5	54.9	54.3	54.2	54.3	54.5
Females	40.9	41.5	42.5	44.0	44.5	45.1	45.7	45.8	45.7	45.5
Unemployment rate (% of civilian labour force)										
All persons	8.5	8.3	11.3	17.9	19.9	21.5	24.9	26.2	24.5	22.1
Males	6.4	6.4	10.1	17.8	19.7	21.2	24.7	25.8	23.8	20.9
Females	11.4	10.7	12.8	18.1	20.2	21.8	25.1	26.7	25.5	23.6
CIVIL. EMPL. - PROFESSIONAL STATUS, thousands										
All activities	**19 853**	**20 491**	**20 373**	**19 000**	**18 619**	**18 321**	**17 536**	**17 052**	**17 249**	**17 776**
Employees	16 304	16 879	16 764	15 774	15 487	15 293	14 476	13 982	14 190	14 684
Employers and persons working on own account	3 264	3 381	3 387	3 042	2 970	2 882	2 928	2 946	2 948	2 987
Unpaid family workers	267	221	210	173	153	138	123	115	103	100
Employees as % of civilian employment	**82.1**	**82.4**	**82.3**	**83.0**	**83.2**	**83.5**	**82.6**	**82.0**	**82.3**	**82.6**
Part-time employment (%)										
Part-time as % of employment	10.7	10.5	10.9	11.6	12.2	12.7	13.6	14.7	14.7	14.5
Male share of part time employment	21.0	20.0	19.8	21.2	22.1	23.6	24.0	26.6	26.0	26.7
Female share of part time employment	79.0	80.0	80.2	78.8	77.9	76.4	76.0	73.4	74.0	73.3
Male part-time as % of male employment	3.8	3.6	3.8	4.4	4.9	5.4	6.0	7.3	7.1	7.2
Female part-time as % of female employment	20.4	20.1	20.4	20.7	21.2	21.4	22.4	23.4	23.6	23.1
Duration of unemployment (% of total unemployment)										
Less than one month	18.1	18.6	16.0	9.6	7.5	7.4	6.3	5.8	5.9	6.5
More than 1 month and less than 3 months	28.0	28.5	29.7	21.7	17.6	16.2	15.0	13.3	13.4	14.5
More than 3 months and less than 6 months	18.0	18.1	20.6	22.1	17.2	16.2	15.3	13.9	12.8	13.0
More than 6 months and less than 1 year	14.3	14.4	15.7	22.8	21.1	18.6	19.0	17.3	15.0	14.4
More than 1 year	21.6	20.4	18.0	23.8	36.6	41.6	44.4	49.7	52.8	51.6

Note: Detailed metadata: http://metalinks.oecd.org/lfs/20170518/6a330, http://metalinks.oecd.org/lfs/20170518/87289, http://metalinks.oecd.org/lfs/20170518/e201f and http://metalinks.oecd.org/lfs/20170518/4854e.
Disclaimer: http://oe.cd/disclaimer

SPAIN

Table 2. Participation rates and unemployment rates by age and sex

Annual average estimates, percentage

	2006	2007	2008	2009	2010	2011	2012	2013	2014	2015
Participation rates										
Males										
15-19	33.6	34.9	32.9	28.9	24.5	21.4	19.0	18.6	16.2	16.6
20-24	72.5	72.2	72.7	69.8	67.4	64.9	63.1	62.1	60.3	58.9
25-34	92.4	92.6	92.6	92.1	92.2	92.2	92.7	92.2	92.2	91.6
35-44	94.2	94.2	94.0	93.8	94.5	94.6	94.3	94.4	94.6	94.9
45-54	90.4	90.4	90.3	90.2	90.1	90.3	90.5	90.4	90.5	90.9
55-59	76.1	76.3	78.3	78.1	79.4	78.7	79.6	79.5	79.2	80.2
60-64	48.7	47.7	49.8	48.0	46.5	46.6	45.6	44.8	46.6	49.4
15-24	57.1	57.3	56.6	53.0	49.6	46.7	44.5	43.7	41.5	40.6
25-54	92.4	92.5	92.4	92.2	92.4	92.5	92.6	92.4	92.6	92.6
55-64	63.3	62.8	64.7	63.6	63.7	63.5	63.6	63.3	64.3	66.2
65 and over	3.4	3.3	3.1	2.9	2.7	2.6	2.7	2.4	2.3	2.4
15-64	82.5	82.6	82.8	82.0	81.8	81.5	81.2	80.9	80.7	80.9
Females										
15-19	24.8	24.5	25.1	20.3	18.3	17.1	15.8	14.5	13.3	13.0
20-24	63.2	62.6	63.4	63.1	61.8	61.4	59.3	57.3	55.2	54.5
25-34	80.0	80.7	82.6	83.5	84.7	84.9	85.3	86.0	86.1	85.1
35-44	72.3	73.8	75.8	78.7	79.8	81.4	83.3	84.0	84.4	84.6
45-54	60.7	63.5	65.8	68.2	71.1	72.4	74.6	75.5	75.9	76.8
55-59	39.8	41.7	44.2	47.9	48.9	53.1	56.0	57.8	58.7	61.1
60-64	21.6	22.9	23.7	25.8	27.4	29.5	30.6	31.1	33.3	35.6
15-24	48.1	47.5	48.1	45.8	44.1	43.2	41.3	39.6	37.6	36.8
25-54	71.8	73.3	75.3	77.2	78.8	79.7	81.1	81.8	82.0	82.0
55-64	31.2	32.7	34.2	37.1	38.4	41.8	43.9	45.2	46.9	49.4
65 and over	1.1	1.1	1.4	1.4	1.5	1.5	1.6	1.4	1.3	1.4
15-64	61.6	62.8	64.5	66.0	67.1	68.3	69.3	69.7	69.8	70.0
All persons										
15-24	52.7	52.5	52.4	49.5	46.9	44.9	43.0	41.7	39.6	38.8
25-54	82.3	83.1	84.0	84.8	85.7	86.2	86.9	87.2	87.3	87.4
55-64	46.8	47.4	49.1	50.0	50.7	52.4	53.5	54.1	55.4	57.6
65 and over	2.1	2.0	2.1	2.1	2.0	2.0	2.1	1.8	1.7	1.9
15-64	72.1	72.8	73.8	74.1	74.6	74.9	75.3	75.3	75.3	75.5
Unemployment rates										
Males										
15-19	23.8	23.9	35.8	54.8	60.1	64.4	72.0	72.3	65.8	64.7
20-24	12.3	12.4	19.8	34.5	38.7	44.3	50.2	52.7	51.0	45.2
25-34	6.8	6.5	11.0	19.9	22.1	23.8	28.7	29.4	26.4	24.0
35-44	4.9	4.9	8.0	15.3	16.7	17.9	20.7	21.4	19.5	16.4
45-54	4.0	4.7	7.3	12.6	14.6	16.4	20.0	21.5	20.2	17.8
55-59	5.1	5.1	6.6	11.6	15.0	15.9	18.9	21.1	22.0	19.7
60-64	4.7	4.9	6.1	10.8	13.3	14.4	16.5	18.6	17.2	16.2
15-24	15.0	15.2	23.6	39.1	43.1	48.2	54.1	56.2	53.4	48.6
25-54	5.4	5.5	8.9	16.1	17.9	19.4	23.0	23.8	21.7	18.9
55-64	4.9	5.0	6.5	11.3	14.4	15.4	18.1	20.3	20.4	18.5
65 and over	1.6	1.1	1.4	3.0	3.4	1.6	4.0	6.4	4.4	4.1
15-64	6.4	6.5	10.1	17.7	19.7	21.2	24.7	25.7	23.7	20.9
Total	6.3	6.4	10.1	17.6	19.6	21.0	24.6	25.6	23.6	20.8
Females										
15-19	36.7	35.9	44.4	55.9	62.9	63.5	73.2	76.3	72.2	70.7
20-24	17.7	18.1	20.5	31.8	34.9	40.2	47.4	50.7	49.6	43.9
25-34	11.5	10.1	12.6	18.4	21.1	23.1	26.4	28.7	27.2	25.3
35-44	9.8	9.4	11.8	16.2	18.8	20.0	23.0	24.1	23.0	21.0
45-54	8.8	8.6	9.8	14.5	16.3	17.9	21.2	23.0	22.4	21.5
55-59	8.2	8.2	9.4	14.4	15.1	16.2	19.0	20.1	20.8	19.5
60-64	5.5	6.8	8.2	11.1	11.6	11.8	15.8	18.9	16.6	17.2
15-24	21.5	21.7	25.5	36.1	39.6	44.0	51.4	54.6	52.9	48.0
25-54	10.3	9.5	11.6	16.6	18.9	20.5	23.6	25.2	24.1	22.4
55-64	7.3	7.7	9.0	13.3	13.9	14.7	17.9	19.7	19.4	18.7
65 and over	2.0	2.2	4.3	2.5	1.3	2.7	4.1	6.2	6.3	4.1
15-64	11.4	10.7	12.9	18.2	20.3	21.9	25.2	26.8	25.5	23.7
Total	11.3	10.7	12.8	18.1	20.2	21.8	25.0	26.7	25.4	23.5
All persons										
15-24	17.9	18.1	24.5	37.7	41.5	46.2	52.9	55.5	53.2	48.3
25-54	7.5	7.2	10.1	16.3	18.4	19.9	23.3	24.5	22.8	20.6
55-64	5.8	6.0	7.4	12.1	14.2	15.1	18.0	20.0	20.0	18.6
65 and over	1.7	1.4	2.5	2.8	2.5	2.1	4.0	6.3	5.2	4.1
15-64	8.5	8.3	11.3	18.0	20.0	21.5	24.9	26.2	24.6	22.2

Note: Detailed metadata at:http://metalinks.oecd.org/lfs/20170518/6f97b
Disclaimer: http://oe.cd/disclaimer

Table 3. Civilian employment and employees: breakdown by activity - ISIC Rev. 4

Annual average estimates

		2006	2007	2008	2009	2010	2011	2012	2013	2014	2015
	CIVILIAN EMPLOYMENT										
	By activity, thousands										
A-U	**All activities**	**19 852.7**	**20 491.2**	**20 372.5**	**18 999.6**	**18 618.9**	**18 320.6**	**17 535.6**	**17 051.9**	**17 248.6**	**17 776.3**
A	Agriculture, hunting and forestry	893.4	866.2	828.2	788.1	786.1	755.3	743.4	736.6	735.8	736.8
B-F	**Industry**	**5 881.2**	**6 010.4**	**5 696.5**	**4 697.3**	**4 301.8**	**4 008.6**	**3 645.1**	**3 385.0**	**3 373.5**	**3 556.0**
B	Mining and quarrying	66.3	59.5	52.7	44.4	45.6	42.0	37.0	29.9	31.5	33.6
C	Manufacturing	3 017.5	2 996.3	2 986.3	2 549.4	2 405.4	2 349.7	2 223.9	2 118.7	2 141.4	2 225.0
D	Electricity, gas, steam, air cond. supply	79.2	74.0	74.4	80.5	80.0	80.5	84.6	78.7	93.8	92.3
E	Water supply, sewerage, waste mgt, remediation	133.1	133.7	123.2	133.3	119.5	132.5	138.2	128.2	113.3	131.4
F	Construction	2 585.1	2 747.0	2 459.9	1 889.8	1 651.4	1 403.9	1 161.4	1 029.5	993.5	1 073.7
G-U	**Services**	**13 078.2**	**13 614.6**	**13 847.9**	**13 514.2**	**13 531.0**	**13 556.8**	**13 147.1**	**12 930.3**	**13 139.3**	**13 483.5**
G	Wholesale, retail trade, vehicle, motorcycle repair	2 969.4	3 115.0	3 222.2	2 990.5	2 936.6	2 962.5	2 860.5	2 846.6	2 866.8	2 921.4
H	Transportation and storage	946.2	965.8	969.0	923.8	925.9	899.3	852.2	831.7	852.8	870.5
I	Accommodation and food service activities	1 405.2	1 457.6	1 457.8	1 423.2	1 383.2	1 401.0	1 336.9	1 332.6	1 403.8	1 505.2
J	Information and communication	536.0	566.5	575.2	533.3	527.7	533.3	534.7	522.9	515.6	530.3
K	Financial and insurance activities	480.7	508.3	515.1	487.5	476.7	464.6	435.7	454.1	452.7	454.1
L	Real estate activities	104.8	108.6	119.2	91.9	84.3	96.3	97.2	92.1	99.5	104.1
M	Professional, scientific and technical activities	805.1	876.1	905.1	881.7	874.7	853.0	858.4	836.6	851.4	890.6
N	Administrative and support service activities	876.2	940.3	934.3	911.6	910.5	914.7	894.3	882.8	899.3	927.9
O	Public administration, defence, social security	1 153.0	1 170.1	1 202.8	1 280.6	1 333.5	1 352.0	1 253.9	1 190.6	1 213.9	1 235.5
P	Education	1 141.4	1 148.7	1 164.3	1 180.1	1 211.0	1 206.1	1 208.1	1 163.4	1 151.3	1 182.2
Q	Human health and social work activities	1 189.6	1 244.3	1 287.0	1 352.6	1 397.2	1 462.5	1 416.2	1 365.5	1 416.4	1 442.0
R	Arts, entertainment and recreation	300.0	308.4	321.0	312.3	341.2	325.2	316.0	315.7	350.3	365.2
S	Other service activities	409.9	434.6	429.9	424.4	390.1	395.2	424.4	419.6	405.5	424.3
T	Households as employers and own-use activities	754.8	768.6	743.0	718.6	735.4	686.9	653.5	669.8	657.0	627.8
U	Activities of extraterritorial organizations, bodies	5.9	1.7	2.1	2.0	2.9	4.3	5.0	6.6	3.0	2.4
	EMPLOYEES										
	By activity, thousands										
A-U	**All activities**	**16 304.2**	**16 879.3**	**16 764.1**	**15 773.9**	**15 486.7**	**15 293.4**	**14 476.3**	**13 982.0**	**14 190.2**	**14 683.7**
A	Agriculture, hunting and forestry	457.3	464.3	425.6	421.6	438.8	426.5	415.7	408.4	428.8	447.5
B-F	**Industry**	**4 972.0**	**5 094.5**	**4 797.9**	**3 938.8**	**3 604.7**	**3 381.4**	**3 017.1**	**2 801.2**	**2 804.7**	**2 962.9**
B	Mining and quarrying	63.2	55.3	48.3	41.4	43.8	39.7	31.3	26.7	30.4	32.4
C	Manufacturing	2 646.2	2 638.4	2 627.8	2 246.1	2 138.1	2 090.3	1 960.3	1 876.4	1 898.4	1 987.2
D	Electricity, gas, steam, air cond. supply	78.0	72.4	73.1	79.0	77.7	78.9	81.5	76.6	90.2	88.1
E	Water supply, sewerage, waste mgt, remediation	125.0	127.1	118.5	127.4	113.1	125.4	130.9	122.4	106.2	120.8
F	Construction	2 059.6	2 201.2	1 930.2	1 444.8	1 231.9	1 047.1	813.0	699.0	679.5	734.4
G-U	**Services**	**10 875.0**	**11 320.5**	**11 540.6**	**11 413.5**	**11 443.3**	**11 485.5**	**11 043.6**	**10 772.3**	**10 956.8**	**11 273.3**
G	Wholesale, retail trade, vehicle, motorcycle repair	2 153.1	2 281.9	2 358.3	2 217.3	2 181.0	2 191.5	2 072.5	2 041.9	2 086.8	2 148.3
H	Transportation and storage	734.0	758.9	780.3	765.5	751.6	735.9	695.1	677.4	691.6	705.6
I	Accommodation and food service activities	1 076.9	1 106.6	1 101.9	1 080.3	1 048.8	1 079.3	1 030.0	1 022.5	1 068.9	1 165.8
J	Information and communication	461.9	492.2	500.8	471.9	464.8	464.6	467.5	463.9	449.4	468.1
K	Financial and insurance activities	437.9	453.0	462.4	452.1	438.2	425.1	401.3	419.4	420.8	413.3
L	Real estate activities	70.5	69.9	70.5	54.3	50.8	58.6	60.0	54.9	56.0	59.8
M	Professional, scientific and technical activities	640.1	694.7	593.5	584.2	581.2	560.4	559.8	523.9	528.4	567.1
N	Administrative and support service activities	673.4	727.7	861.9	842.4	837.4	850.1	829.8	809.4	825.6	848.2
O	Public administration, defence, social security	1 153.0	1 170.1	1 202.8	1 280.6	1 333.5	1 352.0	1 253.9	1 190.6	1 213.9	1 235.5
P	Education	1 083.2	1 087.4	1 101.8	1 129.6	1 161.8	1 157.7	1 151.2	1 105.4	1 094.0	1 112.8
Q	Human health and social work activities	1 105.7	1 165.0	1 211.9	1 279.4	1 316.3	1 383.5	1 341.3	1 284.5	1 323.3	1 351.7
R	Arts, entertainment and recreation	244.8	247.3	266.7	259.6	281.5	271.1	256.1	253.1	286.4	297.2
S	Other service activities	283.5	296.9	284.7	277.6	260.8	268.5	271.5	255.5	253.6	271.8
T	Households as employers and own-use activities	754.8	768.6	743.0	718.6	735.4	686.9	653.5	669.8	657.0	627.8
U	Activities of extraterritorial organizations, bodies	2.2	0.4	0.2	0.0	0.1	0.4	0.0	0.1	1.1	0.2

Note: Detailed metadata at: http://metalinks.oecd.org/lfs/20170518/44a47.
Disclaimer: http://oe.cd/disclaimer

SWEDEN

Table 1. Labour force

Annual average estimates

	2006	2007	2008	2009	2010	2011	2012	2013	2014	2015
Civilian labour force, thousands										
All persons	4 671	4 838	4 898	4 907	4 948	5 016	5 060	5 116	5 183	5 223
Males	2 444	2 540	2 574	2 581	2 621	2 645	2 660	2 688	2 725	2 736
Females	2 227	2 299	2 324	2 326	2 328	2 371	2 400	2 428	2 459	2 487
Unemployed, thousands										
All persons	330	298	305	408	425	390	403	411	411	386
Males	170	149	152	222	227	207	218	220	222	206
Females	160	148	152	186	198	184	185	191	189	180
Civilian employment, thousands										
All persons	4 341	4 541	4 593	4 499	4 524	4 626	4 657	4 705	4 772	4 837
Males	2 273	2 390	2 422	2 359	2 394	2 438	2 442	2 468	2 503	2 530
Females	2 067	2 150	2 171	2 140	2 130	2 188	2 215	2 237	2 270	2 307
Civilian employment (%)										
All persons	100.0	100.0	100.0	100.0	100.0	100.0	100.0	100.0	100.0	100.0
Males	52.4	52.6	52.7	52.4	52.9	52.7	52.4	52.4	52.4	52.3
Females	47.6	47.3	47.3	47.6	47.1	47.3	47.6	47.6	47.6	47.7
Unemployment rate (% of civilian labour force)										
All persons	7.1	6.2	6.2	8.3	8.6	7.8	8.0	8.0	7.9	7.4
Males	7.0	5.9	5.9	8.6	8.7	7.8	8.2	8.2	8.2	7.5
Females	7.2	6.4	6.5	8.0	8.5	7.7	7.7	7.9	7.7	7.2
CIVIL. EMPL. - PROFESSIONAL STATUS, thousands										
All activities	**4 341**	**4 541**	**4 593**	**4 499**	**4 524**	**4 626**	**4 657**	**4 705**	**4 772**	**4 837**
Employees	3 908	4 060	4 115	4 018	4 028	4 144	4 170	4 206	4 279	4 341
Employers and persons working on own account	425	468	466	471	484	473	476	488	483	484
Unpaid family workers	8	13	12	10	11	10	11	10	10	12
Employees as % of civilian employment	**90.0**	**89.4**	**89.6**	**89.3**	**89.0**	**89.6**	**89.5**	**89.4**	**89.7**	**89.7**
Part-time employment (%)										
Part-time as % of employment	13.4	14.4	14.4	14.6	14.5	14.3	14.3	14.3	14.2	14.1
Male share of part time employment	32.7	35.0	35.4	35.8	37.0	37.3	38.0	38.8	38.9	39.3
Female share of part time employment	67.3	65.0	64.6	64.2	63.0	62.7	62.0	61.2	61.1	60.7
Male part-time as % of male employment	8.4	9.5	9.6	10.0	10.1	10.1	10.3	10.6	10.5	10.6
Female part-time as % of female employment	19.0	19.7	19.6	19.8	19.4	19.0	18.6	18.4	18.3	18.0
Duration of unemployment (% of total unemployment)										
Less than one month	..	30.9	34.5	25.6	24.2	25.0	25.5	25.4	27.3	27.6
More than 1 month and less than 3 months	..	25.0	24.1	25.3	23.2	24.6	24.5	24.3	24.0	23.9
More than 3 months and less than 6 months	..	17.3	16.2	19.7	17.7	16.8	17.0	17.3	16.7	16.0
More than 6 months and less than 1 year	..	14.1	13.1	16.6	17.6	15.4	15.5	16.0	15.1	14.9
More than 1 year	..	12.8	12.1	12.8	17.3	18.2	17.5	17.0	16.8	17.6

Note: Detailed metadata: http://metalinks.oecd.org/lfs/20170518/8a1fb, http://metalinks.oecd.org/lfs/20170518/87289, http://metalinks.oecd.org/lfs/20170518/1fdf3 and http://metalinks.oecd.org/lfs/20170518/85b64.

Disclaimer: http://oe.cd/disclaimer

Table 2. Participation rates and unemployment rates by age and sex

Annual average estimates, percentage

	2006	2007	2008	2009	2010	2011	2012	2013	2014	2015
Participation rates										
Males										
15-19	36.9	30.2	30.0	28.1	28.8	29.1	26.3	28.9	30.3	28.8
20-24	74.5	76.2	77.6	75.6	74.9	75.5	73.7	74.3	74.2	73.3
25-34	91.7	92.3	92.5	92.1	91.2	91.4	91.4	91.5	91.6	91.6
35-44	94.7	95.1	95.1	94.5	95.1	95.2	95.7	96.0	95.4	95.0
45-54	90.9	91.0	91.5	91.6	92.1	92.7	93.2	93.2	93.4	93.4
55-59	85.5	85.1	86.7	87.6	88.1	88.3	89.2	89.5	89.1	89.5
60-64	66.4	67.8	67.4	68.9	71.3	72.2	72.9	74.1	74.0	74.1
15-24	56.6	51.5	52.4	50.9	51.6	53.0	51.6	53.7	54.7	53.6
25-54	92.5	92.9	93.1	92.8	92.9	93.2	93.5	93.6	93.5	93.3
55-64	76.2	76.4	76.7	77.9	79.4	80.1	81.0	81.8	81.7	82.0
65 and over	14.1	15.2	16.6	16.4	18.7	18.0	19.3	18.8	21.9	21.2
15-64	82.8	81.4	81.6	81.3	81.8	82.4	82.6	83.3	83.6	83.5
Females										
15-19	43.4	36.9	38.2	34.7	34.0	34.5	35.4	36.8	37.6	38.0
20-24	68.9	70.7	69.5	68.1	68.3	69.7	69.0	69.9	70.2	70.5
25-34	84.2	85.0	85.3	84.1	83.4	84.3	83.8	84.0	84.8	84.9
35-44	87.7	88.8	89.6	89.4	88.9	89.2	89.8	90.9	90.4	90.9
45-54	86.7	87.2	87.5	87.4	87.2	88.1	88.8	89.1	88.7	89.3
55-59	80.4	80.2	80.6	81.6	82.1	83.4	83.3	82.4	83.6	84.4
60-64	58.6	59.3	58.6	59.4	59.6	61.9	63.3	64.7	66.6	66.9
15-24	56.8	52.6	53.0	50.8	51.1	52.7	53.4	55.0	55.9	56.3
25-54	86.2	87.1	87.5	87.1	86.6	87.3	87.6	88.1	88.0	88.3
55-64	69.8	69.6	69.3	70.0	70.4	72.3	73.1	73.5	75.2	75.7
65 and over	6.8	7.6	8.3	9.2	8.6	9.5	11.4	11.1	12.3	12.6
15-64	77.7	76.8	77.0	76.4	76.2	77.4	77.9	78.8	79.3	79.9
All persons										
15-24	56.7	52.1	52.7	50.8	51.4	52.8	52.5	54.3	55.3	54.9
25-54	89.4	90.0	90.4	90.0	89.8	90.3	90.6	90.9	90.8	90.9
55-64	73.0	73.0	73.0	74.0	74.9	76.2	77.1	77.7	78.4	78.9
65 and over	10.3	11.3	12.3	12.7	13.5	13.7	15.3	14.9	17.0	16.8
15-64	80.3	79.1	79.3	78.9	79.0	79.9	80.3	81.1	81.5	81.7
Unemployment rates										
Males										
15-19	29.3	30.5	32.5	37.9	37.8	35.1	39.1	39.3	38.5	34.3
20-24	16.7	13.2	13.9	21.4	21.3	19.0	20.6	20.1	19.7	17.1
25-34	6.8	5.2	5.1	8.5	7.9	7.3	8.2	7.8	7.9	7.6
35-44	4.4	3.7	3.3	5.2	5.4	4.7	4.9	5.4	5.2	5.0
45-54	4.3	3.5	3.7	5.7	5.6	5.2	5.4	5.0	5.0	4.8
55-59	4.5	3.8	3.7	5.8	6.6	6.0	5.5	5.7	5.8	5.5
60-64	5.3	5.0	4.5	6.0	6.7	5.8	5.9	6.1	6.6	6.7
15-24	20.6	18.6	19.6	26.1	25.9	23.3	25.0	24.8	24.3	21.2
25-54	5.1	4.1	4.0	6.4	6.3	5.6	6.1	6.0	6.0	5.8
55-64	4.9	4.3	4.1	5.8	6.6	5.9	5.7	5.8	6.2	6.0
65 and over	1.5	1.2	1.8	1.6	1.5	1.6	1.7	1.5	2.2	2.1
15-64	6.9	6.0	6.0	8.8	8.9	8.0	8.4	8.4	8.4	7.8
Total	6.8	5.9	5.9	8.6	8.7	7.8	8.2	8.2	8.2	7.5
Females										
15-19	30.9	29.4	31.8	33.8	34.2	33.8	34.5	34.5	33.9	31.5
20-24	16.2	14.0	14.0	18.2	18.2	16.9	16.8	17.0	16.3	14.3
25-34	7.4	6.6	6.3	7.7	8.4	7.5	7.7	8.3	7.4	7.3
35-44	5.3	4.6	4.2	5.5	6.3	5.6	5.1	5.3	5.7	5.6
45-54	3.8	3.2	3.6	4.8	5.4	4.7	4.7	4.9	4.7	4.5
55-59	3.7	3.1	3.3	4.3	4.7	4.3	4.3	4.1	4.5	4.4
60-64	4.0	4.1	3.6	4.9	5.0	4.7	5.0	4.3	4.7	4.9
15-24	21.5	19.8	20.8	23.7	23.6	22.2	22.3	22.3	21.5	19.4
25-54	5.5	4.7	4.7	6.0	6.6	5.8	5.7	6.1	5.9	5.8
55-64	3.8	3.5	3.4	4.6	4.8	4.5	4.6	4.2	4.6	4.6
65 and over	3.3	2.9	2.5	3.2	3.0	2.6	4.0	2.7	3.9	2.7
15-64	7.2	6.5	6.6	8.1	8.6	7.8	7.8	8.0	7.8	7.4
Total	7.1	6.5	6.6	8.0	8.5	7.7	7.7	7.9	7.7	7.2
All persons										
15-24	21.1	19.2	20.2	24.9	24.8	22.8	23.7	23.6	22.9	20.3
25-54	5.3	4.4	4.3	6.2	6.4	5.7	5.9	6.1	6.0	5.8
55-64	4.4	3.9	3.8	5.2	5.8	5.2	5.2	5.1	5.4	5.3
65 and over	2.1	1.8	2.0	2.2	2.0	2.0	2.5	1.9	2.8	2.3
15-64	7.1	6.2	6.3	8.5	8.7	7.9	8.1	8.2	8.1	7.6

Note: Detailed metadata at:http://metalinks.oecd.org/lfs/20170518/6f97b

Disclaimer: http://oe.cd/disclaimer

Table 3. Civilian employment and employees: breakdown by activity - ISIC Rev. 4

Annual average estimates

		2006	2007	2008	2009	2010	2011	2012	2013	2014	2015
	CIVILIAN EMPLOYMENT										
	By activity, thousands										
A-U	**All activities**	..	..	**4 593.0**	**4 499.0**	**4 523.7**	**4 626.0**	**4 657.3**	**4 705.0**	**4 772.3**	**4 837.2**
A	Agriculture, hunting and forestry	..	..	97.0	98.0	95.0	92.3	96.2	95.4	94.5	98.8
B-F	**Industry**	..	..	**976.0**	**904.0**	**898.6**	**918.4**	**911.0**	**897.9**	**884.6**	**881.9**
B	Mining and quarrying	..	..	9.0	9.0	8.5	9.1	9.8	11.3	10.0	9.4
C	Manufacturing	..	..	621.0	560.0	545.2	556.5	538.2	525.4	509.9	504.3
D	Electricity, gas, steam, air cond. supply	..	..	22.0	23.0	23.3	22.5	24.2	24.9	25.9	30.5
E	Water supply, sewerage, waste mgt, remediation	..	..	18.0	18.0	19.2	20.2	20.9	19.1	21.4	23.4
F	Construction	..	..	306.0	294.0	302.4	310.1	317.9	317.2	317.4	314.3
G-U	**Services**	..	..	**3 520.0**	**3 497.0**	**3 530.1**	**3 615.3**	**3 650.1**	**3 711.7**	**3 793.2**	**3 856.5**
G	Wholesale, retail trade, vehicle, motorcycle repair	..	..	559.0	551.0	554.2	564.3	554.5	550.4	557.2	564.3
H	Transportation and storage	..	..	237.0	239.0	243.8	237.9	238.3	246.4	245.6	246.1
I	Accommodation and food service activities	..	..	148.0	144.0	153.7	144.6	145.8	154.1	158.8	167.4
J	Information and communication	..	..	182.0	180.0	175.1	191.5	200.5	196.7	197.4	202.8
K	Financial and insurance activities	..	..	94.0	98.0	95.9	96.2	95.6	96.8	98.0	97.6
L	Real estate activities	..	..	65.0	67.0	64.4	64.6	67.5	70.6	76.1	71.6
M	Professional, scientific and technical activities	..	..	335.0	339.0	349.1	363.5	371.5	382.3	402.4	413.4
N	Administrative and support service activities	..	..	208.0	198.0	197.7	213.1	217.1	216.6	219.0	228.9
O	Public administration, defence, social security	..	..	261.0	267.0	270.9	276.6	282.7	294.8	306.9	313.1
P	Education	..	..	489.0	480.0	488.5	502.6	513.5	519.8	536.3	556.0
Q	Human health and social work activities	..	..	714.0	701.0	701.5	721.1	717.7	718.2	736.6	739.8
R	Arts, entertainment and recreation	..	..	106.0	108.0	111.8	108.9	108.7	116.2	120.8	118.7
S	Other service activities	..	..	111.0	114.0	115.4	115.3	120.5	130.0	124.3	123.9
T	Households as employers and own-use activities	..	..	1.0	0.0	0.7	0.8	0.8	1.2	0.7	0.6
U	Activities of extraterritorial organizations, bodies	..	..	1.0	1.0	1.4	1.6	1.9	2.5	1.6	0.9
	EMPLOYEES										
	By activity, thousands										
A-U	**All activities**	..	..	**4 115.0**	**4 018.0**	**4 028.2**	**4 143.9**	**4 170.3**	**4 206.0**	**4 279.1**	**4 341.1**
A	Agriculture, hunting and forestry	..	..	34.0	37.0	35.4	36.7	37.3	40.2	38.4	37.3
B-F	**Industry**	..	..	**880.0**	**808.0**	**796.9**	**819.2**	**811.1**	**799.2**	**786.9**	**790.0**
B	Mining and quarrying	..	..	9.0	9.0	8.3	8.9	9.5	10.9	9.5	9.1
C	Manufacturing	..	..	584.0	525.0	509.6	523.8	505.6	492.7	478.6	476.7
D	Electricity, gas, steam, air cond. supply	..	..	22.0	23.0	23.0	22.3	24.0	24.6	25.6	30.3
E	Water supply, sewerage, waste mgt, remediation	..	..	18.0	18.0	18.4	19.5	20.4	18.8	20.7	22.4
F	Construction	..	..	247.0	233.0	237.6	244.7	251.6	252.2	252.5	251.5
G-U	**Services**	..	..	**3 201.0**	**3 173.0**	**3 195.9**	**3 288.0**	**3 321.9**	**3 366.6**	**3 453.8**	**3 513.8**
G	Wholesale, retail trade, vehicle, motorcycle repair	..	..	484.0	476.0	478.5	490.9	480.7	478.3	489.0	497.1
H	Transportation and storage	..	..	216.0	218.0	222.0	219.3	220.7	226.9	228.0	228.6
I	Accommodation and food service activities	..	..	124.0	121.0	126.0	121.5	125.8	132.0	136.1	143.2
J	Information and communication	..	..	160.0	157.0	154.7	167.3	175.8	170.8	170.9	174.6
K	Financial and insurance activities	..	..	91.0	95.0	91.8	92.5	92.0	92.3	93.9	93.7
L	Real estate activities	..	..	55.0	57.0	55.3	55.8	57.5	58.9	65.1	61.3
M	Professional, scientific and technical activities	..	..	262.0	263.0	269.8	282.8	291.1	301.5	316.8	321.4
N	Administrative and support service activities	..	..	192.0	181.0	181.3	199.0	201.2	196.2	200.1	211.6
O	Public administration, defence, social security	..	..	260.0	266.0	270.4	276.1	282.4	294.6	306.8	312.9
P	Education	..	..	480.0	473.0	479.1	492.6	505.7	510.2	526.0	545.2
Q	Human health and social work activities	..	..	698.0	684.0	683.2	703.8	698.8	700.7	719.3	723.2
R	Arts, entertainment and recreation	..	..	85.0	87.0	89.4	86.8	85.4	91.3	96.3	94.9
S	Other service activities	..	..	85.0	88.0	86.8	85.6	90.0	96.6	93.0	94.2
T	Households as employers and own-use activities	..	..	1.0	0.0	0.7	0.7	0.8	1.1	0.6	0.5
U	Activities of extraterritorial organizations, bodies	..	..	1.0	1.0	1.4	1.6	1.9	2.5	1.6	0.9

Note: Detailed metadata:http://metalinks.oecd.org/lfs/20170518/87289
Disclaimer: http://oe.cd/disclaimer

SWITZERLAND

Table 1. Labour force

Annual average estimates

	2006	2007	2008	2009	2010	2011	2012	2013	2014	2015
Civilian labour force, thousands										
All persons	4 469	4 567	4 666	4 733	4 758	4 845	4 925	5 004	5 103	5 182
Males	2 461	2 516	2 553	2 578	2 608	2 665	2 706	2 733	2 775	2 808
Females	2 008	2 051	2 113	2 155	2 151	2 181	2 219	2 271	2 327	2 373
Unemployed, thousands										
All persons	170	157	150	193	204	184	193	205	215	219
Males	79	69	70	96	101	91	98	108	112	115
Females	91	88	80	98	103	93	94	97	104	104
Civilian employment, thousands										
All persons	4 299	4 410	4 516	4 540	4 555	4 662	4 732	4 800	4 887	4 963
Males	2 382	2 446	2 483	2 483	2 507	2 574	2 607	2 625	2 663	2 693
Females	1 917	1 963	2 033	2 057	2 048	2 088	2 125	2 174	2 224	2 270
Civilian employment (%)										
All persons	100.0	100.0	100.0	100.0	100.0	100.0	100.0	100.0	100.0	100.0
Males	55.4	55.5	55.0	54.7	55.0	55.2	55.1	54.7	54.5	54.3
Females	44.6	44.5	45.0	45.3	45.0	44.8	44.9	45.3	45.5	45.7
Unemployment rate (% of civilian labour force)										
All persons	3.8	3.4	3.2	4.1	4.3	3.8	3.9	4.1	4.2	4.2
Males	3.2	2.8	2.7	3.7	3.9	3.4	3.6	3.9	4.0	4.1
Females	4.5	4.3	3.8	4.5	4.8	4.2	4.3	4.3	4.5	4.4
CIVIL. EMPL. - PROFESSIONAL STATUS, thousands										
All activities	**4 277**	**4 389**	**4 500**	**4 543**	**4 555**	**4 662**	**4 732**	**4 800**	**4 887**	**4 963**
Employees	3 800	3 881	4 002	4 062	4 074	4 172	4 243	4 302	4 398	4 517
Employers and persons working on own account	389	411	416	388	397	399	400	404	399	359
Unpaid family workers	89	97	83	93	84	91	90	94	90	87
Employees as % of civilian employment	**88.8**	**88.4**	**88.9**	**89.4**	**89.5**	**89.5**	**89.7**	**89.6**	**90.0**	**91.0**
Part-time employment (%)										
Part-time as % of employment	25.5	25.4	25.9	26.5	26.1	25.9	26.0	26.4	26.9	26.8
Male share of part time employment	18.8	18.7	18.8	18.8	19.6	19.8	20.0	20.0	21.5	21.7
Female share of part time employment	81.2	81.3	81.2	81.2	80.4	80.2	80.0	80.0	78.5	78.3
Male part-time as % of male employment	8.8	8.7	9.0	9.2	9.4	9.4	9.6	9.8	10.8	10.9
Female part-time as % of female employment	45.7	45.6	45.9	46.7	46.1	45.5	45.6	45.7	45.6	45.0
Duration of unemployment (% of total unemployment)										
Less than one month	8.9	7.9	11.6	10.5	8.6	10.8	11.6	8.5	10.0	8.7
More than 1 month and less than 3 months	15.1	15.3	16.6	19.6	18.0	17.0	19.1	20.1	17.1	18.7
More than 3 months and less than 6 months	17.4	20.2	22.5	21.9	17.5	15.5	18.2	17.9	15.5	16.8
More than 6 months and less than 1 year	19.5	15.8	15.0	17.9	22.7	17.9	15.9	20.3	19.6	17.1
More than 1 year	39.1	40.8	34.3	30.1	33.1	38.8	35.3	33.2	37.7	38.6

Note: Detailed metadata: http://metalinks.oecd.org/lfs/20170518/011d0, http://metalinks.oecd.org/lfs/20170518/87289, http://metalinks.oecd.org/lfs/20170518/f3325 and http://metalinks.oecd.org/lfs/20170518/1700d.

Disclaimer: http://oe.cd/disclaimer

SWITZERLAND

Table 2. Participation rates and unemployment rates by age and sex

Annual average estimates, percentage

	2006	2007	2008	2009	2010	2011	2012	2013	2014	2015
Participation rates										
Males										
15-19	56.9	55.9	56.9	54.9	56.8	58.6	58.1	58.6	58.8	55.7
20-24	83.2	83.7	79.3	77.2	80.9	79.1	78.8	77.6	76.6	75.2
25-34	95.3	95.4	95.5	95.3	94.8	95.3	95.2	94.3	94.6	94.8
35-44	96.8	97.3	97.5	97.3	97.2	97.2	97.2	97.1	97.0	97.1
45-54	94.1	94.6	94.5	95.2	95.0	95.2	95.4	95.2	95.7	96.1
55-59	89.5	90.0	90.0	90.4	90.7	91.0	91.5	91.2	90.6	91.4
60-64	62.4	66.0	66.8	68.0	69.8	71.7	71.0	72.0	70.6	71.9
15-24	70.2	70.2	68.1	66.1	69.1	69.3	69.3	68.8	68.2	65.9
25-54	95.5	95.8	95.9	96.0	95.7	95.9	95.9	95.6	95.8	96.0
55-64	77.1	78.4	78.9	79.5	80.5	81.7	82.0	82.4	81.4	82.5
65 and over	12.1	13.2	13.5	14.5	13.5	14.9	15.2	15.1	16.3	16.5
15-64	87.8	88.2	88.0	87.8	88.3	88.7	88.8	88.6	88.5	88.5
Females										
15-19	53.3	51.5	52.0	56.2	54.4	54.6	51.2	53.3	53.0	54.4
20-24	80.8	78.3	80.5	80.4	78.1	79.0	78.9	78.5	78.6	78.7
25-34	82.3	82.2	84.1	83.9	83.6	83.8	84.2	84.6	86.2	86.9
35-44	79.8	80.8	82.4	83.0	81.7	81.7	83.0	83.5	84.1	84.5
45-54	81.9	83.0	84.5	84.8	85.2	84.7	85.1	85.3	86.6	86.3
55-59	71.9	74.5	76.4	74.2	74.2	74.3	76.7	78.3	79.1	81.5
60-64	44.0	44.6	46.3	47.1	46.3	49.0	49.6	51.6	52.2	54.5
15-24	67.0	64.5	66.1	68.5	66.5	67.0	65.4	66.5	66.6	67.6
25-54	81.2	81.9	83.6	83.9	83.5	83.4	84.1	84.5	85.7	85.9
55-64	58.6	60.3	61.6	61.0	60.6	62.1	63.5	65.4	66.5	69.1
65 and over	5.5	5.7	6.6	6.7	6.2	6.2	6.7	7.5	8.2	8.2
15-64	74.7	75.0	76.6	77.1	76.4	76.7	77.2	78.0	79.0	79.8
All persons										
15-24	68.6	67.4	67.1	67.3	67.8	68.2	67.4	67.7	67.4	66.7
25-54	88.3	88.9	89.8	90.0	89.6	89.7	90.0	90.1	90.8	91.0
55-64	67.7	69.3	70.2	70.2	70.5	71.9	72.7	73.9	74.0	75.8
65 and over	8.2	8.8	9.5	10.0	9.3	10.0	10.4	10.8	11.7	11.8
15-64	81.2	81.6	82.3	82.5	82.4	82.8	83.0	83.3	83.8	84.1
Unemployment rates										
Males										
15-19	7.8	6.8	6.2	7.6	7.0	6.9	7.7	8.8	7.8	8.4
20-24	8.0	6.8	7.0	8.2	7.4	8.1	9.4	8.7	9.2	9.7
25-34	3.7	2.9	2.4	5.1	5.1	4.2	4.8	5.6	5.6	4.4
35-44	2.0	2.0	2.3	2.8	3.7	2.9	2.7	3.3	3.2	3.5
45-54	2.7	2.1	2.0	2.2	2.9	2.7	2.8	3.0	3.4	3.7
55-59	2.0	1.8	2.0	3.3	3.7	2.6	2.9	3.1	3.0	4.7
60-64	4.2	3.7	3.2	2.6	3.4	3.9	3.3	3.0	4.0	3.9
15-24	7.9	6.8	6.7	7.9	7.3	7.6	8.8	8.8	8.6	9.2
25-54	2.7	2.3	2.2	3.3	3.8	3.2	3.4	3.9	4.1	3.8
55-64	2.8	2.6	2.5	3.0	3.6	3.2	3.1	3.1	3.4	4.4
65 and over	0.8	0.7	0.7	0.7	0.9	0.5	0.8	0.7	0.7	1.4
15-64	3.5	3.0	2.9	3.9	4.3	3.8	4.1	4.4	4.5	4.6
Total	3.4	2.9	2.8	3.8	4.2	3.7	3.9	4.3	4.4	4.5
Females										
15-19	8.0	7.0	8.1	8.8	7.8	9.2	7.7	8.8	8.6	9.1
20-24	7.1	7.7	6.9	9.0	8.9	6.9	8.3	8.0	8.5	7.4
25-34	5.3	4.9	4.1	5.5	6.3	4.9	5.2	5.2	5.8	5.2
35-44	4.7	4.3	3.8	3.9	4.7	4.1	4.0	4.2	4.4	4.4
45-54	3.4	3.3	3.0	3.1	3.5	3.3	3.5	3.4	3.4	3.6
55-59	2.7	3.7	2.6	2.5	3.5	3.7	3.1	3.1	3.3	3.6
60-64	4.4	3.9	2.7	2.0	3.3	2.8	3.1	2.5	2.7	3.1
15-24	7.5	7.4	7.4	9.0	8.4	7.8	8.1	8.3	8.5	8.0
25-54	4.5	4.1	3.6	4.1	4.7	4.1	4.2	4.2	4.5	4.4
55-64	3.3	3.8	2.7	2.3	3.4	3.4	3.1	2.9	3.1	3.4
65 and over	1.2	1.3	1.7	0.8	0.4	1.2	0.8	0.7	0.6	1.2
15-64	4.8	4.6	4.0	4.6	5.1	4.5	4.6	4.6	4.8	4.7
Total	4.7	4.5	4.0	4.5	5.0	4.4	4.5	4.5	4.7	4.6
All persons										
15-24	7.7	7.1	7.0	8.4	7.8	7.7	8.4	8.5	8.6	8.6
25-54	3.5	3.1	2.9	3.7	4.2	3.6	3.7	4.1	4.2	4.1
55-64	3.0	3.1	2.6	2.7	3.5	3.3	3.1	3.0	3.3	3.9
65 and over	0.9	0.9	1.1	0.7	0.7	0.7	0.8	0.7	0.6	1.3
15-64	4.1	3.7	3.4	4.2	4.6	4.1	4.3	4.5	4.7	4.7

Note: Detailed metadata at:http://metalinks.oecd.org/lfs/20170518/6f97b
Disclaimer: http://oe.cd/disclaimer

Table 3. Civilian employment and employees: breakdown by activity are not available for Switzerland

TURKEY

Table 1. Labour force

Annual average estimates

	2006	2007	2008	2009	2010	2011	2012	2013	2014	2015
Civilian labour force, thousands										
All persons	22 751	23 114	23 805	24 748	25 641	26 725	27 339	28 271 |	28 786	29 678
Males	16 836	17 098	17 475	17 897	18 257	18 867	19 147	19 597 |	20 057	20 453
Females	5 916	6 016	6 330	6 850	7 383	7 859	8 192	8 674 |	8 729	9 225
Unemployed, thousands										
All persons	2 328	2 376	2 611	3 471	3 046	2 615	2 518	2 747 |	2 853	3 057
Males	1 671	1 716	1 877	2 491	2 088	1 730	1 635	1 714 |	1 813	1 891
Females	658	660	734	979	959	885	883	1 033 |	1 040	1 167
Civilian employment, thousands										
All persons	20 423	20 738	21 194	21 277	22 594	24 110	24 821	25 524 |	25 933	26 621
Males	15 165	15 382	15 598	15 406	16 170	17 137	17 512	17 883 |	18 244	18 562
Females	5 258	5 356	5 596	5 871	6 425	6 973	7 309	7 641 |	7 689	8 058
Civilian employment (%)										
All persons	100.0	100.0	100.0	100.0	100.0	100.0	100.0	100.0 |	100.0	100.0
Males	74.3	74.2	73.6	72.4	71.6	71.1	70.6	70.1 |	70.4	69.7
Females	25.7	25.8	26.4	27.6	28.4	28.9	29.4	29.9 |	29.6	30.3
Unemployment rate (% of civilian labour force)										
All persons	10.2	10.3	11.0	14.0	11.9	9.8	9.2	9.7 |	9.9	10.3
Males	9.9	10.0	10.7	13.9	11.4	9.2	8.5	8.7 |	9.0	9.2
Females	11.1	11.0	11.6	14.3	13.0	11.3	10.8	11.9 |	11.9	12.7
CIVIL. EMPL. - PROFESSIONAL STATUS, thousands										
All activities	**20 423**	**20 738**	**21 194**	**21 277**	**22 594**	**24 110**	**24 821**	**25 524 |**	**25 933**	**26 621**
Employees	12 028	12 534	12 937	12 770	13 762	14 876	15 619	16 353 |	17 125	17 827
Employers and persons working on own account	5 717	5 576	5 573	5 637	5 750	5 931	5 933	5 955 |	5 651	5 643
Unpaid family workers	2 678	2 628	2 684	2 870	3 083	3 303	3 268	3 216 |	3 155	3 151
Employees as % of civilian employment	**58.9**	**60.4**	**61.0**	**60.0**	**60.9**	**61.7**	**62.9**	**64.1 |**	**66.0**	**67.0**
Part-time employment (%)										
Part-time as % of employment	7.6	8.1	8.5	11.1	11.5	11.7	11.8	12.3	10.6	9.9
Male share of part time employment	41.5	40.4	41.3	41.6	42.0	40.0	40.0	40.1	42.3	41.8
Female share of part time employment	58.5	59.6	58.7	58.4	58.0	60.0	60.0	59.9	57.7	58.2
Male part-time as % of male employment	4.2	4.4	4.8	6.4	6.7	6.6	6.7	7.0	6.4	5.9
Female part-time as % of female employment	17.3	18.6	19.0	23.5	23.4	24.3	24.2	24.5	20.6	19.0
Duration of unemployment (% of total unemployment)										
Less than one month	2.1	2.7	3.3	2.9	4.1	4.4	3.9	4.3	5.0	5.2
More than 1 month and less than 3 months	23.3	26.1	27.4	25.1	26.3	29.2	29.7	29.4	36.9	36.1
More than 3 months and less than 6 months	23.4	24.9	26.7	27.0	24.0	23.5	25.9	26.2	24.3	23.2
More than 6 months and less than 1 year	15.5	16.0	15.7	19.7	17.1	16.4	15.6	15.7	13.1	14.3
More than 1 year	35.7	30.3	26.9	25.3	28.6	26.5	24.9	24.4	20.6	21.2

Note: Detailed metadata: http://metalinks.oecd.org/lfs/20170518/eb867, http://metalinks.oecd.org/lfs/20170518/87289, http://metalinks.oecd.org/lfs/20170518/616fd and http://metalinks.oecd.org/lfs/20170518/fc5cb.

Disclaimer: http://oe.cd/disclaimer

TURKEY

Table 2. Participation rates and unemployment rates by age and sex

Annual average estimates, percentage

	2006	2007	2008	2009	2010	2011	2012	2013	2014	2015
Participation rates										
Males										
15-19	35.2	36.3	36.6	37.0	35.6	35.8	34.6	35.3	37.8	37.5
20-24	71.5	71.4	71.8	72.3	71.6	72.9	70.7	72.7	73.8	74.5
25-34	93.2	93.3	93.5	93.7	93.9	93.8	92.8	93.5	92.7	93.3
35-44	93.5	93.8	94.2	94.4	94.6	94.6	94.3	94.5	94.4	94.5
45-54	73.6	72.8	73.4	74.5	76.4	78.3	78.6	79.5	80.0	81.4
55-59	49.2	47.1	48.3	49.7	50.6	53.6	54.2	54.2	54.4	56.7
60-64	37.1	37.0	37.7	38.0	40.0	41.3	42.2	40.4	42.5	42.4
15-24	51.2	51.6	51.7	52.2	50.9	52.3	50.8	51.9	54.0	54.2
25-54	88.3	88.1	88.5	88.8	89.5	90.0	89.5	90.0	89.8	90.4
55-64	44.0	42.9	43.8	44.8	46.1	48.4	49.1	48.2	49.3	50.3
65 and over	20.2	18.9	19.4	19.6	19.9	20.9	20.2	20.5	19.3	19.9
15-64	74.4	74.4	74.8	75.2	75.4	76.4	75.8	76.3	76.6	77.0
Females										
15-19	17.3	16.6	17.1	17.3	17.0	17.0	15.8	16.6	17.1	18.4
20-24	31.2	32.1	33.2	34.5	36.0	37.1	36.8	39.5	39.1	42.2
25-34	30.8	31.2	32.5	35.3	36.9	37.9	39.9	41.3	42.6	43.5
35-44	29.4	29.5	30.7	33.1	36.7	38.4	39.9	42.1	41.5	43.6
45-54	21.5	21.3	22.7	23.9	26.2	29.0	30.0	31.3	30.0	31.8
55-59	16.6	15.9	16.5	17.8	19.1	20.2	20.1	20.8	20.2	21.2
60-64	12.8	13.3	13.2	14.3	15.0	15.7	16.0	16.2	15.1	14.9
15-24	24.3	24.4	25.1	25.8	26.3	26.8	25.9	27.5	27.7	29.8
25-54	28.0	28.0	29.3	31.6	34.0	35.7	37.3	38.9	38.8	40.3
55-64	14.9	14.8	15.0	16.3	17.3	18.2	18.3	18.8	17.9	18.3
65 and over	5.7	5.7	5.7	5.9	5.9	6.5	6.4	6.1	5.4	5.8
15-64	25.6	25.7	26.7	28.4	30.2	31.5	32.3	33.7	33.6	35.0
All persons										
15-24	37.4	37.7	38.1	38.7	38.3	39.3	38.2	39.6	40.8	42.0
25-54	58.2	58.2	59.0	60.3	61.8	62.9	63.5	64.5	64.4	65.5
55-64	28.8	28.3	28.9	30.1	31.4	33.0	33.4	33.2	33.4	34.2
65 and over	12.0	11.5	11.7	11.9	12.0	12.8	12.4	12.4	11.4	11.9
15-64	49.8	49.8	50.6	51.7	52.7	53.8	54.0	55.0	55.1	56.1
Unemployment rates										
Males										
15-19	17.1	20.1	20.1	24.2	19.0	16.0	14.9	15.9	16.1	15.6
20-24	19.0	19.3	20.1	26.2	22.4	17.8	17.1	17.6	17.0	17.1
25-34	10.2	10.1	11.0	14.5	11.5	9.3	8.7	9.0	9.2	9.1
35-44	7.3	7.1	8.0	10.7	8.9	6.9	6.2	6.4	6.4	7.1
45-54	7.7	7.7	8.1	10.5	9.3	7.5	7.3	6.9	7.6	7.8
55-59	6.5	6.1	7.5	9.7	8.6	7.3	6.4	6.9	8.2	8.3
60-64	3.8	4.2	4.8	5.5	5.7	4.0	4.2	5.3	6.0	7.3
15-24	18.3	19.6	20.1	25.4	21.0	17.1	16.3	16.9	16.6	16.5
25-54	8.6	8.5	9.3	12.2	10.1	8.0	7.5	7.6	7.8	8.1
55-64	5.5	5.4	6.6	8.2	7.5	6.1	5.6	6.3	7.4	7.9
65 and over	1.0	1.3	1.0	1.9	2.1	1.7	1.5	1.5	2.4	3.1
15-64	10.1	10.2	11.0	14.2	11.7	9.4	8.7	8.9	9.2	9.4
Total	9.9	10.0	10.7	13.9	11.4	9.2	8.5	8.7	9.0	9.2
Females										
15-19	18.1	18.9	18.7	22.2	18.6	15.5	14.9	17.4	16.0	18.3
20-24	22.0	21.7	22.5	26.5	25.2	23.2	22.2	24.0	22.5	24.1
25-34	13.0	12.4	13.2	16.8	15.4	13.6	13.7	14.4	14.3	15.0
35-44	6.9	7.1	7.9	10.8	9.7	8.4	7.8	9.2	9.7	9.8
45-54	3.2	3.4	4.6	6.0	6.0	5.1	4.6	5.5	6.3	7.1
55-59	1.4	1.4	1.7	2.3	1.7	2.2	2.7	3.3	2.7	4.2
60-64	0.0	0.7	0.7	0.6	1.1	1.0	0.5	1.8	1.4	2.2
15-24	20.7	20.8	21.2	25.0	23.0	20.7	19.9	21.9	20.4	22.2
25-54	8.9	8.8	9.6	12.5	11.4	9.9	9.6	10.6	10.9	11.4
55-64	0.9	1.1	1.3	1.6	1.5	1.7	1.8	2.7	2.2	3.4
65 and over	0.0	0.0	0.6	0.0	0.0	0.0	0.0	0.0	1.1	0.5
15-64	11.4	11.3	11.9	14.7	13.3	11.6	11.0	12.2	12.1	12.9
Total	11.1	11.0	11.6	14.3	13.0	11.3	10.8	11.9	11.9	12.7
All persons										
15-24	19.1	20.0	20.5	25.3	21.7	18.4	17.5	18.7	17.9	18.5
25-54	8.7	8.5	9.4	12.3	10.4	8.6	8.1	8.5	8.7	9.1
55-64	4.3	4.3	5.1	6.4	5.8	4.9	4.5	5.3	6.0	6.7
65 and over	0.7	0.9	0.9	1.4	1.5	1.2	1.1	1.0	2.0	2.4
15-64	10.5	10.5	11.2	14.3	12.1	10.0	9.4	9.9	10.1	10.5

Note: Detailed metadata at:http://metalinks.oecd.org/lfs/20170518/6f97b

Disclaimer: http://oe.cd/disclaimer

TURKEY

Table 3. Civilian employment and employees: breakdown by activity - ISIC Rev. 4

Annual average estimates

		2006	2007	2008	2009	2010	2011	2012	2013	2014	2015
	CIVILIAN EMPLOYMENT										
	By activity, thousands										
A-U	**All activities**	..	..	..	**21 277.0**	**22 594.0**	**24 110.0**	**24 821.0**	**25 524.0 |**	**25 932.0**	**26 620.0**
A	Agriculture, hunting and forestry	..	..	..	5 240.0	5 683.0	6 143.0	6 097.0	6 015.0 |	5 470.0	5 483.0
B-F	**Industry**	..	..	..	**5 385.0**	**5 926.0**	**6 380.0**	**6 459.0**	**6 737.0 |**	..	..
B	Mining and quarrying	..	..	..	97.0	114.0	125.0	113.0	105.0 |	134.0	119.0
C	Manufacturing	..	..	..	3 870.0	4 215.0	4 367.0	4 420.0	4 632.0 |	4 936.0	4 956.0
D	Electricity, gas, steam, air cond. supply	..	..	..	112.0	165.0	212.0	217.0	218.0 |	245.0	256.0
E	Water supply, sewerage, waste mgt, remediation	..	..	..	0.0	0.0	0.0	0.0	0.0	..	..
F	Construction	..	..	..	1 306.0	1 432.0	1 676.0	1 709.0	1 782.0 |	1 912.0	1 914.0
G-U	**Services**	..	..	..	**10 652.0**	**10 985.0**	**11 587.0**	**12 265.0**	**12 772.0 |**	..	..
G	Wholesale, retail trade, vehicle, motorcycle repair	..	..	..	3 381.0	3 326.0	3 476.0	3 502.0	3 518.0 |	3 586.0	3 692.0
H	Transportation and storage	..	..	..	986.0	1 008.0	1 044.0	1 095.0	1 152.0 |	1 119.0	1 108.0
I	Accommodation and food service activities	..	..	..	1 050.0	1 084.0	1 141.0	1 207.0	1 308.0 |	1 351.0	1 449.0
J	Information and communication	..	..	..	156.0	204.0	211.0	237.0	255.0 |	227.0	251.0
K	Financial and insurance activities	..	..	..	273.0	274.0	281.0	264.0	288.0 |	301.0	294.0
L	Real estate activities	..	..	..	63.0	61.0	154.0	184.0	186.0 |	205.0	212.0
M	Professional, scientific and technical activities	..	..	..	399.0	428.0	427.0	507.0	553.0 |	684.0	751.0
N	Administrative and support service activities	..	..	..	600.0	766.0	777.0	924.0	1 020.0 |	1 154.0	1 290.0
O	Public administration, defence, social security	..	..	..	1 207.0	1 292.0	1 337.0	1 458.0	1 461.0 |	1 384.0	1 441.0
P	Education	..	..	..	967.0	1 019.0	1 106.0	1 224.0	1 247.0 |	1 320.0	1 410.0
Q	Human health and social work activities	..	..	..	591.0	590.0	693.0	808.0	858.0 |	972.0	1 052.0
R	Arts, entertainment and recreation	..	..	..	130.0	102.0	100.0	108.0	121.0 |	132.0	149.0
S	Other service activities	..	..	..	849.0	831.0	840.0	747.0	804.0 |	800.0	793.0
T	Households as employers and own-use activities	..	..	..	0.0	0.0	0.0	0.0	0.0	..	..
U	Activities of extraterritorial organizations, bodies	..	..	..	0.0	0.0	0.0	0.0	0.0	..	..
	EMPLOYEES										
	By activity, thousands										
A-U	**All activities**	..	..	..	**12 770.0**	**13 762.0**	**14 876.0**	**15 619.0**	**16 353.0 |**	**17 126.0**	**17 827.0**
A	Agriculture, hunting and forestry	..	..	..	454.0	527.0	623.0	605.0	591.0 |	546.0	599.0
B-F	**Industry**	..	..	..	**4 491.0**	**4 951.0**	**5 396.0**	..	..	..	..
B	Mining and quarrying	..	..	..	93.0	111.0	121.0	109.0	102.0 |	130.0	113.0
C	Manufacturing	..	..	..	3 282.0	3 595.0	3 765.0	3 841.0	4 010.0 |	4 246.0	4 280.0
D	Electricity, gas, steam, air cond. supply	..	..	..	93.0	113.0	143.0	157.0	162.0 |	172.0	179.0
E	Water supply, sewerage, waste mgt, remediation	..	..	..	0.0	0.0	0.0	..	..	..	..
F	Construction	..	..	..	1 023.0	1 132.0	1 367.0	1 399.0	1 470.0 |	1 583.0	1 582.0
G-U	**Services**	..	..	..	**7 825.0**	**8 284.0**	**8 857.0**	..	..	..	..
G	Wholesale, retail trade, vehicle, motorcycle repair	..	..	..	1 827.0	1 898.0	2 022.0	2 073.0	2 133.0 |	2 171.0	2 274.0
H	Transportation and storage	..	..	..	651.0	671.0	696.0	735.0	785.0 |	801.0	805.0
I	Accommodation and food service activities	..	..	..	762.0	789.0	847.0	906.0	1 002.0 |	1 017.0	1 127.0
J	Information and communication	..	..	..	145.0	168.0	178.0	205.0	218.0 |	191.0	211.0
K	Financial and insurance activities	..	..	..	253.0	257.0	264.0	250.0	272.0 |	275.0	274.0
L	Real estate activities	..	..	..	25.0	26.0	115.0	141.0	142.0 |	150.0	163.0
M	Professional, scientific and technical activities	..	..	..	254.0	289.0	295.0	357.0	400.0 |	524.0	570.0
N	Administrative and support service activities	..	..	..	571.0	725.0	737.0	806.0	882.0 |	1 026.0	1 143.0
O	Public administration, defence, social security	..	..	..	1 207.0	1 292.0	1 337.0	1 458.0	1 461.0 |	1 383.0	1 441.0
P	Education	..	..	..	957.0	1 007.0	1 092.0	1 205.0	1 229.0 |	1 297.0	1 389.0
Q	Human health and social work activities	..	..	..	567.0	571.0	671.0	787.0	836.0 |	953.0	1 030.0
R	Arts, entertainment and recreation	..	..	..	81.0	74.0	76.0	81.0	92.0 |	94.0	104.0
S	Other service activities	..	..	..	525.0	517.0	527.0	504.0	566.0 |	567.0	543.0
T	Households as employers and own-use activities	..	..	..	0.0	0.0	0.0	..	..	..	..
U	Activities of extraterritorial organizations, bodies	..	..	..	0.0	0.0	0.0	..	..	..	..

Note: Detailed metadata at: http://metalinks.oecd.org/lfs/20170518/141d9.
Disclaimer: http://oe.cd/disclaimer

UNITED KINGDOM

Table 1. Labour force

Annual average estimates

	2006	2007	2008	2009	2010	2011	2012	2013	2014	2015
Civilian labour force, thousands										
All persons	30 540	30 729	31 116	31 268	31 394	31 728	31 981	32 210	32 513	32 630
Males	16 437	16 600	16 781	16 811	16 808	17 011	17 140	17 200	17 309	17 336
Females	14 104	14 130	14 334	14 457	14 587	14 717	14 841	15 009	15 205	15 293
Unemployed, thousands										
All persons	1 648	1 623	1 646	2 413	2 451	2 501	2 542	2 485	2 031	1 815
Males	952	925	963	1 475	1 460	1 446	1 448	1 425	1 127	999
Females	696	698	683	938	990	1 055	1 094	1 059	904	816
Civilian employment, thousands										
All persons	28 892	29 106	29 470	28 855	28 944	29 227	29 439	29 725	30 482	30 815
Males	15 484	15 674	15 818	15 336	15 347	15 565	15 692	15 775	16 182	16 338
Females	13 408	13 432	13 652	13 518	13 597	13 662	13 747	13 950	14 301	14 477
Civilian employment (%)										
All persons	100.0	100.0	100.0	100.0	100.0	100.0	100.0	100.0	100.0	100.0
Males	53.6	53.9	53.7	53.2	53.0	53.3	53.3	53.1	53.1	53.0
Females	46.4	46.1	46.3	46.8	47.0	46.7	46.7	46.9	46.9	47.0
Unemployment rate (% of civilian labour force)										
All persons	5.4	5.3	5.3	7.7	7.8	7.9	7.9	7.7	6.2	5.6
Males	5.8	5.6	5.7	8.8	8.7	8.5	8.5	8.3	6.5	5.8
Females	4.9	4.9	4.8	6.5	6.8	7.2	7.4	7.1	5.9	5.3
CIVIL. EMPL. - PROFESSIONAL STATUS, thousands										
All activities	**28 892**	**29 106**	**29 470**	**28 855**	**28 944**	**29 227**	**29 439**	**29 725**	**30 482**	**30 815**
Employees	25 111	25 230	25 528	24 945	24 934	25 150	25 126	25 428	25 777	26 213
Employers and persons working on own account	3 691	3 779	3 831	3 814	3 921	3 984	4 205	4 187	4 596	4 506
Unpaid family workers	90	98	110	96	89	93	108	110	110	96
Employees as % of civilian employment	**86.9**	**86.7**	**86.6**	**86.4**	**86.1**	**86.1**	**85.4**	**85.5**	**84.6**	**85.1**
Part-time employment (%)										
Part-time as % of employment	23.1	22.9	23.0	23.9	24.6	24.7	25.0	24.6	24.1	24.0
Male share of part time employment	22.4	22.8	23.8	24.0	25.0	25.2	26.1	26.2	25.8	26.3
Female share of part time employment	77.6	77.2	76.2	76.0	75.0	74.8	73.9	73.8	74.2	73.7
Male part-time as % of male employment	9.7	9.7	10.2	10.8	11.6	11.7	12.3	12.2	11.7	11.9
Female part-time as % of female employment	38.5	38.2	37.7	38.7	39.3	39.3	39.4	38.7	38.1	37.7
Duration of unemployment (% of total unemployment)										
Less than one month	17.5	16.5	16.7	12.5	10.4	10.5	10.9	11.0	12.7	14.5
More than 1 month and less than 3 months	24.1	25.2	24.8	22.5	19.7	19.9	18.8	19.4	19.7	22.4
More than 3 months and less than 6 months	18.7	18.3	18.2	20.3	17.4	17.8	16.8	16.4	15.6	16.7
More than 6 months and less than 1 year	17.4	16.2	16.1	20.2	20.0	18.3	18.8	17.1	16.3	15.8
More than 1 year	22.4	23.8	24.2	24.5	32.6	33.5	34.7	36.2	35.7	30.7

Note: Detailed metadata: http://metalinks.oecd.org/lfs/20170518/69e0c, http://metalinks.oecd.org/lfs/20170518/87289, http://metalinks.oecd.org/lfs/20170518/9e826 and http://metalinks.oecd.org/lfs/20170518/a05b9.

Disclaimer: http://oe.cd/disclaimer

Table 2. Participation rates and unemployment rates by age and sex

Annual average estimates, percentage

	2006	2007	2008	2009	2010	2011	2012	2013	2014	2015
Participation rates										
Males										
15-19	55.1	53.3	53.4	51.4	48.1	46.2	47.5	44.2	40.7	42.6
20-24	81.0	81.0	80.0	78.9	77.6	78.9	79.1	77.5	78.5	77.8
25-34	92.9	93.1	93.2	92.5	92.8	92.5	92.9	93.2	93.4	92.1
35-44	92.4	92.6	92.5	92.5	91.9	92.4	93.7	92.7	93.2	93.5
45-54	89.6	89.2	89.3	89.6	89.5	90.0	89.4	90.2	90.6	89.8
55-59	78.3	77.7	80.0	81.7	81.1	79.1	79.8	81.4	81.7	80.4
60-64	56.0	59.2	60.0	59.3	58.0	58.4	58.7	58.6	59.0	60.5
15-24	69.5	68.7	68.2	66.7	64.6	64.8	65.6	63.4	62.7	63.1
25-54	91.7	91.7	91.7	91.5	91.4	91.6	92.0	92.0	92.4	91.7
55-64	68.3	68.8	70.0	70.3	69.3	68.5	69.3	70.4	70.9	71.1
65 and over	9.9	10.0	10.9	10.5	11.3	12.2	12.6	13.5	13.3	13.7
15-64	83.4	83.3	83.5	83.2	82.5	82.5	83.1	82.9	83.1	82.8
Females										
15-19	55.6	53.1	53.1	49.6	50.2	46.9	48.6	45.7	44.6	47.1
20-24	71.0	70.1	69.6	68.9	67.5	68.7	68.4	69.1	70.2	70.7
25-34	76.3	75.6	76.5	76.2	76.7	77.7	76.8	77.5	78.0	78.2
35-44	77.9	78.0	78.1	78.7	78.7	78.6	79.2	79.7	80.0	80.0
45-54	79.3	79.0	80.1	80.4	80.4	80.6	80.9	81.5	81.9	81.8
55-59	64.3	65.4	65.4	67.2	67.9	68.0	69.0	71.1	70.3	71.2
60-64	33.0	33.2	34.5	34.8	34.2	34.8	36.9	38.4	41.4	41.4
15-24	64.3	62.7	62.5	60.6	60.1	59.5	60.2	59.4	59.6	60.9
25-54	77.8	77.5	78.2	78.5	78.6	79.0	79.0	79.6	80.0	80.0
55-64	50.1	49.9	50.0	50.7	50.6	50.9	53.0	55.1	56.4	57.1
65 and over	4.5	4.4	4.7	5.5	6.3	6.4	6.5	6.8	7.7	7.5
15-64	70.4	69.8	70.2	70.2	70.2	70.4	70.9	71.6	72.1	72.5
All persons										
15-24	66.9	65.7	65.4	63.6	62.4	62.2	62.9	61.4	61.2	62.0
25-54	84.7	84.5	84.9	84.9	84.9	85.2	85.4	85.7	86.1	85.8
55-64	59.0	59.2	59.8	60.4	59.8	59.6	61.0	62.6	63.5	64.0
65 and over	6.8	6.9	7.5	7.7	8.6	9.0	9.3	9.8	10.3	10.3
15-64	76.8	76.5	76.8	76.6	76.3	76.4	76.9	77.2	77.6	77.6
Unemployment rates										
Males										
15-19	21.8	23.5	22.8	29.5	32.0	33.5	32.9	34.5	27.2	26.4
20-24	12.2	11.7	12.4	17.8	16.6	17.3	20.1	18.9	15.2	13.7
25-34	5.2	4.4	5.0	8.9	8.5	8.2	7.4	7.5	5.6	5.4
35-44	4.0	3.5	3.8	5.8	6.1	5.2	5.4	4.8	4.3	3.2
45-54	3.6	3.2	3.5	5.6	5.6	5.8	5.2	5.7	4.3	3.7
55-59	3.5	4.6	3.9	6.5	6.1	6.6	5.7	5.5	4.6	3.9
60-64	2.9	3.5	2.7	5.3	6.4	5.7	5.9	5.5	4.4	3.4
15-24	15.6	15.8	16.0	21.8	21.6	22.3	24.0	23.5	18.5	17.3
25-54	4.3	3.7	4.1	6.8	6.7	6.4	6.0	6.0	4.7	4.1
55-64	3.3	4.1	3.4	6.0	6.2	6.2	5.8	5.5	4.6	3.7
65 and over	2.6	3.1	2.3	3.3	2.8	2.0	2.0	3.3	2.8	1.9
15-64	5.8	5.6	5.8	8.9	8.8	8.7	8.6	8.4	6.6	5.9
Total	5.8	5.5	5.7	8.7	8.6	8.4	8.4	8.2	6.5	5.7
Females										
15-19	16.0	17.9	16.3	22.0	24.9	25.1	25.9	24.1	23.4	19.1
20-24	9.3	9.4	9.6	12.5	12.8	14.4	14.1	15.8	9.8	10.6
25-34	4.9	4.7	4.7	6.9	6.7	7.7	8.0	6.4	6.4	4.9
35-44	4.2	3.8	3.6	5.0	5.4	5.9	5.8	5.9	4.6	4.4
45-54	2.6	2.9	2.8	4.0	4.4	4.1	4.3	4.5	3.9	3.6
55-59	2.5	2.3	2.4	3.1	3.7	3.6	4.2	4.3	4.2	3.3
60-64	2.2	1.9	1.4	2.2	1.7	2.0	3.2	3.0	3.2	2.9
15-24	11.8	12.5	12.0	15.9	17.1	17.9	18.1	18.4	14.0	13.3
25-54	3.9	3.8	3.7	5.3	5.4	5.8	6.0	5.6	4.9	4.3
55-64	2.4	2.2	2.1	2.8	3.0	3.0	3.8	3.8	3.8	3.2
65 and over	1.4	1.6	1.2	1.7	1.1	1.4	1.6	0.6	1.4	1.8
15-64	5.0	5.0	4.8	6.6	6.9	7.3	7.5	7.2	6.1	5.4
Total	4.9	4.9	4.8	6.5	6.8	7.2	7.4	7.0	5.9	5.3
All persons										
15-24	13.8	14.2	14.1	19.0	19.5	20.2	21.2	21.1	16.3	15.4
25-54	4.1	3.8	3.9	6.1	6.1	6.1	6.0	5.8	4.8	4.2
55-64	2.9	3.3	2.8	4.6	4.8	4.8	4.9	4.8	4.2	3.5
65 and over	2.2	2.6	1.9	2.7	2.1	1.8	1.8	2.3	2.2	1.9
15-64	5.4	5.3	5.3	7.8	7.9	8.0	8.1	7.9	6.4	5.7

Note: Detailed metadata at:http://metalinks.oecd.org/lfs/20170518/6f97b
Disclaimer: http://oe.cd/disclaimer

Table 3. Civilian employment and employees: breakdown by activity - ISIC Rev. 4

Annual average estimates

		2006	2007	2008	2009	2010	2011	2012	2013	2014	2015
	CIVILIAN EMPLOYMENT										
	By activity, thousands										
A-U	**All activities**	**28 711.0**	**28 859.0**	**29 177.0**	**28 630.0**	**28 742.2**	**29 020.0**	**29 163.4**	**29 423.9**	**30 211.0**	**30 578.3**
A	Agriculture, hunting and forestry	271.0	299.0	325.0	311.4	341.4	342.4	353.1	308.0	395.0	340.3
B-F	**Industry**	**6 532.0**	**6 660.0**	**6 406.0**	**5 643.8**	**5 544.1**	**5 586.3**	**5 623.0**	**5 551.3**	**5 723.6**	**5 758.3**
B	Mining and quarrying	110.0	132.0	128.0	113.2	107.1	99.3	123.4	135.1	121.5	167.4
C	Manufacturing	3 558.0	3 551.0	3 346.0	2 775.5	2 874.4	2 867.7	2 920.0	2 868.6	2 996.8	3 013.7
D	Electricity, gas, steam, air cond. supply	117.0	144.0	140.0	152.4	171.6	191.3	180.5	177.4	186.1	174.7
E	Water supply, sewerage, waste mgt, remediation	213.0	216.0	205.0	217.2	183.9	229.6	228.5	213.9	203.6	208.9
F	Construction	2 534.0	2 617.0	2 587.0	2 385.3	2 207.0	2 198.4	2 170.6	2 156.3	2 215.6	2 193.5
G-U	**Services**	**21 908.0**	**21 900.0**	**22 446.0**	**22 674.8**	**22 856.8**	**23 091.3**	**23 187.3**	**23 564.7**	**24 092.4**	**24 479.7**
G	Wholesale, retail trade, vehicle, motorcycle repair	4 195.0	4 106.0	4 269.0	3 989.0	4 004.2	4 051.0	4 102.3	4 024.4	3 995.0	3 991.4
H	Transportation and storage	1 563.0	1 567.0	1 598.0	1 510.5	1 442.8	1 445.0	1 413.1	1 454.5	1 464.2	1 530.6
I	Accommodation and food service activities	1 271.0	1 298.0	1 282.0	1 359.9	1 460.2	1 458.1	1 496.2	1 505.1	1 631.9	1 658.8
J	Information and communication	1 140.0	1 168.0	1 150.0	1 014.8	979.5	1 073.4	1 098.4	1 161.8	1 172.4	1 235.3
K	Financial and insurance activities	1 254.0	1 266.0	1 281.0	1 234.9	1 174.9	1 173.0	1 228.7	1 142.7	1 154.7	1 214.9
L	Real estate activities	262.0	243.0	253.0	268.1	262.2	307.6	327.6	343.8	358.0	337.4
M	Professional, scientific and technical activities	1 500.0	1 564.0	1 635.0	1 881.6	1 893.0	1 851.0	1 945.0	2 023.1	2 138.6	2 135.7
N	Administrative and support service activities	1 091.0	1 147.0	1 204.0	1 301.1	1 325.5	1 321.3	1 356.9	1 423.0	1 438.7	1 494.0
O	Public administration, defence, social security	1 919.0	1 909.0	1 929.0	1 837.6	1 777.5	1 724.3	1 672.5	1 742.6	1 698.5	1 704.6
P	Education	2 672.0	2 645.0	2 681.0	2 928.2	3 129.4	3 128.7	3 077.2	3 102.4	3 213.3	3 253.1
Q	Human health and social work activities	3 541.0	3 419.0	3 593.0	3 737.5	3 848.0	3 930.7	3 869.5	4 026.8	4 099.5	4 143.3
R	Arts, entertainment and recreation	731.0	743.0	756.0	758.1	760.8	745.0	784.1	753.1	754.0	829.8
S	Other service activities	631.0	695.0	668.0	755.4	706.3	772.1	728.9	771.0	844.0	861.0
T	Households as employers and own-use activities	125.0	120.0	137.0	68.7	63.3	69.8	60.7	67.0	93.7	59.6
U	Activities of extraterritorial organizations, bodies	13.0	10.0	10.0	29.7	29.3	40.3	26.5	23.4	35.9	30.2
	EMPLOYEES										
	By activity, thousands										
A-U	**All activities**	**24 946.0**	**25 003.0**	**25 271.0**	**24 738.5**	**24 747.8**	**24 958.4**	**24 867.5**	**25 153.1**	**25 520.3**	**25 995.8**
A	Agriculture, hunting and forestry	129.0	140.0	150.0	125.9	145.2	144.8	150.7	129.7	167.3	169.1
B-F	**Industry**	**5 414.0**	**5 485.0**	**5 241.0**	**4 570.9**	**4 478.5**	**4 535.8**	**4 526.1**	**4 462.9**	**4 575.0**	**4 598.6**
B	Mining and quarrying	102.0	124.0	120.0	108.6	98.9	93.7	109.9	123.3	112.7	150.6
C	Manufacturing	3 329.0	3 341.0	3 130.0	2 590.7	2 689.3	2 686.0	2 727.8	2 655.1	2 781.4	2 779.8
D	Electricity, gas, steam, air cond. supply	115.0	141.0	133.0	148.4	163.6	181.6	176.0	171.3	177.6	163.5
E	Water supply, sewerage, waste mgt, remediation	206.0	209.0	196.0	207.1	174.6	219.8	212.9	206.4	191.0	195.7
F	Construction	1 662.0	1 670.0	1 662.0	1 516.1	1 352.1	1 354.7	1 299.5	1 306.9	1 312.3	1 309.1
G-U	**Services**	**19 403.0**	**19 378.0**	**19 880.0**	**20 041.8**	**20 124.1**	**20 277.8**	**20 190.7**	**20 560.5**	**20 777.9**	**21 228.1**
G	Wholesale, retail trade, vehicle, motorcycle repair	3 773.0	3 690.0	3 837.0	3 597.8	3 598.9	3 661.9	3 676.7	3 619.5	3 570.2	3 609.7
H	Transportation and storage	1 308.0	1 329.0	1 352.0	1 240.7	1 185.7	1 192.9	1 151.9	1 202.1	1 188.2	1 269.2
I	Accommodation and food service activities	1 152.0	1 162.0	1 147.0	1 225.9	1 308.1	1 320.0	1 342.8	1 364.9	1 487.2	1 496.4
J	Information and communication	965.0	989.0	1 000.0	867.1	836.2	882.1	901.3	951.4	950.8	1 007.1
K	Financial and insurance activities	1 211.0	1 210.0	1 222.0	1 167.5	1 106.0	1 096.9	1 144.1	1 068.0	1 057.6	1 112.0
L	Real estate activities	204.0	198.0	201.0	224.1	220.9	253.3	266.3	278.9	286.1	260.1
M	Professional, scientific and technical activities	1 133.0	1 176.0	1 227.0	1 434.1	1 409.1	1 371.6	1 426.1	1 496.3	1 566.3	1 569.5
N	Administrative and support service activities	871.0	931.0	983.0	1 059.6	1 069.7	1 066.3	1 049.1	1 127.5	1 106.0	1 167.4
O	Public administration, defence, social security	1 897.0	1 883.0	1 896.0	1 809.6	1 748.6	1 697.5	1 639.8	1 708.4	1 662.0	1 667.3
P	Education	2 546.0	2 518.0	2 547.0	2 738.2	2 943.3	2 926.7	2 866.3	2 905.6	2 968.6	3 018.8
Q	Human health and social work activities	3 288.0	3 175.0	3 339.0	3 472.0	3 550.1	3 639.1	3 588.9	3 706.5	3 772.6	3 817.6
R	Arts, entertainment and recreation	554.0	571.0	566.0	598.5	600.0	575.2	585.5	560.0	543.1	600.5
S	Other service activities	436.0	488.0	483.0	538.6	480.5	511.7	493.3	517.8	547.1	573.7
T	Households as employers and own-use activities	54.0	49.0	70.0	40.2	38.4	43.5	33.2	31.8	37.4	31.8
U	Activities of extraterritorial organizations, bodies	11.0	9.0	10.0	27.6	28.8	39.0	25.3	21.9	34.7	26.8

Note: Detailed metadata:http://metalinks.oecd.org/lfs/20170518/87289
Disclaimer: http://oe.cd/disclaimer

UNITED STATES

Table 1. Labour force

Annual average estimates

	2006	2007	2008	2009	2010	2011	2012	2013	2014	2015
Civilian labour force, thousands										
All persons	151 428	153 124	154 287	154 142	153 889	153 617	154 975	155 389	155 922	157 130
Males	81 255	82 136	82 519	82 123	81 985	81 975	82 327	82 667	82 882	83 620
Females	70 173	70 988	71 767	72 019	71 904	71 642	72 648	72 722	73 040	73 509
Unemployed, thousands										
All persons	7 001	7 078	8 924	14 265	14 825	13 747	12 506	11 460	9 616	8 296
Males	3 753	3 882	5 033	8 453	8 626	7 684	6 771	6 314	5 190	4 490
Females	3 247	3 196	3 891	5 811	6 199	6 063	5 734	5 146	4 427	3 807
Civilian employment, thousands										
All persons	144 427	146 047	145 363	139 878	139 064	139 869	142 469	143 929	146 305	148 833
Males	77 502	78 254	77 486	73 670	73 359	74 290	75 555	76 353	77 692	79 131
Females	66 926	67 792	67 876	66 208	65 705	65 579	66 914	67 577	68 613	69 703
Civilian employment (%)										
All persons	100.0	100.0	100.0	100.0	100.0	100.0	100.0	100.0	100.0	100.0
Males	53.7	53.6	53.3	52.7	52.8	53.1	53.0	53.0	53.1	53.2
Females	46.3	46.4	46.7	47.3	47.2	46.9	47.0	47.0	46.9	46.8
Unemployment rate (% of civilian labour force)										
All persons	4.6	4.6	5.8	9.3	9.6	8.9	8.1	7.4	6.2	5.3
Males	4.6	4.7	6.1	10.3	10.5	9.4	8.2	7.6	6.3	5.4
Females	4.6	4.5	5.4	8.1	8.6	8.5	7.9	7.1	6.1	5.2
CIVIL. EMPL. - PROFESSIONAL STATUS, thousands										
All activities	**144 427**	**146 047**	**145 362**	**139 877**	**139 064**	**139 869**	**142 469**	**143 929**	**146 305**	**148 833**
Employees	133 736	135 503	135 161	129 956	129 267	130 315	132 830	134 420	136 861	139 225
Employers and persons working on own account	10 586	10 413	10 080	9 831	9 681	9 449	9 529	9 408	9 358	9 509
Unpaid family workers	105	131	122	91	117	106	110	101	86	100
Employees as % of civilian employment	**92.6**	**92.8**	**93.0**	**92.9**	**93.0**	**93.2**	**93.2**	**93.4**	**93.5**	**93.5**
Part-time employment (%)										
Part-time as % of employment	..	..	..	..	..	..	..	..	..	..
Male share of part time employment	..	..	..	..	..	..	..	..	..	..
Female share of part time employment	..	..	..	..	..	..	..	..	..	..
Male part-time as % of male employment	..	..	..	..	..	..	..	..	..	..
Female part-time as % of female employment	..	..	..	..	..	..	..	..	..	..
Duration of unemployment (% of total unemployment)										
Less than one month	37.3	35.9	32.8	22.2	18.7	19.5	21.1	22.6	25.7	28.9
More than 1 month and less than 3 months	30.3	31.5	31.4	26.8	22.0	21.8	22.9	24.1	25.3	27.8
More than 3 months and less than 6 months	14.8	15.0	16.0	19.5	16.0	15.0	14.9	15.8	15.6	15.3
More than 6 months and less than 1 year	7.6	7.6	9.1	15.3	14.3	12.4	11.8	11.7	10.5	9.4
More than 1 year	10.0	10.0	10.6	16.3	29.0	31.3	29.3	25.9	23.0	18.7

Note: Detailed metadata: http://metalinks.oecd.org/lfs/20170518/af600, http://metalinks.oecd.org/lfs/20170518/87289, http://metalinks.oecd.org/lfs/20170518/fd503 and http://metalinks.oecd.org/lfs/20170518/7169f.

Disclaimer: http://oe.cd/disclaimer

Table 2. Participation rates and unemployment rates by age and sex

Annual average estimates, percentage

	2006	2007	2008	2009	2010	2011	2012	2013	2014	2015
Participation rates										
Males										
15-19	43.7	41.1	40.1	37.3	34.9	33.7	34.0	34.2	33.5	34.2
20-24	79.6	78.7	78.7	76.2	74.5	74.7	74.5	73.9	73.9	73.0
25-34	91.7	92.2	91.5	90.3	89.7	89.2	89.5	89.2	88.7	88.8
35-44	92.1	92.3	92.2	91.7	91.5	90.9	90.7	90.7	90.5	90.3
45-54	88.1	88.2	88.0	87.4	86.8	86.2	86.0	85.5	85.6	85.9
55-59	77.7	77.7	78.8	78.0	78.5	78.2	78.0	78.0	76.8	77.1
60-64	58.6	59.2	59.9	60.9	60.0	59.1	60.5	60.5	61.9	61.5
15-24	63.3	61.5	61.0	58.5	56.7	56.6	56.5	56.6	56.4	56.2
25-54	90.6	90.9	90.5	89.7	89.3	88.7	88.7	88.4	88.2	88.3
55-64	69.6	69.6	70.4	70.3	70.0	69.3	69.9	70.0	69.9	69.8
65 and over	20.3	20.5	21.5	21.9	22.1	22.8	23.6	23.5	23.0	23.4
15-64	81.9	81.7	81.4	80.4	79.6	78.9	78.8	78.7	78.5	78.5
Females										
15-19	43.6	41.5	40.2	37.7	35.0	34.6	34.6	34.7	34.5	34.4
20-24	69.5	70.1	70.0	69.6	68.2	67.8	67.4	67.6	67.7	68.3
25-34	74.4	74.5	75.2	75.0	74.7	73.9	74.1	73.5	73.8	73.4
35-44	75.9	75.5	76.1	75.9	75.2	74.7	74.8	74.0	74.1	74.3
45-54	76.0	76.0	76.1	76.0	75.7	75.4	74.7	74.1	73.8	73.4
55-59	66.7	66.6	67.7	68.5	68.4	67.8	67.3	67.2	66.4	66.3
60-64	47.0	47.9	48.7	49.9	50.7	50.3	50.4	50.0	50.2	49.8
15-24	57.9	57.2	56.5	55.2	53.5	53.3	53.2	53.5	53.6	53.8
25-54	75.5	75.4	75.8	75.6	75.2	74.7	74.5	73.9	73.9	73.7
55-64	58.2	58.3	59.1	60.0	60.2	59.5	59.4	59.2	58.8	58.5
65 and over	11.7	12.6	13.3	13.6	13.8	14.0	14.4	14.9	15.1	15.3
15-64	69.3	69.1	69.3	69.0	68.4	67.8	67.6	67.2	67.1	66.9
All persons										
15-24	60.6	59.4	58.8	56.9	55.2	55.0	54.9	55.0	55.0	55.0
25-54	82.9	83.0	83.1	82.6	82.2	81.6	81.4	81.0	80.9	80.9
55-64	63.7	63.8	64.5	64.9	64.9	64.2	64.5	64.4	64.1	63.9
65 and over	15.4	16.0	16.8	17.2	17.4	17.9	18.5	18.7	18.6	18.9
15-64	75.5	75.3	75.3	74.6	73.9	73.3	73.1	72.8	72.7	72.6
Unemployment rates										
Males										
15-19	16.8	17.6	21.2	27.8	28.8	27.2	26.8	25.5	21.4	18.4
20-24	8.7	8.9	11.4	17.0	17.8	15.7	14.3	14.0	12.2	10.8
25-34	4.5	4.7	6.1	10.9	10.9	9.7	8.2	7.6	6.4	5.5
35-44	3.3	3.3	4.6	8.6	8.5	7.4	6.4	5.8	4.6	4.0
45-54	3.1	3.1	4.2	8.2	8.6	7.4	6.2	5.7	4.4	3.6
55-59	3.2	3.2	3.8	7.2	7.8	7.0	6.4	5.7	4.4	4.0
60-64	2.8	3.2	3.7	7.1	8.2	7.4	6.1	5.6	4.7	3.9
15-24	11.2	11.6	14.4	20.1	20.8	18.7	17.6	17.1	14.5	12.8
25-54	3.6	3.7	5.0	9.2	9.3	8.2	6.9	6.4	5.2	4.4
55-64	3.0	3.2	3.7	7.2	8.0	7.1	6.3	5.6	4.5	3.9
65 and over	2.8	3.4	4.5	6.7	7.1	6.5	6.2	5.5	4.6	3.8
15-64	4.7	4.8	6.2	10.5	10.7	9.5	8.3	7.8	6.4	5.5
Total	4.6	4.7	6.1	10.3	10.5	9.4	8.2	7.6	6.3	5.4
Females										
15-19	13.8	13.8	16.2	20.7	22.8	21.6	21.1	20.3	17.7	15.5
20-24	7.6	7.3	8.8	12.3	13.0	13.4	12.1	11.5	10.1	8.5
25-34	4.9	4.6	5.5	8.6	9.1	9.1	8.4	7.3	6.6	5.5
35-44	3.9	3.6	4.5	7.1	7.7	7.2	6.8	6.0	4.9	4.4
45-54	3.1	3.2	3.9	6.0	6.8	6.7	6.2	5.5	4.5	3.8
55-59	2.9	3.1	3.8	6.0	6.2	6.1	5.6	5.0	4.2	3.5
60-64	2.9	2.8	3.5	6.1	6.3	6.2	5.6	5.0	4.1	3.7
15-24	9.7	9.4	11.2	14.9	15.8	15.7	14.7	13.9	12.2	10.4
25-54	3.9	3.8	4.6	7.2	7.8	7.6	7.1	6.3	5.3	4.6
55-64	2.9	3.0	3.7	6.0	6.2	6.1	5.6	5.0	4.2	3.6
65 and over	3.0	3.1	4.0	6.1	6.2	6.6	6.3	5.1	4.7	3.9
15-64	4.7	4.6	5.5	8.2	8.7	8.5	8.0	7.2	6.1	5.3
Total	4.6	4.5	5.4	8.1	8.6	8.5	7.9	7.1	6.1	5.2
All persons										
15-24	10.5	10.5	12.8	17.6	18.4	17.3	16.2	15.5	13.4	11.6
25-54	3.8	3.7	4.8	8.3	8.6	7.9	7.0	6.3	5.2	4.5
55-64	3.0	3.1	3.7	6.6	7.1	6.6	5.9	5.3	4.3	3.8
65 and over	2.9	3.3	4.2	6.4	6.7	6.5	6.2	5.3	4.6	3.8
15-64	4.7	4.7	5.8	9.4	9.8	9.1	8.2	7.5	6.3	5.4

Note: Detailed metadata at:http://metalinks.oecd.org/lfs/20170518/6f97b
Disclaimer: http://oe.cd/disclaimer

Table 3. Civilian employment and employees: breakdown by activity are not available for United States

BRAZIL

Table 1. Labour force

Annual average estimates

	2006	2007	2008	2009	2010	2011	2012	2013	2014	2015
Civilian labour force, thousands										
All persons	95 643	96 829	98 824	100 551	..	100 219	101 184	102 170	105 537	..
Males	53 610	54 370	55 530	56 166	..	56 622	57 143	57 540	58 867	..
Females	42 033	42 459	43 294	44 385	..	43 597	44 041	44 630	46 670	..
Unemployed, thousands										
All persons	8 036	7 839	7 010	8 325	..	6 718	6 244	6 637	7 254	..
Males	3 414	3 264	2 870	3 444	..	2 758	2 637	2 857	3 142	..
Females	4 622	4 575	4 140	4 881	..	3 960	3 607	3 780	4 112	..
Civilian employment, thousands										
All persons	87 607	88 990	91 814	92 226	..	93 501	94 940	95 533	98 283	..
Males	50 196	51 105	52 660	52 722	..	53 864	54 506	54 682	55 725	..
Females	37 411	37 884	39 154	39 504	..	39 637	40 434	40 851	42 558	..
Civilian employment (%)										
All persons	..	..	..	..	..	..	..	..	..	..
Males	57.3	57.4	57.4	57.2	..	57.6	57.4	57.2	56.7	..
Females	42.7	42.6	42.6	42.8	..	42.4	42.6	42.8	43.3	..
Unemployment rate (% of civilian labour force)										
All persons	8.4	8.1	7.1	8.3	..	6.7	6.2	6.5	6.9	..
Males	6.4	6.0	5.2	6.1	..	4.9	4.6	5.0	5.3	..
Females	11.0	10.8	9.6	11.0	..	9.1	8.2	8.5	8.8	..
CIVIL. EMPL. - PROFESSIONAL STATUS, thousands										
All activities	**87 607**	**88 990**	**91 814**	**92 226**	**..**	**93 501**	**94 940**	**95 533**	**98 283**	**..**
Employees	56 234	58 074	60 792	61 533	..	63 939	65 297	65 772	66 561	..
Employers and persons working on own account	26 820	26 407	27 044	26 886	..	26 789	27 060	27 634	29 198	..
Unpaid family workers	4 553	4 509	3 978	3 807	..	2 772	2 583	2 127	2 524	..
Employees as % of civilian employment	**64.2**	**65.3**	**66.2**	**66.7**	**..**	**68.4**	**68.8**	**68.8**	**67.7**	**..**
Part-time employment (%)										
Part-time as % of employment	19.2	18.3	18.0	17.8	..	16.0	16.2	16.4	17.1	..
Male share of part time employment	32.0	32.4	32.2	32.5	..	34.9	35.6	35.8	35.2	..
Female share of part time employment	68.0	67.6	67.8	67.5	..	65.1	64.4	64.2	64.8	..
Male part-time as % of male employment	10.7	10.3	10.1	10.1	..	9.7	10.0	10.2	10.6	..
Female part-time as % of female employment	30.6	29.1	28.7	28.1	..	24.6	24.6	24.7	25.6	..
Duration of unemployment (% of total unemployment)										
Less than one month	..	..	..	..	..	..	..	..	..	..
More than 1 month and less than 3 months	..	..	..	..	..	..	..	..	..	..
More than 3 months and less than 6 months	..	..	..	..	..	..	..	..	..	..
More than 6 months and less than 1 year	..	..	..	..	..	..	..	..	..	..
More than 1 year	..	..	..	..	..	..	..	..	..	..

Note: Detailed metadata: http://metalinks.oecd.org/lfs/20170518/2f692, http://metalinks.oecd.org/lfs/20170518/87289, http://metalinks.oecd.org/lfs/20170518/02b2d and http://metalinks.oecd.org/lfs/20170518/f480b.

Disclaimer: http://oe.cd/disclaimer

BRAZIL

Table 2. Participation rates and unemployment rates by age and sex

Annual average estimates, percentage

	2006	2007	2008	2009	2010	2011	2012	2013	2014	2015
Participation rates										
Males										
15-19	58.4	58.1	56.1	55.3	..	50.2	50.7	47.7	50.2	..
20-24	88.1	87.2	88.4	88.1	..	86.2	85.3	84.8	85.8	..
25-34	94.4	94.2	94.7	94.6	..	93.4	93.4	93.1	93.4	..
35-44	94.7	94.3	94.3	94.9	..	94.2	93.8	94.2	93.8	..
45-54	89.0	89.0	89.9	90.0	..	89.5	89.0	89.0	89.5	..
55-59	77.1	77.2	77.9	77.6	..	78.2	78.2	78.7	79.6	..
60-64	64.8	65.6	65.4	63.9	..	63.2	62.0	63.2	65.0	..
15-24	73.1	72.3	71.9	71.4	..	67.4	67.2	65.0	66.9	..
25-54	93.1	92.8	93.3	93.4	..	92.6	92.3	92.3	92.4	..
55-64	71.9	72.3	72.5	71.7	..	71.6	70.9	71.8	72.8	..
65 and over	36.8	33.8	34.3	33.6	..	29.8	30.0	29.9	31.1	..
15-64	85.2	84.9	85.1	85.1	..	83.5	83.3	82.8	83.5	..
Females										
15-19	42.5	41.5	40.0	39.4	..	35.3	36.5	33.7	36.5	..
20-24	67.1	67.8	68.6	68.8	..	66.8	65.8	65.3	66.7	..
25-34	72.6	73.0	73.1	74.3	..	72.2	71.8	72.2	73.7	..
35-44	72.9	72.7	72.7	73.9	..	71.3	72.0	72.5	73.3	..
45-54	64.0	63.3	63.2	65.0	..	62.7	63.3	63.5	65.9	..
55-59	47.9	46.9	49.2	48.1	..	45.7	45.5	46.6	50.1	..
60-64	34.3	32.4	34.9	32.7	..	29.2	30.0	31.3	32.4	..
15-24	54.8	54.7	54.2	54.0	..	50.8	50.7	48.9	51.0	..
25-54	70.4	70.2	70.2	71.5	..	69.2	69.4	69.7	71.2	..
55-64	41.9	40.6	42.8	41.4	..	38.4	38.5	39.7	41.9	..
65 and over	14.9	14.6	14.7	13.6	..	11.5	11.7	11.3	13.3	..
15-64	63.0	62.8	62.9	63.5	..	60.8	60.8	60.7	62.4	..
All persons										
15-24	63.9	63.6	63.2	62.7	..	59.2	59.0	57.1	59.0	..
25-54	81.3	81.1	81.2	82.0	..	80.4	80.4	80.6	81.4	..
55-64	55.9	55.4	56.5	55.5	..	54.0	53.5	54.6	56.2	..
65 and over	24.4	22.9	23.1	22.3	..	19.4	19.7	19.4	21.0	..
15-64	73.7	73.5	73.7	73.9	..	71.8	71.7	71.4	72.6	..
Unemployment rates										
Males										
15-19	17.8	16.8	15.4	18.5	..	16.1	15.6	16.8	19.1	..
20-24	11.1	10.2	9.5	10.8	..	9.5	8.6	9.4	10.3	..
25-34	5.6	5.3	4.6	5.8	..	4.3	4.4	4.8	4.9	..
35-44	3.3	3.4	2.8	3.6	..	2.9	2.6	3.1	3.1	..
45-54	3.5	3.5	2.7	3.0	..	2.3	2.1	2.3	2.7	..
55-59	3.4	3.1	2.1	2.9	..	2.3	2.0	2.4	2.1	..
60-64	3.4	2.8	2.3	2.2	..	2.0	2.1	1.8	2.0	..
15-24	13.8	12.9	11.8	13.8	..	12.1	11.4	12.3	13.8	..
25-54	4.3	4.2	3.5	4.3	..	3.3	3.1	3.5	3.7	..
55-64	3.4	3.0	2.2	2.6	..	2.2	2.1	2.2	2.0	..
65 and over	1.5	1.7	1.2	1.9	..	1.2	1.3	1.4	1.2	..
15-64	6.5	6.1	5.3	6.3	..	5.0	4.7	5.1	5.5	..
Total	6.3	6.0	5.1	6.1	..	4.9	4.6	4.9	5.3	..
Females										
15-19	28.6	28.1	26.6	29.1	..	26.5	25.3	25.3	28.5	..
20-24	19.3	18.2	16.9	19.6	..	16.1	15.2	15.1	16.8	..
25-34	11.5	11.5	10.4	12.0	..	10.0	8.6	9.5	9.7	..
35-44	7.0	7.4	6.2	7.2	..	6.3	5.4	6.1	6.0	..
45-54	4.6	5.0	4.2	5.4	..	3.9	3.6	3.8	3.8	..
55-59	3.2	2.9	3.0	4.0	..	2.9	3.1	2.7	2.7	..
60-64	2.1	2.4	2.4	2.3	..	1.6	2.1	2.2	2.1	..
15-24	22.9	21.9	20.5	23.1	..	19.8	18.9	18.7	21.2	..
25-54	8.2	8.5	7.4	8.6	..	7.1	6.2	6.8	6.8	..
55-64	2.8	2.7	2.8	3.4	..	2.5	2.7	2.6	2.5	..
65 and over	1.3	1.0	1.4	1.4	..	1.6	1.4	2.4	1.4	..
15-64	11.3	11.0	9.8	11.3	..	9.3	8.4	8.6	9.0	..
Total	11.0	10.8	9.6	11.0	..	9.1	8.2	8.5	8.8	..
All persons										
15-24	17.7	16.8	15.5	17.8	..	15.3	14.6	15.0	17.0	..
25-54	6.1	6.1	5.2	6.3	..	5.0	4.5	5.0	5.1	..
55-64	3.2	2.9	2.4	3.0	..	2.3	2.3	2.3	2.2	..
65 and over	1.5	1.4	1.3	1.8	..	1.3	1.3	1.7	1.2	..
15-64	8.6	8.3	7.3	8.5	..	6.9	6.3	6.6	7.1	..

Note: Detailed metadata at:http://metalinks.oecd.org/lfs/20170518/6f97b
Disclaimer: http://oe.cd/disclaimer

Table 3. Civilian employment and employees: breakdown by activity - ISIC Rev. 3

Annual average estimates

		2006	2007	2008	2009	2010	2011	2012	2013	2014	2015
	CIVILIAN EMPLOYMENT										
	By activity, thousands										
A-X	**All activities**	**87 607**	**88 990**	**91 814**	**92 226**	..	**93 501**	**94 940**	**95 533**	**98 283**	..
A	Agriculture, hunting and forestry	16 144	15 581	15 300	14 932	..	13 863	13 077	13 062	13 556	..
B	Fishing	387	359	394	461	..	460	492	506	469	..
C	Mining and quarrying	346	380	362	388	..	381	395	372	403	..
D	Manufacturing	12 371	12 928	13 334	12 887	..	11 888	12 636	12 170	12 173	..
E	Electricity, gas and water supply	396	360	377	404	..	350	335	363	389	..
F	Construction	5 820	6 070	6 928	6 933	..	7 888	8 334	8 848	9 072	..
G	Wholesale, retail trade: vehicle repair, household gds	15 461	15 992	15 991	16 379	..	16 712	16 933	17 055	17 906	..
H	Hotels and restaurants	3 318	3 282	3 548	3 593	..	4 559	4 534	4 414	4 595	..
I	Transport, storage and communication	4 034	4 328	4 615	4 459	..	5 170	5 331	5 393	5 441	..
J	Financial intermediation	1 066	1 173	1 166	1 145	..	1 234	1 254	1 334	1 303	..
K	Real estate, renting and business activities	5 396	5 445	6 017	6 052	..	6 978	7 173	6 838	7 289	..
L	Public adm., defence; social sec., excl. armed forces	4 186	4 256	4 299	4 511	..	4 921	4 896	5 006	4 807	..
M	Education	4 861	5 042	5 146	5 289	..	5 131	5 318	5 747	5 896	..
N	Health and social work	3 149	3 305	3 444	3 475	..	3 598	3 912	4 165	4 303	..
O	Other community, social, personal service activities	3 753	3 665	4 087	3 930	..	3 559	3 802	3 769	4 175	..
P	Private households with employed persons	6 703	6 616	6 605	7 183	..	6 674	6 446	6 423	6 439	..
Q	Extra-territorial organisations and bodies	4	3	3	4	..	4	5	5	2	..
X	Not classifiable by economic activities	212	208	197	199	..	131	70	63	65	..
	By sector, thousands										
A-B	Agriculture	16 531	15 940	15 694	15 393	..	14 323	13 569	13 568	14 025	..
C-F	Industry	18 934	19 738	21 001	20 612	..	20 506	21 700	21 754	22 036	..
G-Q	Services	51 931	53 105	54 922	56 021	..	58 540	59 602	60 149	62 156	..
	By sector, percentages										
A-B	Agriculture	18.9	17.9	17.1	16.7	..	15.3	14.3	14.2	14.3	..
C-F	Industry	21.6	22.2	22.9	22.3	..	21.9	22.9	22.8	22.4	..
G-Q	Services	59.3	59.7	59.8	60.7	..	62.6	62.8	63.0	63.2	..
	EMPLOYEES										
	By activity, thousands										
A-X	**All activities**	**56 233**	**58 074**	**60 792**	**61 533**	..	**63 939**	**65 297**	**65 772**	**66 561**	..
A	Agriculture, hunting and forestry	4 711	4 703	4 710	4 738	..	4 148	4 118	3 969	3 874	..
B	Fishing	57	52	53	75	..	67	63	61	67	..
C	Mining and quarrying	305	336	321	357	..	363	369	346	369	..
D	Manufacturing	9 176	9 798	10 128	9 743	..	9 451	10 056	9 544	9 426	..
E	Electricity, gas and water supply	391	356	374	400	..	347	333	358	387	..
F	Construction	2 948	3 020	3 683	3 608	..	4 241	4 413	4 789	4 751	..
G	Wholesale, retail trade: vehicle repair, household gds	8 888	9 365	9 701	10 053	..	10 599	10 781	11 013	11 450	..
H	Hotels and restaurants	1 877	1 936	2 081	2 121	..	2 901	2 789	2 774	2 883	..
I	Transport, storage and communication	2 707	2 903	3 211	3 050	..	3 687	3 821	3 900	3 894	..
J	Financial intermediation	986	1 077	1 085	1 058	..	1 169	1 169	1 253	1 207	..
K	Real estate, renting and business activities	3 951	4 112	4 537	4 542	..	5 429	5 636	5 271	5 601	..
L	Public adm., defence; social sec., excl. armed forces	4 173	4 244	4 282	4 496	..	4 917	4 892	5 002	4 799	..
M	Education	4 597	4 775	4 862	5 023	..	4 893	5 068	5 473	5 636	..
N	Health and social work	2 634	2 797	2 927	2 952	..	3 173	3 415	3 682	3 750	..
O	Other community, social, personal service activities	2 110	1 922	2 178	2 108	..	1 825	1 906	1 891	2 010	..
P	Private households with employed persons	6 702	6 616	6 605	7 183	..	6 674	6 446	6 423	6 439	..
Q	Extra-territorial organisations and bodies	4	3	3	4	..	4	5	5	2	..
X	Not classifiable by economic activities	16	61	49	22	..	51	17	18	18	..
	By sector, thousands										
A-B	Agriculture	4 768	4 755	4 763	4 813	..	4 216	4 180	4 030	3 941	..
C-F	Industry	12 820	13 510	14 507	14 107	..	14 401	15 172	15 037	14 932	..
G-Q	Services	38 628	39 749	41 473	42 591	..	45 272	45 928	46 686	47 670	..
	By sector, percentages										
A-B	Agriculture	8.5	8.2	7.8	7.8	..	6.6	6.4	6.1	5.9	..
C-F	Industry	22.8	23.3	23.9	22.9	..	22.5	23.2	22.9	22.4	..
G-Q	Services	68.7	68.4	68.2	69.2	..	70.8	70.3	71.0	71.6	..

Note: Detailed metadata:http://metalinks.oecd.org/lfs/20170518/87289
Disclaimer: http://oe.cd/disclaimer

COLOMBIA

Table 1. Labour force

Annual average estimates

	2006	2007	2008	2009	2010	2011	2012	2013	2014	2015
Civilian labour force, thousands										
All persons	19 206	19 258	19 655	20 935	21 777	22 446	23 091	23 292	23 654	24 173
Males	11 411	11 470	11 670	12 236	12 580	12 933	13 183	13 283	13 481	13 722
Females	7 795	7 788	7 985	8 699	9 197	9 513	9 907	10 009	10 173	10 452
Unemployed, thousands										
All persons	2 311	2 152	2 214	2 515	2 564	2 426	2 394	2 243	2 151	2 156
Males	1 049	1 001	1 035	1 142	1 127	1 058	1 034	977	940	924
Females	1 262	1 151	1 178	1 373	1 437	1 369	1 360	1 267	1 211	1 232
Civilian employment, thousands										
All persons	16 895	17 106	17 442	18 420	19 213	20 020	20 696	21 048	21 503	22 017
Males	10 362	10 469	10 635	11 094	11 453	11 875	12 149	12 306	12 541	12 798
Females	6 533	6 637	6 807	7 326	7 760	8 144	8 547	8 742	8 962	9 220
Civilian employment (%)										
All persons	100.0	100.0	100.0	100.0	100.0	100.0	100.0	100.0	100.0	100.0
Males	61.3	61.2	61.0	60.2	59.6	59.3	58.7	58.5	58.3	58.1
Females	38.7	38.8	39.0	39.8	40.4	40.7	41.3	41.5	41.7	41.9
Unemployment rate (% of civilian labour force)										
All persons	12.0	11.2	11.3	12.0	11.8	10.8	10.4	9.6	9.1	8.9
Males	9.2	8.7	8.9	9.3	9.0	8.2	7.8	7.4	7.0	6.7
Females	16.2	14.8	14.8	15.8	15.6	14.4	13.7	12.7	11.9	11.8
CIVIL. EMPL. - PROFESSIONAL STATUS, thousands										
All activities	**16 895**	**17 106**	**17 442**	**18 420**	**19 213**	**20 020**	**20 696**	**21 048**	**21 503**	**22 017**
Employees	8 890	9 227	8 603	8 692	8 894	9 178	9 633	9 979	10 373	10 719
Employers and persons working on own account	7 225	7 137	8 112	8 795	9 305	9 750	9 926	9 985	10 085	10 277
Unpaid family workers	780	742	726	933	1 014	1 091	1 138	1 084	1 045	1 021
Employees as % of civilian employment	**52.6**	**53.9**	**49.3**	**47.2**	**46.3**	**45.8**	**46.5**	**47.4**	**48.2**	**48.7**
Part-time employment (%)										
Part-time as % of employment	..	14.5	14.0	15.1	16.3	16.9	18.0	17.8	16.5	..
Male share of part time employment	..	38.7	35.4	34.3	34.5	34.0	34.1	33.5	32.5	..
Female share of part time employment	..	61.3	64.6	65.7	65.5	66.0	65.9	66.5	67.5	..
Male part-time as % of male employment	..	9.2	8.1	8.6	9.4	9.7	10.4	10.2	9.2	..
Female part-time as % of female employment	..	22.8	23.1	24.8	26.3	27.3	28.6	28.4	26.6	..
Duration of unemployment (% of total unemployment)										
Less than one month	..	19.7	19.4	18.4	19.4	21.9	23.6	24.1	24.7	24.2
More than 1 month and less than 3 months	..	34.7	34.5	34.2	34.0	35.3	35.9	36.4	36.3	38.4
More than 3 months and less than 6 months	..	17.9	19.4	19.1	19.0	18.1	17.7	17.6	16.9	17.0
More than 6 months and less than 1 year	..	15.7	16.5	16.9	15.7	14.3	13.3	13.2	13.0	12.7
More than 1 year	..	12.0	10.2	11.4	11.9	10.4	9.5	8.7	9.1	7.7

Note: Detailed metadata: http://metalinks.oecd.org/lfs/20170518/0eeca, http://metalinks.oecd.org/lfs/20170518/87289, http://metalinks.oecd.org/lfs/20170518/26573 and http://metalinks.oecd.org/lfs/20170518/80c84.

Disclaimer: http://oe.cd/disclaimer

Table 2. Participation rates and unemployment rates by age and sex

Annual average estimates, percentage

	2006	2007	2008	2009	2010	2011	2012	2013	2014	2015
Participation rates										
Males										
15-19	..	38.6	37.9	42.2	42.9	44.5	45.9	43.6	43.1	43.0
20-24	..	81.7	82.6	84.9	85.6	86.6	87.3	85.7	85.7	86.1
25-34	..	95.2	95.5	96.3	96.6	96.7	96.5	96.3	96.1	96.2
35-44	..	96.5	96.9	97.3	97.5	97.4	97.4	97.1	97.3	96.9
45-54	..	93.4	93.9	94.8	95.4	95.2	95.6	95.4	95.4	95.1
55-59	..	84.7	85.9	88.4	87.9	89.0	88.9	90.0	90.4	90.8
60-64	..	68.5	70.6	72.3	74.6	75.3	76.3	75.5	76.8	78.0
15-24	..	58.2	57.5	61.3	62.0	63.7	64.8	63.2	63.1	63.4
25-54	..	95.2	95.5	96.2	96.5	96.5	96.5	96.3	96.2	96.1
55-64	..	77.7	79.3	81.3	82.0	82.9	83.3	83.5	84.3	85.1
65 and over	..	38.5	38.7	42.6	44.2	44.8	44.3	43.9	44.1	44.3
15-64	..	82.6	82.8	84.5	84.9	85.6	86.0	85.5	85.7	85.8
Females										
15-19	..	23.9	24.0	27.5	28.4	29.1	30.1	29.1	29.2	28.9
20-24	..	55.8	55.7	59.8	61.7	62.2	64.0	63.6	62.8	62.7
25-34	..	66.0	66.7	70.3	72.7	72.9	74.0	74.2	74.3	75.3
35-44	..	66.8	67.0	71.0	73.3	74.2	75.3	75.4	75.4	76.5
45-54	..	58.4	59.9	64.0	66.2	67.7	69.3	68.9	69.2	70.4
55-59	..	41.1	43.0	46.9	49.1	51.9	54.5	53.9	53.9	55.6
60-64	..	27.7	29.4	30.9	35.2	37.8	40.3	41.1	41.2	42.4
15-24	..	39.5	39.2	42.9	44.3	45.0	46.6	46.0	46.1	46.0
25-54	..	64.2	64.9	68.8	71.1	71.8	73.1	73.1	73.2	74.3
55-64	..	35.2	37.1	40.0	43.0	45.8	48.3	48.3	48.3	49.7
65 and over	..	12.1	12.1	13.9	15.8	16.2	17.4	17.8	18.1	18.5
15-64	..	54.2	54.8	58.5	60.5	61.5	63.0	62.8	62.9	63.7
All persons										
15-24	..	48.8	48.3	52.1	53.2	54.4	55.8	54.6	54.6	54.7
25-54	..	79.1	79.7	82.0	83.4	83.7	84.4	84.3	84.4	84.9
55-64	..	55.2	57.0	59.4	61.4	63.1	64.7	64.7	65.1	66.1
65 and over	..	24.3	24.3	27.1	28.7	29.3	29.6	29.7	29.9	30.2
15-64	..	68.0	68.4	71.1	72.4	73.2	74.2	73.9	74.0	74.5
Unemployment rates										
Males										
15-19	..	20.8	20.9	20.6	20.5	19.0	18.0	16.3	17.1	14.7
20-24	..	16.1	16.5	17.1	16.8	15.8	14.3	13.5	13.1	12.4
25-34	..	8.1	8.8	8.7	8.3	7.4	7.1	6.8	6.4	6.4
35-44	..	5.3	5.4	5.8	5.5	4.7	4.9	4.8	4.3	4.4
45-54	..	6.1	5.9	6.5	5.9	5.4	5.3	5.0	4.5	4.4
55-59	..	6.0	6.3	7.9	6.3	6.4	6.1	5.9	5.6	5.7
60-64	..	7.0	6.0	6.9	8.2	6.0	6.4	5.6	5.7	5.5
15-24	..	17.8	18.1	18.4	18.2	17.0	15.7	14.6	14.6	13.2
25-54	..	6.6	6.8	7.1	6.7	5.9	5.9	5.7	5.2	5.2
55-64	..	6.3	6.2	7.5	7.1	6.2	6.2	5.8	5.6	5.6
65 and over	..	5.3	5.0	5.9	5.7	6.0	5.5	5.1	4.7	4.8
15-64	..	8.9	9.1	9.5	9.2	8.3	8.0	7.5	7.1	6.9
Total	..	8.7	8.9	9.4	9.0	8.2	7.9	7.4	7.0	6.8
Females										
15-19	..	32.0	34.9	35.1	34.9	33.0	31.7	27.3	27.9	26.1
20-24	..	27.0	27.1	28.7	28.2	26.7	25.1	24.5	22.6	22.8
25-34	..	16.2	15.9	16.8	16.7	15.8	15.4	14.0	12.8	13.2
35-44	..	11.3	10.8	12.2	11.9	10.5	10.1	9.3	9.0	9.0
45-54	..	7.6	8.0	9.0	9.2	8.3	8.0	7.7	7.2	7.0
55-59	..	5.6	6.1	7.0	7.0	6.6	6.3	5.9	5.7	5.8
60-64	..	3.8	3.8	4.9	6.1	5.7	4.9	4.4	4.0	4.4
15-24	..	28.6	29.6	30.9	30.5	28.9	27.3	25.4	24.3	23.8
25-54	..	12.3	12.0	13.1	13.0	11.9	11.6	10.7	10.0	10.1
55-64	..	5.0	5.3	6.3	6.7	6.3	5.8	5.4	5.1	5.2
65 and over	..	2.4	2.8	2.8	4.3	3.9	2.6	2.1	3.1	2.4
15-64	..	15.1	15.1	16.2	16.0	14.8	14.2	13.1	12.3	12.2
Total	..	14.8	14.8	15.8	15.7	14.5	13.8	12.7	12.0	11.8
All persons										
15-24	..	22.2	22.8	23.5	23.3	21.9	20.5	19.1	18.7	17.7
25-54	..	9.0	9.0	9.7	9.5	8.6	8.4	7.9	7.3	7.4
55-64	..	5.9	5.9	7.1	6.9	6.2	6.1	5.6	5.4	5.5
65 and over	..	4.5	4.4	5.0	5.3	5.4	4.6	4.1	4.2	4.0
15-64	..	11.5	11.5	12.3	12.1	11.1	10.7	9.9	9.4	9.2

Note: Detailed metadata at:http://metalinks.oecd.org/lfs/20170518/6f97b

Disclaimer: http://oe.cd/disclaimer

COLOMBIA

Table 3. Civilian employment and employees: breakdown by activity - ISIC Rev. 3

Annual average estimates

		2006	2007	2008	2009	2010	2011	2012	2013	2014	2015
	CIVILIAN EMPLOYMENT										
	By activity, thousands										
A-X	**All activities**	**16 895**	**17 106**	**17 442**	**18 420**	**19 213**	**20 020**	**20 696**	**21 048**	**21 503**	**22 017**
A	Agriculture, hunting and forestry	3 226	3 142	3 176	3 440	3 561	3 634	3 622	3 549	3 495	3 544
B	Fishing	0	0	0	0	0	0	0	0	0	0
C	Mining and quarrying	195	180	202	184	213	244	235	224	214	204
D	Manufacturing	2 218	2 300	2 317	2 416	2 455	2 604	2 656	2 533	2 586	2 606
E	Electricity, gas and water supply	78	73	73	79	96	109	108	109	121	117
F	Construction	852	901	889	969	1 047	1 145	1 242	1 220	1 302	1 375
G	Wholesale, retail trade: vehicle repair, household gds	4 166	4 301	4 489	4 764	5 038	5 286	5 535	5 777	5 859	6 042
H	Hotels and restaurants	0	0	0	0	0	0	0	0	0	0
I	Transport, storage and communication	1 277	1 419	1 453	1 535	1 619	1 660	1 721	1 742	1 793	1 805
J	Financial intermediation	207	226	223	220	240	238	260	290	290	298
K	Real estate, renting and business activities	810	949	1 117	1 190	1 212	1 303	1 386	1 489	1 560	1 676
L	Public adm., defence; social sec., excl. armed forces	3 510	3 602	3 477	3 609	3 725	3 794	3 924	4 111	4 280	4 349
M	Education	0	0	0	0	0	0	0	0	0	0
N	Health and social work	0	0	0	0	0	0	0	0	0	0
O	Other community, social, personal service activities	0	0	0	0	0	0	0	0	0	0
P	Private households with employed persons	0	0	0	0	0	0	0	0	0	0
Q	Extra-territorial organisations and bodies	0	0	0	0	0	0	0	0	0	0
X	Not classifiable by economic activities	355	12	25	13	8	3	6	4	3	2
	By sector, thousands										
A-B	Agriculture	3 226	3 142	3 176	3 440	3 561	3 634	3 622	3 549	3 495	3 544
C-F	Industry	3 343	3 454	3 482	3 648	3 811	4 102	4 242	4 085	4 224	4 302
G-Q	Services	9 971	10 498	10 759	11 318	11 833	12 280	12 826	13 410	13 781	14 170
	By sector, percentages										
A-B	Agriculture	19.1	18.4	18.2	18.7	18.5	18.2	17.5	16.9	16.3	16.1
C-F	Industry	19.8	20.2	20.0	19.8	19.8	20.5	20.5	19.4	19.6	19.5
G-Q	Services	59.0	61.4	61.7	61.4	61.6	61.3	62.0	63.7	64.1	64.4
	EMPLOYEES										
	By activity, thousands										
A-X	**All activities**	**8 890**	**9 227**	**8 603**	**8 692**	**8 894**	**9 178**	**9 633**	**9 979**	**10 373**	**10 719**
A	Agriculture, hunting and forestry	1 499	1 579	1 348	1 238	1 243	1 254	1 228	1 210	1 146	1 136
B	Fishing	0	0	0	0	0	0	0	0	0	0
C	Mining and quarrying	113	110	124	95	109	133	124	130	140	126
D	Manufacturing	1 329	1 388	1 287	1 305	1 304	1 363	1 400	1 412	1 472	1 500
E	Electricity, gas and water supply	72	68	69	69	86	97	99	100	109	107
F	Construction	437	456	416	452	492	563	633	624	657	678
G	Wholesale, retail trade: vehicle repair, household gds	1 621	1 716	1 640	1 749	1 828	1 904	2 031	2 139	2 250	2 361
H	Hotels and restaurants	0	0	0	0	0	0	0	0	0	0
I	Transport, storage and communication	539	593	537	550	572	582	613	644	661	679
J	Financial intermediation	183	196	192	194	208	209	223	257	254	264
K	Real estate, renting and business activities	439	521	533	555	542	585	691	752	815	915
L	Public adm., defence; social sec., excl. armed forces	2 486	2 593	2 448	2 479	2 506	2 487	2 586	2 711	2 867	2 953
M	Education	0	0	0	0	0	0	0	0	0	0
N	Health and social work	0	0	0	0	0	0	0	0	0	0
O	Other community, social, personal service activities	0	0	0	0	0	0	0	0	0	0
P	Private households with employed persons	0	0	0	0	0	0	0	0	0	0
Q	Extra-territorial organisations and bodies	0	0	0	0	0	0	0	0	0	0
X	Not classifiable by economic activities	171	7	9	5	3	2	3	1	0	0
	By sector, thousands										
A-B	Agriculture	1 499	1 579	1 348	1 238	1 243	1 254	1 228	1 210	1 146	1 136
C-F	Industry	1 950	2 022	1 896	1 922	1 991	2 156	2 257	2 265	2 379	2 411
G-Q	Services	5 269	5 619	5 351	5 527	5 657	5 767	6 145	6 503	6 847	7 171
	By sector, percentages										
A-B	Agriculture	16.9	17.1	15.7	14.2	14.0	13.7	12.7	12.1	11.0	10.6
C-F	Industry	21.9	21.9	22.0	22.1	22.4	23.5	23.4	22.7	22.9	22.5
G-Q	Services	59.3	60.9	62.2	63.6	63.6	62.8	63.8	65.2	66.0	66.9

Note: Detailed metadata:http://metalinks.oecd.org/lfs/20170518/87289
Disclaimer: http://oe.cd/disclaimer

RUSSIAN FEDERATION

Table 1. Labour force

Annual average estimates

	2006	2007	2008	2009	2010	2011	2012	2013	2014	2015
Civilian labour force, thousands										
All persons	74 419	75 289	75 700	75 694	75 478	75 779	75 676	75 529	75 428	76 588
Males	37 594	38 119	38 594	38 501	38 601	38 717	38 720	38 720	38 729	39 433
Females	36 825	37 170	37 106	37 193	36 877	37 063	36 956	36 809	36 700	37 155
Unemployed, thousands										
All persons	5 250	4 519	4 697	6 284	5 544	4 922	4 131	4 137	3 889	4 264
Males	2 788	2 421	2 492	3 430	3 034	2 684	2 250	2 242	2 123	2 296
Females	2 463	2 097	2 206	2 854	2 510	2 238	1 881	1 896	1 766	1 968
Civilian employment, thousands										
All persons	69 169	70 770	71 003	69 410	69 934	70 857	71 545	71 391	71 539	72 324
Males	34 807	35 698	36 103	35 071	35 566	36 032	36 470	36 478	36 605	37 137
Females	34 362	35 073	34 901	34 339	34 367	34 824	35 075	34 913	34 934	35 187
Civilian employment (%)										
All persons	100.0	100.0	100.0	100.0	100.0	100.0	100.0	100.0	100.0	100.0
Males	50.3	50.4	50.8	50.5	50.9	50.9	51.0	51.1	51.2	51.3
Females	49.7	49.6	49.2	49.5	49.1	49.1	49.0	48.9	48.8	48.7
Unemployment rate (% of civilian labour force)										
All persons	7.1	6.0	6.2	8.3	7.3	6.5	5.5	5.5	5.2	5.6
Males	7.4	6.4	6.5	8.9	7.9	6.9	5.8	5.8	5.5	5.8
Females	6.7	5.6	5.9	7.7	6.8	6.0	5.1	5.2	4.8	5.3
CIVIL. EMPL. - PROFESSIONAL STATUS, thousands										
All activities	**69 169**	**70 770**	**71 003**	**69 410**	**69 934**	**70 857**	**71 545**	**71 391**	**71 539**	**72 324**
Employees	63 961	65 593	65 814	64 266	65 158	65 827	66 598	66 197	66 378	67 109
Employers and persons working on own account	5 150	5 100	5 099	4 917	4 479	4 825	4 664	4 930	4 883	4 951
Unpaid family workers	58	78	90	228	297	204	284	265	278	263
Employees as % of civilian employment	**92.5**	**92.7**	**92.7**	**92.6**	**93.2**	**92.9**	**93.1**	**92.7**	**92.8**	**92.8**
Part-time employment (%)										
Part-time as % of employment	5.3	5.1	5.0	4.7	4.3	4.1	4.1	4.3	4.0	4.2
Male share of part time employment	35.7	35.2	35.5	34.8	35.7	34.6	35.5	34.5	34.9	35.1
Female share of part time employment	64.3	64.8	64.5	65.2	64.3	65.4	64.5	65.5	65.1	64.9
Male part-time as % of male employment	3.8	3.5	3.5	3.3	3.0	2.8	2.9	2.9	2.7	2.9
Female part-time as % of female employment	6.9	6.6	6.5	6.2	5.6	5.4	5.4	5.8	5.3	5.6
Duration of unemployment (% of total unemployment)										
Less than one month	10.3	10.9	13.0	12.6	11.3	10.6	11.4	11.9	12.3	11.5
More than 1 month and less than 3 months	15.2	16.7	19.5	22.1	18.7	19.4	21.4	21.6	21.9	22.7
More than 3 months and less than 6 months	13.7	13.8	15.1	20.3	22.6	17.1	18.7	16.6	17.0	17.8
More than 6 months and less than 1 year	18.5	18.0	17.2	16.2	17.4	20.0	17.5	18.8	20.7	20.6
More than 1 year	42.3	40.6	35.2	28.7	30.0	32.9	30.9	31.0	28.1	27.3

Note: Detailed metadata: http://metalinks.oecd.org/lfs/20170518/f6233, http://metalinks.oecd.org/lfs/20170518/87289, http://metalinks.oecd.org/lfs/20170518/616b5 and http://metalinks.oecd.org/lfs/20170518/c2a5d.

Disclaimer: http://oe.cd/disclaimer

Table 2. Participation rates and unemployment rates by age and sex

Annual average estimates, percentage

	2006	2007	2008	2009	2010	2011	2012	2013	2014	2015
Participation rates										
Males										
15-19	17.3	16.8	17.4	15.6	13.9	12.5	11.0	10.3	9.5	10.2
20-24	66.7	66.6	70.5	69.5	68.3	68.3	65.5	66.4	65.2	64.0
25-34	92.7	93.6	93.7	93.5	94.2	94.3	94.6	94.9	95.1	95.6
35-44	92.1	93.1	93.6	93.5	93.9	93.9	94.5	94.4	94.6	94.9
45-54	88.0	89.3	89.5	89.2	89.7	90.0	90.5	90.1	90.8	91.2
55-59	75.4	76.3	76.3	76.2	76.3	77.0	77.8	77.4	77.9	78.3
60-64	38.7	43.9	43.9	40.9	40.0	38.8	38.5	38.8	38.6	39.1
15-24	42.2	42.7	46.2	45.8	45.5	45.7	43.8	44.1	43.0	41.9
25-54	90.9	92.0	92.2	92.1	92.6	92.8	93.3	93.2	93.6	94.0
55-64	63.7	66.3	65.5	63.3	61.6	60.6	60.6	60.4	60.5	61.0
65 and over	15.7	16.4	14.6	14.1	12.7	14.0	14.1	14.3	13.9	14.6
15-64	75.7	76.9	77.9	77.6	77.7	77.8	78.1	78.1	78.6	79.1
Females										
15-19	13.7	12.6	12.3	11.2	9.2	8.6	7.5	7.6	6.6	7.1
20-24	56.8	57.3	58.5	59.3	56.5	55.8	53.1	53.6	52.4	52.3
25-34	83.9	84.4	82.5	82.1	82.2	82.8	83.2	81.6	81.7	81.4
35-44	90.0	89.9	89.8	89.8	89.9	89.9	90.0	89.5	89.7	89.4
45-54	85.7	85.9	86.1	86.2	86.4	86.6	87.2	86.8	87.4	87.5
55-59	50.5	53.0	51.6	51.2	50.7	51.8	52.9	53.6	53.3	53.8
60-64	22.8	26.7	26.9	27.2	25.4	25.9	24.9	25.6	26.1	26.8
15-24	35.5	36.0	37.4	38.3	36.7	36.7	35.1	35.4	34.3	33.7
25-54	86.5	86.6	86.0	85.9	86.0	86.3	86.7	85.8	86.1	85.9
55-64	40.8	44.2	42.9	41.9	39.9	40.1	40.0	40.7	40.7	41.2
65 and over	9.6	9.5	9.3	8.8	7.8	8.7	8.9	9.6	9.9	10.5
15-64	68.5	69.2	68.9	68.8	68.0	68.1	68.2	67.9	68.1	68.2
All persons										
15-24	38.9	39.4	41.8	42.1	41.2	41.3	39.5	39.8	38.7	37.9
25-54	88.6	89.2	89.0	88.9	89.2	89.4	89.9	89.4	89.7	89.9
55-64	50.6	53.7	52.6	51.1	49.2	48.8	48.8	49.1	49.1	49.6
65 and over	11.8	12.0	11.2	10.7	9.5	10.6	10.8	11.3	11.4	12.0
15-64	72.0	72.9	73.2	73.0	72.7	72.8	73.0	72.8	73.1	73.4
Unemployment rates										
Males										
15-19	24.6	23.2	22.7	27.4	28.5	28.1	26.0	23.0	24.7	28.6
20-24	13.5	12.4	11.2	16.5	14.9	13.4	13.2	12.3	12.2	13.8
25-34	7.0	5.8	6.0	8.5	7.7	6.7	5.4	5.5	5.1	5.4
35-44	6.6	5.4	5.4	7.4	6.2	5.4	4.5	4.6	4.3	4.6
45-54	5.8	4.8	5.0	7.2	6.3	5.6	4.6	4.7	4.4	4.7
55-59	4.1	3.7	4.7	6.8	6.1	5.5	4.5	4.5	4.6	4.8
60-64	3.0	2.9	4.1	4.8	4.4	4.1	3.0	3.4	3.6	3.2
15-24	15.7	14.5	13.2	18.1	16.6	15.0	14.5	13.3	13.3	15.3
25-54	6.5	5.4	5.5	7.7	6.8	6.0	4.9	5.0	4.7	5.0
55-64	3.9	3.5	4.6	6.3	5.6	5.1	4.1	4.2	4.4	4.3
65 and over	2.7	2.5	4.0	4.2	3.5	3.1	3.3	3.1	2.7	2.8
15-64	7.5	6.4	6.5	9.0	7.9	7.0	5.8	5.8	5.5	5.9
Total	7.4	6.4	6.5	8.9	7.9	6.9	5.8	5.8	5.5	5.8
Females										
15-19	30.6	26.9	30.5	36.1	37.0	34.9	31.5	30.4	33.1	38.2
20-24	14.0	11.9	12.4	16.3	15.0	13.4	13.6	13.1	12.5	14.9
25-34	6.3	5.6	5.7	7.8	7.1	6.4	5.6	5.5	5.3	5.9
35-44	5.7	4.8	4.8	5.9	5.2	4.5	3.7	3.9	3.6	3.9
45-54	4.9	4.1	4.4	5.8	5.2	4.8	3.7	3.9	3.6	3.8
55-59	3.6	2.5	3.4	4.9	4.1	3.6	2.5	3.0	2.6	2.9
60-64	2.7	3.1	3.4	4.4	4.0	3.7	2.4	3.2	2.9	3.2
15-24	17.1	14.4	15.1	18.9	17.3	15.5	15.1	14.5	14.1	16.9
25-54	5.6	4.8	5.0	6.5	5.8	5.2	4.4	4.4	4.2	4.6
55-64	3.4	2.6	3.4	4.8	4.1	3.7	2.5	3.1	2.7	3.0
65 and over	2.4	1.7	3.5	4.1	3.8	2.8	3.1	2.6	3.0	2.8
15-64	6.8	5.7	6.0	7.7	6.8	6.1	5.1	5.2	4.8	5.3
Total	6.7	5.6	5.9	7.7	6.8	6.0	5.1	5.2	4.8	5.3
All persons										
15-24	16.4	14.4	14.0	18.5	16.9	15.2	14.8	13.8	13.7	16.0
25-54	6.0	5.1	5.2	7.1	6.3	5.6	4.6	4.7	4.4	4.8
55-64	3.7	3.1	4.0	5.6	4.9	4.4	3.3	3.7	3.6	3.7
65 and over	2.6	2.1	3.7	4.1	3.6	2.9	3.2	2.8	2.8	2.8
15-64	7.1	6.1	6.2	8.4	7.4	6.5	5.5	5.5	5.2	5.6

Note: Detailed metadata at:http://metalinks.oecd.org/lfs/20170518/6f97b

Disclaimer: http://oe.cd/disclaimer

Table 3. Civilian employment and employees: breakdown by activity - ISIC Rev. 3

Annual average estimates

		2006	2007	2008	2009	2010	2011	2012	2013	2014	2015
	CIVILIAN EMPLOYMENT										
	By activity, thousands										
A-X	**All activities**	**69 169**	**70 770**	**71 003**	**69 410**	**69 934**	**70 857**	**71 545**	**71 391**	**71 539**	**72 324**
A	Agriculture, hunting and forestry	6 642	6 071	5 920	5 618	5 302	5 322	5 123	4 880	4 698	4 725
B	Fishing	189	197	139	120	116	124	118	112	112	128
C	Mining and quarrying	1 192	1 330	1 333	1 362	1 406	1 446	1 451	1 541	1 526	1 505
D	Manufacturing	12 441	12 321	11 721	10 590	10 646	10 607	10 718	10 562	10 382	10 343
E	Electricity, gas and water supply	2 117	2 052	2 110	2 245	2 296	2 292	2 378	2 299	2 358	2 335
F	Construction	4 483	4 932	5 406	4 912	5 053	5 106	5 320	5 392	5 419	5 475
G	Wholesale, retail trade: vehicle repair, household gds	10 576	11 059	10 770	10 583	10 894	11 246	11 503	11 495	11 469	11 513
H	Hotels and restaurants	1 406	1 348	1 472	1 436	1 372	1 495	1 532	1 616	1 728	1 802
I	Transport, storage and communication	6 274	6 629	6 581	6 540	6 522	6 690	6 711	6 767	6 775	6 883
J	Financial intermediation	1 077	1 256	1 332	1 254	1 332	1 427	1 463	1 579	1 592	1 573
K	Real estate, renting and business activities	4 205	4 487	4 486	4 516	4 512	4 755	4 726	4 829	5 032	5 220
L	Public adm., defence; social sec., excl. armed forces	4 936	4 913	5 368	5 522	5 669	5 467	5 397	5 259	5 203	5 330
M	Education	6 246	6 473	6 458	6 522	6 580	6 508	6 617	6 534	6 577	6 667
N	Health and social work	4 951	5 220	5 269	5 513	5 528	5 570	5 721	5 623	5 626	5 717
O	Other community, social, personal service activities	2 407	2 467	2 591	2 648	2 681	2 769	2 738	2 875	3 019	3 079
P	Private households with employed persons	24	16	44	29	22	28	22	25	21	23
Q	Extra-territorial organisations and bodies	4	0	5	2	1	2	7	3	2	5
X	Not classifiable by economic activities	0	0	0	0	0	0	0	0	0	0
	By sector, thousands										
A-B	Agriculture	6 831	6 268	6 058	5 739	5 418	5 446	5 242	4 992	4 811	4 853
C-F	Industry	20 232	20 635	20 569	19 109	19 402	19 452	19 867	19 794	19 685	19 658
G-Q	Services	42 106	43 867	44 376	44 563	45 114	45 958	46 437	46 605	47 044	47 812
	By sector, percentages										
A-B	Agriculture	9.9	8.9	8.5	8.3	7.7	7.7	7.3	7.0	6.7	6.7
C-F	Industry	29.3	29.2	29.0	27.5	27.7	27.5	27.8	27.7	27.5	27.2
G-Q	Services	60.9	62.0	62.5	64.2	64.5	64.9	64.9	65.3	65.8	66.1
	EMPLOYEES										
	By activity, thousands										
A-X	**All activities**	**63 961**	**65 593**	**65 814**	**64 266**	**65 158**	**65 827**	**66 598**	**66 197**	**66 378**	**67 109**
A	Agriculture, hunting and forestry	3 930	3 574	3 722	3 545	3 418	3 276	3 158	2 886	2 814	2 789
B	Fishing	151	163	118	99	104	104	102	97	95	108
C	Mining and quarrying	1 189	1 324	1 332	1 357	1 402	1 443	1 447	1 538	1 523	1 502
D	Manufacturing	12 203	12 086	11 412	10 245	10 303	10 292	10 409	10 232	10 091	10 058
E	Electricity, gas and water supply	2 114	2 046	2 102	2 236	2 288	2 284	2 370	2 293	2 350	2 329
F	Construction	4 267	4 689	5 104	4 624	4 805	4 796	4 994	5 024	5 006	5 041
G	Wholesale, retail trade: vehicle repair, household gds	9 187	9 594	9 232	9 094	9 482	9 845	10 124	10 072	10 087	10 130
H	Hotels and restaurants	1 374	1 306	1 428	1 392	1 323	1 451	1 485	1 563	1 660	1 739
I	Transport, storage and communication	5 997	6 270	6 180	6 118	6 137	6 275	6 265	6 291	6 282	6 411
J	Financial intermediation	1 070	1 250	1 327	1 245	1 323	1 420	1 456	1 571	1 582	1 567
K	Real estate, renting and business activities	4 096	4 377	4 340	4 354	4 342	4 569	4 549	4 627	4 808	4 988
L	Public adm., defence; social sec., excl. armed forces	4 936	4 913	5 368	5 522	5 668	5 466	5 397	5 259	5 203	5 330
M	Education	6 225	6 455	6 439	6 493	6 556	6 484	6 588	6 507	6 544	6 634
N	Health and social work	4 922	5 186	5 233	5 462	5 488	5 525	5 684	5 575	5 573	5 668
O	Other community, social, personal service activities	2 274	2 343	2 431	2 450	2 499	2 571	2 543	2 636	2 739	2 789
P	Private households with employed persons	24	16	44	25	19	25	20	23	19	20
Q	Extra-territorial organisations and bodies	4	0	5	2	1	2	7	3	2	5
X	Not classifiable by economic activities	0	0	0	0	0	..	..	..	..	..
	By sector, thousands										
A-B	Agriculture	4 080	3 738	3 839	3 645	3 522	3 381	3 260	2 983	2 909	2 897
C-F	Industry	19 774	20 144	19 949	18 463	18 798	18 815	19 221	19 087	18 970	18 931
G-Q	Services	40 107	41 711	42 026	42 158	42 838	43 632	44 118	44 127	44 499	45 282
	By sector, percentages										
A-B	Agriculture	6.4	5.7	5.8	5.7	5.4	5.1	4.9	4.5	4.4	4.3
C-F	Industry	30.9	30.7	30.3	28.7	28.8	28.6	28.9	28.8	28.6	28.2
G-Q	Services	62.7	63.6	63.9	65.6	65.7	66.3	66.2	66.7	67.0	67.5

Note: Detailed metadata:http://metalinks.oecd.org/lfs/20170518/87289
Disclaimer: http://oe.cd/disclaimer

ORGANISATION FOR ECONOMIC CO-OPERATION AND DEVELOPMENT

The OECD is a unique forum where governments work together to address the economic, social and environmental challenges of globalisation. The OECD is also at the forefront of efforts to understand and to help governments respond to new developments and concerns, such as corporate governance, the information economy and the challenges of an ageing population. The Organisation provides a setting where governments can compare policy experiences, seek answers to common problems, identify good practice and work to co-ordinate domestic and international policies.

The OECD member countries are: Australia, Austria, Belgium, Canada, Chile, the Czech Republic, Denmark, Estonia, Finland, France, Germany, Greece, Hungary, Iceland, Ireland, Israel, Italy, Japan, Korea, Latvia, Luxembourg, Mexico, the Netherlands, New Zealand, Norway, Poland, Portugal, the Slovak Republic, Slovenia, Spain, Sweden, Switzerland, Turkey, the United Kingdom and the United States. The European Commission takes part in the work of the OECD.

OECD Publishing disseminates widely the results of the Organisation's statistics gathering and research on economic, social and environmental issues, as well as the conventions, guidelines and standards agreed by its members.

OECD PUBLISHING, 2, rue André-Pascal, 75775 PARIS CEDEX 16
(01 2017 02 1 P) ISBN 978-92-64-27116-6 – 2017

www.ingramcontent.com/pod-product-compliance
Lightning Source LLC
Chambersburg PA
CBHW061216240926
51846CB00006B/1247
* 9 7 8 9 2 6 4 2 7 1 1 6 6 *